THE MEMOIRS AND MEMORIALS OF JACQUES DE COUTRE

Security, Trade and Society in
16th- and 17th-century Southeast Asia

THE MEMOIRS AND MEMORIALS OF JACQUES DE COUTRE

Security, Trade and Society in 16th- and 17th-century Southeast Asia

Edited with an Introduction by Peter Borschberg
Translated by Roopanjali Roy

NUS PRESS
SINGAPORE

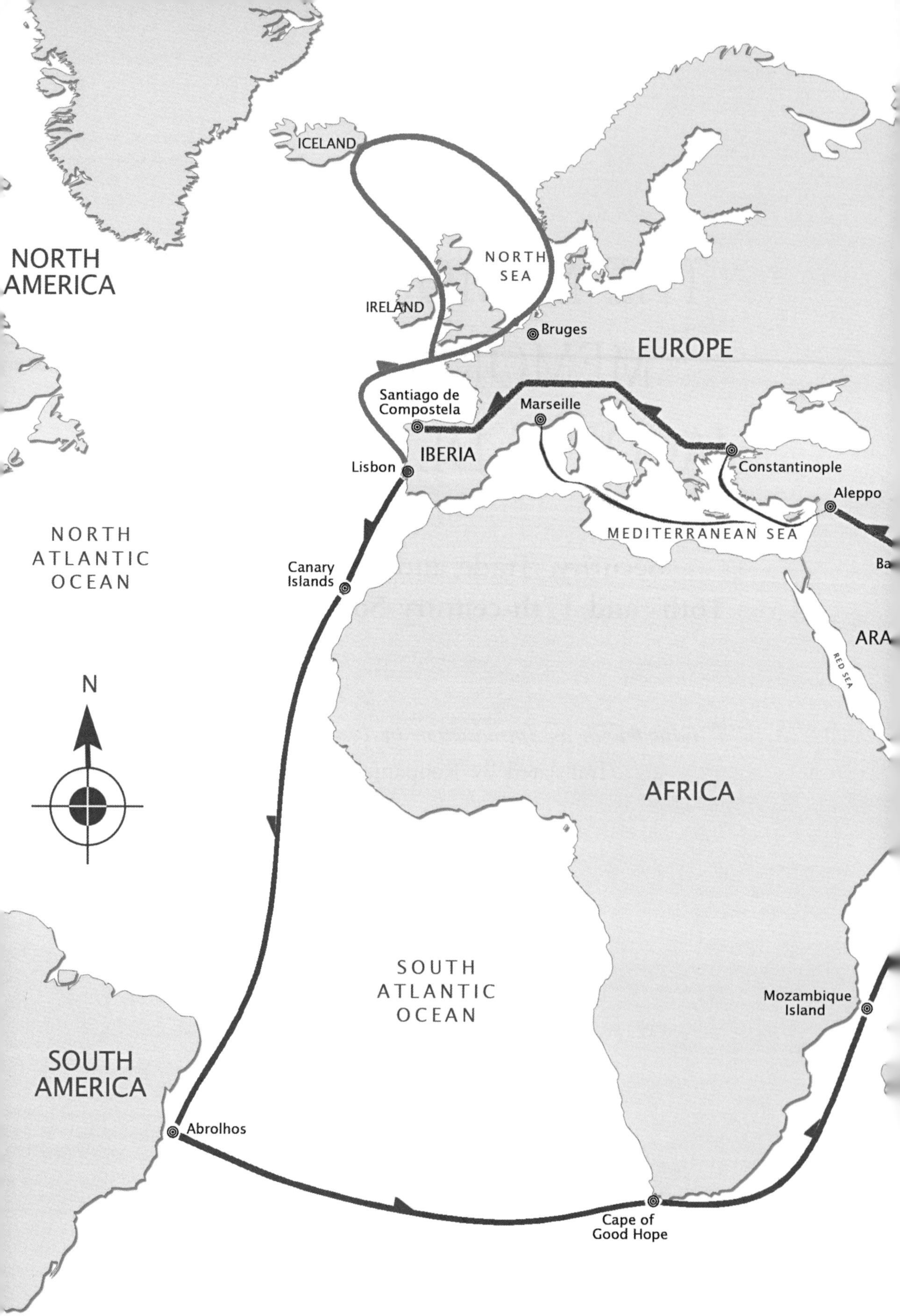

ICELAND
NORTH AMERICA
NORTH SEA
IRELAND
Bruges
EUROPE
Santiago de Compostela
Marseille
IBERIA
Lisbon
Constantinople
Aleppo
MEDITERRANEAN SEA
NORTH ATLANTIC OCEAN
Canary Islands
Ba
ARA
RED SEA
N
AFRICA
SOUTH ATLANTIC OCEAN
Mozambique Island
SOUTH AMERICA
Abrolhos
Cape of Good Hope

Jacques de Coutre's Travels

Europe – India – Southeast Asia

1591–1623

Published by:

NUS Press
National University of Singapore
AS3-01-02, 3 Arts Link
Singapore 117569

Fax: (65) 6774-0652
E-mail: nusbooks@nus.edu.sg
Website: http://www.nus.edu.sg/nuspress

ISBN 978-9971-69-528-6 (Paper)
ISBN 978-9971-69-783-9 (Case)

National Library Board, Singapore Cataloguing-in-Publication Data

Coutre, Jacques de, 1577–1640.
The memoirs and memorials of Jacques de Coutre : security, trade and society in 16th- and 17th-century Southeast Asia / [Jacques de Coutre] ; edited with introduction by Peter Borschberg ; translated by Roopanjali Roy. – Singapore : NUS Press, c2014.
pages cm.
ISBN : 978-9971-69-528-6 (paperback)
978-9971-69-783-9 (case)

1. Asia – Description and travel – Early works to 1800. 2. Coutre, Jacques de, 1577-1640 – Travel – Asia. 3. Singapore – History – 16th century. 4. Singapore – History – 17th century. 5. Malacca, Strait of – History – 16th century. 6. Malacca, Strait of – History – 17th century. 7. Southeast Asia – History – 16th century. 8. Southeast Asia – History – 17th century.
I. Borschberg, Peter.
II. Roy, Roopanjali.
III. Title.

DS522.2
959 -- dc23 OCN847505492

Front cover: Hand-coloured depiction of a Portuguese couple with their servants, halberds in hand, on their way to church at night. Taken from the first edition of Jan Huyghen van Linschoten's *Itinerario* and *Reysgeschrift* printed in 1596. (The Hague, KB, 1702 B 4, insert after p. 48).

Back cover: Map of the East Indies by Abraham Ortelius, c.1570. (Washington, D.C., Library of Congress).

Typeset by: International Typesetters Pte Ltd
Printed by: Mainland Press Pte Ltd

CONTENTS

MEMORIALS OF JACQUES DE COUTRE TO THE CROWN AND VICEROY

APPENDICES

LIST OF ABBREVIATIONS

AA	Jacques de Coutre, *Andanzas asiáticas*, ed. E. Stols, B. Teensma and J. [V]erbeckmoes (Madrid: História 16, 1991).
AJSS	Asian Journal of Social Sciences
ANTT	Arquivo Nacional da Torre do Tombo, Lisbon
AO	Jacques de Coutre, *Aziatische Omzwervingen. Het levensverhaal van Jaques de Coutre, een Brugs diamantenhandelaar, 1591–1626*, tr. J. Verbeckmoes and E. Stols (Berchem: EPO, 1988).
BKI	*Bijdragen en Mededelingen van het Koninklijk Instituut voor Taal-, Land- en Volkenkunde*, Leiden
BLB	The British Library, London
BMH	*Bijdragen en Mededelingen van het Historisch Genootschap*
BNE	Biblioteca Nacional de España
BNP	Biblioteca Nacional de Portugal
BOC	Pieter van Dam, *Beschryvinge van de Oostindische Compagnie,* ed. F.W. Stapel, 8 vols. (The Hague: Martinus Nijhoff, 1931–43).
BSB	Bayerische Staatsbibliothek, München
BUR	I.H. Burkhill, *A Dictionary of the Economic Products of the Malay Peninsula,* 2 vols. (Kuala Lumpur: Governments of Malaysia and Singapore, Ministry of Agriculture and Cooperatives, 1966).
BV	Isaac Commelin, *Begin ende Voortgang Vande Vereenigde Neerlandsche Geoctroyeerde Oost-Indische Compagnie*, facsimile of the edition printed by Johannes Janssonius in 1646 in 4 vols. (Amsterdam: Facsimile Uitgaven Nederland, 1969).

CRE	Jacques de Coutre, *Como Remediar o Estado da Índia? Being the Appendices of the Vida de Jaques de Coutre* (Madrid: Biblioteca Nacional, Ms. 2780), ed. Benjamin N. Teensma (Leiden: Centre for the History of European Expansion, 1989).
CSV	Arquivo Nacional da Torre do Tombo, Collecção de São Vicente, Lisbon
CTCB	Shantha Hariharan, *Cotton Textiles and Corporate Buyers in Cottonopolis: A Study of Purchases and Prices in Gujarat, 1600–1800* (New Delhi: Manak Publications, 2002).
DAS	Jaap R. de Bruijn, Femme S. Gaastra and Ivo Schöffer, ed., *Dutch-Asiatic Shipping in the 17th and 18th Centuries,* 3 vols. (The Hague: Martinus Nijhoff, 1979–87).
DLM	Humberto Leitão and J. Vicente Lopes, *Dicionário da Linguagem de Marinha Antiga e Actual,* 2nd edn. (Lisbon: Centro de Estudos Históricos Ultramarinos da Junta de Investigações Científicas do Ultramar, 1974).
DRI	Arquivo Nacional da Torre do Tombo, Documentos Remetidos da Índia, Lisbon
DUP	*Documentação Ultramarina Portuguesa,* 2 vols. (Lisbon: Centro de Estudos Históricos Ultramarinos,1960–62).
EFS	Anthony Farrington and Dhiravat na Pombejra, ed., *The English Factory in Siam, 1612–1685,* 2 vols. (London: The British Library, 2007).
ENI	J. Paulus, ed., *Encyclopaedie van Nederlandsch-Indië,* 2nd edn., 8 vols. (The Hague and Leiden: Martinus Nijhoff and E.J. Brill, 1917–39).
GLA	Mons. Sebastião Rodolfo Dalgado, *Glossário Luso-Asiático,* 2 vols. (Coimbra: Imprensa da Universidade, 1919–21).
GPFT	Peter Borschberg, *Hugo Grotius, the Portuguese and Free Trade in the East Indies* (Singapore and Leiden: NUS Press and KITLV Press, 2011).
GVOC	*VOC Glossarium. Verklaringen van Termen, verzamelt uit de Rijksgeschiedkundige Publicatiën die betrekking hebben op de Verenigde*

	Oost-Indische Compagnie (The Hague: Instituut voor Nederlandse Geschiedenis, 2000).
HJ	Henry Yule and A.C. Burnell, *Hobson-Jobson: A Glossary of Colloquial Anglo-Indian Words and Phrases*, reprint (Sittingbourne: Linguasia, 1994).
IMM	K.M. Nadkarni, *Indian Materia Medica. With Ayurverdic, Unani-Tibbi, Siddha, Allopathic, Homeopathic, Naturopathic and Home Remedies, Appendices and Indexes,* 2 vols. (Bombay and Panvel: Popular Book Depot and Dhootapapeshwar Prakashan, 1955).
JMBRAS	Journal of the Malaysian Branch of the Royal Asiatic Society
JO	J.K.J. de Jonge, *Opkomst van het Nederlandsch gezag in Oost-Indië. Verzameling van onuitgegeven stukken uit het oud-coloniaal archief,* 16 vols. (The Hague: Martinus Nijhoff, 1862–1925).
JSEAH	Journal of Southeast Asian History
JSEAS	Journal of Southeast Asian Studies
KB	Koninklijke Bibliotheek, The Hague
LGT	Visconde de Lagoa, *Glossário Toponímico da Antiga Historiografia Portuguesa Ultramarina,* vol. I, Ásia e Oceania (Lisbon: Ministério das Colónias, Junta de Investigações Coloniais, 1953).
lit.	Literally
LM	Pato, R.A. de Bulhão and António da Silva Rego, ed., *Documentos Remettidos da Índia ou Livros das Monções,* 10 vols. (Lisbon: Typographia da Academia Real das Sciencias and Imprensa Nacional—Casa de Moeda, 1880–1982).
MNI	George Roques, *La manière de négocier aux Indes, 1676–1691: La compagnie des Indes de l'art du commerce,* ed. and tr. Valéry Bérinstain (Paris: École française d'Extrême-Orient—Maisonneuve & Larose, 1996).
Ms.	Manuscript
NAN	Nationaal Archief van Nederland, The Hague

PI	Emma H. Blair and James A. Robertson, ed., *The Philippine Islands, 1493–1898*, 55 vols. (Cleveland: A.H. Clark Co., 1903–09).
PMS	Paulo Jorge de Sousa Pinto, *The Portuguese and the Straits of Melaka, 1575–1619: Power, Trade and Diplomacy* (Singapore: NUS Press, 2012).
RC	*Revista de Cultura*, Macao.
SMS	Peter Borschberg, *The Singapore and Melaka Straits: Violence, Security and Diplomacy in the 17th Century* (Singapore and Leiden: NUS Press and KITLV Press, 2010).
UB	Universitätsbibliothek or Universiteitsbibliotheek, the German and Dutch terms respectively for University Library
VOC	Vereenigde Oost-Indische Compagnie; United Netherlands East India Company
WMSA	Pierre le Roux, Bernard Sellato and Jacques Ivanoff, ed., *Poids e mesures en Asie du Sud-Est—Weights and Measures in Southeast Asia*, 2 vols. (Paris: École française d'Extrême-Orient and Institut de Recherche sur le Sud-Est Asiatique, 2004–08).

LIST OF ILLUSTRATIONS

PREFACE

This book is an annotated source translation that brings an important eyewitness account of early modern Southeast Asia closer to a contemporary, general Asian readership. The documents contained in this volume are by Jacobus van de Koutere, alias Jacques de Coutre (and later also Jaques do Couto), who was a native of Bruges in present-day Belgium. Jacques spent more than three decades of his adult life in Asia. Between 1594 and 1603, he lived first in Melaka and then for about two years in Manila. He was an independent trader, dealing chiefly in precious stones, bezoars and Indian textiles. Apart from the problematic Mendes Pinto, his account of Ayutthaya is arguably the oldest surviving eyewitness account of the old Thai royal capital written by a European visitor. Moreover, taken as a whole, De Coutre's writings also offer the single most comprehensive European account of Singapore before 1800.

A selection of materials taken from his autobiography (book 1 of 3), as well as four memorials to the Spanish crown and to the Portuguese viceroy in Goa are translated into English for the first time. They touch on Jacques' life in, knowledge of, and personal experience with Southeast Asia. These texts position Melaka and the region of the Malay Peninsula, including the Singapore and Melaka Straits, into a vast web of trading relations maintained by Portugal and Spain that spanned from the eastern coast of Africa to the Japanese islands. In the first half of the 17th century this network was being seriously challenged by traders from the Dutch Republic. After 1602, the Portuguese were presented with a formidable military force and economic competitor in the form of the United Netherlands East India Company, better known by its historic initials VOC. Jacques was clearly interested in more than just trade and commerce. He provided an astonishingly detailed overview of the peoples, cultures and regions he came into personal contact with, yielding rare glimpses into a pre-colonial Asian world that has long been eclipsed by imperialism and the Industrial Revolution.

ACKNOWLEDGEMENTS

This publication could not have been completed without research time spent on a sabbatical year in 2012. I would first like to acknowledge the support I have received from the project "Baltic Borderlands: Shifting Boundaries of Mind and Culture in the Borderlands of the Baltic Sea Region" based at the Universities of Greifswald (Germany), Lund (Sweden) and Tartu (Estonia) and funded by the German Research Council (Deutsche Forschungsgemeinschaft, DFG). Professor Michael North, Chair of Modern History at the Ernst-Moritz-Arndt Universität Greifswald, together with his research team have developed a strong interest in maritime history and European-Asian cultural interactions. My special thanks go out to him not only for hosting me as a visiting professor (Gastprofessor) in 2012 and 2013, but also for the excellent working synergy that has developed over the past decade.

My three other associates in completing this project, Kwa Chong Guan (Singapore), Roderich Ptak (Ludwig-Maximilians-Universtität, Munich); and Pedro Pinto (Universidade Nova, Lisbon), deserve my sincere gratitude. Their input has been proof that translation projects of this complexity require the active collaboration of experts across different academic disciplines, as well as from different sub-fields of history.

Partial translation of Jacques de Coutre's memoirs (*Vida*) and memorials has been facilitated through funding made available from the National Archives of Singapore (NAS). A special word of gratitude is extended to Mr Pitt Kuan Wah, the former head of the NAS, and especially to the philanthropist and entrepreneur Dr Lee Seng Tee of the Lee Foundation (Singapore) for encouraging and co-financing an in-depth study of Singapore, the Straits and the surrounding regions before 1800.

For post-editing the translation, as well as compiling the notes and glossaries, I relied on a number of established and junior members of the academic community who gave input according to their fields of expertise.

In this context, I would like to thank (in alphabetical order) Chris Baker (Bangkok); Cheah Boon Kheng (Universiti Sains Malaysia, Penang); Choo Lip Sin (Singapore); Pamela Cross (Canterbury, U.K.); Dhiravat na Pombejra (Chulalongkorn University, Bangkok); Alexander Drost (Ernst-Moritz-Arndt Universität, Greifswald); Khir Johari (independent researcher, Singapore); Mohd. Effendy bin Abdul Hamid (University of Hawai'i at Manoa); Anton van der Lem (Leiden University Library); Ruth Llobet (NUS); Bruce Lockhart (NUS); Pius Malekandathil (JNU, New Delhi); António Vasconcelos de Saldanha (University of Macao); and Sebastian Song (National Library, Singapore).

Among the institutions and special collections departments deserving separate mention are the Biblioteca Nacional de España in Madrid, owner of Jacques de Coutre's manuscripts, and the *Journal of the Malaysian Branch of the Royal Asiatic Society* for granting permission to publish a substantially reworked article that now forms part of the introduction to this volume. Thanks are also extended to Amsterdam University Library; Greifswald University Library; Koninklijke Bibliotheek, The Hague; Nationaal Archief van Nederland, The Hague; Leiden University Library; Arquivo Nacional da Torre do Tombo, Lisbon; Biblioteca de Academia das Ciências de Lisboa; Biblioteca Nacional de Portugal, Lisbon; Arquivo Histórico de Macau, Macao; Biblioteca Nacional de España, Madrid; Bayerische Staatsbibliothek, Munich; the Huntington Library, San Marino; Archivo General, Simancas; the Central Library of the National University of Singapore; and the National Archives of Singapore.

TIMELINE

1572/5	Estimated date of birth of Jacques de Coutre in Bruges, Flanders, in present-day Belgium.
1577	(5 March) Baptized in Bruges.
1591	(22 June) Farewell at Sluis; proceeded to Flushing via Middelburg.
1591	(after 1 August) Brief stint fishing for cod in the North Sea.
1592	(Spring) Headed for Lisbon; met his older brother Paul; proceeded with his brother Joseph to Goa via the Abrolhos Islands and the Cape of Good Hope.
1592	(14 September) Arrived in Goa.
1593	(28 September) Arrived in Melaka.
	Voyage by sea via Singapore to Pahang.
1595	(8 May–about December) Departure on diplomatic mission to Siam; eight-month sojourn in and around Ayutthaya.
1596	Brief return to Melaka via Cambodia.
1600	Headed for Manila via Brunei, Palawan and Mindoro.
1600–02	Life in Manila; witnessed battle at sea between the Spanish armada and the ships of Olivier van Noort in Manila Bay (14 December 1600); acted as translator for Lambert Biesman.
1602	Returned to Melaka via Borneo and Riau Islands.
1602	(Spring) Brief stay at Melaka; travelled with Júlio de Barros to Patani to trade in textiles. There he met Jacob van Neck, Jacob van Heemskerck, and evidently also Simon Lambertsz. Mau.
1602–03	Returned to Melaka via Batu Sawar; witnessed unfolding of a political crisis between Johor and Portuguese Melaka that ended in the massacre of Christian prisoners.
1603	(March or April) Headed for Goa to get married; travelled by sea via Baticalao and Tuticorin.

1603	(2 May) Arrival in Goa; wed his sister-in-law Dona Catarina (Cathalina) do Couto within one week of his arrival in Goa.
1606	First overland voyage to Europe via Hormuz, Basra, Baghdad, the ruins of Babylon, Aleppo, toward Marseille via Cyprus, Malta and Pantelleria. Jacques was captured off the north African coast by Tunesian pirates, and ransomed for 1,000 escudos in gold. After he was released, he continued his journey toward Marseille, Bayonne, Irún, Valladolid, Segovia, Madrid, Santiago de Compostela and Lisbon.
1609	Return voyage from Lisbon to Goa via the sea route, departing from Lisbon on 22 March and arriving in Goa on 15 November that year.
1620–21	Second overland voyage to Europe via Baghdad, Aleppo, Constantinople, and from there overland to Spain. Jacques returned to Goa via Baghdad, Isfahan, Shiraz, and the Persian coast, and from there via sea to Goa.
1623	Arrested in Goa and deported (1 April 1623) together with his brother Joseph and the German Cristóvão Luís van Undiston to Lisbon.
1623–28	Wrote the *Vida de Jaques de Coutre* and the Memorials.
1628	(29 December) Date of last memorial.
1632	(29 June) Exonerated by the Council of Portugal.
1640	(July) Died in Zaragoza; buried in San Andrés Hospital, Madrid.

INTRODUCTION

In the autumn of the year 1593, a young Fleming from Bruges in his early twenties named Jacobus van de Koutere, alias Jacques de Coutre or Jaques do Couto, disembarked in the Portuguese-held port of Melaka.[1] The first person to greet him after disembarking was one Sequin Martinela, whom de Coutre described as a gem merchant from Venice, residing in Melaka. The ageing Italian took Jacques under his wing and through the good services of Melaka's Portuguese Captain[2] Francisco de Silva de Meneses,[3] lodgings were quickly arranged.

De Coutre's arrival in the famous entrepôt of spice and commerce marked the beginning of his sojourn in and travels across much of insular and mainland Southeast Asia. De Coutre would have almost certainly been forgotten, had he not later in life decided to put pen to paper and with the assistance of his son Esteban written down his life's story. Who was Jacques de Coutre? Why should historians and anthropologists of Southeast Asia today bother to study his writings? And in what ways do the insights gained from his writings compare with similar travel accounts, rutters[4] and general commercial information about Asia written by De Coutre's late 16th and early 17th-century contemporaries?

This introduction is divided into eight basic parts. In the first I will provide a summary of the Fleming's biography by contextualising historically

[1] Concerning the different meanings of this name here and in other parts of the book, see also the list of place names (*Malaca*).

[2] The "governor" of Portuguese Melaka held the military rank of captain or captain-major. See the glossary (*capitão-mór*).

[3] Silva de Meneses, who served as captain of Melaka between 1594 and 1597, was subsequently imprisoned. See Paulo Jorge de Sousa Pinto, *The Portuguese and the Straits of Melaka, 1575–1619: Power, Trade and Diplomacy* (Singapore: NUS Press, 2012), p. 191.

[4] A manual containing instructions for navigation and trade. See also the glossary (*rutter*).

information gleaned from the *Vida de Jaques de Coutre* (The Life of Jacques de Coutre). The original Spanish-language manuscript is preserved in the National Library of Spain in Madrid. In the second part, I will provide a synopsis of the bundle of manuscripts preserved in Madrid and known as Ms. 2780. In addition to the *Vida* it also contains a series of politico-commercial memorials written in the late 1620s and 1630s for the crowns of Spain and Portugal.[5] Part three looks at the work on and with the manuscripts and in part four, I turn to explore the contents and arguments contained in this source translation. In part five, I will briefly comment on the preparation of the English translations and the policy for annotating the texts. Parts six and seven furnish summaries of Book I of the *Vida* and of the memorials respectively; and finally I provide a synopsis of the appendices.

I

JACQUES DE COUTRE: HIS LIFE AND TIMES

Jacobus van de Koutere, better known in present times from his writings as Jacques de Coutre (and later also as Jaques do Couto), was the natural son of a broom maker, Jacques senior, and Anna van Houven, and was born in the Flemish city of Bruges. According to surviving records, he was baptized on 5 March 1577; however, his actual date of birth remains unknown.[6] Based on chapter 1 of the *Vida*, Benjamin Teensma placed it in the year 1575, but according to De Coutre's testimony to the Inquisition in Goa in 1610, it can be calculated back to 1572.[7] Economically, socially and politically, these were difficult times not only for the city of Bruges and the county of Flanders, but also for much of western and central Europe as a whole. Different waves of the Protestant Reformation were rapidly altering the religious, social, political, and economic landscape of Europe—not least in the Low Countries, where

---

[5] The latter, however, are addressed to the Portuguese viceroy in Goa.

[6] Jacques de Coutre, *Aziatische Omzwervingen. Het levensverhaal van Jaques de Coutre, een Brugs diamantenhandelaar, 1591–1626*, tr. Johan Verbeckmoes and Eddy Stols (Berchem: EPO, 1988), p. 25; Benjamin N. Teensma, *De politieke en economische ideeën van de Bruggeling Jacques de Coutre (1575–1640) alsmede enige tekstkritiek* (Leiden: 1994), p. 3.

[7] ANTT, Inquisição de Lisboa, Processo 4941 (dated 1 December 1610) fol. 101 verso–3 recto, minutes of Jacques de Coutre's statements presented before the Inquisition of Goa in a case involving the appraised value of certain emeralds. These had been presented to a bailiff of the Inquisition (as a bribe?) by some New Christians. The bailiff wanted to make a necklace for his wife. In the minutes, De Coutre claims to be 38 years old in 1610, which places his year of birth in or around 1572.

religious disturbances spilled over into a full-fledged revolt against their overlord, Philip II of Spain. As Philip dispatched armies to the Netherlands to quell the disturbances, his policies to stamp out Protestantism and especially the decision of his governor in the Low Countries, the Duke of Alva, to levy a controversial sales tax, eventually led to Philip's deposition by the rebelling provinces in 1581. The 17 provinces of the Low Countries that had been created as a distinct administrative unit within the borders of the Holy Roman Empire came to division. While ten southern provinces were reconciled with Spain and Spanish-Catholic rule (the Spanish Netherlands), the seven provinces in the north—led by the Protestant-dominated provinces of Holland and Zeeland and their Stadholder, William of Orange—continued their revolt and eventually became the Dutch Republic. The Low Countries remained a battle ground for decades, with the Scheldt River, the port city of Antwerp and the border separating the Spanish Netherlands (now Belgium and Luxembourg) from the Dutch Republic (now the Netherlands) remaining a heavily armed and heavily garrisoned area.

Beyond the borders of the Low Countries, the situation was hardly less troubled. Neighbouring France was being torn apart by a civil war that was ostensibly motivated by the Protestant-Catholic divide. The debate was not just about the role and social space for each religious group, but crucially also about the sovereignty of France, the function and powers of the monarchy (supported by the Catholics), the power of the estates (largely supported by the Huguenots) and a group of pragmatists (the so-called *Politiques*) who aimed at strengthening the monarchy and pursuing a political agenda that was above factional (religious) interests.

England had admittedly entered a period of relative political and social stability during the reign of the last Tudor monarch, Queen Elizabeth I. But her legitimacy and reign were initially uncertain, and the socio-religious unrest unleashed after the death of her father, Henry VIII (especially due to the policies under the brief rule of Elizabeth's half-sister Mary before 1558) lingered for years. In the Holy Roman Empire—of which the Low Countries were formally an integral but self-administering part—the Protestant Reformation and the Catholic Counter-Reformation after 1563 continued to undermine the social and constitutional fabric of the German heartland. Policies of the Habsburg monarchs to champion the cause of the Counter-Reformation and their efforts at "rolling back" Protestantism in the Empire only served to invite hostile action from the Ottoman Empire and

Printed Portrait of Queen Elizabeth I of England taken from Emanuel van Meteren's *Commentariën ofte Memoriën* (Commentaries or Memoirs), 1652. (Private collection, Peter Borschberg).

Printed etching of the Duke of Alva, Spanish governor of the Low Countries, taken from Emanuel van Meteren's *Commentariën ofte Memoriën* (Commentaries or Memoirs), 1652. (Private collection, Peter Borschberg).

their efforts in Europe united Habsburg enemies in a protracted period of armed conflict known as the Thirty Years War (1618–48).

On the Iberian Peninsula, Spain and Portugal were reaping the fruits of their early colonial enterprise that had started in earnest during the late 15th century. The Portuguese had reaped significant benefits from their dominance of the spice trade with Asia, and defended themselves valiantly against Spanish incursions into traditional Portuguese markets in Southeast Asia. In 1580, Philip II invaded Portugal and became its king. Thus began the Union of the Two Crowns of Spain and Portugal that would last for a period of six decades until 1640. Though ruled by the same monarch—Philip II of Spain, for example, came to rule as Philip I of Portugal—the two countries and their respective colonial empires, the Spanish and the Portuguese, remained separate entities with minimal political and strategic coordination. In fact, Spain and Portugal during this period faced each other as stiff competitors in the Indies.

During the third quarter of the 16th century, gold and silver bullion imports to Spain reached their apex, and ultimately created an illusion of wealth. Within only a few years—especially in view of the protracted and costly warfare in the Low Countries and the naval wars in the Mediterranean against the Ottoman Turks—Spain's finances had become seriously over-stretched. Spain was forced to cease payments on its debt several times, but the default of 1606 forced the Spanish to negotiate with the "rebels" from the Netherlands.

It is against the backdrop of these broader, long-term geo-political and religious developments in Europe and the early European colonial empires of Spain and Portugal that we should place the decision of Jacques and his brother Joseph to seek their fortune outside Flanders, first fishing in the North Sea, then briefly in Lisbon and later in Portuguese India. Fate—and certainly personal choice—brought the two brothers to Lisbon, and in 1592 to Goa.[8] Here in the "Rome of the East", the capital of the Portuguese Estado da Índia,[9] the two brothers appeared to have parted ways for a few years. Joseph married a daughter of an established Christian family of limited means and settled in Goa, while Jacques ventured on his own to the

[8] Teensma, *De politieke en economische ideeën*, p. 3.

[9] The Portuguese colonial possessions around the Indian Ocean littoral. See the glossary for an explanation (*Estado da Índia*).

Hand-coloured bird's-eye view of Goa taken from the first edition of Jan Huyghen van Linschoten's *Itinerario* and *Reysgeschrift* printed in 1596. (The Hague, KB, 1702 B 4, inserted after p. 42).

Portuguese emporium and colony of Melaka. It served as his home base for most of the time between 1593 and his departure for Goa in 1603. Towards the end of Chapter II, Jacques recounted how an ageing gem merchant from Venice (by the name of Sequin Martinela) greeted him as he disembarked at Melaka on 28 September 1593. The two became close friends and with many years of hindsight Jacques reminisced, "I expressed my heartfelt thanks to old Sequin Martinela", and adjoined with an evident sense of fondness, "and from then on we were great friends, he was more of a father to me than my own father, and we lived together for a long time."[10]

Hand-coloured depiction of a Portuguese nobleman or crown official on a horse with his servants. Taken from the first edition of Jan Huyghen van Linschoten's *Itinerario* and *Reysgeschrift* printed in 1596. (The Hague, KB, 1702 B 4, insert after p. 46).

Thus began in September 1593 Jacques de Coutre's life in Southeast Asia, where he would spend about one decade from his early twenties until his early thirties. This was a period in Melaka's history that saw its apex under

[10] See ch. II of the *Vida de Jaques de Coutre.*

Hand-coloured depiction of a Portuguese couple with their servants, halberds in hand, on their way to church at night. Taken from the first edition of Jan Huyghen van Linschoten's *Itinerario* and *Reysgeschrift* printed in 1596. (The Hague, KB, 1702 B 4, insert after p. 48).

Portuguese rule, the arrival of the Dutch in Southeast Asian waters, as well as the beginnings of the Luso-Dutch conflict. The latter would invariably shape the politics, commerce and diplomacy across the region during the first half of the 17th century.

Book I of the *Vida,* which is translated here in its entirety, recounts Jacques' seaborne voyages across much of maritime Southeast Asia, the *orang laut* of the Old Strait of Singapore, the town of Pahang,[11] an extended adventure in Siam, as well as his impressions of the royal capital Ayutthaya. These impressions and observations of Siam and especially Ayutthaya arguably rank as the oldest surviving testimony by a European eyewitness. Jacques also wrote about his sojourn of nearly two years in the Philippines, where he met Dr Antonio de Morga and witnessed Olivier van Noort's

[11] See also the list of place names (*Pam*).

Hand-coloured depiction of servants carrying a Portuguese woman, or a daughter of a Portuguese nobleman, on a palanquin. Taken from the first edition of Jan Huyghen van Linschoten's *Itinerario* and *Reysgeschrift* printed in 1596. (The Hague, KB, 1702 B 4, insert after p. 48).

seaborne attack on Cavite in the Bay of Manila on 14 December 1600.[12] Jacques returned to Melaka on a journey that brought him along the coast of Borneo. Driven off course by a typhoon, Jacques and his mates found themselves hopelessly lost in the Riau Archipelago.[13] After sailing for about a month among the maze of islands and islets, with fresh water and food supplies almost depleted, they resorted to desperate measures, ambushing and kidnapping a fisherman whom they promised rich rewards for acting as a pilot and guide. In a subsequent voyage, Jacques ventured to

---

[12] Morga himself is the author of an important historical work on the early Spanish colonial Philippines. See Antonio de Morga, *The Philippine Islands, Moluccas, Siam, Cambodia, Japan and China at the Close of the Sixteenth Century*, ed. L.V. de Torres and H.E.J. Stanley (London: Hakluyt Society, 1868); *Sucesos de las Islas Filipinas,* tr. and ed. J.S. Cummins (Cambridge: Cambridge University Press for the Hakluyt Society, 1971) and Cummins, "Antonio de Morga and his *Sucesos de Las Islas Filipinas*", *JSEAH* 10, 3 (1969): 564–65.

[13] For further details and background information, see also the list of place names (*Islas de Linga*).

Patani,[14] where he escaped death and lost his fortune to the conniving Dutch. There he rubbed shoulders with the Dutch Admirals Jacob van Neck and Jacob van Heemskerck, whose men sank his fully laden junk[15] by drilling holes into the hull at night. Jacques mentioned the seizure of the Portuguese carrack *Santa Catarina* off the coast of Singapore in February 1603, around the same time he escaped a massacre of Christians in the Johor royal administrative centre of Batu Sawar.[16] Book I ends with Jacques marrying his sister-in-law, Dona Catarina do Couto, in a ceremony without pomp and fanfare held at the church of Nossa Senhora de Merces (Our Lady of Mercy) sometime in or around May 1603.[17]

With his marriage to Dona Catarina do Couto, Jacques relocated permanently to Goa where his brother Joseph also lived. The two Flemings integrated well into society there, gave generously to the local Santa Casa de Misericórdia (Holy House of Mercy), and contributed financially towards equipping an armada in 1605 that the Portuguese viceroy, Martim Afonso de Castro, dispatched to Melaka in response to an imminent Dutch maritime siege and blockade. The armada would engage the well-armed vessels of Dutch Admiral Cornelis Matelieff de Jonge in 1606 in the Melaka Straits near Cape Rachado (present-day Tanjung Tuan)[18] and again off Pulau Butom (present-day Mu Ko A Dang-Ra Wi).[19] With the benefit of hindsight, the Estado da Índia had embarked on a long, painful retreat, yielding forts, ports and settlements to the VOC,[20] which was ever-growing through its commercial prowess, diplomatic savvy and successful armed engagements

---

[14] See the list of place names (*Patane*).

[15] See the glossary (*junk*).

[16] See the *Vida,* ch. XIX; and the explanation in the list of place names *(Batusavar).* Concerning the seizure of the *Santa Catarina* in general and its impact both in Europe and Southeast Asia, see SMS, pp. 68–75; Borschberg, "The Seizure of the *Santa Catarina* off Singapore", *Revista de Cultura,* International Edition 11 (2004): 1–25; "The Seizure of the *Santa Catarina* Revisited", *JSEAS* 33, 1 (2002): 31–62, esp. 48–50; Martine van Ittersum, "Hugo Grotius in Context", *AJSS* 31, 3 (2003): 511–48 and more extensively in her book *Profit and Principle.*

[17] See the *Vida,* ch. XX. Teensma falsely claimed that Jacques married the wife of his brother Paul. See CRE, p. iii.

[18] See the list of place names (*Cabo Rachado*).

[19] Island group off the southwestern coast of present-day Thailand near the border with Malaysia. See also the list of place names (*Pulau Butom*) as well as the forthcoming title: *Journals, Memorials and Letters of Cornelis Matelieff de Jonge: Security, Diplomacy and Commerce in 16th- and 17th-century Southeast Asia,* ed. and intr. P. Borschberg and tr. Corinna Vermeulen (Singapore: NUS Press, 2014).

[20] The United Netherlands East India Company, formed in 1602. See also the glossary (*VOC*).

Printed etching of King Philip III/II of Spain and Portugal taken from Emanuel van Meteren's *Commentariën ofte Memoriën* (Commentaries or Memoirs), 1652. (Private collection, Peter Borschberg).

at sea. But the year 1606 also marked the beginning of important changes in the European homeland. In that year, the Castilian treasury suspended interest payments on its huge accumulated debt, as a result of which King Philip III/II was forced to negotiate for peace with the "rebels" in the Netherlands. The negotiations were acrimonious, and although the Spanish were willing to grant the Dutch "rebels" their independence, they sought to exact guarantees for the free exercise of the Roman Catholic faith in the Dutch Republic and—the most controversial of all—a complete withdrawal of Dutch merchants from trading activities in the West and East Indies.

By August 1608, discussions for peace almost grounded to a halt and eventually collapsed over the Dutch refusal to give in to such demands.[21] That was simply not acceptable to the Dutch merchants who urged the senior statesman Johan van Oldenbarnevelt not to yield. The outcome was not a permanent peace settlement, but a truce signed at Antwerp that was to last for a period of 12 years (1609–21). Although the East and West Indies were to be covered by the clauses of the agreement, developments in Asia ensured that the Twelve Years Truce became a dead letter east of the Cape of Good Hope by 1613 at the very latest.[22]

Irrespective of whether the Truce ever had a realistic chance of holding in Asia—and influential historians such as Jonathan Israel have expressly argued against this—the arrival of Dutch traders in the East Indies and the extension of their war against Spain and Portugal into the Asian theatre had certainly changed the fortunes of the Portuguese Estado da Índia for the worse. For sure, there was a debate among the officers of the Portuguese crown in Asia as well as in the Lusitanian homeland about the perceived decay of the Estado da Índia, which since the late 16th century was seen as a victim of myopic and greedy officials. But as is so often the case in times of crisis, such introspection was supplanted by the search for a scapegoat, a person or a group of persons who could be clearly identified and dealt with. As fleets of the VOC stepped up their pressure by attacking hard (fortifications and installations) and soft (ships and persons) Portuguese targets and routinely plundered richly laden commercial vessels in Asian waters, mistrust mounted against other European foreigners living in the Portuguese settlements. Suspicions were particularly strong against members of communities with roots in and connections to northern Europe, such as the Flemings, Brabanders (who were also subjects of King Philip III/II of Spain and Portugal), and also the Germans, who were subjects of the Holy Roman Emperor, a cousin of the Iberian monarch.

---

[21] Borschberg, "The Johor-VOC Alliance and the Twelve Years Truce", *IILJ Working Paper* 8 (2009): 7. See also *Johan van Oldenbarnevelt. Bescheiden betreffende zijn staatkundig beleid en zijn familie,* ed. Sikko P. Haak and Augustus J. Veenendaal, 3 vols. (The Hague: Martinus Nijhoff, 1934–67), II, pp. 174 et seq., where Van Oldenbarnevelt recorded his discussions with the Spanish delegates over the East Indies trade. See also Jonathan I. Israel, *Dutch Primacy in World Trade, 1585–1740* (Oxford: Clarendon Press, 1989), p. 81.

[22] Borschberg, "The Johor-VOC Alliance and the Twelve Years Truce": 8, note 17. See also the list of place names *(Cabo de Boa Esperansa).*

Printed etching of King Philip IV/III of Spain and Portugal. (BNE, public domain).

At the dawn of the 17th century, a number of royal ordinances were passed by the Portuguese crown that progressively marginalised members of the community who were not Portuguese subjects. They tightened the rules and severely restricted who could obtain a licence to organise and conduct annual concession voyages (*viagens*) or purchase a safe-conduct pass (*cartaz*).[23] This tightening of regulations was followed shortly thereafter by a decree that expelled European settlers in the Portuguese colonies. On 28 November 1606, Philip III/II wrote to his viceroy in India, Dom Martim Afonso de Castro, instructing him to implement a law (promulgated on 18 March 1605) that instructed the expulsion of foreigners from the Portuguese settlements of the Estado da Índia, including especially the "many foreigners from diverse nations [who] live in those lands, Italians, French, Germans and Flemish, most of whom ... have gone there overland through Persia and Turkey and few through Portugal."[24] Although the law was to be implemented without exception, the monarch also advised caution as the expellees could "go to the enemy Moors" and pass on to them "information about my fortresses that are near them, teaching them tricks and means" that could endanger the security of the fortresses and implicitly of the nearby resident population.[25] As members of the community in Goa—who in 1605 had contributed towards outfitting a fleet dispatched to assist Melaka that came under the attack of Dutch Admiral Cornelis Matelieff de Jonge—the De Coutre brothers managed to avoid immediate eviction from their adopted home of Goa.[26] Their surviving petitions to the Lusitanian crown testify that they fought hard against deportation for many years, arguing for an exemption on the grounds that they had already lived in Goa for 15 years and had founded families and settled there. Jacques, importantly, had also stressed his loyalty to the Portuguese and reminded officials that he had carried important letters by the viceroy on his trips overland to Europe.[27] Surviving evidence from

---

[23] See also the glossary (*cartaz, viagem*).

[24] GPFT, pp. 175, 177.

[25] GPFT, p. 177.

[26] On this point see also S. Subrahmanyam, "An Augsburger in Ásia Portuguesa: Further Light on the Commercial World of Ferdinand Cron, 1587–1624", *Emporia, Commodities and Entrepreneurs in Asian Maritime Trade, 1400–1750,* ed. Roderich Ptak and Dietmar Rothermund (Stuttgart: Franz Steiner Verlag, 1991), p. 406, note 18.

[27] Lisbon, ANTT, DRI, Livro 4, fol. 98, letter by the king of Portugal Philip II to Viceroy Rui Lourenço de Távora, 8 February 1611; see also Pato, Raymundo A. de Bulhão, and António da Silva Rego, ed., *Documentos Remettidos da Índia ou Livros das Monções*, 10 vols. (Lisbon: Typographia da Academia Real das Sciencias and Imprensa Nacional—Casa de Moeda, 1880–1982), II, pp. 16–7.

the Lisbon Inquisition also reveals that De Coutre had assisted in estimating the value of some emeralds that had been given by certain New Christians as a bribe to the Goa Inquisition.[28] Importantly, additional testimonies appended to the minutes of the Inquisition by witnesses corroborate De Coutre's statements and add details relating to his activities in his workshop.[29] Other services he rendered to the Portuguese crown included spying on the Dutch.

Jacques travelled to the Iberian Peninsula on at least two occasions. In 1606 he embarked on the first of his two return voyages via Hormuz,[30] Babylon and Aleppo. Captured by Tunisian pirates, he managed to buy himself freedom and returned to Goa some years later. He embarked on a second, similar voyage to Europe in the year 1620.

The sense of xenophobia that had pervaded Goa did not dissipate—to the contrary—and by 1621, when the Twelve Years Truce had formally expired, officers of the crown and the merchant community both in Europe and Asia had long begun to take stock of developments. They faced the prospect of a full-blown war with much trepidation and a great deal of uncertainty. The British historian Jonathan Israel reported that by the expiry of the Truce and the onset of the third decade of the 17th century, the "almost universal conviction among Spaniards of all classes by around 1620 [was] that the Twelve Years Truce had been a disaster".[31] Evidently such sentiments were widespread, and one commentator, Sancho de Monçada, had already lamented in 1619: "The damage to Spain arises from the new commerce of the foreigners ... For in every prosperity in Spain, the foreigner intervenes and sucks it forth depriving Spain of it and carrying it to all her enemies."[32] The sentiment and xenophobia in the Portuguese colonies were hardly any different.

It was against the broader canvas of this uncertainty—and the heightened sense of xenophobia accompanying the expiry of the Truce—that the brothers Jacques and Joseph de Coutre were arrested and detained

---

[28] ANTT, Inquisição de Lisboa, Processo 4941 (1 December 1610) fol. 101 verso–3.

[29] Ibid., fol. 1–6.

[30] Port city in present-day Iran. See also the list of place names (*Ormus*).

[31] Jonathan I. Israel, *The Dutch Republic and the Hispanic World, 1606–1661* (Oxford: Clarendon Press, 1982), p. 55.

[32] Israel, *The Dutch Republic,* p. 54.

before being deported to Lisbon. From documentary evidence preserved in the Arquivo Nacional-Torre de Tombo in Lisbon, it transpired that earlier attempts to have the brothers deported based on the law of 1606 had been successfully resisted.[33] Eddy Stols and Benjamin Teensma have argued that the De Coutre brothers were arrested on suspicion of colluding with the Dutch and spying for the VOC,[34] but Teotónio de Sousa has significantly highlighted that their arrest and detention at Fort Ponda for a period of six months was "for reasons that have no mention of the Dutch or [De Coutre's] involvement with them."[35] As the VOC was in the process of consolidating its foothold on the Indian subcontinent during the early 1620s, Jacques and Joseph may very well have willingly or unwillingly passed sensitive trade and security information to the VOC—and may have leaked entire documents to the Dutch—as George Winius and Carrie Chorba have surmised.[36]

Be this as it may, Jacques and Joseph were deported to Europe on 1 April 1623.[37] In earlier years, their deportation from Goa had been conditioned by the law of 1605, but they had managed to stall for time by petitioning the viceroy; now charges had been lodged against them for colluding with the Dutch, accusations they vehemently denied.

The brothers set out to prove their innocence. Perhaps they were just the victims of some plot or had been made convenient scapegoats in a political and economic environment that was rapidly deteriorating. They were most certainly not the only ones. Jacques' *Vida* also mentioned the fate of one German named Christóvão Luís van Undiston who had earlier worked for

---

33 DRI, Livro 4 (8 February 1611), fol. 98; DRI, Livro 6 (28 March 1613), fol. 153; LM, II, pp. 16–7, 411.

34 Jacques de Coutre, *Andanzas asiáticas*, ed. E. Stols, B. Teensma and J. [V]erbeckmoes (Madrid: História 16, 1991), bk. 3, ch. 13, pp. 339–40; AO, pp. 237–38; Teensma, *De politieke en economische ideeën*, p. 14; Winius and Chorba, "Literary Invasions in *La vida de Jaques de Coutre*", p. 716, note 14; Stefan Halikowski-Smith, "Globalisation before Globalisation: the case of the Portuguese world empire, 1415–1808", in *World and Global History: Research and Teaching*, ed. Seija Jalagin, Susanna Tavera and Andrew Dilley (Pisa: Edizioni Plus—Pisa University Press, 2011), p. 38.

35 Teotónio R. de Souza, "Embassies and Surrogates: Case-Study of a Malacca Embassy to Siam in 1595", *Indica* 26, 1/2 (1989): 43.

36 George D. Winius and Carrie C. Chorba, "Literary Invasions in *La vida de Jaques de Coutre*: do they prejudice its value as an historical source?", *A Carreira da Índia e as Rotas dos Estreitos. Actas do VIII Seminário Internacional de História Indo-Portuguesa,* ed. Artur Teodoro de Matos and Luís Filipe R. Thomaz (Angra do Heroísmo: Barbosa & Javier, 1998), p. 716.

37 CRE, p. 10. "... partimos de lá [Goa] em primero de abril de 1623 ..." (We departed from there [Goa] on 1 April 1623).

the Dutch and was taken as a prisoner of war by the Spanish in Manila. As part of the conditions for release, Van Undiston was not permitted to re-enter employment with the VOC, and so he headed for Goa where he was arrested yet again and subsequently deported to Lisbon.[38] According to surviving documents, Van Undiston evidently took his revenge. Under cross-examination he denounced various persons, including Dom Filipe de Sousa and others, for their suspected dealings with the Dutch. The names of these alleged collaborators were revealed in a letter by King Philip III/II of Portugal to his viceroy of India.

In addition to Jacques and Joseph de Coutre, as well as Christóvão Luís van Undiston, the plan of the Goa authorities was to deport a fourth person. This was another German who once had acted as the Indian agent of the Fugger and Welser and had since become a fabulously wealthy merchant in Goa by his own right. He was Ferdinand Cron (sometimes spelled Kron) from Augsburg.[39] Given that De Coutre and Cron were both active in the gem trade in Goa around the same time, it is not surprising that they knew and did business with one another, but it is evident that their relationship was patchy and not (always) cordial.[40] Cron was by all accounts a colourful character who has elicited considerable interest in recent decades, especially

---

[38] AA, bk. 3, ch. 15, pp. 352–53; AO, p. 247. See also Gijs Kruijtzer, *Xenophobia in Seventeenth Century India* (Leiden: Leiden University Press, 2009), p. 20.

[39] For works touching on Cron in general, see the useful studies by Malekandathil, *The Germans, the Portuguese and India,* (Münster: LIT Verlag, 1999), esp. pp. 97–111; Reinhard Hildebrandt, *Die Georg Fuggerischen Erben* (Berlin: Duncker & Humblot, 1966); Maximilian Kalus, *Pfeffer—Kupfer—Nachrichten. Kaufmannsnetzwerke und Handelsstrukturen im europäisch-asiatischen Handel am Ende des 16. Jahrhunderts,* Dissertation zur Erlangung des akademischen Grades doctor rerum politicarum (Jena: Wissenschaftliche Fakultät, Friedrich-Schiller-Universität, 2009); Kalus, "Tracing Business Patterns in Sixteenth Century European-Asian Trade. New Methods Using Semantic Networking Models", XIV International Economic History Congress, 21–25 August 2006; Hermann Kellenbenz, "Cron, Ferdinand, 1559–1637", in J. Serrão, *Dicionário de história de Portugal,* I (Lisbon: Iniciatiras Editoriais, 1963), pp. 752–53; Kellenbenz, "Ferdinand Cron" in *Lebensbilder aus dem Bayerischen Schwaben,* ed. Wolfgang Zorn, 3, 9 (1974): 95–96; Kellenbenz, "Autour de 1600: Le commerce du poivre des Fugger et le marché international du poivre", *Annales, Histoire, Sciences Sociales* 11, 1 (1956): 1–28; Kellenbenz, "German Trade Relations with the Indian Ocean from the End of the Eighteenth Century to 1870", *JSEAS* 13, 1 (1982): 133–52; Kellenbenz, "From Melchior Manlich to Ferdinand Cron. German Levantine and Oriental Trade Relations (Second Half of 16th and Beginning of 17th Century), *Journal of European Economic History* 19, 3 (1990): 611–22; Kellenbenz, "Ferdinand Cron, 1559–1637" in *Lebensbilder aus dem Bayrischen Schwaben,* ed. Wolfgang Zorn (München: Max Hueber Verlag, 1966), pp. 194–210; S. Subrahmanyam, "An Augsburger", pp. 401–25; Teensma, *De politieke en economische ideeën,* p. 13.

[40] On this point see also Subrahmanyam, "An Augsburger", p. 406, note 18.

among scholars researching in India and Germany. After 1591, he took over from the Fuggers and Welsers an information network that he further built up and expanded to cover much of the Indian Ocean region spanning from the eastern Mediterranean in the west to Melaka and Macao in the east.[41] Cron was capable of transmitting information overland within weeks between India, Iran, the Ottoman Empire and Europe, and with his network he could circumvent naval blockades of European ports and even pre-empt information arriving via the maritime route around the Cape.[42] He had used his information network in 1605–06 to alert the viceroy about Dutch fleet movements and imminent attacks.[43] This gave the Portuguese a head start in making preparations to counter an attack on Melaka by Admiral Cornelis Matelieff de Jonge in 1606. Like De Coutre, Cron had contributed money towards arming and equipping Portuguese naval campaigns and had generously donated or sponsored gemstones for altarpieces in Goa and as far away as Macao.[44] Last but not least, he was—since its founding in 1611—the agent in India for the *Real Monasterio de la Incarnación* in Madrid, founded by Philip III/II's wife Margareta of Austria, and Cron also served as the queen's procurator.[45] Licences for commercial voyages had been conceded to the monastery as a way of raising funds for the construction of its new premises in Madrid. These voyage concessions were managed by Cron, and profits generated were supposed to be channelled back to Madrid to fund the construction work.[46] That scheme, alas, had not quite worked according to plan, as Cron allegedly used profits as seed capital to fund his personal business ventures in the gem trade. It would appear that Cron may have become too powerful and too wealthy for comfort. The Goa treasury officially owed him considerable sums of money at one time—20,000 ducats[47] or

---

[41] Malekandathil, *The Germans, the Portuguese and India,* p. 100; Malekandathil, *Maritime India: Trade, Religion and Polity in the Indian Ocean* (New Delhi: Primus Books, 2010), pp. xxi–xxii, 156.

[42] Concerning Cron's familiarity with developments in West Asia, see also Sanjay Subrahmanyam, "Manila, Melaka, Mylapore...: A Dominican Voyage through the Indies, ca.1600", *Archipel* 57 (1999): 229.

[43] Malekandathil, *The Germans, the Portuguese and India*, pp. 99, 100–1.

[44] London British Library, Egerton Ms. 1646, fol. 239; DUP, I, p. 621; Subrahmanyam, "An Augsburger", p. 408.

[45] Malekandathil, *The Germans, the Portuguese and India*, p. 103; Subrahmanyam, "An Augsburger", pp. 407–8.

[46] Malekandathil, *The Germans, the Portuguese and India*, p. 103.

[47] A gold-based currency unit. See also the glossary (*ducat*).

the equivalent of 70 kilograms of mint-grade gold.[48] As in the case of the De Coutre brothers some years later, Cron was charged in 1619 with secretly maintaining relations with the Dutch[49]—nay, at one time he was even rumoured to have exchanged correspondence with the Dutch Stadholder Prince Maurice of Nassau.[50] One rumour circulating in Japan had him scheming to betray the Estado da Índia and delivering up *Ásia Portuguesa* to the VOC for the sum of 40,000 cruzados.[51] Although the charges of collusion were subsequently withdrawn (on the grounds that they had been made to avoid torture), Cron was arrested at the orders of Viceroy João Coutinho, the Count of Redondo, and stripped of his possessions, only to have them restored to him within months by the viceroy's successor, Fernão de Albuquerque. But in the three months he languished in prison, Cron lost both his brother-in-law (who was imprisoned with him) as well as his wife.[52] But this apparent rehabilitation and protection from De Albuquerque was not to last, and after the latter's tenure as viceroy had come to an end, the case against Cron was reopened. All sorts of new rumours were swirling between Goa, Lisbon and Madrid. One had Viceroy De Albuquerque illicitly obtaining loans from Cron;[53] and on hearing rumours that the German was walking freely through the streets of Goa, King Philip IV/III angrily issued fresh instructions to his new viceroy, Francisco da Gama, the Conde de Vidigueira, for Cron's immediate arrest. From a letter the viceroy wrote to Philip IV/III in 1624, it transpires that the *patache* deporting the De Coutre brothers (and implicitly Van Undiston) to Lisbon in March 1623 was allegedly "too small", so Cron was to be taken to Europe on a larger vessel during the next sailing season.

The ship deporting Cron was named the *São Tomé* and it departed Goa on 1 February 1624.[54] On arrival in Europe, Cron was placed under house

---

[48] Malekandathil, *The Germans, the Portuguese and India,* p. 105.

[49] Charles Ralph Boxer, "Uma raridade bibliográfica sobre Fernão Cron", *Boletim Internacional de Bibliografia Luso-Brasileira* 12, 3 (1971): 343; Malekandathil, *The Germans, the Portuguese and India,* pp. 105–6.

[50] CSV, Livro 19 (25 January 1624), fol. 320–26. This rumour reportedly was circulating in Jambi. On the alleged complicity with the Dutch, see also Subrahmanyam, "An Augsburger", pp. 420–21.

[51] Ibid. About 1.16 metric tons of coin-grade silver. See also the glossary (*cruzado*).

[52] DRI, Livro 12 (9 February 1620), fol. 506.

[53] DRI, Livro 21 (21 February 1625), fol. 70 recto–verso.

[54] DRI, Livro 19 (January 1624), fol. 18; LM, X, p. 47; Malekandathil, *The Germans, the Portuguese and India,* p. 108; Sanjay Subrahmanyam, "An Augsburger", pp. 418–19.

arrest and in 1627 was transferred to Madrid to give advice to the king on plans to set up a Portuguese East India Company.[55] He expressed his doubts whether any company could handle the complex trade of Asia, and whether enough capital could be raised for the operations.[56] Cron was eventually acquitted. In the same year he famously defended his dealings in India in a work published in 1629.[57]

Due to the pressure and intervention of the Flemish merchant community in Lisbon, Jacques and Joseph were released from prison in Lisbon and transferred to Madrid. This was based on the reasoning that, being natives of Bruges, they were also direct subjects of the King of Spain in his capacity as the Count of Flanders.[58] The brothers defended their dealings and personal reputation in a memorial submitted to the Spanish crown in December 1624. In what was evidently an attempt at demonstrating loyalty against charges of treason and collaborating with the Dutch "rebels", Jacques penned a number of memorials during this period in which he furnished a sweeping overview of trading activities across the Indian Ocean and broadly staked out commercial and strategic priorities for the Iberian powers for eastern Africa and Asia.

The crown duly investigated the case lodged against the De Coutre brothers, and according to a royal decree dated 29 June 1632, they were exonerated by the *Conselho de Portugal* (Council of Portugal).[59] In the words of Stefan Halikowski-Smith, however, overturning of the expulsion order from Goa "did not bring the brothers and their economic activities back to Goa".[60] Still, Jacques' steadfast belief in proving his innocence and loyalty to the Iberian monarch yielded dividends, and as Winius and Chorba have underscored, he received great honours from the Spanish crown and was elevated to the status of a Knight of the Order of Santiago.[61] Around eight years after his exoneration—in July 1640—Jacques de Coutre passed away

---

[55] Boxer, "Uma raridade": 339; Malekandathil, *The Germans, the Portuguese and India,* p. 108.

[56] James C. Boyajian, *Portuguese Trade in Asia under the Habsburgs, 1580–1640* (Baltimore and London: Johns Hopkins University Press, 1993), p. 191.

[57] BNP, *Collecção Pombalina,* no. 647, fol. 210–19; also Boxer, "Uma raridade": 323–64; Malekandathil, *The Germans, the Portuguese and India,* p. 109; Subrahmanyam, "An Augsburger", p. 401, note 3.

[58] AA, bk. 3, ch. 15, p. 354; AO, p. 248.

[59] AA, appendix 1, p. 361; Teensma, *De politieke en economische ideeën,* p. 13.

[60] Halikowski-Smith, *Globalisation before Globalisation,* p. 38.

[61] Winius and Chorba, "Literary Invasions", p. 717.

Hand-drawn draft for the title page of the *Vida de Jaques de Coutre* (Life of Jacques de Coutre). (BNE, Ms. 2780).

in Zaragoza, Spain.[62] Although his exact date and year of birth remains uncertain, he would have probably been in his early to mid-60s, a ripe old age for a person living in his time and circumstances.[63] De Coutre's remains were brought to Madrid and he was interred in the church of the San Andrés Hospital which is said to have served the Flemish community in the Spanish capital.[64] Its premises were built in the 1520s during the rule of Charles V/I and were located outside the city walls adjacent to the Puerta del Sol ("Sun Gate"). The San Andrés Hospital was demolished in 1864.

[62] Winius and Chorba, "Literary Invasions", p. 715.

[63] AO, p. 33.

[64] AA, appendix 2, "Licentia Funeranda", p. 363.

II

SYNOPSIS OF THE SURVIVING MANUSCRIPTS

This section examines a bundle of manuscripts ascribed to Jacques de Coutre that is preserved in the Biblioteca Nacional de España (National Library of Spain) in Madrid and is shelved as Ms. 2780.[65]

As has been earlier observed by other researchers, the bundle Ms. 2780 can be divided into two basic parts: first, the *Vida* or autobiography of Jacques de Coutre written in a neat, scribal hand; and second, a series of documents and memorials (allegedly) written in De Coutre's own hand. All of the manuscripts contained in this bundle were written in the second half of the 1620s, in other words after Jacques and Joseph had been deported to Europe. This would also place the texts in a period before their exoneration in 1632.

The autobiography commonly known as the *Vida de Jaques de Coutre*, spans the first 242 folios of Ms. 2780. It is written in a neat and legible hand that features the occasional marginalia written by an unknown person and that summarize points of interest encountered in the text. There is a coloured coat-of-arms in addition to what appears to be a draft title page for a printed version of the text. As the ornate draft title page states (see p. 22), the text of the *Vida* was edited by Jacque's son, Esteban de Coutre. The latter's more precise role in crafting the *Vida* is not known with certainty, and this is a point to which I will return later in this introduction.

The second part of the manuscript is formed by a set of appendices or annexes to the main text of the *Vida*. These span folios 252 through 294. In his introduction to his *Como Remediar o Estado da Índia?* (How to Remedy the Estado da Índia), Benjamin Teensma described these as "appendices of a more general character, in which the author gives concrete advice to the King of Spain and the Count of Linhares—who in 1628 was appointed Viceroy of Portuguese Asia—on how to restore the former colonial prosperity."[66] Teensma regards these appendices or annexes as documents in rough draft

[65] For a detailed description of the Madrid manuscript, see Jacques de Coutre, *Como Remediar o Estado da Índia? Being the Appendices of the Vida de Jaques de Coutre* (Madrid: Biblioteca Nacional, Ms. 2780), ed. Benjamin N. Teensma (Leiden: Centre for the History of European Expansion, 1989), p. iv. Concerning the composition of the seven memorials between 1625 and 1629, see ibid., p. vii. See also Teensma, *De politieke en economische ideeën*, p. 4.

[66] CRE, pp. v, vii.

that are written carelessly in terms of style and grammar and are littered with "Lusitanianisms" or Portuguese idioms.[67] Unlike the *Vida,* the appendices are not written in a neat hand and are very difficult to decipher. Teensma has concluded that they are written in De Coutre's own hand, in one long narrative and "rarely pausing to introduce new paragraphs".[68] The first two documents are written in Portuguese and the remaining five in Spanish. The headings or titles of these seven appendices have been translated into English as follows:[69]

1. How to seriously damage the Dutch should Your Majesty license our merchant-vassals to prepare ships for the East Indies, and where they might find prizes and do their trading. But it will be necessary that Your Majesty leave the pepper to the merchants. In doing so He will inflict great war upon the Dutch, because then our ships will bring large quantities to Spain, and the rebels will make smaller profit as pepper is their principal merchandise.[70] (*See Memorial I in this edition*)
2. Information presented to Your Majesty by Joseph and Jacques de Coutre, citizens of the city of Bruges.[71]
3. In order that Your Excellency be cognizant of the commerce that used to exist in the Indies, especially in Malacca, before the Dutch went there.[72] (*See Memorial II in this edition*)
4. Information urging the building of some castles or fortifications in the Singapore Strait and other parts of the South.[73] (*See Memorial III in this edition*)
5. Information to your Majesty to remedy the State of the East Indies.[74] (*See Memorial IV in this edition*)

---

[67] CRE, p. vii.

[68] CRE, p. vii.

[69] CRE, pp. vi–vii, as translated by Benjamin Teensma. AO, p. vi. In AA, these memorials are featured as Appendices III through IX, pp. 365–438.

[70] Ms. 2780, fol. 252–61. According to John Villiers, "Review of Jacques de Coutre, Como Remediar o Estado da Índia?, ed. Benjamin N. Teensma, Leiden: Center for the History of European Expansion, 1989", *JSEAS* 21, 2 (1990): 455, this memorial was addressed to the Portuguese viceroy in Goa.

[71] Ms. 2780, fol. 262–66 verso. Villiers, "Review": 455, also opines that this memorial was addressed to the viceroy in Goa.

[72] Ms. 2780, fol. 268–69.

[73] Ms. 2780, fol. 270–74 verso. A map of the straits region indicating the selected sites, perhaps drawn by De Coutre himself, was once appended to this document but is now missing.

[74] Ms. 2780, fol. 277–87. According to Villiers, "Review": 455, this memorial is addressed to the viceroy in Goa.

6. List of what the rebels take to the East Indies (*See Memorial IV in this edition*).[75]
7. Copy of some recommendations given by Jacques de Coutre to the Count of Liñares,[76] Viceroy, who in this year of 1629 went to India.[77]

The Madrid manuscript bundle Ms. 2780 thus contains two sets of materials: an autobiography generally known as the *Vida* and an appendix comprising seven documents. Before I turn to delve further into the subject of authorial intentions, it would be opportune to intoduce and summarise some of the work that has been done on Ms. 2780 over the course of about four and a half decades.

III
WORK ON AND WITH THE DE COUTRE MANUSCRIPTS

Although Ms. 2780 has long been in the possession of the Biblioteca Nacional, the texts had aroused little interest among the scholarly community until the mid- to late 1960s when they were featured in the *Inventario General de Manuscritos de la Biblioteca Nacional de Madrid* (1965).[78] The manuscripts eventually caught the eye—and soon fired the imagination—of several researchers in Belgium and the Netherlands, notably Eddy O. Stols, Johan Verbeckmoes, Benjamin N. Teensma, and George Winius.

In the early 1970s, Stols drew scholarly attention to the Madrid bundle, and referred expressly to Jacques de Coutre both in his work *De Spaanse Brabanders* (The Spanish Brabanders) published in 1971,[79] as well as in an entry he had written for the *Nationaal Biografisch Woordeboek* (Dictionary of National Biography) of Belgium published in 1974.[80] Stols is perhaps best remembered for spearheading the 1991 Spanish edition

[75] Ms. 2780, fol. 288.

[76] This represents an Hispanicised spelling of Manuel de Noronha, Conde de Linhares. He served as the Portuguese viceroy of India in the late 1620s and early 1630s.

[77] Ms. 2780, fol. 290–94 verso. See Teensma's introduction to CRE, p. vii. This memorial dated 29 December 1628 is the most recent of the seven.

[78] Winius and Chorba, "Literary Invasions", p. 711.

[79] Eddy Stols, *De Spaanse Brabanders of de Handelsbetrekkingen der Zuidelijke Nederlanden met de Iberische Wereld, 1598–1648. Tekst en Bijlagen* (Brussels: Paleis der Academiën, 1971).

[80] *Nationaal Biographisch Woordenboek van België,* 15 vols. (Brussels: Paleis der Academiën, 1964–96), see vol. VI, pp. 151–4.

published as a volume in the *Crónicas de America* (Chronicles of the Americas), a series produced to coincide with the quincentennial celebrations commemorating the "discovery" of the Americas in 1992.[81] This Spanish edition contains both the *Vida* as well as the full set of memorials, to which the editors added as appendices 1–2 a copy of the sentence issued in 1623 against Joseph and Jacques de Coutre as well as the funerary licence issued on the death of Jacques in 1640.[82] Publication of the *Vida* and memorials was not only misplaced in a series like the *Crónicas de América* (vol. 61), but this Spanish edition itself is faulty. In one instance a paragraph from book I, chapter IV, of the *Vida* has been omitted.[83] In addition, the annotations reveal a generally poor command of Asian geography, languages, and occasionally, the commodities of trade. All in all, the Spanish edition remains by and large unfamiliar, as well as inaccessible to students and researchers in (English-speaking) Asia.

The first translation of the *Vida* was published in 1988 in a Flemish-Dutch edition prepared by the Belgian academics Stols and Verbeckmoes (the latter is a specialist in 17th century Spanish literature and especially the picaresque and Byzantine literary genres). This edition, titled *Aziatische Omzwervingen* (Asian Peregrinations) is certainly very useful, but it suffers from three distinct shortcomings. First, corrupted Asian names and titles are reproduced as they appear in the text without further explanation or clarification. This renders the text largely inaccessible to non-specialists. Second, the translation of the Spanish text is in parts too free or even inaccurate. Moreover, the Flemish-Dutch translation—unlike its Spanish counterpart—contains only the text of the *Vida* and has omitted the memorials. In his review of the *Aziatische Omzwervingen* published in 1992, Christian Koninckx had few genuinely critical comments to make about the translation, but conceded that it is not something suitable for "the average reader", and therefore, not a text for the uninitiated and non-specialist.[84]

---

[81] AA.

[82] AA, pp. 359–62, "Copia de la sentencia que se dio en favor de Ioseph de Coutre, y su hermano Iaques de Coutre ...", and pp. 363–4, "Licencia Funeranda".

[83] See p. 82 below where the missing passage has been identified and marked.

[84] Christian Koninckx, "Review of Eddy Stols and Johan Verbeckmoes. Aziatische omzwervingen. Het leven van Jacques de Coutre, een Brugs diamanthandelaar 1591–1627", *Revue Belge de philologie et d'histoire* 70, 4 (1992): 1052–3. The term used by Koninckx on p. 1052 is "doorsnee-lezer".

The task of preparing a transcript of the appendices with critical annotations was completed by Benjamin Teensma in 1989.[85] This edition was published as part of the Leiden Centre for the History of European Expansion's *Intercontinenta* series (vol. 10), but due to a small print run, it is not widely available in public depository institutions, and moreover, is rarely found outside of Europe. In a review published in the Singapore-based *Journal of Southeast Asian Studies* in 1990, the British academic John Villiers had only a few good words to spare about the quality of Teensma's transcript and edition. He faulted the annotations as inadequate, and criticised that no English translation had been prepared of the Spanish and Portuguese original texts.[86] Villiers thought it of very limited use to rush "into a typescript with a work that will neither satisfy specialists who wish to use Jacques de Coutre as a primary source, nor meet the requirements of those with a more general interest in the histories of the Portuguese and Spanish empires in Asia."[87] Unlike the autobiographical section of the manuscript, which is written in neat hand, the memorials prove admittedly difficult to decipher and display a generally problematic command of the Spanish language.[88] Over the years I have been working with the microfilm of Ms. 2780 as well as Teensma's published transcript, and I have spotted several errors over and above those already identified by Villiers.[89] Some are significant enough to merit special mention in the present context.

The first concerns the location of the Old Strait of Singapore.[90] Teensma followed early modern cartographical materials—in this instance Gerrit de Haan's *Lichtende Zeefakkel*—of 1760, the copy of which is preserved in the Nationaal Archief van Nederland (National Archives of the Netherlands) in the Hague—to place the Old Strait to the north of the main island of Singapore. As a result of this unfortunate misidentification, Teensma concluded that the island situated between the Old and the New Strait of Singapore (which De Coutre called *Ysla de Arena*, or present-day Sentosa) must therefore be Pulau Ubin. The size of that island, he further contended,

---

85 CRE.

86 Villiers, "Review": 454–6.

87 Villiers, "Review": 456.

88 Teensma, *De politieke en economische ideeën*, p. 25.

89 Villiers, "Review": 456.

90 See also the list of place names (*Estrecho de Sincapura, Estrecho Viejo*).

used to be larger than it is today.[91] The confusion of the Tebrau or Johor Strait with the Old Strait of Singapore is a common error started, to the best of my knowledge, in Dutch cartography of the second or third quarter of the 17th century.[92] In fact, the Old Strait and its sister, the New Strait, ran along the southern coast of Singapore and present-day Sentosa, as corroborated by early 17th-century Portuguese materials, such as the *Declaraçam de Malaca* (Description of Melaka) by Manoel Godinho de Erédia (see p. 76) and the *Décadas da Ásia* by João de Barros.[93] I have written previously on this phenomenon and to which I refer for further information.[94]

The second concerns the location of a port named *Arisbaya.* Teensma —erroneously—equated Arisbaya with Surabaya.[95] But Arisbaya was in fact a historic port situated along the western shores of Madura, an island located off the northeastern coast of Java. Similarly, Teensma misread *Daquão* as the Deccan rather than the city of Dhaka.[96]

The third researcher to delve more deeply into Ms. 2780 is George Winius. In an article published in 1985 titled "The Life of Jaques de Couttre: A Prime Source Emerges from the Shades", Winius expressed beaming optimism about the potential value of De Coutre as a newly rediscovered primary source.[97] He expressed confidence that the retrieval and future publication of the manuscript was truly momentous, and that the De Coutre would soon establish himself as a travel "classic" in the league of Jan Huyghen van Linschoten's *Itinerario* and the *Travels* of François Pyrard de Laval.[98] Writing some years later Winius appeared to have lost his initial enthusiasm for the *Vida* and candidly conceded:

---

[91] CRE, p. xi.

[92] SMS, pp. 38–41.

[93] Brussels, Bibliothèque Royale, Ms. 39015A, fol. 61 recto. Manoel Godinho de Erédia, *Declaraçam de Malaca*, c.1613; Manoel Godinho de Erédia, *Malaca L'Inde Méridionale e le Cathay: Manuscrit original autographe de Godinho de Eredia appartenant à la Bibliothèque Royale de Bruxelles*, tr. M. Léon Janssen (Bruxelles: Librairie Européenne C. Muquardt, 1882); João de Barros and Diogo do Couto, *Da Ásia. Dos feitos que os Portuguezes fizeram no conquista, e descubrimento das terras e mares do Oriente*, 24 vols. (Lisbon: Na Regia Officina Typographia, 1777–78).

[94] Peter Borschberg, *The Singapore and Melaka Straits: Violence, Security and Diplomacy in the 17th Century* (Singapore and Leiden: NUS Press and KITLV Press, 2010), pp. 17–59, esp. p. 44.

[95] CRE, p. 44.

[96] CRE, p. 52.

[97] George Winius, "The Life of Jacques de Couttre: A Prime Source Emerges from the Shades", *Itinerario* 9 (1985): 137–44.

[98] Ibid., p. 144.

> I quickly became one of its [the *Vida*] champions and was one of the first to use it extensively in my writings. My instincts did not lead me into any egregious errors, yet I will admit enough *naïveté* that I might have been served better if I had known more about that manuscript, such as one already knows about similar, but more familiar narratives, such as the *Itinerario* of Jan Huyghen van Linschoten, the *Voyages* of François Pyrard de Laval, the *Peregrinação* of Frei Sebastião Manrique, or the abovementioned travels of [Niccolao] Manucci and [Fernão de] Mendes Pinto. We all recognize that these are sources to be used with varying degrees of caution (Winius and Chorba, p. 709).

Sighing with relief that in the end he had not fallen into any serious traps by liberally using and citing from De Coutre's *Vida*, Winius conceded on hindsight that caution is advised when using a text whose provenance or pedigree remains sparsely known. This is true for De Coutre as much as it is for any other piece of travel literature dating from the early modern period. For although such texts contain "history"—sometimes great and fascinating nuggets of historical information and veracity—we must always remember why and in what specific context a particular text was written. Travel literature from the early modern period often represents a collage of information plucked from different sources and from different periods —printed, manuscript or hearsay—and it is far from simple to ascertain which passages represents genuine autobiographical memory, and which were adduced to enrich one's personal experience for information or entertainment of the reader. De Coutre did not write his text to aid his own memory, nor is the text evidently designed as a testimony of a man with clear, undetached objectivity. At this juncture it is important to distinguish more clearly between the autobiography or *Vida* and the memorials. The authorial intentions—what the author wanted to achieve with these texts—is thus the topic of the following section.

IV

AUTHORIAL INTENTIONS OF MS. 2780

Why does a person write or compile something when he does? This is one of the fundamental questions underlying modern historical research methodologies. Even if this question may be simple and straightforward, a clear answer is not always forthcoming—especially where there is no correspondence or other concrete statements of purpose, function or general intention. In this case, historians are often compelled to explore the immediate historical context to find their answers.

With reference to Ms. 2780, it is imperative to distinguish not only the form but also the authorial intentions of the two basic constituent parts: the autobiography or *Vida* and the memorials. With reference first to the *Vida,* the questions for further exploration are these: What was the role of Esteban de Coutre in giving shape and revising the manuscript of the *Vida?* For whom or what sort of readership was this manuscript destined?

Let us first turn to the question concerning the role of Esteban. That he even had a role is evidenced by a short statement that follows the title of the *Vida de Jaques de Coutre* on fol. 3 recto of the manuscript. There we read: "Puesto en la forma que està por su hijo Don[99] Estevan de Coutre" (Put into the current form by his son Esteban de Coutre). This statement raises some additional questions: Was Esteban just lending a helping hand to his ageing father and assisted him to compile and possibly to transcribe some pre-existing notes or drafts, or perhaps even to record a dictated narrative? Given the heavy Portuguese influence in the text, was Esteban perhaps a little more than a "translator" of his father's notes from Portuguese into Spanish?[100] Did he streamline the text by organising the manuscript into the different books and chapters?[101] Or did he assume a more proactive role by (re-) writing the text from a set of pre-existing notes and documents? Did he transcribe the testimonies that he strung together into a more coherent narrative? And did he take licence to embellish the text with imagination or extrapolated information from other sources to make the *Vida* more interesting and readable? Those researchers who have worked closely with the text differ in their reading of Esteban's statement. All agree, however, that while Esteban may have exercised a (heavy) editorial hand in giving shape to the narrative, he almost certainly did not write it himself.[102] The narrative is written in a personal, reflective way, employing the Spanish personal pronoun *yo* (I). The memorials appended to the *Vida* were not subjected to his editorial activities as they are thought to have been written in Jacques' own hand. Crucially,

[99] A Spanish title or salutation. See also the glossary (*Don*).

[100] This is suggested in Teensma, *De politieke en economische ideeën,* pp. 4, 23.

[101] Winius and Chorba, "Literary Invasions", p. 712.

[102] Ibid., p. 718; see also AO, p. 33.

why was the *Vida* written at all? Verbeckmoes surmised that writing the memorials had prompted Jacques to reflect on his lifelong experiences in Asia and to have these recorded on paper.[103]

This brings us to the second set of questions: For whom was the text or were the texts written? Is the *Vida* just the personal reflections of an ageing European, a testimony of his many years in Asia that was intended for personal use, and at the same time to be used as a reference for family, descendants and friends? Or is it an autobiographical account intended for the eyes of Spanish crown officials who were also readers of the memorials?

The fact that the *Vida* is written in neat hand and appears to include a draft title page (see p. 22) has led researchers to conclude that Esteban edited the *Vida* with the intention of having it published. For this reason the book was written in Spanish (Castilian), not Portuguese, although the latter would have been Jacques' working language in Melaka and Goa and also Esteban's native tongue. If the book was indeed meant for publication, then the preparation of the text in the Spanish language was done with an eye cast on the size of prospective readership and sales. There were far more people in Europe at the time who were sufficiently proficient in Spanish, including in De Coutre's home in the Spanish Netherlands. Besides—as the London-based academic Joan-Pau Rubiés has also highlighted—it was not at all unusual for Portuguese-language authors of this period to choose the Spanish language as the preferred medium to reach their readers.[104]

The intention to have the book published, together with the fact that the *Vida* was written in Spanish brings us to one more important observation. In their joint article titled *Literary Invasions in La vida de Jaques de Coutre,* George Winius and Carrie Chorba raised questions about the value and reliability of the autobiography as an historical source. They underscored that the *Vida* displayed strong features of the *picaresca* (picaresque novel). This literary genre characterizes fiction and biography in the Golden Age of Spanish literature during the first half of the 17th century, and therefore was a genre prevalent in De Coutre's own lifetime. It would appear that

---

[103] AO, p. 35.

[104] Joan-Pau Rubiés, "The Spanish Contribution to Ethnology of Asia in the Sixteenth and Seventeenth Centuries", *Asian Travel in the Renaissance,* ed. Daniel Carey (Malden and Oxford: Blackwell Publishing, 2004), p. 121.

Jacques—and to an extent his "editor" Esteban—streamlined the *Vida* in such a way that it fitted the popular literary taste of its day. This can be taken as another indication that the text was meant for publication and wider circulation, and the literary genre of the *picaresca* also befits the choice of the Spanish language.[105] Verbeckmoes was the first to establish a link between De Coutre's *Vida* and that literary genre, and it is a point subsequently repeated by Stols, Teensma, Winius and Chorba.[106] Another significant literary influence is the Byzantine novel, a genre known from Miguel de Cervantes' *Don Quixote.* Winius and Chorba raised the question of whether these "literary invasions" compromise, or seriously diminish, the value of De Coutre's *Vida* as a primary source. This issue remains fundamentally problematic, and it seems that Winius and Chorba left it up to their readers to draw their own conclusions. While there is really nothing unusual about streamlining a biography to suit the literary tastes of the day, it is—like with all biographies and travel literature dating from any period—important to be cognizant of the more immediate context and the intended purpose of a given text.

Exploring the forms of self-presentation remains fundamental for deconstructing any autobiography or piece of travel literature. De Coutre presented himself to the reader as a quixotic character who was haplessly drawn into adverse and dangerous situations.[107] He was always able to survive—sometimes by the skin of his teeth—because he could successfully outsmart his adversaries. Given the approximate date when the *Vida* was written—that is, before the exoneration by the *Conselho de Portugal* (Council of Portugal) in 1632—De Coutre was also keen to underscore his unwavering and devoted loyalty to the Spanish-Habsburg monarchs, who were, after all, also the rightful overlords of his native Flanders. De Coutre could hardly contain his disappointment with the Portuguese—whom he generally portrayed in a negative light—and expressed far more confidence in the abilities of the Spaniards. The latter is especially evident from his recommendations contained in the memorial appendices.

We should not be fooled by the self-effacing poise, the clever escapes from mortal danger, or the repeated demonstrations of loyalty to the Spanish

---

105 Winius and Chorba, "Literary Invasions", pp. 711–2.

106 CRE, p. iv; Winius and Chorba, "Literary Invasions", p. 714.

107 Ibid., p. 713.

crown. A closer look at the *Vida*, and especially the memorials, also evidenced that De Coutre revelled in self-promotion and self-glorification. He paraded his knowledge of Asia, his experience as a merchant, his quick-wittedness and his ability to think on his feet. The clear, sober style of the text also revealed a good dose of humour and irony. De Coutre wanted his readers to understand that he had something to say, had important knowledge to impart, and he certainly wanted to be taken seriously. The question that remains is this: Was this clever, self-promoting author, the true Jacques de Coutre, or were his writings the self-defensive carping of a man awaiting a crucial verdict? Whatever the case may be, it is clear from De Coutre's life story that he was really nothing less than "a very shrewd operator".[108]

These observations bring us to the seven memorials that have been appended to Ms. 2780. When were they written and why were they written? And what purpose do they serve here in the manuscript?

Researchers today agree that De Coutre appears to be the author of the seven memorials; and according to Teensma, they are also written in his hand and feature his signature. The genesis of the seven memorials is to be placed between 1623 and December 1628, in other words over a period of about five years. This also means that the different memorials were almost certainly written with an eye cast on his future exoneration and rehabilitation. Only the genesis of the seventh memorial is precisely known, namely 29 December 1628.[109] As for the others, there are references within the running texts that enable a *postquam* dating. For example, De Coutre mentioned the large fleet dispatched by Portugal and Spain in 1625 to oust the Dutch from Bahia in Brazil.[110] Based on the closing lines, Teensma concluded that memorial IV in this volume represents a commissioned report and most probably dates from the year 1628.[111]

While all of the memorials are different, they also share certain common traits and agendas. What binds these texts together in purpose and intention are three facets: 1) De Coutre's first-hand familiarity with the vast trading networks across the Indian Ocean and the South China Sea; 2) the more concrete trading opportunities offered by these; and 3) the new geopolitical

---

108 Winius and Chorba, "Literary Invasions", p. 718.
109 CRE, p. vii.
110 Ibid.
111 Ibid.

security situation impacting the main maritime trading arteries on the arrival of the VOC (and other Europeans) in Asian waters after 1595. Deeper knowledge of the actual situation on the ground enabled De Coutre to offer a set of specific recommendations to reverse what he thought was the decline of the Estado da Índia.[112] Among the concrete measures that he recommended was to clean up corruption, smuggling and weak military discipline within the vice-regal administration in Goa and the Estado at large. He recommended fundamentally a three-pronged approach: radical internal administrative reforms, heightened security in and around major trading ports, and serious economic reforms that would enable the Portuguese to respond to—if not reverse—the threat from European competitors and especially the Dutch. But De Coutre's recommendations are not exactly spelt out in any one single memorial—even if the fourth would seem to indicate this via its header or title. His recommendations are in fact found scattered among the different memorials.

Researchers today also agree that his opinions and recommendations "were almost certainly known" [113] among officials at the Madrid court. But as Teensma and Villiers have duly highlighted, there was "no shortage of arbitristas in the seventeenth century" who "thought themselves experts in the most diverse subjects" and who "flooded the royal chanceries with every kind of advice about all sorts of current difficulties".[114] The fact is that the memorials, broadly speaking, contain few nuggets of hitherto unknown information about the Portuguese in Asia during the first half of the 17th century.[115] Still, if Teensma's appraisal is indeed correct that memorial IV[116] represents a commissioned report, then Jacques' advice was actively solicited by officials at very senior levels. One can also surmise that the knighthood of the Order of Santiago was awarded in return for his good services to the Spanish crown.

We now turn to the question of what purpose the memorials serve here as appendices to the *Vida de Jaques de Coutre.* As mentioned, these texts—and

[112] See also Subrahmanyam, "Manila, Melaka, Mylapore": 228, esp. for Subrahmanyam's comparison of De Coutre with Diogo do Couto; also his reference to Francisco Rodrigues Silveira, *Reformação da Milícia do Governo do Estado da Índia Oriental,* ed. Benjamin N. Teensma (Lisbon: Fundação Oriente, 1996).

[113] Winius and Chorba, "Literary Invasions", p. 715.

[114] CRE, p. xxvi; Villiers, "Review": 455.

[115] Villiers, "Review": 455.

[116] This features as memorial 3 in the present edition.

perhaps also the autobiography—were written during an approximately five-year window between late 1623 and late 1628. This also placed the genesis of the seven memorials well within the period before the exoneration and rehabilitation of the De Coutre brothers in 1632. Taken as a collection and also in conjunction with the autobiography, these materials contained in Ms. 2780 demonstrate (or at least aim to demonstrate) that Jacques was a loyal subject and had at heart the greater geostrategic interests and well-being of the united crowns of Spain and Portugal. He was not a boasting fraud, but a person who acquired and shared with desk-bound officials in Europe his valuable first-hand experience in Asia in understanding the broader commercial and political situation across the Indian Ocean and the South China Sea regions. He openly addressed the internal administrative, structural, commercial and strategic issues at hand and was well acquainted with the Iberian competitors, especially the VOC's prowess as a trading organisation and a military machine.

V

TRANSLATION AND ANNOTATED ENGLISH SOURCE EDITION

It is unfortunate that the existing Spanish and Flemish-Dutch language translations of De Coutre's materials remain inaccessible to the vast majority of students and researchers in Asia. The present annotated English translation introduces De Coutre as a primary source worthy of further study and examination. It should be noted at the outset that the main target group is Southeast Asia-oriented historians and area studies specialists, and bearing this geographic focus in mind, only book I of the *Vida de Jaques de Coutre* is published in the present source edition. This first part of the autobiography deals specifically with De Coutre's life and early career in Southeast Asia. It spans the decade between approximately 1592 and 1603 from when Jacques left his hometown of Bruges in search of a better life in Asia until his marriage to Dona Catarina (or Cathalina) do Couto and his permanent relocation to Goa. The chapters cover his life in Portuguese Melaka and Manila, with key undertakings or adventures reported in Pahang, Siam, Cambodia, Patani and Batu Sawar (Johor).

Of the memorials appended to the *Vida,* four have been selected for translation. Omitted are memorials II and VII because they do not feature a sufficient focus on Southeast Asia. The selected texts contain the most valuable information about the Southeast Asian region at large and specifically how Southeast Asian ports fit within the larger context of trading networks that spanned the Indian Ocean and the South China Sea regions. They contain De Coutre's assessment of security and geopolitics and also feature recommendations aimed at reversing the perceived declining fortunes of the Estado da Índia in Asia. The information and insights put to paper in these memorials overlap to varying degrees.

Although there are existing editions and translations of the manuscripts, the discovery of at least one serious lacuna made it necessary to work very closely with a microfilm prepared from the original manuscript bundle in Madrid. In this way it could be ensured that the texts would be translated without significant gaps. Working with large printouts of the original manuscript also helped clarify uncertain readings and other problems with the original Spanish text. With reference to the memorials, the handwriting is generally problematic, and where serious doubts over the reading of a particular word or letter occurred, cross references were made to the 1989 and 1991 transcripts.

Roopanjali Roy was commissioned to prepare the primordial English translation of all the Portuguese and Spanish language materials selected. Over the years of her living and working in Portugal, she has acquired valuable experience in translating early modern texts and documents from Portuguese, Spanish and Italian. Substantial editorial work on the translation saw the clarification of obscure or difficult passages and the identification of early modern place names (some of which are garbled beyond recognition in the texts), commodities, textiles, weapons, weights and measures. These are featured and explained in the glossary. In preparing this glossary and the annotations, recourse to contemporaneous accounts (and their annotated texts, where available) proved immensely useful and beneficial. Also, I am much obliged to my colleagues in the NUS Department of History—and fellow researchers worldwide—many of whom helped clarify the most challenging problems relating to Lusitanianisms, garbled place names, garbled titles of officials, obscure commodities or medicinal substances, and technical details of early modern firearms.

It should be emphasised that this is an annotated source translation and not a critical edition of the *Vida* and memorials. Footnoting is limited to providing cross references or indicating the original term employed by

De Coutre in the manuscript. Lengthy and more detailed explanations of names, titles, commodities, and place names are featured in the two glossaries. The first provides explanations of weights, measures, commodities and objects; and the second is a list of toponyms encountered in the *Vida* and the memorials.

In order to ensure a smooth reading experience, objects and commodity names have been translated into English, providing of course that an English term is both available and (still) widely familiar. For example, the names *freydera* or *payones* have been left standing because De Coutre subsequently also explained these terms in the text of the *Vida*. To avoid confusing the contemporary reader, place names are rendered as far as possible in their commonly used present-day spelling—*Malaca* is spelled *Melaka* and *Bantam* as *Banten*. Where cities or geographical features have been renamed, the rule of the greatest present-day familiarity applies, with the notable exception of Jayakerta (sometimes also Jacatra), which was renamed Batavia by the Dutch in the early 17th century and renamed Jakarta at the time of Indonesia's independence. In this instance the original, pre-colonial name has been deliberately retained. Thus the *Estrecho de Mecca* becomes the *Bab-el-Mandeb Strait,* with a corresponding explanation in the list of place names. Where names represent a European corruption of indigenous toponyms, the indigenous name is employed in the main body of the text with a reference to the original spelling in the footnote. In this way, *Marmacin* and other spellings becomes *Banjarmasin, Jaquetera* becomes *Jayakerta, Yudia* becomes *Ayutthaya,* and *Cinquapura* and other spellings become *Singapura.* When a place name cannot be positively identified, the original is left in the main text, and a suggested modern equivalent is placed in a footnote.

Titles and names of persons have been left as far as possible in their original form in order to preserve the integrity of the text, except when these names or titles offer a garbled rendition from another (Asian) language. For example, the sultans of Aceh, Banten or Johor are all titled "kings"—as indeed they commonly were in European documents of the early modern period. Titles or functions have been left intact, but spelling has been adapted to modern usage.

De Coutre had the propensity to begin many sentences with the word "and". In order to ensure a fluent reading experience, this word has been omitted in the present translation, unless otherwise warranted. His frequent employment of *dicho/dicha* (said, aforementioned), especially in Memorial IV has also been omitted.

VI

SYNOPSIS OF BOOK I OF THE *VIDA DE JAQUES DE COUTRE*

In the opening chapter of the book, Jacques de Coutre spoke about his family background and also briefly about his home in Flanders. He and his brother Joseph had left home in search of a better life. After a brief stint on a cod fishing vessel in the stormy waters of the North Sea, Jacques headed for Lisbon when he reunited with his brother Joseph and there decided to embark on a voyage to the East Indies.

Chapter II describes in some detail the voyage aboard the Goa-bound carrack *Nossa Senhora de Nazaré* (Our Lady of Nazareth) captained by one Bras Correia. The route plied by this carrack on its way to India can be considered standard during the age of sail. After heading south to the Canary Islands and Cape Verde, the ship headed across the Atlantic towards Brazil, passing the Abrolhos[117] islands, and then heading back across over the Atlantic towards the Cape of Good Hope. Following the coast of southern Africa's Natal,[118] the ship arrived at the Portuguese fortress and colony at Mozambique.[119] By this stage the gruelling voyage had taken the lives of about 200 men who had originally set sail with the ship, with many more ill and requiring recuperation in a local hospital, including the De Coutre brothers. Jacques admitted that he and his brother Joseph were demoralized—a state worsened by the fact that their clothes were stolen whilst recuperating in hospital—but they consoled themselves that life in Goa had to be better. When the brothers arrived in Goa on 14 September 1592, Joseph had to be hauled with ropes over the deck and into a vessel waiting to ferry the brothers to shore—he was simply too ill to climb over. But he recovered, and within three months of arriving in Goa, Joseph married into a family of Old Christians. Driven, however, by the desire to see the world, Jacques—this time evidently without his brother—headed off again and reached Melaka on 28 September 1593. He described how almost immediately upon disembarking in that famed city of spice and trade he was greeted by one Sequin Martinela, an ageing gem dealer from

[117] Island group off the coast of Brazil. See the list of place names (*Abrolhos*).

[118] See also the list of place names (*Natal*).

[119] Southeastern Africa. See also the list of place names (*Monsanbique*).

Venice.[120] Jacques, it would seem, had fallen into benevolent hands. The captain of Melaka, Francisco de Silva de Meneses, arranged for lodgings to be allocated to the young Jacques. At the end of the chapter De Coutre reminisced fondly of his long, enduring friendship with Martinela, who he said was like a father to him.

Within six months of arriving in Melaka, Jacques joined an embassy led by Martim Teixeira and set off on a major trip to Pahang by sea. Chapter III describes this voyage along the western coast of the Malay Peninsula, past the Batu Pahat River, Pulau Pisang, around Tanjung Bulus in view of the Karimun Islands and then through the Old Strait of Singapore.[121] At this juncture Jacques displayed his keen sense of observation by describing in detail the area around the Old Strait (running between present-day Sentosa and Keppel Harbour), the *orang laut* who lived here, their boats and their fishing techniques. Arguably this chapter also contains one of the oldest eyewitness references to the settlement that Jacques named *Sabandaría*—after the presence of the *shahbandar,*[122] or port master, on what would be on the main island of present-day Singapore.[123] The settlement's residents along with the *orang laut* who lived around the nearby Straits and islands paid tribute to the ruler of Johor. Jacques' maritime journey continued past Tioman and Pulau Tinggi[124] to the Pahang River estuary and a settlement that he identified as Beruas.[125]

Pahang, Jacques continued in chapter IV, is a small polity with one major settlement and a petty ruler who styled himself king. The chapter delves into the surroundings, weapons, money and dress of the local inhabitants, both men and women. Jacques was evidently appalled by the punishments he saw meted out by the local ruler of Pahang. After a misdemeanour committed by one of the Portuguese on a pretty woman in the market square and a skirmish with weapons, De Coutre and his comrades were in some serious trouble. The story continues in much the same vein in chapter V

[120] Teotónio R. de Souza, "Embassies and Surrogates": 46.

[121] See also the list of place names (*Rio Fermoso, Pula Pisan, Pula Quiliman, Tangonburi, Estrecho Nuevo, Estrecho Viejo*).

[122] See also the glossary (*shahbandar*) and the list of place names (*Sabandaria*).

[123] The presence of a shahbandar's compound is also indicated on the 1604 sketch of Singapore Island and the Straits by Manoel Godinho de Erédia dating from 1604. See the image on p. 76.

[124] See also the list of place names (*Pulatimom, Pulatinga*).

[125] See also the list of place names (*Baroas*).

with Friar Manuel Ferreira mistaking a woman for his slave. The incident alerted the royal guards and senior officials of Pahang. Local inhabitants could not positively identify the culprit and could only recall that he had *mata kucing* or "cat's eyes".

In chapter VI, De Coutre reminisces about the fraud of one Don[126] Luis del Castillo who claimed to be a relative of the king of Spain and Portugal and travelled incognito in Asia. In reality he had been banned from Mexico. He managed to fool the king of Johor, Raja Ali Jalla bin Abdul Jalil,[127] the Portuguese captain of Melaka and even the bishop, at least for a short while. But when he promised Johor military support against Aceh,[128] and Johorese ambassadors came to Melaka to enquire about the preparations for the expeditionary fleet, an arrest warrant was issued for Don Luis. He fled to Aceh and subsequently sought to reach Pegu[129] by ship when he was killed together with his slaves by members of the crew. Jacques also used this episode to say a few words about the kingdom of Johor,[130] especially Dom Paulo Lima de Pereira's campaign of 1587, the transfer of the royal administrative centre from Johor Lama to Batu Sawar, and Johor's conflict with Aceh.[131]

Chapter VII marks the first of five chapters touching on a voyage from Melaka to Ayutthaya and the Portuguese embassy to Siam during the rule of King Naresuan.[132] De Coutre's description of Siam and Ayutthaya in particular are arguably the oldest surviving accounts of the old royal capital by a European eyewitness. The purpose of this mission was to negotiate with the monarch about certain Portuguese Catholics he had deported from Cambodia, and Jacques accompanied the embassy charged by the captain or "governor" of Melaka to purchase gemstones.[133] This chapter

[126] A Spanish title or salutation. See also the glossary (*Don*).

[127] Concerning the identity of Raja Ali Jalla, see also GPFT, appendix 13, pp. 213–14.

[128] See the list of place names (*Achem*).

[129] It is uncertain whether De Coutre refers here to the city or polity named Pegu. See also the list of place names (*Pegu, Taungoo Dynasty Kingdom*).

[130] See the list of place names (*Jor*).

[131] See significantly Denys Lombard, *Le Sultanat d'Atjéh au temps d'Iskandar Muda 1607–1636* (Paris: École français d'Extrême-Orient, 1967).

[132] A summary of this embassy is also found in Teotónio R. de Souza, "Embassies and Surrogates": 39–55. George Winius claimed that De Coutre's description "provides the first eyewitness account of the Siamese court". Winius, "Review of Miroslav Krása, Joseph Polišenský, and Peter Rakoš, European Expansion 1494–1519. The Voyages of Discovery in the Bratislava Manuscript Lyc. 515/18 (Codex Bratislavensis), Prague: Charles University, 1986", *The Hispanic American Historical Review* 68, 4 (1988): 821.

[133] See also De Souza, "Embassies and Surrogates": 46–47.

touches on the preparations for the embassy as well as the actual voyage by sea through the Singapore Strait. The men called at Ligor, [134] engaged in armed combat against pirates in the Gulf of Siam and finally reached the Chao Phraya River estuary.

Chapter VIII explains that the leaders of the embassy, Manuel Pereira de Abreu and Friar Jorge de Mota[135] experienced cold feet upon arriving in Siam and contemplated diverting the mission to Cochinchina[136] instead. Jacques and the friar proceeded to Ayutthaya to seek permission to present the embassy before King Naresuan, but they were informed that the king was away on a hunt. Not wanting to wait for the monarch's return, they embarked on a new journey to meet the royal hunting party, only to learn a few days later that Naresuan had already returned to Ayutthaya. The two headed back to the royal capital in the company of Franciscan monks whom they had met on their journey.

Summoned before the king, De Mota—with the help of two translators of European origin—began to spin a web of lies. He claimed to have arrived in the company of a relative of the Iberian monarch Philip II/I of Spain and Portugal. This relative (ambassador Pereira de Abreu) was supposedly a man with high military credentials who had come to assist in Siam's war against Pegu. Naresuan requested to see the ambassador at once, and arrangements were made to bring the rest of the Portuguese embassy to Ayutthaya.

The formal reception at Ayutthaya is the subject of chapter IX.[137] This consisted of reading out a formal letter in Malay (which was then translated

---

[134] Present-day Nakhon Si Thammarat in Thailand. See also the list of place names (*Lugor*).

[135] This appears to be the same Dominican friar named Jorge de la Mota who is also mentioned by Antonio de Morga. See Morga, *Sucesos*, pp. 189–90, "There was a Portuguese Dominican friar [Jorge de la Mota] in Odia [i.e. Ayutthaya], who had been there for two years, ministering the Portuguese traders there, amongst whom were some that the king had brought out from Cambodia and Pigu [i.e. Pegu], when he had been at war with these nations. These, and the other Portuguese also, had been involved in some rioting against the locals in the city and they had killed one of the servants of the king, who, not being a forgiving man, had burnt some of those involved. Moreover, he refused to allow the Dominican friar or the others to leave either the city or the kingdom, although they insisted and begged his permission to do so. Consequently, finding themselves without liberty, less well treated than before, and under daily threats, they arranged with Friar Joan Maldonado that when he left that kingdom he should smuggle them out with him. ... The friar left a letter for his superiors in the order of Saint Dominic in the Philippines; this had been written a few days before his death to recount his travels and trials and the circumstances leading up to his death."

[136] A historic polity in present-day southern-central Vietnam. See also the list of place names (*Cochinchina*).

[137] A paraphrase of the account found in the *Vida* is also found in De Souza, "Embassies and Surrogates": 39–54.

into Thai for the king) professing friendship and promising assistance in the war against Pegu. But what had been read out in Malay and what had been translated into Thai were two completely different stories. Some Capuchin monks who had been present and understood both Malay and Thai warned Friar De Mota of the potential consequences of his deceit. The members of the Portuguese embassy were given a reception with much pomp and ceremony accompanied by an exchange of lavish gifts.

The story surrounding the reception of the Portuguese embassy continues in chapter X. Though he clearly had his doubts, King Naresuan made preparations for sending his own embassy to Lisbon and began to load a large junk[138] with goods and royal presents.[139] Some Portuguese began to fear for their lives, and De Coutre together with the factor[140] of Melaka, Simão Peres, approached Naresuan's powerful consort to blow the whistle on De Mota and Pereira de Abreu. Their lies fell apart like a house of cards. King Naresuan, who had been suspicious all along, was furious. He had senior military officers executed as a punishment, and left town on another royal hunt. The Portuguese, fearing the worst, first sought to kill the whistle-blowers De Coutre and Peres, but later took out their anger on the Siamese in a skirmish instead.

The time to flee Siam had arrived. Chapter XI tells of the different plans concocted by De Mota and Pereira de Abreu. Jacques joined forces again with Peres and some other friends. They set out in boats hoping to reach the sea by following the course of a small, unnamed river. This may have been one of the tributaries of the Chao Phraya. Their scheme to reach the Gulf of Siam was foiled. Thinking on their feet in this moment of crisis, they showed a (draft) petition addressed to the king and requested permission to leave. They were then taken on a voyage upstream to the location of Naresuan's royal hunt. As the king could not immediately grant them an audience, they became spectators of the royal hunting party until the king placed a junk at their disposal to take them home together with members of his own embassy to Portuguese Melaka. The harrowing episode in Siam, Jacques recalled at the end of the chapter, had lasted a total of eight months.

---

[138] A type of cargo vessel. See also the glossary (*junk*).

[139] Concerning a further definition of sappanwood, white or almond benzoin, vermilion and alum, and their role in Asian trade, see the glossary.

[140] A leading official at a so-called factory. See also the glossary (*factor*).

The homebound voyage forms the backbone of chapter XII. The junk headed out of the Chao Phraya estuary and sailed southward along the coast of Cambodia. Calling at one of the unnamed ports in Cambodia, Jacques and his friends learnt of the adventures of Diogo Veloso and Blas Ruiz, who on behalf of Cambodia's King Sâtha had been sent to Manila to seek assistance from the Spanish there.[141] What they achieved, instead, was the intervention by Laos in Cambodian affairs, and specifically against a powerful Malay chieftain, Okhna de Chu, whom De Coutre does not refer to by his name, but by his title Laksamana.[142]

On arriving in Melaka, Jacques and his friends found that Pereira de Abreu had returned and had already ingratiated himself with the new captain, Martim Afonso de Melo. Despite amiable airs and gestures, the two conspired to have Jacques removed from the scene by a hired killer—unsuccessfully, one should immediately add. Jacques reported with evident satisfaction that De Mota and Pereira de Abreu found their just retribution during another visit to Siam. The friar died in a skirmish with the Spanish on the Chao Phraya River, while the severely injured ambassador died later on his return to Melaka. Jacques, too was hit by a bout of bad luck. A fire that consumed more than a thousand homes in Melaka's suburbs also destroyed his home together with his stash of valuable benzoin.[143] The house "burnt to the ground", Jacques lamented, and "nothing escaped the flames."

The following two chapters—XIII and XIV—act as a series of supplementary afterthoughts on the eight-month sojourn in Siam. They are chiefly devoted to describing the royal administrative centre at Ayutthaya, the royal court, the king's elephants, temples and offering ceremonies,

---

[141] Concerning the episode of Veloso and Ruiz, and Spanish intervention in Cambodia at the close of the 16th century, see the useful article by Lawrence Palmer Briggs, "Spanish Intervention in Cambodia, 1593–1603", *T'Oung Pao* second series 39, 1/3 (1950): 132–60. Scattered references are also found in Subrahmanyam, "Manila, Melaka, Mylapore": 223–42. The mission Manila is mentioned on pp. 141–2 and 148–9. In return for Spanish aid against Siam, King Sâtha in a letter to the Spanish governor in Manila dated 20 July 1593 promised to become a Christian and accept some form of vassalage or overlordship from the Spanish. There was no ready aid as the Manila governor was preparing for an expedition to the Maluku islands. See also the account of Blas Ruiz and Diogo Veloso in Bartolomé Leonardo de Argensola's *Conquista de las Islas Molucas* (Conquest of the Maluku Islands, 1609) in PI, XVI, esp. pp. 264–9.

[142] See Morga, *Sucesos*, pp. 87, 189, "Ocuña Lacasamana" (Oknea Laksamana, grand-admiral). According to Briggs his name was Oknha de Chu and was a native of Johor. See Briggs, "Spanish Intervention", p. 150. See also the glossary *(laksamana)*.

[143] An odoriferous resin. See also the glossary *(benzoin)*.

cruel punishments and executions, as well as a number of curiosities that included notably the *bungkals* or penis bells "worn" by the Siamese and Peguan men.

Chapter XV continues the narrative left off at the end of chapter XII. It tells of how Jacques reinvented himself after the devastating fire that had destroyed his house and wiped out his possessions. Days after the tragedy, he boarded a ship bound for Manila via Brunei Bay, Palawan and Mindoro.[144] The description of the palace and port of Brunei is one of the oldest European eyewitness accounts written. The envoys from Melaka were received by the ruler with "scant ceremony". The palace was described as an islet made of bamboo surrounded by the settlement "which was very large" and densely populated. The principal place of commerce was a sprawling floating market. The king, one is informed, made a living by robbing and plundering and this rendered him "more of a pirate than a king". In addition, there were some observations made on the weapons used on Borneo—small culverins,[145] blowpipes with poisoned darts, spears made from wild palms, lances and krisses[146]—as well as a brief account of Jacques' efforts to attend to the ailing king of Jailolo.

En route to Manila off the coast of Mindoro, the ship was caught in a dreadful storm—perhaps a typhoon—that caused serious damage. After taking shelter in a bay and making the necessary repairs, Jacques and some friends who were fetching fresh water on land were mistaken for pirates and pursued by the local population.

In Manila, it appears from chapter XVI that Jacques' fortunes quickly changed for the better, and he was able to recoup part of his fortune lost in the fire. The chapter describes the city of Manila, both inside the walls and outside in the suburb of Parián, home at the time to about 40,000 Chinese. "They are all merchants and professionals of all mechanical trades", Jacques noted, "very ingenious and hardworking people, as all the Chinese generally are."

About three weeks after arriving in Manila, Jacques witnessed a confrontation in the Bay of Manila between ships of the Spanish governor

[144] Three islands, the latter two of which today belong to the Philippines. See also the list of place names (*Borneo, Paragua, Mindoro*).

[145] A type of weapon. See the glossary (*culebrina*).

[146] A Malay dagger. See the glossary (*keris*).

and vessels under the supreme command of Admiral Olivier van Noort.[147] Considerable space is given in this chapter in recounting the battle at sea, which resulted in the sinking of Dr Antonio de Morga's galleon[148] and the capture of the *Eendracht* (Unity, Concordia). Lambert Biesman and 18 members of his crew were taken prisoner by the Spanish authorities.[149] Jacques put his language skills to work as an interpreter for the captured Dutch. With the exception of six boys (who had been spared on account of their youth), these Dutchmen were subsequently executed by the Spanish. Those who had converted to Catholicism in the face of death were subsequently buried in the chapel of Santa Potenciana.[150]

After about two years in Manila, Jacques set sail for Melaka on a ship belonging to the captain of Melaka, Fernão de Albuquerque. The plan was to head for Goa to get married. Off the coast of Borneo, however, the ship got into a terrible storm "and [it was] on the verge of sinking because the gutters were clogged with the skins of the many fruits we had eaten during the voyage". The ship had come off course and headed into the Riau Archipelago where the crew found themselves hopelessly lost and disoriented. All attempts to make contact with the local population failed. After about a month, when provisions were running low, Jacques and the crew resorted to a desparate measure and kidnapped one of the local fishermen. Although they kept him in shackles they offered him a reward of money and fabrics to show them out of the islands, which he did. Near the coast of Johor—where the route and the environment became familiar—the captive was set free and paid the reward he had been promised. On arrival in Melaka, Jacques successfully disposed of the cargo of cloves he had brought from Manila, but found that there was a shortage of vessels available for Goa and that

---

[147] Pieter Anton Tiele, "De Europeërs in den Maleischen Archipel", *BKI* part VI, 30 (1882): 160–1.

[148] A type of ship. See the glossary *(galleon).*

[149] See appendix IV and also Fred Swart,"Lambert Biesman (1573–1601) of the Company of Trader Adventurers, the Dutch Route to the East Indies, and Olivier van Noort's Circumnavigation of the Globe", *Journal of the Hakluyt Society* (2007): 1–21.

[150] *Santa Potenciana* was a Spanish royal foundation for poor (female) orphans. Domingo de Navarrete claimed it also featured a house "for honest Women to retire". See *The Travels and Controversies of Fray Domingo de Navarrete, 1618–86,* ed. J.S. Cummins, 2 vols. (London and Cambridge: Hakluyt Society and Cambridge University Press, 1960–62), I, p. 94. See also Otto van den Muijzenberg, "Philippine-Dutch Social Relations, 1600–1800", *BKI* 157, 3 (2001): 475, note 7; Morga, *Sucesos*, p. 182, note 2.

the carracks from China would arrive late. His marriage would have to be put off until the following year.

Chapter XVII tells the story of how Jacques took his profits from the sale of cloves and hoped to turn a quick profit with textiles in Patani. On this voyage he joined forces with Júlio de Barros, a nephew of the bishop of Melaka, and one Domingo Gonçalves. When their vessel arrived at the western entrance of the Old Strait of Singapore, they found riding at anchor several carracks that were waiting for conditions to improve for their onward voyage to China.[151] Here at the western entrance to the Old Strait around present-day Labrador Park and Fort Siloso, Jacques and his fellow travellers received news that four Dutch ships were riding at anchor off Patani. As the Dutch were not attacking the Portuguese, they decided to continue their onward journey. At Patani the ships of Admiral Jacob van Neck were still waiting for a cargo of pepper[152] when they arrived.[153] Through the services of António de Saldanha,[154] a *casado*[155] from Melaka residing in Patani, Jacques and his companions received lodgings and an audience with the queen of Patani. There they presented the letter of Fernão de Albuquerque in which the captain had expressed his desire to mend relations with Patani and procure foodstuffs for the Portuguese colony. The queen honoured this request.

The remainder of the chapter recounts Jacques' conversations with Admiral Van Neck, especially on developments in the Malukus[156] and the

---

[151] This practice of anchoring off present-day Fort Siloso on Sentosa and awaiting the change of weather and tidal conditions is also described in Memorial III below.

[152] Van Neck had arrived in Patani from China and Vietnam on 7 November 1601. See H.A. van Foreest and A. de Booy, ed., *De Vierde Schipvaart der Nederlanders naar Oost-Indië onder Jacob Wilkens en Jacob van Neck (1599–1604)* (The Hague: Martinus Nijhoff, 1980), I, "Journaal Roelof Roelofsz", p. 254; Rui Manuel Loureiro, *Nas Partes da China. Colectânea de Estudos Dispersos* (Lisbon: Centro Científico e Cultural de Macau, 2009), pp. 298–99, where he delved into the encounter between Admiral Van Neck and De Coutre.

[153] Concerning the presence of Van Neck at Patani and the beginnings of the Dutch factory there, see the older but still very useful account by Heert Terpstra, *De Factorij der Oostindische Compagniee te Patani* (The Hague: Martinus Nijhoff, 1938), esp. pp. 4–17.

[154] Loureiro, "European Encounters and Clashes in the South China Sea", II, *Revista de Cultura,* International Edition 12 (2004): 154, described him as "A Portuguese living and married in Malacca in 1600."

[155] A married settler. See also the glossary (*casado*).

[156] The "Spice Islands"; a sub-group of the Indonesian Archipelago. See also the list of place names (*Maluquo*).

earlier fate of several members of his crew at Macao.[157] The Admiral was evidently very agitated about what the Portuguese had done to his men, and Jacques made up a story to soothe him.[158] Just as Jacques and his friends were loading their cargo onto a junk purchased from Saldanha, another Dutch commander entered with his ships into the port of Patani[159]—Jacob van Heemskerck.[160] Upon his arrival the situations began to deteriorate rapidly for the Portuguese in Patani. On hearing rumours of Van Heemskerck's plan to seize his vessel, Jacques took precautions by moving his junk closer to shore and sleeping on land. The next morning he found that the Dutch had come and drilled holes into the hull. The junk was filled with so much water it was almost entirely submerged. Jacques had, once again, lost his entire fortune.

Chapter XVIII tells of how Jacques and his Portuguese friends escaped town by the skin of their teeth following the assassination of António de Saldanha. With the help of one powerful woman named Cik Tangan,[161] Jacques and Júlio de Barros managed to escape alive on board one of her relatives' ships. The crew of the vessel, fearing revenge by the Portuguese in Melaka, first tried to leave Jacques behind on Pulau Redang, and later plotted—unsuccessfully—to kill him aboard the junk. When the crew encountered Portuguese naval patrols around the Straits of Singapore, they decided to enter the Johor River. Jacques disembarked at Batu Sawar hoping to find another ship that would take him to Melaka.

At Batu Sawar, Jacques found himself in the midst of an unfolding political crisis between Johor and Melaka. Portuguese naval patrols had seized a junk and killed the Johorese envoy to the king of Perak;[162] and another Johorese vessel was later seized at Melaka. Infuriated by this escalation of violence, Johor's ruler Ala'uddin Ri'ayat Shah III ordered that all

---

[157] For the account of Admiral Van Neck in which he also mentioned his conversations with De Coutre, see appendix 1. Concerning the episode at Macao, see also Leonard Blussé, "Brief Encounter at Macao", *Modern Asian Studies* 22, 3 (1988): 647–64.

[158] This is similarly recounted in Van Foreest and De Booy, *Vierde Shipvaart,* I, "Journaal van Jacob van Neck", p. 221. See also Leonard Blussé, "Brief Encounter at Macao": 662–3.

[159] Van Heemskerck arrived at Patani on 26 May 1602. See Van Foreest and De Booy, ed., *De Vierde Schipvaart*, I, "Journaal Roelof Roelofsz", p. 257.

[160] See also Van Heemskerck's account of his actions before and after his time in Patani in appendix 2.

[161] The name *Enchetangan* (Encik or Cik Tangan) already broadly translates into English as "powerful woman"; "Madam Powerful". See also the glossary (*Enchetangan*).

[162] See also the list of place names (*Pera*).

the Portuguese and Christians from Melaka be rounded up and taken to the compound of the shahbandar who was empowered to pronounce justice over them. Various parties sought to mediate, and eventually the following simple proposal was made: If Melaka released the people and merchandise from the two junks the Portuguese naval patrols had seized, then the Johorese would also release the Portuguese and Christians they were holding prisoner together with their merchandise. Júlio de Barros was to convey this message to Melaka.

Upon the exhortations of Khoja[163] Ibrahim, a merchant and ambassador of the Portuguese at Batu Sawar, Jacques was instructed to leave the Johor capital at once. Near Johor Lama his path crossed with Júlio de Barros who was just returning from Melaka with a reply from Fernão de Albuquerque. Júlio implored Jacques to wait for him until the next morning when he would return from Batu Sawar. When Júlio had handed over the reply from De Albuquerque to the king of Johor, he was ordered killed with all the Portuguese and Christians held prisoner by the shahbandar in Batu Sawar. Khoja Ibrahim's life was spared because he was reportedly a Muslim.[164] Jacques soberly reminisced: "If I had been there [in Batu Sawar] I would have undoubtedly perished with all the rest".

Roughly around the same time as the slaughter of the Portuguese and Christians took place in Johor, a carrack sailing from Japan and China and owned by Sebastião Serrão was seized by Admiral Van Heemskerck off the eastern coast of Singapore island. This was the seizure of the *Santa Catarina* on 25 February 1603.[165]

---

[163] An honorific or title. See the glossary (*Khoja*).

[164] According to Paulo Pinto, however, Khoja Ibrahim was executed by the Portuguese for treason during the seaborne siege of Melaka by the fleet of Admiral Cornelis Matelieff de Jonge in 1606. See Pinto, *The Portuguese and the Straits of Melaka*, p. 181.

[165] See esp. SMS, pp. 68–75. Borschberg, "The Seizure of the *Santa Catarina* off Singapore", *RC*, International Edition 11 (2004): 11–25; "The Seizure of the *Santa Catarina* Revisited", *JSEAS* 33, 1 (2002): 31–62, esp. pp. 48–50; "A Portuguese-Dutch Naval Battle in the Johor River Delta", *Zeitschrift der Deutschen Morgenländischen Gesellschaft* 153, 1 (2003): 157–75; "Luso-Johor-Dutch Relations in the Straits of Malacca and Singapore", *Itinerario* 28, 2 (2004): 15–33, as well as van Ittersum, "Hugo Grotius in Context", *AJSS* 31, 3 (2003): 511–48 and more extensively in her book *Profit and Principle: Hugo Grotius, Natural Rights Theories and the Rise of Dutch Power in the East Indies, 1595–1615* (Leiden: E.J. Brill, 2006). Other references are also found in Charles Ralph Boxer, *Fidalgos in the Far East, 1550–1770: Fact and Fancy in the History of Macao* (The Hague: Martinus Nijhoff, 1948), as well as in Dirk van der Cruysse, *Louis XIV et le Siam* (Paris: Fayard, 1991) and its English translation titled *Siam and the West, 1500–1700,* tr. Michael Smithies (Seattle: University of Washington Press, 2002).

In the final chapter of book I, Jacques recalls how, without a penny to his name, he made his way to Goa to get married. Here in chapter XX, he also takes stock of his life in Southeast Asia over a course of almost one decade, recounting the places he had visited and the vast trade Portuguese Melaka still enjoyed in those years. "It was the largest stopover and trade that took place in all of the East Indies", and from this trade, Jacques reminded his readers emphatically that "the Portuguese viceroy in Goa reaped considerable tax revenue".

Jacques arrived at Goa on 2 May 1603, and within one week, he wed his sister-in-law, Dona Catarina do Couto in the church of *Nossa Senhora de Merces* (Our Lady of Mercy). Unlike the pomp and processions characteristic of Indian weddings and baptisms, Jacques and Catarina wed without grand "celebrations or a lot of noise".

VII

SYNOPSIS OF THE TRANSLATED MEMORIALS

The first memorial, addressed to the Portuguese viceroy in Goa,[166] explored the possibilities by which the Iberians could deal a serious blow to their Dutch competitors in Asia. In the opening lines, De Coutre urged the viceroy to relinquish the royal monopoly in pepper and to permit private merchants to trade in this commodity. Such a move, he contended, would flood the market in Europe with pepper, reduce its price and as a result significantly diminish the profits which the Dutch reap from the pepper trade. "This", the Fleming underscored, "is the main commodity in which they trade." What follows is a sweeping overview of geopolitics and trading opportunities around the Indian Ocean rim and the western Pacific, starting at the southern Cape of Good Hope, the eastern African coast, Arabia, Persia, India, Ceylon, Pegu, the Malay Peninsula, Sumatra, Borneo, Java and the Malukus, Siam, China and Japan. For each port or region, De Coutre described the commodities or textiles that could be bought or sold. This synopsis appears to fulfil twin objectives. The first is to show what the Iberian powers—particularly the Portuguese—gained, retained and had lost in terms of trade to the Dutch (and other competitors) across Asia and the Indian Ocean region. The other is to highlight what the Dutch had gained or what they

[166] Villiers, "Review": 455.

were doing in a given port or place. Occasionally, Jacques described the activities of Iberia's European or Asian competitors. He clearly had an eye on the English and in at least one instance reported on the Turks and Arabs from Aden.[167] He ended his memorial with these candid words:

> All this is no more than a recommendation to do damage to the [Dutch] rebels and an indication of the ports where we could capture ships and trade, and the wares that are traded between different lands.

The second, shorter memorial expanded on the theme of what the Portuguese once had enjoyed and what they had lost to the Dutch in terms of trade. Similar to the previous exposé, Jacques provided a sweeping overview of the vast trading network but focused specifically on the emporium Melaka, which stood at the centre of the network he described. As the opening line makes clear, this is "about the commerce that used to take place in India before the Dutch went to that state", in other words he was illustrating Melaka's commercial state at the close of the 16th century when Jacques lived in the city. What is described, however, had been clearly lost to the Dutch within a period of around three decades. In what appears to be an afterthought or a post-script, the memorial added a list of wares that the Dutch brought to the Indies from Europe.

With the third memorial Jacques delved more deeply into the subjects of geopolitics and security. From the opening lines it is clear that the measures he recommended were aimed specifically at the Dutch who had seriously disrupted a network of trade centred in Melaka that extended to many other ports in Asia. He listed a number of ports located to the east of the Singapore Strait with which Melaka carried out regular seaborne trade: Johor, Pahang, Patani, Ligor, Siam, Cambodia, Champa, Cochinchina, China, Manila, Japan, Borneo and the Ryukyu Islands.[168] If maritime traffic in Melaka from these eastern ports was to be revived, it was necessary to step up security in and around the Singapore Straits with the construction of a citadel or fortress. De Coutre then proceeded to identify and justify his preferred site for this proposed fortification: on an island located at the confluence of the Old and New Strait of Singapore which he called *Ysla de Arena*

[167] Port in present-day Yemen. See also the list of place names (*Ada*).
[168] Concerning the Ryukyus, see the list of place names (*Ryukyu*).

(present-day Sentosa).[169] More specifically, he singled out an area off the northwestern tip of the island which he called *Surgídera.*[170] This is exactly where Fort Siloso stands today—built by the British in 1878 to guard the western entrance to Singapore's New Harbour, later known as Keppel Harbour. The *Ysla de Arena,* De Coutre continued, had good fresh water, offered an excellent point of anchorage, and yielded ample building materials such as stone, wood, and coral that could be pounded up to be used as mortar.[171] The local population, the *orang laut,* could be enticed into cooperation. A fleet of rowed galleys[172] could be based at the fortress to patrol the nearby islands and waterways as well as to control maritime traffic. In this way, the Dutch would no longer be able to harass shipping coming from the east. In fact they would have a hard time conducting their own business at nearby ports, specifically in pepper.

A second fortification was proposed for the Johor River estuary mainly with an eye on controlling the fluvial traffic for the upstream towns (such as Johor Lama and Batu Sawar) and the eastern entrance of the Tebrau Strait. This second fortress was to be located on the northeastern side of what De Coutre called the *Ysla de la Sabandaria Vieja* (present-day Singapore island).[173] The proximity of the two recommended fortifications, as is underscored, would facilitate the lending of mutual assistance in times of need. A third, smaller fortification could be built on one of the shoals in the lower reaches of the Johor River. There are also a number of comments touching on the history of the kingdom of Johor, the Portuguese destruction of Johor Lama in 1578, and the subsequent construction of the new royal residence at Batu Sawar further upstream. There is specific mention of the 1613 Acehnese attack and invasion, as a result of which Johor had become a "vassal state" of Aceh. This situation, De Coutre opined, would facilitate a political takeover of Johor by which its ruler could be made a vassal of Portugal, just as the king of Hormuz had been between 1515 and 1622. A fourth fortification is recommended for the Muar River estuary.

In closing his document, it is recommended that 40 galleons be despatched from Europe. De Coutre expressed his conviction that, together

---

[169] For further particulars, see the list of place names (*Ysla de Arena*).

[170] See the list of place names (*Surgídera*).

[171] See the glossary (*karang*).

[172] A type of craft. See also the glossary (*galley*).

[173] See the list of place names (*Ysla de la Sabandaria Vieja*).

with the fortifications, the fleet would succeed in ousting the Dutch "rebels" from the East Indies once and for all.

The fourth and final memorial in this volume made a series of recommendations for reversing the decline of the Estado da Índia. It is divided into two basic parts or sections that De Coutre titled "chapters". Judging by the opening lines of these "chapters", they foresaw two distinct scenarios: Luso-Spanish efforts to evict the Dutch from the East Indies with the help of a massive armada on the one hand and intervention with a more modest naval force on the other.

In the first chapter, a scenario is staked out for a large-scale naval intervention comprising well-equipped and well-manned galleons from Europe "like the fleet Your Majesty sent to Brazil". This was a reference to the large Luso-Spanish fleet sent to Bahia de Todos os Santos in 1624–25 under the command of Don Fadrique Álvarez de Toledo y Osorio with the aim of expelling the Dutch from Brazil.[174] The number of ships recommended—namely 40 galleons—also establishes a direct link to the third memorial on security in the Singapore Straits, the Johor River region and the Muar River estuary. De Coutre provided a fairly detailed operational plan for attacks on Dutch and local Asian positions in the East Indies. He recommended sailing to the Sunda Strait and forging friendly relations with the king of Banten[175] as soon as possible in order to ensure the availability of provisions and fresh water supplies. He explained that the Dutch have their base in Jayakerta (later renamed Batavia) and can therefore be expected to have ships calling regularly at ports all around the northern coast of Java and Palembang.[176] If an attack on Batavia was not feasible, then the fleet should proceed to Ambon and seek to wrest that island from Dutch control. If that too was not possible—due to adverse winds for example—then the fleet should proceed to Melaka and prepare an attack on Aceh, an important pepper port for the Dutch, as well as for the Turks and Arabs.

In the event that it were not possible to immediately proceed to the Sunda Strait, then the fleet should head for Aceh before continuing to Melaka. It is important, De Coutre underscored, to attack Aceh by surprise.

---

[174] Concerning this episode, see Meuwese, M., *Brothers in Arms, Partners in Trade: Dutch-Indigenous Alliances in the Atlantic World, 1595–1674* (Leiden: E.J. Brill, 2012), pp. 34–36.

[175] Port and polity in western Java. See also the list of place names (*Bantan*).

[176] Port and polity in central-eastern Sumatra. See also the list of place names (*Pelibam*).

If all the scenarios above were not feasible, the next prioritized target would have to be Patani. An attack on this port city would not be difficult, he assured. It would be possible to attack and seize many Dutch vessels and in any case take a significant amount of booty from the city as well as from the unfortified suburbs where all the merchants lived. Additional attacks could be launched on Ligor and Ayutthaya. An attack on the latter, however, would have to be conducted with rowed galleys. De Coutre thought that a sack of Ayutthaya would "not be very difficult". A successful attack, moreover would be able to supply ample provisions for the European troops as the king of Siam had warehouses well stocked with victuals.

From Siam, the fleet could then proceed to subcontinental India and launch attacks on Masulipatam and Pulicat.[177] There would be opportunities here to seize vessels belonging to the English, Dutch as well as Muslim merchants. Reinforcements could also be brought in from Portuguese settlements such as São Tomé (Mylapur).[178] De Coutre opined that the indigenous population would also support such an attack, as the locals were dissatisfied with Dutch business practices, which he proceeded to explain in some detail. He warned that the fleet should make these conquests in the Coromandel Coast region first before proceeding to Goa, as many of the soldiers tended to seek other opportunities as well as join the smuggling ships or *pimenteiros*. It would also be necessary to shanghai additional soldiers in India.

The Dutch were able to sustain large fleets due to their capture of an abundance of booty coupled with their trading activities. In the Indian subcontinent, De Coutre suggested that focus be placed on the Dutch settlements along the Coromandel Coast—Pulicat and Masulipatam. If for any reason the Iberian fleet were detained and needed to dock for the winter, they should call at Nagapattinam or Tuticorin[179] where provisions could be purchased inexpensively and in copious amounts.

There is a distinct anti-Portuguese tone to this section of the memorial. De Coutre warned that the Estado da Índia must be remedied, but with substantial Spanish aid. Fortresses in the East Indies were to be preferably placed under the command of a Spanish officer, and soldiers were to be

---

[177] Ports along the Coromandel Coast. See also the list of place names (*Cheramandel, Mosolopatão, Paleacate*).

[178] Port along the Coromandel Coast. See also the list of place names (*Melapor*).

[179] Two ports in southeastern India. See also the list of place names (*Negapatão, Totoçarin*).

rewarded and promoted as in Manila or in Flanders. Due to incompetency and the sale of important military offices to young men with little or no experience, the Portuguese had lost many positions around the Indian Ocean region including Solor, Syriam, Hormuz, Bahrein, Gombrun, Qeshm and Julfar.[180] Tidore and Ternate were saved, but only because of Spanish intervention from Manila. There had also been major setbacks for the Portuguese in India.

In Chapter II De Coutre walks the reader through the scenario in which equipping a large fleet is not a viable option for the foreseeable future. In this section he suggested a series of other measures—both strategic and commercial—to reverse, or at least stem, the declining fortunes of the Estado da Índia. The first possible measure was to annually send 20 or 30 caravels to the East Indies. Oared vessels such as galleys could be constructed in India and the men brought to Asia on the caravels could help man these. Immediately adjoining this measure was a plea to open up trade and abolish the concession voyages (*viagens*).[181] Sailing routes should be made accessible to any merchant who wished to sail to the East Indies from Portugal or Spain, or within the Indian Ocean region. This could be accomplished in conjunction with the liberalisation of the pepper trade. The suggested reform of the trading system was conceived as a way of spreading trade risks over several smaller vessels. If one were to be caught, the potential loss was modest in comparison to the seizure of large, ocean-going vessels (such as carracks) used by the Portuguese between India and Europe. The Dutch who outfitted their vessels and extracted great profits from plundering would thus find their "returns" significantly diminished. De Coutre expressed his conviction that the merchants in the Dutch Republic would as a result be far less willing to pour money into ventures if prospective returns were largely lessened. In turn, the Iberians were to step up their attacks on Dutch vessels that ride at anchor in ports around the East Indies, especially at ports where the ships have to anchor relatively far out at sea due to shallow coastal waters.

The next step saw the construction or upgrading of fortresses. Goa, De Coutre explained, "is open like Madrid" and lacked defences. Despite efforts undertaken during the rule of Philip II/I to have an engineer survey

---

[180] For further background information see the list of place names (*Solor, Serião, Ormuz, Gombrun, Quexome* and *Gulfar*).

[181] See the glossary (*viagem*).

the city and devise plans for Goa's defences, the Portuguese have only begun to build a wall that is haphazard and does not provide adequate protection. De Coutre lamented the state of the Reis Magos fortress[182] and recommended that its stones be reused to construct another fortification, and he also urged the upgrading of the Aguada Fortress.[183] Similarly, fortifications along the Malabar Coast[184] were in urgent need of attention as the forts were "open, falling down, or built in the old fashioned way". Materials and labour to accomplish this were plentiful and the reader is assured that "you can do more with one ducat there than with twenty ducats here" in Spain.

In Bardez,[185] it was important to dig a channel linking two rivers, the São Christóvão and Coluale.[186] This was to help protect the 16 towns under Goa's jurisdiction from being invaded by neighbouring Muslim overlords. More also had to be done to stop the rampant smuggling that went on in Bardez and that ultimately deprived Goa of its rightful fees and duties. The smuggling took place overland and also at sea.

Moving from the Indian subcontinent to the Malay Peninsula, the memorial turns to the situation in Portuguese Melaka. It recommended the construction of a fortification on the Ilha das Naus—which was a significant place of anchorage located "a cannon shot away from the city".[187] Spanish galleys from Manila should be deployed to patrol the nearby maritime channels and capture enemy ships in the Strait of Kundur as well as the Singapore Straits. There was reportedly "no shortage of men there to serve as crews on the galleys." As already outlined in greater detail in memorial III, a fortification should be constructed on a "triangular island" (present-day Sentosa) located between the New and Old Straits with some vessels dispatched to patrol the nearby waters. In order to reduce Melaka's dependence on imports, De Coutre advised that the Portuguese invite ethnic Chinese to settle these lands. He recounted how Captain Francisco da Silva de Meneses permitted the Chinese to settle on the opposite bank of the Melaka River, but at the time competition from the Chinese evoked

---

[182] A Portuguese fortification near Goa. See also the list of place names (*Reis Magos*).

[183] See the list of place names (*Aguada*).

[184] Southwestern coast of India. See also the list of place names (*Costa de Malavar*).

[185] See the list of place names (*Bardez*).

[186] Rivers in the Goa region around Bardez. See also the list of place names (*São Christóvão River, Coluale River*).

[187] For further particulars, see also the list of place names (*Ysla das Naus*).

considerable opposition from the Melaka *casados* who grossly inflated the prices of imported foodstuffs. Still, settlement by the Chinese was seen as something both urgent and imperative. Finally, the entrances of Melaka should be garrisoned just as in the case of Manila. De Coutre attested: "I lived for many years in Melaka, and most of the time the entrances were completely unguarded."

The memorial then changes tack and speaks of smuggling and its suppression. Soldiers who arrived in the East Indies were lured away to work for the smugglers, especially between India and the Arabian Peninsula. If commerce were opened to supply the goods legally, and for which there was evidently a demand, then taxation could be derived from legitimate businesses and the Dutch would suffer as a consequence.

Finally De Coutre lamented the loss of trade at Melaka. He listed the range of goods and commodities that were brought in from all across the region, from as far as China, Japan and India. But that was in the past, and he assured "Your Majesty has lost all this trade which is now in the hands of the rebels. They have grown rich in this commerce by means of their robberies, and the Portuguese in India have become impoverished and lost a lot". For this reason, action must be taken "in the manner that I [Jacques] have described, so as not to lose the lands and the many Christian communities that are there in them."

The memorial closes with what appears to be a postscript to the main text similar to Memorial II—a "list of goods that the Dutch take to the East Indies". Teensma treats this short paragraph as a separate document by its own right.

VIII

APPENDICES TRANSLATED FROM DUTCH

This volume also contains four appendices featuring documents that touch on Jacques de Coutre and some of the events that he recounted in book one of his *Vida.* All of the documents presented here are found in a bound manuscript volume preserved at the Nationaal Archief van Nederland in the Hague and titled *Boeck Tracterende vande Wreede, Verradische ende Hostile proceduren der Portugesen in Oost-Indien* (Book Concerning the Evil, Treasonous and Hostile Proceedings of the Portuguese in the East Indies). The volume which forms part of the Baron H. van Zuylen van Nyevelt collection, was specially prepared by the VOC and forwarded to the Dutch humanist Hugo Grotius in or around October 1604, that is approximately the time he received his commission to write an apology for Jacob van Heemskerck's seizure of the Portuguese carrack *Santa Catarina* off the eastern coast of Singapore in the preceding year.

The first appendix, an affidavit filed by Admiral Jacob van Neck on 28 September 1604, recounts his voyage to the East Indies. On arriving in Banten, Van Neck was warned not to proceed to the Banda islands on the grounds that the Portuguese had turned all the rulers of Java against the Dutch. Rumour had it that the Portuguese were also equipping vessels at the time with the objective of ousting the Dutch from the Spice Islands. Despite this, Van Neck and his ships sailed to the Malukus where they were cordially welcomed by the king of Ternate—much to his surprise and evidently to that of the Portuguese on the neighbouring island Tidore who made strenuous efforts to discredit the Dutch. In fact—as Van Neck pointed out—most of the atrocities in the Indies had been committed by the Portuguese and not by the Dutch. As there was no stock of cloves at hand, Van Neck's ships had to drop anchor to wait for a new harvest. After waiting for one month with no clove harvest in sight, they set sail for China via the Philippines. They arrived off the coast near Macao, but did not realise that they were near this Portuguese settlement. A sloop[188] was sent to shore to reconnoitre the situation but its crew members soon found themselves arrested by the Portuguese authorities.[189] A second vessel—a yacht[190] or cutter—was sent out the next day and its crew was also captured. The Dutch prisoners were subsequently executed by hanging and drowning with the exception of one Martin Apius.[191]

The ships then weighed anchor and headed for Patani, a port on the Gulf of Siam. It was here that Van Neck met Jacques who had just recently returned from Manila. There the Fleming had visited a Dutch prisoner—Lambert Biesman—who along with other crew members had been taken from the pinnace[192] *Eendracht* (Unity, Concordia) belonging to the fleet of Olivier van Noort. It was De Coutre who informed the admiral about Biesman's execution together with most of his shipmates by the Spanish in Manila.

---

188 See the glossary (*sloop*).

189 See the more extensive account in Van Foreest and De Booy, ed., *De Vierde Schipvaart*, I, pp. 100–6.

190 See the glossary (*yacht*).

191 See Martin Apius, "Incidente em Macau, 1601", ed. and tr. Arie Pos, *Revista de Cultura* 12 (2004): 61–7.

192 See the glossary (*pinnace*).

Towards the end of his testimony the admiral noted that during his first voyage to the East Indies in 1598, there were no clashes with the Portuguese, unlike his second voyage. He had heard at the time of a large Portuguese naval expedition against Banten—to punish the Bantanese and the Dutch—but the Portuguese were successfully repelled.

The second appendix, an affidavit by Jacob van Heemskerck, links into the preceding testimony of Admiral Van Neck, not least with reference to the execution of members of Van Neck's crew by the Portuguese. Van Heemskerck recounted his departure in April 1600 from Europe, how they ran into a Spanish naval squadron near the Canary Islands, and the subsequent armed engagement at sea. Having arrived at Banten, Van Heemskerck had learnt of a Portuguese naval attack on the city under Admiral André Furtado de Mendonça and his engagement at sea with five Dutch ships under Admiral Wolfert Hermanszoon. After failing in his mission at Banten to evict the Dutch from that important trading city, Furtado de Mendonça then proceeded to Ambon—where he harassed the people of Hitu who had recently established friendly relations with the Dutch—and subsequently also to Ternate. Here he was supported by two Spanish ships from Manila.

Van Heemskerck recounted several more incidents involving the Portuguese who either acted directly against "peaceful" Dutch traders or instigated others to use violence against them. These incidents included the execution of members of Van Necks' crew at Macao, an attack in Cochinchina instigated by a Portuguese monk, an incident in Ambon, and the deceit of the ruler of Demak who first invited Van Heemskerck to trade in his realm, but on his arrival attacked the Dutch. The latter was repulsed by force, and in the skirmish that ensued Van Heemskerck took a Johorese junk and some prisoners. He also wrote to the king of Johor, offering his apologies. He offered to come to trade in Johor, if feasible, and had already hired a pilot to lead the way. He also offered to reimburse the seized cargo of the Johorese junk.

At Patani Van Heemskerck received a letter from the king of Johor inviting the Dutch to conduct trade in his kingdom. Here he also held conversations with one of the Johorese princes, Raja Siak, who repeated the invitation and gave Van Heemskerck some information as to where and when to lie in wait for Portuguese merchantmen arriving from China. Van Heemskerck proceeded to wait in the waters around Tioman, and here he received an embassy from Johor bearing gifts and a letter stating that the Portuguese had learnt of his plans and as a result, had dispatched an ambassador to Johor to issue threats against its king should he proceed to forge friendly trading relations with the Dutch. The king of Johor rebuffed these threats, and now invited Van Heemskerck to await the arrival of ships from China around the Johor River estuary, where he would stand a better chance of seizing and plundering a Portuguese vessel than in the open waters around Tioman. This invitation, so Van Heemskerck claimed, was to help the king of Johor exact revenge on the Portuguese for their misdeeds against his people and to forge an alliance with the Dutch. After taking up the king's invitation and moving his three vessels to the waters around the Johor River estuary, Van Heemskerck as promised reimbursed the king of Johor for the damages caused by the earlier seizure of the junk at Demak.

The third appendix makes a connection with the information provided by Van Neck, and particularly the information he had learnt from De Coutre at Patani about the execution of Lambert Biesman and his men at Manila. This affidavit, filed by Simon Lambertsz. Mau, told of how the vessel commanded by Biesman was taken in Manila Bay by the Spanish. Mau also confessed that he personally had conversed with a person "who had lived in the East Indies on a permanent basis"—this is most probably a reference to De Coutre—and had visited Biesman in prison before he was garrotted with most of the other prisoners.[193]

Finally, the fourth appendix is related to the seizure of the *Santa Catarina* off Singapore in February 1603. Although Van Heemskerck had mentioned nothing about this incident in his own affidavit, it happened around the time De Coutre was in Batu Sawar. Penned by the captain of Melaka, Fernão de Albuquerque, on 26 March 1603—that is almost one month to the day after the *Santa Catarina* incident—he sought to muster the support of Van Heemskerck in negotiating the release of some Portuguese and Christian hostages in Johor. For this purpose De Albuquerque dispatched the assistance of Filipe Lobo[194] and

---

[193] See also Morga, *Sucesos*, p. 182, note 2.

[194] Filipe Lobo is mentioned as one of the six Portuguese captives earlier held aboard Van Heemskerck's vessel. See bk. I, ch. XVII of the *Vida*; and separately also appendix IV. Loureiro described him as a "Portuguese captured by the Dutch in Insulíndia in 1600". See Loureiro, "European Encounters and Clashes in the South China Sea", II, *Revista de Cultura,* International Edition 12 (2004): 157.

Pero Mascarenhas. In book I, chapter XVII, of the *Vida,* De Coutre mentioned that in Patani he had met, aboard Van Heemskerck's flagship, a Portuguese prisoner from Melaka by the name of Filipe Lobo. This would have probably been the same individual. Lobo was sent by the Portuguese governor of Melaka to mediate in what was apparently a severe political crisis where several Christians from Melaka and their belongings had been taken by the Johorese. This is with great likelihood the same or a related crisis described by De Coutre in chapter XIX of his *Vida.*

After these summary outlines of the individual chapters, memorials and appendices, we now turn to the translated and annotated texts, starting with book I of the *Vida,* or "Life of Jacques de Coutre".

JACQUES DE COUTRE'S LIFE IN SOUTHEAST ASIA

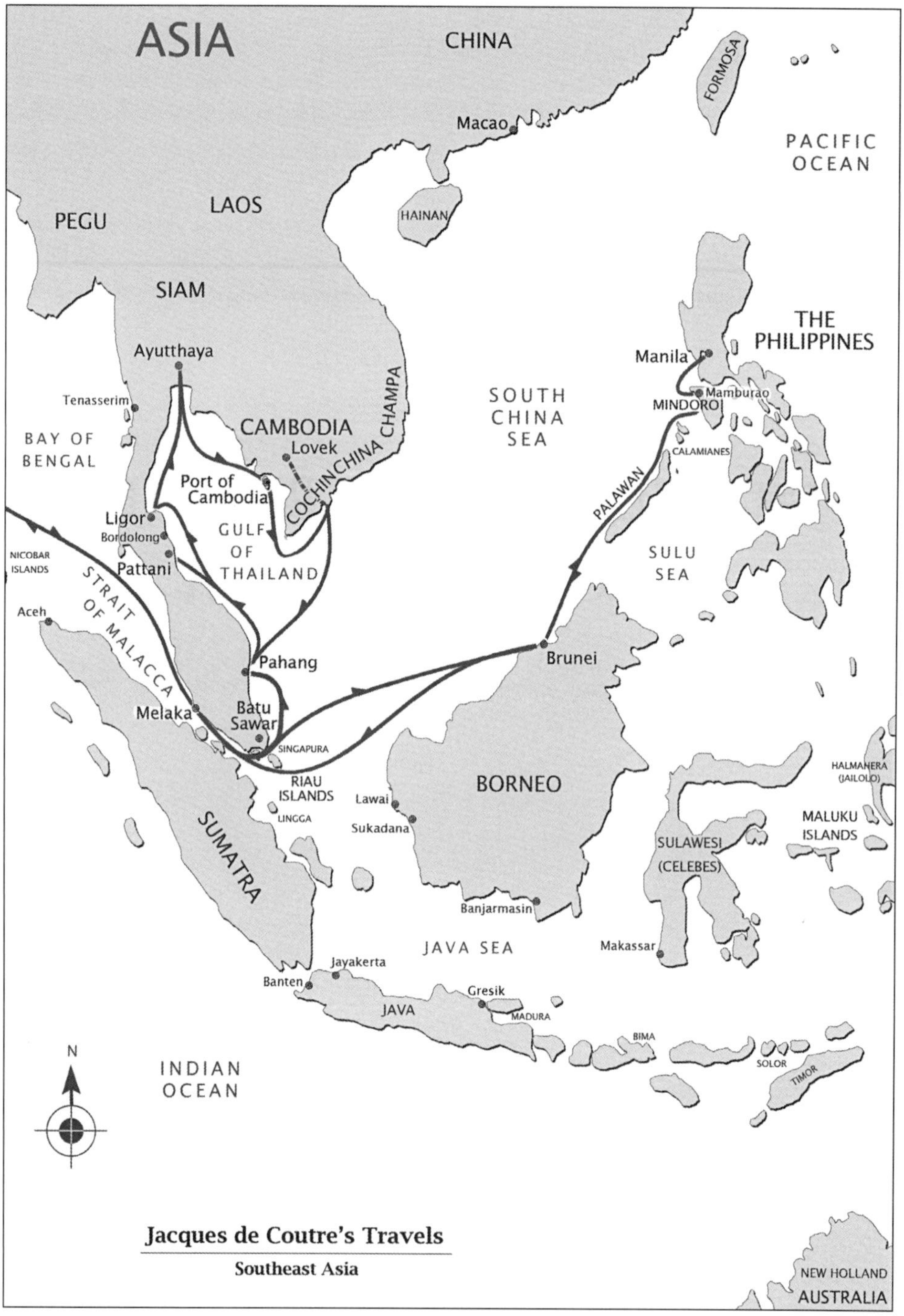

Jacques de Coutre's Travels

Southeast Asia

CHAPTER

I

How I left my parents' house and my homeland, and what happened to me until I reached Spain[1]

I was born in the noble city of Bruges, in the county of Flanders, and my parents were Jacques de Coutre and Anna van Houven, citizens and natives of the said city. Shortly after my father died, my mother decided to send me to Spain, seeing that I was inclined toward a military career,[2] and to spare me the wars that were then raging in those states, since most of my relatives and siblings had been killed in these wars. Before saying farewell to my homeland, I went to the city of Ghent and to the town of Antwerp and on the way I visited an uncle who lived there. I returned to Bruges, from where I set out for the city of Sluis,[3] accompanied by my mother and a brother. At the time I was between 15 and 16 years old. On 22 June 1591, I bid farewell to her and to my brother in Sluis, and with a passport I went to Zeeland aboard a boat. I arrived in the city of Middelburg, which is the main city on that island, and after having seen the cities of Arnemuiden[4] and Veere I went to Vlissingen,[5] and from there

---

[1] BCE, Ms. 2780, fol. 3 recto–5 verso.

[2] Ms. lit. *toward arms.*

[3] Ms. here and subsequently: *Enclusa.*

[4] Ms. *Hermua.*

[5] In English also: *Flushing.*

I set out for Spain on 1 August 1591 aboard a carrack[6] that was called *León Roxo*,[7] captained by Gaspar Yances, who ensured that it was very well outfitted, with 20 pieces of artillery and four *pedreros*,[8] 30 sailors and soldiers, and there were 36 passengers on board.

We set out from the port with favourable weather. We sailed around[9] England, Scotland,[10] Ireland and Iceland until we reached the Norwegian Sea,[11] where we spent more than a month with adverse winds, and we anchored at [a spot where the water was] 50 *brazas*[12] [deep]. There we caught a large quantity of herring and codfish, in such large quantities [in fact] that we had to return them to the sea owing to a lack of salt, taking only what was necessary for that day. As we were tired of battling such adverse weather, the fishing was a welcomed relief and good entertainment, and more than 200 fishing vessels were doing the same thing within sight of our ship. Here, while I was fishing, a lad of my age fell into the sea from the capstan,[13] who, not knowing how to swim, floated face up on the surface of the water. When I saw him I yelled at him to grab the fishing line with which I was fishing, but he could not hear me because of the distance and the carrack[14] was being buffeted by stiff winds. To grip the fishing line more firmly I twisted it countless times around my hands. God willed that the fishing line managed to get entangled around the boy's legs. When he felt it, he hastily grabbed it. Hearing my clamours some people came to help me, and my hands were being mangled due to the force of being dragged away by the carrack. Then the vessel suddenly did a sharp turn and the captain threw a rope into the sea and brought the boy back.

We continued sailing until we passed the island[15] of Ireland. In the evening we saw four *baxeles*,[16] and the following day at dawn we saw them on our stern; two of them were English ships and the other two were prizes

[6] Ms. *nao.* A type of ship. See also the glossary (*carrack*).
[7] Meaning: *Red Lion.*
[8] An artillery piece. See also the glossary (*pedrero*).
[9] Ms. lit. *outside.*
[10] Ms. *Escorcia.*
[11] The North Sea.
[12] About 83.5–91.5 metres. See also the glossary (*braça*).
[13] Ms. *tornera.*
[14] Ms. *nao.*
[15] Ms. lit. *region.*
[16] A type of vessel. See also the glossary (*baxel*).

they had captured, one was from Hamburg, and the other was a caravel from Portugal. We took up arms. As soon as they drew near us they yelled that we should surrender to the queen of England.[17] Our captain responded to this by ordering that a large cannon be fired from the stern, which was done very skillfully, hitting the enemy in the middle of their forecastle. Since they wanted to approach us from the windward side, the captain ordered that another cannon be fired from the castle.[18] They fired and hit the enemy in the middle of their ship's stern.[19] When they saw how we were responding, they did another turn and fired upon us with all their artillery. We suffered little damage since there was a lot of sea between us; then we saw the enemy [ship] going under; and they were chasing after the caravel that was a *legua*[20] away from their stern, to save themselves by going aboard that ship. While we were thus engaged, the flagship[21] moved off and the admiral's ship[22] joined in, which also attacked us with so much fury that they killed our captain, blowing away his legs with a [cannon] shot. He remained cheerful until he died. Then when they saw the little success they were having with us, they thought it best to sail away after we had fought for four hours.

With these and other events we reached Lisbon in October 1591, after having been at sea for three months. We anchored near the Belém fortress[23] and the pilot, myself and other men disembarked. We went to the residence of the Count of Fuentes[24]—at the time Cardinal Albert the Archduke [of Austria][25] was governing the kingdom of Portugal—and from there to the house of Herman Vermeire,[26] the Flemish owner of the carrack, who lived in Corpo Santo. When we were in his house, I fainted and fell unconscious to the ground. We returned to the carrack at dawn, since it had not yet

---

[17] Elizabeth I of England.

[18] Ms. *cruzera*. Possibly a reference here to the castle at the aft of the vessel.

[19] Ms. *rueda*.

[20] About 5.5–6 kilometres. See also the glossary (*legua*).

[21] Ms. *capitana*. The flagship of the captain-general of the fleet. See also the glossary (*capitana*).

[22] Ms. *almiranta*. The admiral's ship. See also the glossary (*almiranta*).

[23] A fortification located along the River Tagus (Tejo) that guarded the entrance to the port of Lisbon. See the image on p. 66.

[24] Pedro Enríquez Acevedo, Conde de Fuentes, served as the captain-general of Portugal, 1589–94.

[25] Albert became the first viceroy following Portugal's annexation by King Philip II of Spain in 1580. Albert served in this capacity between 1583 and 1593.

[26] Ms. *Herman Varmere*. According to AA he was a tapestry maker born in Flanders who lived in Lisbon.

been inspected.[27] After returning to the ship my brother, Joseph de Coutre, came aboard. I was very happy to see him as we had not seen each other for more than five years. He took me to his house where we lived together until we went to the East Indies.[28]

The fortress or tower of Belém has guarded the entrance to Lisbon harbour since the Middle Ages. (Private collection, Peter Borschberg).

---

[27] Ms. lit. *visited.*

[28] Ms. here and subsequently: *Índia Oriental.* See the list of place names (*Sur*).

Map of the East Indies by Abraham Ortelius, c.1570. (Washington, D.C., Library of Congress).

CHAPTER

II

My voyage to the East Indies in the company of my brother in the year 1592[1]

Finding myself in Lisbon with such few resources and subject to the work and misery of Europe, my brother and I decided to journey to remote lands where the cost of living was more economical. We chose the East Indies,[2] and to this end we banded together with two companions, one of whom was called Luís López, and the other Christóval Homen. We assembled our provisions by scrimping and saving. Finally, we embarked as soldiers on a carrack that was called *Nossa Senhora de Nazaré*,[3] captained by Brás Correia, and the captain-major of the entire fleet was called Francisco de Melo Caniveado. While boarding I found myself in quite a predicament; it so happened that my brother had already embarked with our companions and the carracks were setting sail, owing to an oversight I was still on land without knowing which carrack my brother was sailing on. I did not speak either Portuguese or Spanish, which was a great pity. I went down to the beach and saw that many people were embarking on a caravel for the carracks, but I did not know to which carrack they were heading. I went aboard with them—God willed that the caravel was taking those people

[1] Ms. fol. 5 verso–9 verso.

[2] Ms. here and subsequently: *Índia Oriental*. See the list of place names (*sur*).

[3] Meaning: *Our Lady of Nazareth*.

to the said carrack, the [*Nossa Senhora de*] *Nazaré*—we reached the vessel. Seeing that there was nobody who could understand me so that I could ask which carrack this was, and nor did I know which carrack I was boarding, I climbed aboard and found a labyrinth of boxes and people without being able to see a single familiar face. I sat down on a ship's beam[4] feeling very melancholic since I thought that my brother had sailed aboard another carrack. After a long while had passed I saw Christóval Homen; I was overjoyed—as one can well imagine—who took me to where my brother was. He was sitting on a crate, with a lot of refreshments, fruit, bread and other things, all piled together in a heap as was customary in the case of poor soldiers. He was as happy as a lark to see me again. There were five carracks going to India, apart from another 50 large and small baxeles, some of which were going to the islands of Madeira, others to the Canary Islands and to Cape Verde, Guinea and Brazil.[5] We went to the Cape [of Good Hope] in a convoy[6] on account of the English fleet that was within sight. They did not dare to come near us. As soon as we lost sight of the English fleet, each ship from our company followed their own route and we then reached the vicinity of Guinea, where we ran into an area with no wind and rough seas, which was why our main mast broke, along with the *cebadera*.[7] Finally, everything was repaired to the greatest extent possible.

We crossed the equator with the trade winds,[8] and after passing the Abrolhos[9]—as they are called—people began to fall sick, so much so that we had to throw three or four corpses into the sea daily until we passed the Cape of Good Hope.[10] We also sailed pass the land of Natal[11] where the seas were tempestuous, but by now there were fewer people dying

---

[4] Ms. *entena.*

[5] The route described here is the standard route taken by vessels outbound from India in the age of sail. De Coutre listed Brazil before Guinea and that is probably an oversight on his part or a copy error made by his son Esteban. The sequence of these two names has been reversed here in the translation in order to match geographic realities.

[6] Ms. *en conserva.*

[7] Ms. *lavadera.* Probably the *cebadera*, the bowsprit yard. See also the glossary (*cebadera*).

[8] Ms. *vientos generales.* The monsoon or trade winds. See also the glossary (*vientos generales*).

[9] Ms. *Abrollos.*

[10] Near the southern tip of Africa. See also the list of place names (*Cabo de Boa Esperansa*).

[11] See the list of place names (*Natal*).

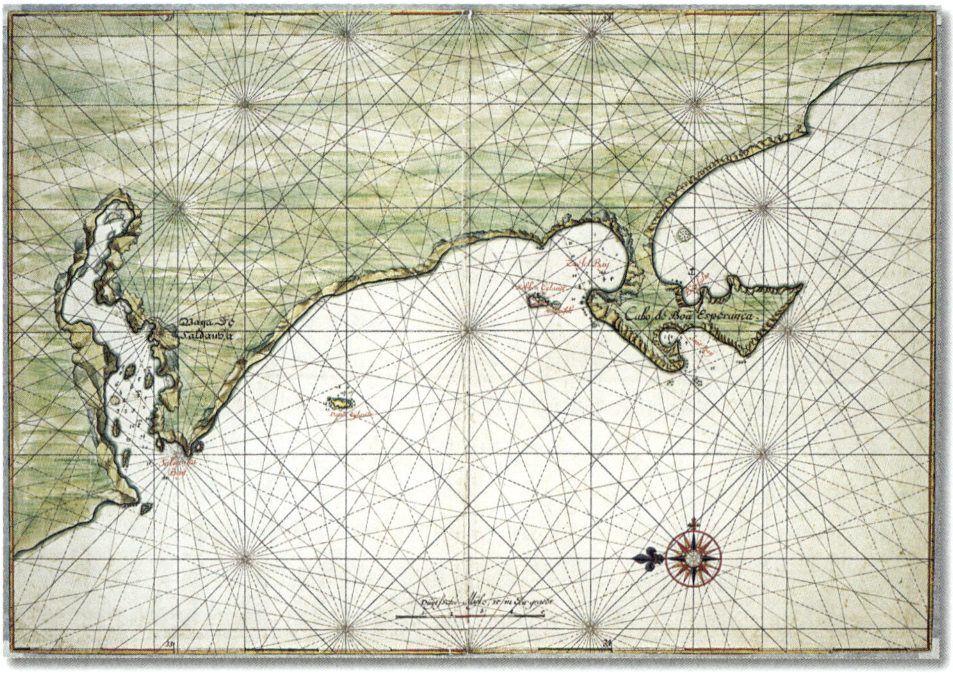

Map of the Cape of Good Hope region featuring Agoada de Saldanha, Table Bay and the Cape of Good Hope. Taken from the Vingboons Atlas, c.1665. (The Hague, NAN, 4.VELH 619, pl. 35).

Hand-coloured plan of the Portuguese fortress and settlement at Mozambique by João Albarnaz I, *Plantas das Cidades, e Fortalezas da Conquista de Índia Oriental* (Maps of the Cities and Fortresses of the Conquest of the East Indies), c.1648. (Munich, BSB, Cod. Icon. 162, pl. 1, fol. 7).

because the air was healthier. We arrived in Mozambique,[12] a fortress of Your Majesty, in July, with 200 less people before we set sail, who had died along the way, and with many people still sick, my brother being one of them, and I myself was not well either. Our two companions and ourselves disembarked aboard a *pangaio*[13]—which is what the boats of that land are called.

When we reached the shore, two native kaffirs,[14] who are blacks like those of Angola, carried my brother on their shoulders since he could not walk, and we went to the hospital in this way. They made us take off the clothes we were wearing, and after giving us a bath, handed each of us a laundered shirt. We left our clothes and firearms on a bench, believing that the hospital warden or our companions would take care to keep an eye on them, and we went to the beds that they indicated to us. Six or seven days after that, I got up to leave the hospital because I was already feeling well. I asked the hospital warden for my clothes, but he did not know how to answer me.[15] Seeing myself in just a shirt, I made such a ruckus until they gave me some linen shorts[16] and some old shoes, and a [thick] cloth[17] cap. Thus arrayed in such a fetching attire, I ran into a lad who was a friend of mine, who lent me a short cape[18] with which I went to see if I could find Luís López, my companion, to find out where my clothes were. I found him in a hut thatched with straw eating and drinking with the rope maker[19] from the carrack and other people. Seeing that he, too, did not know what to tell me about my clothes, I asked him to find some money to get some clothes for my brother, who was still ill. He said he would, but he did not.

As my brother and I were ill, Luís López negotiated for provisions and he spent a lot and ineptly, without wanting to buy us clothes. I later learnt how he had sold our swords, and therefore I could not help but suspect that he himself had taken our clothes. With this and other annoyances, the time when we would have to embark once more drew ever closer. I went one day

---

[12] The Portuguese fortress São Sebastião was located near the so-called Stone Town on the Isle of Mozambique. See also the list of place names (*Monsanbique*) as well as the image on p. 70.

[13] A type of longboat. See also the glossary (*pangaio*).

[14] Ms. *cafres.* See also the glossary (*kaffir*).

[15] Ms. *no me supo dar razon.*

[16] Ms. *calconçillos de lienço.*

[17] Ms. *xerga,* a thick cloth, cloak.

[18] Ms. *herregüelo.* A short military cape.

[19] Ms. *estrinquero.*

at dawn to the hospital to take my brother to the carrack; I did not find him there. When I asked for him they told me that he had left. When I heard this answer I understood that he had died and that they were saying it in this manner to console me. I was very upset but I had to leave, and I ran through the city since people were being hurried to board the carrack. I finally found my brother in the old fort wearing a pair of linen[20] shorts and a shirt, with another cloth cap[21] that had been given to him as alms, with bare feet and legs. On the one hand I rejoiced at having found him but on the other hand tears came into my eyes thinking about the misery and extreme poverty in which we found ourselves, furthermore in alien lands, having been brought up with so much pampering and indulgence. I then said to him: "Brother, we have set out to reach India and reach it we must", and we consoled ourselves in the belief that the city of Goa would be a better land. In this manner we boarded a *pangaio* belonging to the Jesuit fathers. They hauled my brother on board tied with some ropes since he was still ill and could not climb. Since we were sick and had so much work to do, I was unable to see the city and that is the reason why I have nothing to say about it. We left the port in such good weather that we arrived in Goa on 14 September 1592, the day of the Holy Cross.

We disembarked aboard a *manchua*[22] in the same miserable state in which we had found ourselves, along with a chest, which fell into the sea since it had been tied badly; however, it fell lid up. Since there were many *manchuas* in port, God willed that a soldier held it up in the water with his hands until everything that was in it was transferred to the *manchua*. By the time we sailed up the river to the city of Goa night had fallen. We lodged in the house of a *freydera*, a female innkeeper, as that is what they were called in Goa. The following day Luís López took a letter of recommendation that he had brought with him to a very rich man, who, as soon as he learnt that we were there, came to see us, and he rented us a house he owned, situated in front of the house in which he lived, and he lent us money with which we clothed ourselves in silks and finery. Three months later my brother Joseph

---

[20] The term *linen* was often used to designate any cloth of plant origin. See J. Irwin, "Indian Textile Trade in the Seventeenth Century. II. Coromandel Coast", *Journal of Indian Textile History* 2 (1956): 37–8.

[21] Ms. *bonete de xerga.*

[22] A cargo boat. See also the glossary (*manchua*).

de Coutre, married into a leading family in Goa, Old Christians,[23] albeit not very well-off. At about the same time Luís López travelled to Melaka, after which we all moved from the house of Sebastião Pinto de Freixos, which was the name of the man to whom Luís López had taken his letter. I later fell sick, and to cure me they took me to my brother's house. After I recovered, [and] having a natural inclination and desire to see the world (that was what had induced me to leave my homeland) my mother took advantage of this to get me away from the war, even if it meant that I had to survive other and greater perils. My life often hung by a thread, where luck alone saved me from these dangers. However, God always made me successful in everything I did.

Since I found I had this opportunity in my hands I wished to make the most of it. I embarked for the Southern Sea[24] on 28 September of the following year, 1593, sailing as a soldier aboard a carrack owned by Dom Diogo Lobo, who was then the captain of Melaka, and the captain of the carrack was called Diogo Camelo. We set off with excellent weather, it was only while crossing the Gulf of Ceylon[25] that we ran into [so] many storms that we thought the carrack was going to break apart because of these. We finally reached Melaka and we found out that the captain of the fortress was Francisco de Silva de Meneses, since the tenure of Dom Diogo Lobo had come to an end. After disembarking, the first person I saw was an old man from Venice—he was called Sequin[26] Martinela—who spoke to me without knowing me or having seen me before in his life. He offered me a lot [of things] and he took me to the house of a man who was called Gaspar Ximenes to give him some letters. The following day he took me to speak with the captain, Francisco de Silva de Meneses, who was delighted[27] to see me since I had been recommended to him, and he ordered that I be given a house to live in for free. Thus, with his patronage, I set out to earn an honourable livelihood, and he always granted me many favours and held

---

[23] Ms. *Cristianos viejos.* As opposed to "New Christians", who are recent converts.

[24] Ms. here and subsequently: *mar de sur.* Lit. South Sea, Sea of the South. See also the list of place names (*Insulíndia, Mar de sur*).

[25] Ms. *golfo de Zeilan.*

[26] Ms. *Sequin.* According to the editors of AA, this name could possibly represent a corruption of the Italian *Cecchino*, the diminutive of *Cecco*, or abbreviation for Francesco.

[27] Ms. *holgar.* This word does not exist in the sense used by De Coutre, probably to be understood as the Portuguese *folgar,* that is to be delighted, rejoice.

me in respect, and he always offered me a chair to sit down in his presence whenever I went to talk to him, something that he did for [only] very few residents of that city. Since I was a lad of such a tender age, he helped me make my fortune, and not just him [but] also all the other captains who succeeded him. I expressed my heartfelt thanks to old Sequin Martinela, and from then on we were great friends, and he was more of a father to me than my own father, and we lived together for a long time.

CHAPTER

III

The journey I made to the kingdom of Pahang in the year 1594 and the events that I experienced[1]

Six months later I went to the kingdom of Pahang[2] on the orders of Captain Francisco de Silva de Meneses, not just to accompany an embassy that he was sending in the name of Your Majesty to that kingdom but also to buy diamonds and bezoars, because I had some knowledge of such wares. From that point onwards I began to make my fortune, being a soldier and a merchant whenever an occasion presented itself. I set sail aboard his own ship accompanied by Martim Teixeira, which was the ambassador's name, who served as the captain of the ship. As the Southern Sea[3] is never free from storms, on departure from the port, we ran into a tempest that forced us to enter into the Batu Pahat River,[4] which is nearby, [and] where we rode out the storm. The following day we unfurled our sails and we passed the islands Pulau Pisang[5] [and] Pulau Karimun,[6] which is [located] near the Strait[s] of Singapore. [The area][7] is completely covered with large and leafy

[1] Ms. fol. 10 recto–12 recto.
[2] See the list of place names (*Pam*).
[3] Ms. *mar de sur.*
[4] Ms. *Rio Fermoso*; the Batu Pahat River. See also the list of place names (*Rio Fermoso*).
[5] Ms. *Pula Pisan*; Pulau Pisang. See also the list of place names (*Pula Pisan*).
[6] Ms. *Pula Quiliman*; Pulau Karimun. See also the list of place names (*Pula Quiliman*).
[7] Ms. lit. which is.

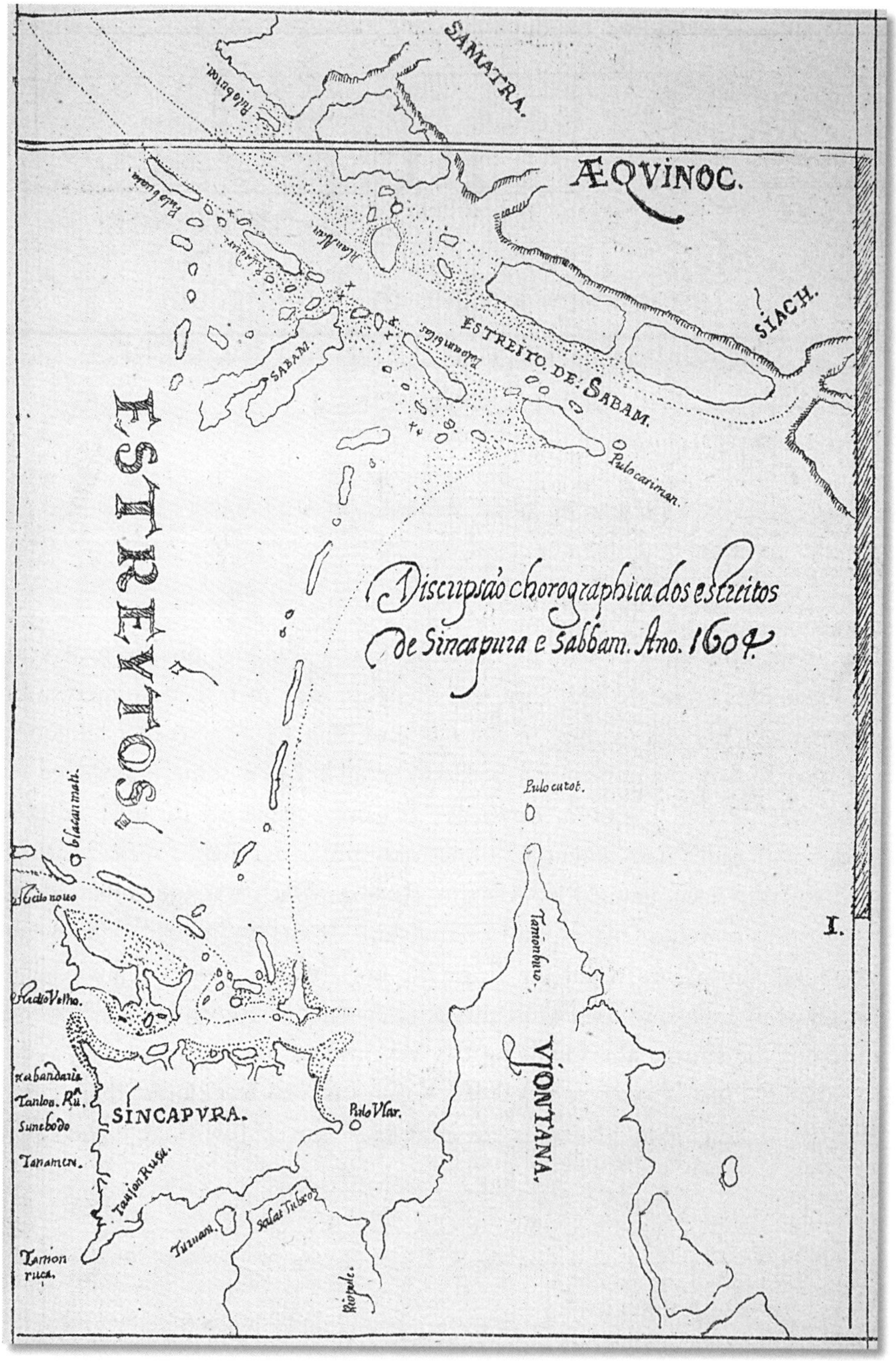

Hand-drawn map of Singapura and the surrounding straits by Manoel Godinho de Erédia. The original is found in the manuscript of the *Declaraçam de Malaca* (Description of Melaka), c.1613. (Brussels, Bibliothèque Royale, Ms. 39015A, fol. 61 recto).

trees, so much so that when ships pass by, the tips of their yards[8] inevitably brush along the branches, especially[9] in the Old Strait [of Singapore]; the passage is very narrow, and there is a great deal of maritime traffic with many ships from different kingdoms. There are two straits side by side, one is called the New Strait,[10] and the other the Old Strait.[11]

Many fishermen live along these straits, who are called *saletes.*[12] While pointing out the strait to us, they came aboard our ship with fresh fish and a lot of local fruits, which are very different from the fruits in Europe, which they pick in the hills.[13] Some are called durians,[14] and others are called mangosteens,[15] and others are called rambutans[16] and *buah duku*;[17] they are all very healthy and tasty. They brought us many parasols made from palm leafs; they call them *payones*;[18] and fresh water. They gave us everything in exchange for rice and old fabrics. They are extremely poor people. They live in sloops[19] that are five or six *varas*[20] long at most, and are very narrow, made of thin, light planks, and on them they have their houses with wives and children, dogs, cats, [and] even hens with their chicks. They raise everything inside the little sloop, which amazed me because these boats are so narrow. When they go fishing, the man sits on the *perahu* with a harpoon and the wife and children paddle very fast and very skillfully. Very old men can be found amongst them; I met some who said that they were all a hundred years old. They are treacherous people by nature. For this reason we deal with them very carefully and with weapons in our hands, because it has happened that they were allowed to come aboard our ships in such numbers, ostensibly to sell fresh fish, and in the blink of an eye they attacked and killed everyone aboard the ship. They are armed with poisoned daggers, which they call *krisses*,[21]

---

[8] Ms. *vergas.*

[9] Ms. lit. mainly.

[10] Ms. *Estrecho Nuevo.* See the list of place names (*Estrecho Neuvo*).

[11] Ms. *Estrecho Viejo.* See the list of place names (*Estrecho Viejo*).

[12] O*rang laut* or sea-gypsies. See also the glossary (*orang laut, saletes*).

[13] Ms. *en los montes*; lit. in the mountains.

[14] Ms. *duriones.*

[15] Ms. *mangostones.*

[16] Ms. *rambeis.*

[17] Ms. *boduques.* A fruit also known as *langsat.* See also the glossary (*buah duku*).

[18] Ms. *caiones.* The term *payung* is Malay for a parasol.

[19] Ms. here and subsequently: *chalupas.* A type of vessel. See also the glossary (*sloop*).

[20] About 5–6 metres. See also the glossary (*vara*).

[21] A Malay dagger. See also the glossary (*keris*).

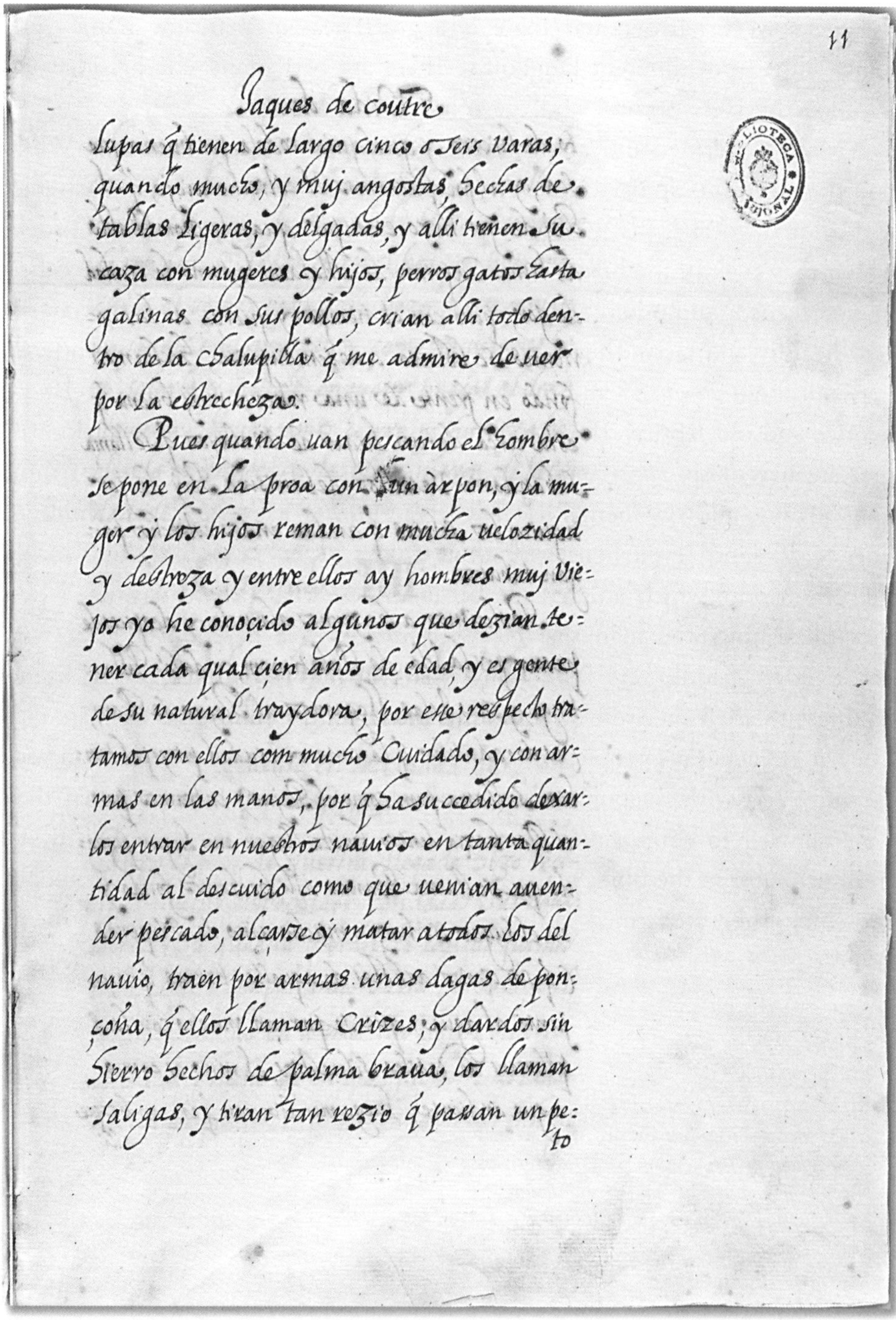

11

Jaques de coutre

lupas q̃ tienen de largo cinco o seis varas; quando mucho, y muy angostas, hechas de tablas ligeras, y delgadas, y alli tienen su caza con mugeres y hijos, perros gatos hasta galinas con sus pollos, crian alli todo dentro de la chalupilla q̃ me admire de ver por la estrecheza.

Pues quando van pescando el hombre se pone en la proa con un arpon, y la muger y los hijos reman con mucha velozidad y destreza y entre ellos ay hombres muy viejos yo he conocido algunos que dezian tener cada qual cien años de edad, y es gente de su natural traydora, por ese respecto tratamos con ellos con mucho cuidado, y con armas en las manos, por q̃ ha succedido dexarlos entrar en nuestros navios en tanta quantidad al descuido como que venian a vender pescado, alçarse y matar a todos los del navio, traen por armas unas dagas de ponçoña, q̃ ellos llaman crizes; y dardos sin hierro hechos de palma brava, los llaman saligas, y tiran tan rezio q̃ passan un pe-
to

Text page from the *Vida de Jaques de Coutre* (autobiography), book 1, chapter 3, describing how the *orang laut* (*saletes, selates*) fish in the Old Strait of Singapore. (Madrid, BNE, Ms. 2780, fol. 11 recto).

and spears made of wild palm, without any iron. They are called *saligas*[22] and they throw them so hard that they can penetrate an iron breastplate and any shield no matter how sturdy they are. Finally we passed through the Old Strait, which the king of Johor had ordered to be obstructed when Dom Paulo Lima de Pereira,[23] captain of Melaka, captured the city of Johor from him;[24] however, with the passage of time and the force of the currents it is now no longer blocked. We anchored in front of a place which is called *Shabandaria*,[25] inhabited by Malays, subjects of the king of Johor, to whom the *saletes*, who sail in the straits, also pay tribute.

We once again set sail and after passing by the island of Tioman[26] and that of Tinggi[27] and other islands, we arrived at the kingdom of Pahang.[28] One can note that the main city, in which the court is located, is also called Pahang,[29] just like the kingdom. We entered by sailing upriver until we arrived at a small place called Beruas[30] [and] we anchored there. In this place they make a lot of wine from nipa [palm]—which are certain trees in those lands that grow along the water—[and] which appear quite similar to wild date palms; the wine is like *aguardente*.[31] They told me later that in the woods nearby there were many wild boars. As I like to hunt, I went ashore that night out of curiosity, under the moonlight, accompanied by two soldiers, and in the woods I built a makeshift shack out of branches so as to be able to shoot from there, and I killed a very large wild boar. As it was Friday, I ordered that it be salted and put into four large earthenware jars. The following day we weighed anchor and we dropped anchor again in front of the main square of the city of Pahang.

---

22 A short spear. See also the glossary (*saliga*).
23 Ms. *Paolo de Lima.*
24 This refers to the events of 1587. See SMS, appendix. 2, pp. 209–28.
25 Ms. *Sabandaria.* Settlement around the house or compound of the shahbandar of Singapura. See also the glossary (*shahbandar*) and the list of place names (*Sabandaria*).
26 Ms. *Pulatimom.* See the list of place names (*Pulatimom*).
27 Ms. *Pulatinga.* See the list of place names (*Pulatinga*).
28 Ms. here and subsequently: *Pam.*
29 Port on the eastern coast of the Malay Peninsula; present-day Pekan.
30 Ms. *Baroas.* See the list of place names (*Baroas*).
31 Ms. *aguardente.* See the glossary (*aguardente*).

CHAPTER

IV

The reception extended to the embassy and other things that happened to us in the city of Pahang[1]

The king learnt of our arrival; he ordered that our ambassador be received with all his knights and his guards, bearing spears. We all went accompanied thus to his palace. He was seated at the highest point of a stage made of cane[2] and mats, and all his knights arrayed themselves below in two rows: one row with swords embellished with gold in their hands and the other row with swords adorned with silver. We climbed up and the king told us to sit amongst them. After the ambassador had presented his embassy and the gift that we had brought, the king gave the ambassador a kris with a golden hilt, and for us he ordered that we be given betel[3]—which are leaves that they eat—and five cows, a lot of rice and many chickens, fruits and sweets, large earthenware jars filled with nipa palm[4] wine, which is similar to *aguardente*,[5] and some houses for us to live in, near our galliot[6]—which is what ships are called in the South.[7] With this he bid us farewell and I took care of the business that I had been commissioned to do by the captain

[1] Ms. *Capitulo IIII* fol. 12 recto–15 verso.
[2] Ms. here and subsequently: *canas.* Probably bamboo.
[3] Ms. *betre.* See the glossary (*betel*).
[4] Ms. *nipera.* A wine of the nipa palm mentioned earlier. See also the glossary (*nipera*).
[5] Ms. *agua ardiente.*
[6] Ms. here and subsequently: *galeota.* A type of oared vessel. See also the glossary (*galliot*).
[7] Ms. *en el Sur.*

of Melaka. I must describe some curious things that happened to us, and something about the kingdom of Pahang.

Pahang is a small kingdom; it has no more than a single city, which bears the same name, where the court is located and where many rich merchants reside in the vicinity, and some other small settlements. It would be more apt to describe it as a duchy, however the ruler has styled himself as a king. The city was entirely surrounded by wooden walls,[8] with a good quantity of bronze artillery, which the natives themselves cast.[9] The majority of the bronze had once belonged to Portuguese carracks that were lost along that coast. They were large pieces of artillery. The natives use barrel guns[10] for arms—but they shoot poorly[11]—[along with] lances, and spears made from wild palms, swords and krisses. There were no horses in the entire kingdom; there were only elephants, albeit very few of them. The king was very poor, he was more of a merchant than a king. He bought most of the wares and merchandise from our ship, and he paid us promptly in *emas*[12]—which are some gold coins. As for the kingdom, even though it was small it was very fertile and verdant, and it even has gold mines. This city is somewhat over 30-odd leguas away from Melaka travelling overland, and about 70 leguas by sea;[13] however, nobody goes overland since it is very hard to get through the forests and there are many swamps,[14] ponds and lagoons; even the Portuguese have never attempted to try this, since it is of very little interest to them. The natives are Muslims, however they are very tactful in their dealings and in their manner of dress. [The men] wear shirts made of *cassa* or *beatilha*[15] dyed in various colours—they call them *bajus*[16]—and as shorts they wear a dyed half-beatilha, which are made for this purpose along the Coromandel Coast,[17] and they wrap it around between their legs in such a way that they look like shorts. They wear another white or coloured scarf as a turban, twisted

[8] Ms. *murada toda de madera.*

[9] Ms. *labrar.*

[10] Ms. here and subsequently: *escopetas.*

[11] Ms. lit. terrible.

[12] Ms. *mazes.* A Malay coinage or currency unit. See also the glossary (*emas*).

[13] About 165–85 kilometres and 385–432 kilometres respectively, depending on the *legua* (or *legoa*) in question. See also the glossary (*legua*).

[14] Ms. *sapal.*

[15] These are types of loosely woven cottons (muslin). See also the glossary (*cassa, beatilha*).

[16] Ms. *bayus.* See the glossary (*baju*).

[17] The southeastern coast of subcontinental India. See also the list of place names (*Cheramandel*).

like a shawl, and they carry a kris in their belt as a dagger. Some of them have a kris with a golden hilt, and others have a wooden hilt, according to what each individual can afford.

{The women also wear a long and narrow blouse which allows a glimpse of their flesh. Some textiles are coloured, others are blue, and you find them in all colours. [They wear] a short tight jacket,[18] which is tailored from very thin material often with elaborate designs and colours. They also tie back their hair in a very curious fashion with multi-coloured ribbons. As they walk barefoot they wear rings on both their fingers and their toes and are very beautiful in their overall appearance.}[19]

I also saw the king when he ventured out, accompanied by some 700 members of his guard, who went before him with lances and krisses, and he rode on a small elephant, controlling [it] with some iron hooks. Behind him was seated a page with a sword, and behind him his brother who was walking with all the knights, who were also on foot, and in this manner he came to our galliot to see it. He left after we gave him a salvo[20] of artillery and musket[21] fire.

In matters of justice he was a tyrant. I saw him order that the testicles of six merchants be cut off because they had gone on a voyage without his permission. Some of them died because they were older men, others had been castrated.[22] He ordered that a woman be thrown before an elephant, which then killed her with its tusks, because she had been unfaithful to her husband. It was an astonishing sight that after she died, many other women fought to cut off her clothes and to take bits of her as souvenirs.[23] He used to habitually decree various forms of punishment such as this, but the most common sentence was to order individuals to be killed with krisses, and one would stab the condemned man where he wished or where he believed he would die faster [and] with less pain. He also used to order that people's heads be flayed from the crown downwards, and the skin be flayed with

---

[18] Ms. *vasquiña.*

[19] The entire paragraph marked in brackets is omitted in AA. This paragraph is found on fol. 13 verso of the manuscript.

[20] Ms. *una salva.*

[21] A type of hand-held firearm. See also the glossary (*musket*).

[22] Ms. *quedaron capones*; lit. became eunuchs.

[23] Ms. *por reliquias*; lit: as relics. These momentos most probably did not have a religious meaning.

Hand-coloured printed map of the world by Pieter Plancius, 1592 (Amsterdam, UB, Special Collections, O.K. 112).

sandpaper, and have needles inserted into people's nails. In the case of those who quarrelled with each other, he would order them to be tied back-to-back and be rolled through the square like a barrel or ball until they were half dead. I observed the most curious form of justice in the whole world, justice the king meted out to married couples when a husband quarrelled with a wife, or the wife with the husband, and if they did not live in harmony. If the husband or the wife complained, he would order both of them to be taken to the square—where there was a very large weighing scale and all the tools and instruments of justice—and they would be placed on the scale to see which of the two weighed more. They would put a stone on the stomach of the individual who weighed less so as to make the weight equal. Once they were evenly balanced, after they had been there for three or four hours and having been made a spectacle in front of everyone, they would cut the rope used to hold up the weighing scale and they would fall with a crash to the ground from a height of four or five *varas*.[24] After having been subjected to that humiliation they were allowed to leave in peace. I saw all these forms of justice being implemented and it was all done verbally, without any cases or appeals and without any paperwork for the purpose.

During the period that we were there it so happened that a soldier[25] from our ship, who must have been insane, got involved in an incident with a pretty woman who was selling eggs in the square. Either by chance or as a joke, he put his hand below her skirt, in the presence of her husband, who was standing nearby with an oar in his hand, because he was a fisherman. Upon seeing this, [the husband] got up and hit the soldier on the head with the oar and left [the latter] very badly injured. At this point we descended to get [the husband]. We were more than 20 armed men who went out to kill the fisherman and to take revenge on those who came across our way. We went running up to the square; [and] after crossing the bridge we were restrained by a Portuguese man, an older man who was sailing aboard our ship; his name was Estévão Correia.[26] He held a halberd[27] in his hand and he told us not to go any further because it would be ruinous to us, since more than 2,000 men with lances and krisses had gathered together

---

[24] About 3.5–5.5 metres.

[25] He is subsequently identified as Martim Rodrigues.

[26] Ms. here and subsequently: *Estevan Correa.*

[27] Ms. *alabarda.* An axe-shaped weapon. See also the glossary (*halberd*).

after hearing the uproar and were waiting for us. In the midst of this, they brought the injured [soldier][28] to us; we returned to the ship. The king learnt of this incident and to make us happy—this should be noted—he sent us the Muslim[29] who had injured Martim Rodrigues—that was the soldier's name—with his hands bound together, telling the ambassador that he could take revenge on him. The ambassador acted very prudently: he did not wish to lay a finger on the Muslim, because the soldier was the one who had been at fault; instead he ordered him to be released immediately and sent him away. The king greatly appreciated the ambassador's clemency and courtesy.

[28] Ms. lit. man.

[29] Ms. here and subsequently: *moro.*

CHAPTER

V

Other events that happened before we reached Melaka[1]

I must describe an incident that happened to me because of a clergyman [who was] the chaplain of our galliot. When I was in the city, the clergyman came to me saying that one of his slaves had escaped and that he had run away and hidden in the house of a prominent Muslim; he asked me to go with him to get him because he did not dare to go alone. Another slave had also escaped from me. Convinced that we would find the two slaves together I agreed and told the clergyman that I would go with him. At this point I went to the galliot to get a broad sword and a buckler[2] with some spears, and I called two more soldiers. One of them was Portuguese and the other was an Indian, but a Christian; and we all went to look for the slave. We arrived at the king's residence and we went inside, where a leading Muslim lived near the gate. We entered into his house and we did not see anyone else apart from his wife, [who was] sitting with a daughter in a cane enclosure in the courtyard,[3] and it had a pergola[4] fashioned like a corridor, because it was night and it was hot. The moment we saw her, and vice versa, she hid her face behind her mother. Upon seeing this action, Manuel Ferreira—that was the clergyman's name—believing that it was his

[1] Ms. fol. 15 verso–17 verso.

[2] Ms. *broquel.*

[3] Ms. *pateo.*

[4] Ms. *ramada.*

slave, told me: "There is Manuel"—which was the name of his slave. I immediately grabbed her by one leg and [began] dragging her down the enclosure. The mother began to scream and the chaplain ran away, fleeing from the scene, as did our other two companions.

When I saw that the person was a girl, by her hair, even though it was at night, I let her go and fled to escape from that fury. The neighbours immediately came running in response to the yelling as did all the royal guards. However, they did not come quickly enough and I still had time to go into a house near the wall. I hid amidst some reeds and walked on past the house, and the moat, all of which was dry since it was summer. I returned to the galliot, aboard it I found two new Muslim sailors who were keeping guard and all the others were asleep. I called out and they threw down the ladder—which was made of cane. I went aboard and lay down on my bed. An hour later the chaplain and our other two companions came back, tired and exhausted, blaming me for everything. I was listening to everything even though I was pretending to be asleep. He asked about me; Estévão Correia answered: "He's sleeping", and he began to say a thousand things about my audacity, and he would have continued ranting if Estévão Correia had not admonished him for making such a racket. We spent the night in this manner, and in the morning the Muslim who was the husband of that woman came [to our ship], accompanied by the overseer of the treasury of that kingdom[5] and other leading Muslims, complaining vehemently about the previous night's discourtesy. However, they did not know who had done the deed; they only said that it was a *mata kucing*,[6] which means a youth with blue eyes, and there were three of us aboard the ship who had blue eyes. In the end they could not ascertain who it was. The Muslims then told the ambassador that it would not have been good if we had been killed and we all agreed fervently. To mollify them, we gave them a lot of preserves and wine from Portugal, which the ambassador ordered to be brought out, and I sat down beside the Muslim who was the father of the girl, inviting him to eat and drink, and he did nothing the whole time except to look intently at my face, suspecting that I was the culprit—and he was not

---

[5] He is subsequently identified as the son of Raja Mudaliar. In Malay polities, the overseer of the treasury holds the title *bendahari*. See also the glossary (*bendahari, Raja Mudaliar*).

[6] Ms. *matecoche*, a corruption of the Malay term *mata kucing* meaning "cat's eyes".

wrong; everyone was most amused to see that I was urging the Muslim to eat, having been the guilty party.

With these and other incidents, many of which could have cost us dearly, the time drew near to return to Melaka. The king ordered that five *lancharas*,[7] which are small baxeles typical of that land, be readied to go with us to Melaka with one of his ambassadors, who was the son of Raja Mudaliar[8]—which was the name of the overseer of the treasury of that kingdom—and he was to sail aboard our galliot. When he later came to board the vessel, that was the moment when Martim Rodrigues decided to avenge the injury he had received in the square. He placed himself at the edge of ship with a sword[9] in his belt. Just when our ambassador was extending his hand to Raja Mudaliar's son to pull him aboard, Martim Rodrigues drew out his sword and stabbed the Muslim twice, once in the head and the second time in the stomach, as a result of which he died instantly. They took him back onto land in this state. Martim Rodrigues did not receive any punishment.

The king saw the injustice of this, and while he did not want to break the peace with the Portuguese, he sent another ambassador in the place of the one who had been killed, with his lancharas to accompany us, complaining to the captain of Melaka. We left that port after having spent six months there. We reached Melaka although the voyage back was not smooth sailing, upon where the ambassador presented his embassy with the complaints against Martim Rodrigues, owing to which the captain ordered him to be arrested. However, he ordered him to be released after six months without any punishment, which caused quite a scandal in Melaka.

---

[7] A type of commercial vessel. See also the glossary (*lancharas*).

[8] Ms. *Raya Modoliar.*

[9] Ms. here and subsequently: *catana.*

CHAPTER

VI

The voyage I made from Melaka to the kingdom of Johor in 1594 and what happened to me[1]

One month after having returned from the kingdom of Pahang, I went to Johor[2] with a consignment of textiles, part of which belonged to me and the other part to the captain [of Melaka], Francisco de Silva de Meneses, to exchange them for diamonds and bezoar stones[3] on behalf of both of us, which is what I actually did when I arrived there.

It so happened that while I was there three Castilian frigates,[4] commanded by Captain Gallinato,[5] came from the kingdom of Cambodia,[6] where they had scored a major[7] victory. To describe the situation succinctly: since wars were raging in Cambodia on account of some uprisings, the native king

[1] Ms. fol. 15 verso–21 recto

[2] De Coutre appears to have gone to Batu Sawar. See also the list of place names (*Batusavar, Jor Nuevo, Jor*).

[3] Ms. *piedras de bazares.* See the glossary (*bezoar*).

[4] Ms. *fragatas.* See the glossary (*frigate*).

[5] Ms. *Galinete.* This is probably Juan Xuárez (or Juárez) Gallinato who is also mentioned by Morga in his *Sucesos*, pp. 82–5, and also by Bartolomé Leonardo de Argensola in his *Conquista de las Islas Molucas* (Conquest of the Maluku Islands) in PI, XVI, p. 264, where he is described as a native of Tenerife (Canary Islands); see also Subrahmanyam, "Manila, Melaka, Mylapore": 235.

[6] Ms. here and subsequently: *Camboya.* Cambodia. See also the list of place names (*Camboya*).

[7] Ms. *grandiosa.*

[Sâtha I], taking advantage of his friendship with the Castilians, requested assistance from the governor of Manila, who sent him those frigates with very skilled[8] people. When Captain Gallinato arrived in Cambodia,[9] believing he would find the rightful king, he found a tyrant[10] in his stead who had killed [Sâtha] and was obeyed by one and all as the [new] king. This tyrant[11] wished to kill Gallinato in treachery. Having sized up the situation, the Castilians attacked. They killed a lot of people and one of the tyrant's sons.[12] After having burnt over 200 baxeles which he encountered in the river, [Captain Gallinato] came to the port of Johor, where he remained for many days. When he decided to return to Manila, he left behind a Castilian, who had asked for permission to go to Melaka. He had a good presence and he disembarked with 14 chests filled with sand, which he pretended were reals-of-eight[13]—considering that he was the greatest liar in the world—with two slaves, and he was very well dressed. He immediately sent a message to the king of Johor [Raja Ali Jalla bin Abdul Jalil] through one of the slaves, saying that he was Don Luis del Castillo, a relative of the King of Spain, and that he had come to those lands incognito so as not to be recognised. He asked his permission to meet with him, since he had important matters to discuss with him. Upon hearing this message, the king believing this to be true, immediately went to look for him, accompanied by all the people in the city, with great fanfare. When Don Luis del Castillo saw the king, he presented him three emerald rings. In recognition of this gift, the king removed the sword[14] that he was wearing on his belt and gave it to him. The scabbard and sword were embellished with gold and precious stones. Don Luis accepted it and then unfastened his [sword], which was worked in silver, and gave it to the king, who pretended that he greatly appreciated the gift. Once the greetings were done with, the king climbed on to a small elephant and Don Luis got on to another. He rode on the right side of the king and they were followed by four of the king's sons

---

[8] Ms. *gente muy luzida.*

[9] Concerning Gallinato's expedition to Cambodia, see Briggs, "Spanish Intervention", p. 154.

[10] Better known as the Laksamana, Oknha de Chu (Rama Chung Prey), a Malay and native of Johor. Briggs, "Spanish Intervention", pp. 146–50. See also the account in Chapter XI.

[11] Ms. lit. who.

[12] Concerning this episode, see Briggs, "Spanish Intervention", pp. 156–7.

[13] A silver coin minted in the Spanish Americas. See also the glossary (*real-of-eight*).

[14] Probably a Malay kris and not a sword. See also the glossary (*keris*).

walking on foot,[15] with all their gentlemen, and all the city's people with their weaponry walked ahead of the group. In this manner they reached the king's residence with all the pomp and pageantry that one can imagine in that land. Since on this occasion they celebrated the baxeles that were in the river with a salvo of artillery and musket-fire,[16] [everything was] festooned with flags, especially the city's[17] artillery. In the five days that Don Luis was hosted by the king he went to see the city's walls with all due ceremony, accompanied by the said king. As the walls were made of wood, he suggested a better layout and strategic way of positioning the artillery so as to defend themselves against the king of Aceh [Raja Buyong], who was waging a war with Johor at the time. Since the king [Raja Ali Jalla] thought that the suggestion was sensible he immediately ordered that it be implemented, and after this became very friendly towards Don Luis.

After five[18] days, Don Luis asked for permission to go to Melaka, promising to come back soon, because he had some important business to resolve with the captain of Melaka. Not only did the king give him permission to leave but he also provided him with a ship and 15 slaves to serve him—of which I bought two slaves. In the end, he went to Melaka accompanied by many ships; I also came back on one of them. As soon as we arrived, the captain[19] and the bishop of Melaka[20] visited Don Luis, greatly honouring him. During the course of the visit Don Luis stated how he had been sent by the King of Spain and the reason why he had travelled through those lands incognito. During the four days that he was there, many festivities and processions were staged, which Don Luis attended in person, walking behind the Holy Sacrament, between the captain and the bishop, with a candle in his hand, accompanied by all of Melaka's citizens and gentlemen.

---

[15] Raja Ali Jalla was known to have had at least six sons, two of whom were killed after a wedding at Patani, and the four who survived were Ala'uddin Ri'ayat Shah III, Raja Bongsu (later Abdullah Ma'ayat Shah), the Raja Siak and Raja Laut. The precise identity of the four sons mentioned by De Coutre cannot be confirmed. Concerning the sons of Raja Ali Jalla, see also GPFT, appendix 13, pp. 211–5.

[16] A type of firearm. See also the glossary (*musket*).

[17] This is a reference to Batu Sawar. De Coutre explained the transfer of the royal residence from Johor Lama to Batu Sawar below. See also the list of place names (*Batusavar*).

[18] Ms. lit. after these five.

[19] Here and subsequently a reference to the captain of Melaka, Francisco de Silva de Meneses.

[20] Here and subsequently a reference to Dom João de Ribeiro Gaio, the Bishop of Melaka. Concerning the career of this controversial cleric, see the brief exposé in Pinto, *The Portuguese and the Straits of Melaka,* pp. 198–200.

After four days he returned to Johor saying how important it was that he do so, and he took letters of recommendation from the captain and the bishop addressed to the king [of Johor, Raja Ali Jalla], declaring and attesting to the quality of Don Luis, [stating] that he was a great nobleman, and that he was going to see His Highness, [and] requesting that they treat him with all the due deference that his person merited. When he arrived in Johor, the king saw that he had returned accompanied by many Portuguese and the aforesaid letters. If the king had given him a grand reception on his first visit, this time he gave him an even more magnificent welcome and showered him with gifts. Three days later he again returned to Melaka, promising the king that he would send him a Portuguese armada to join his fleet to wage war on the king of Aceh. As soon as Don Luis arrived in Melaka he secretly negotiated a light *bantin*[21] to go to Aceh; in the meanwhile two ambassadors who had been sent by the king of Johor arrived, to enquire whether the fleet that Don Luis had promised the king of Johor was being prepared. When the captain came to know of this promise he decided to arrest him to determine on what basis he had made such a promise. Don Luis must have suspected that this would be the case and he fled that night to the kingdom of Aceh, where he also duped the king with other tall stories. The king of Aceh believed these tales to be true and gave him a carrack laden with pepper and a crew of native sailors. He set sail with the carrack and the permission of the king of Aceh and went to the kingdom of Pegu. On the way he mistreated the sailors, who conspired against him and killed him one night, along with all his slaves and those who were accompanying him, and they rebelled on the carrack. Only one of his slaves managed to escape, who brought us the news in Melaka.

This was the fate of Don Luis del Castillo, who claimed that he was a relative of the King of Spain, [but] who [in reality] had Muslim blood and had been flogged in New Spain[22] and banished from the Philippines.

Having become distracted with the story of this charlatan, I have not yet written some of the many things I could relate about the kingdom of Johor. One can note that the city they call Johor Lama[23] was destroyed by Dom Paulo de Lima [de Pereira],[24] as I have stated before, and this success

---

[21] A type of craft. See also the glossary (*bantin*).

[22] Mexico. See also the list of place names (*España Nueva*).

[23] Ms. *Jor Viejo*; Old Johor, Johor Lama. See also the list of place names (*Jor Viejo*).

[24] Concerning the epistolary report of Dom Paulo Lima de Pereira's attack on, and destruction of, Johor Lama in 1587, see SMS, pp. 212–28.

Map of Singapore Island and the Johor River region with its historic upstream towns.

will undoubtedly have been recorded in the chronicles pertaining to India. The king [of Johor] used to have his court in this city. [The settlement] that was built after the city of Johor Lama was ruined is called Batu Sawar.[25] Now we call this other city New Johor. It is a port frequented by many carracks from diverse nations. The native people dress in the same manner as the

[25] Ms. *Battallamar.* See the list of place names (*Batusavar*).

inhabitants of the kingdom of Pahang; they are ethnic[26] Malays and are very smartly dressed. As arms they use lances, harquebuses,[27] spears, swords, *rodelas*,[28] krisses that are typical of the Minangkabau[29] people—which is what they are called—and artillery. It has a beautiful river and a port with many large and small ships, and it is a land where merchants conduct vast volumes of trade and there are abundant provisions. The king is called Raja Ali [Jalla bin Abdul Jalil].[30] His grandfather was once the king of Melaka,[31] which was a city that spanned 12 leguas along the coast.[32] He titled himself "Emperor of the Malays".[33] After his death this title was lost and is now extinguished. The most important monarch in the South today[34] is [the king][35] of Aceh. After I returned to Melaka I went on other journeys, which I have not described since nothing noteworthy happened to me that would merit it being recorded.[36]

---

[26] Ms. lit. by blood.
[27] A type of hand-held firearm. See also the glossary (*harquebus*).
[28] A type of shield. See also the glossary (*rodela*).
[29] Ms. *manecabo*. People and polity in western-central Sumatra. See also the list of place names (*Manecabo*).
[30] Ms. *Raxaly*.
[31] In the time of the Melaka Sultanate before its fall to the Portuguese in 1511.
[32] Ms. *twelve leguas wide*. Probably 66–74 kilometres. See also the glossary (*legua*).
[33] Concerning this title, see also SMS, pp. 226, 323n155; GPFT, pp. 365–6n83.
[34] Ms. lit. now.
[35] Ms. lit. that of.
[36] Ms. lit. written down.

CHAPTER

VII

How I went to the kingdom of Siam, accompanying an embassy that the captain of Melaka sent in the name of Your Majesty. What happened to us before we reached the port of the said kingdom in the year 1595[1]

After I had returned to Melaka from Johor it so happened that the king of Siam captured the kingdom and the city of Cambodia,[2] where there was a Christian community, and many Portuguese, and Franciscan, Augustinian and Dominican monasteries and clergymen. All of them were captured and taken to Siam along with all the finest things in that kingdom. Amongst the Dominican friars, there was one who was called Friar Jorge de Mota, an astute but appalling man, who managed to become friends with a personal servant of the king[3] who was called Phra Choduk.[4] By means of the gifts he gave him, he convinced the king to send him to Melaka with letters for the captain so as to negotiate a peace agreement with the Portuguese. Friar Jorge arrived with the letters in Melaka, he handed them over to Francisco de Silva de Meneses and he informed him about the state

[1] Ms. fol. 321 verso–24 verso.

[2] This is a reference to Lovek which was attacked by King Naresuan (Phra Naret) of Siam in 1593.

[3] Ms. *moço privado del Rey*.

[4] Ms. *Prachidech*. AA erroneously reads the name here and subsequently as a corruption of Phra Naret (King Naresuan of Siam). Most likely Phra Choduk or possibly also Okya Phrasadet. See also the glossary (*Prachidec*).

of the Portuguese in Siam. Then, in order to get him to do his bidding, he sought to tempt him by appealing to his greed and mentioned that in Siam textiles were worth a lot of money, and that there were many rubies, sapphires and many other precious stones and riches that the king had captured in Cambodia and in the wars with Pegu,[5] in such large quantities that they were sold in *chupos*[6]—which are weights that are similar to half a *celamin*[7] used in Siam to measure rice, vegetables and other provisions. To corroborate his words he showed him some ruby rings, which, according to him, he had bought very cheaply and were worth a lot of money, all of which I knew was a lie.

As soon as Captain Francisco de Silva [de Meneses] heard this information he decided to send Friar [Jorge] and an ambassador [Manuel Pereira de Abreu] to King [Naresuan] of Siam to agree on a peace settlement and to free the Christians who were being held captive in that kingdom, and also ordered that he purchase those precious stones that the friar had said were so cheap and to make the most of that occasion.

Very few people wished to go to Siam, since the king has a reputation of a tyrant, fickle and deceitful—and none of those who went there were not motivated by greed. The captain chose one of his retainers to go there as an ambassador, along with a factor [Simão Peres] and nine Portuguese to accompany the embassy. At this stage he called me and asked me to accompany that embassy, and at the same time to buy some rubies and sapphires there on his behalf. I refused and excused myself as much as I could; [however] it proved impossible not to go. In the end the captain made an agreement with me in order to make me more comfortable with the idea, in the presence of Friar Jorge. We set sail from the port in a junk that belonged to the said captain—a junk is a baxel that are used by the natives of the South,[8] and some of them are very large, [they can even be] a thousand *toneladas*[9] or more; the sails are made of palm leaves—on 8 May 1595. Apart from the sailors and officials who were Chinese, the people

---

[5] The Taungoo Dynasty Kingdom. See also the list of place names (*Taungoo Dynasty Kingdom, Pegu*).

[6] See the glossary (*chupo*).

[7] Ms. *selemin*. See the glossary (*celamine*).

[8] Ms. *los naturales del sur*. See the list of place names (*Sur*).

[9] A unit to measure the cargo capacity of a ship. About 793–920 metric tons or more. See also the glossary (*tonelada*).

who sailed aboard the junk included the ambassador, the friar, myself and ten Portuguese; and everything on board was done in accordance to how the friar wanted things done. We reached the Strait of Singapore,[10] and they threw the *batel*[11] into the water. The friar tried to coerce me, forcefully, to go in this *batel* with three companions to fetch fresh water on an island that was called *Ysla de Arena.*[12] We approached it, I got the water. By the time we returned night had fallen; I could not see the junk, they did not light either a lamp nor did they fire any shots, even though I made many signals, until the current carried me out of the New Strait [of Singapore][13] and [there] they were anchored. At the entrance to[14] this strait I came across some *orang laut*[15] vessels, who attacked us in order to capture us, however, we repelled them by means of our barrel guns[16] and one of my companions was injured. We rowed the entire night until we saw the junk at dawn where we managed to reach it feeling annoyed and irritated.

We could not pass through the strait [of Singapore] with the junk because the sea was rising, which tends to happen with the constellation of the moon, and the currents usually last at least two or three days. At this point, and at night, the friar insisted we pass through [the waters]. It would have been a difficult task by day and was even more so at night. He insisted persistently until we weighed anchor, and the junk slammed against a rock, however, the currents only damaged the rudder, which was shattered into 2,000 splinters. It struck the junk right in the middle.[17] At this point we repaired it with some *espadelas*[18] with which we managed to control the junk. After this, after we had passed the islands of Pulau Tioman,[19] we threw [the corpse of] a comrade of mine into the sea, who had died of diarrhoea. He was a

[10] Ms. *estrecho de cincapuro.* Reference to probably the area around the northwestern tip of present-day Sentosa off Fort Siloso, named *Surgídera* in memorial III. See also the list of place names (*Surgídera*).

[11] A small craft. See also the glossary (*batel*).

[12] Ms. *Isla … de Arena.* Present-day Sentosa. See also the list of place names (*Ysla de Arenas*).

[13] Along the southwestern coast of present-day Sentosa. See also the list of place names (*Estrecho Nuevo*).

[14] Ms. lit. mouth of. This is presumably a reference to the area around present-day Fort Siloso at the northwestern tip of present-day Sentosa.

[15] Ms. *saletes.* See the glossary (*saletes*).

[16] Ms. here and subsequently: *escupetas.* See the glossary (*escupeta*).

[17] Ms. *hiziera lo proprio.*

[18] An oar that can also be used as a rudder. See also the glossary (*espadala*).

[19] Ms. *Pula timan.* See the list of place names (*Pulatimom*).

Frenchman who had been born in Avignon and his name was Don Claudio de Godon. We passed by many other islands, which I am not naming so as not to be overly verbose. We reached some uninhabited islands,[20] which were called Pulau *Sanquiuxu*[21] and Pulau Redang.[22] We went ashore to take on fresh water; after having obtained some water, a few people began bathing and washing their clothes on the shore.

When there were no more men left on land beside myself and two other companions, carrying harquebuses, some pirates[23] disembarked on the other side of the island, who at the time were known in the South as the Bajau of Borneo.[24] They made our men go into the sea until we were either waist or neck deep in the water. My companions and I defended [all of] us by firing musket shots until everyone was back aboard the ship. Spears and poisoned darts rained down on us, which the pirates aimed at us with blowpipes, and they killed one of our men and injured two others. The pirates also suffered many casualties, both dead and wounded. With this we turned away from the land and we reached the junk with the water that had been obtained at such a great cost. We sailed along the coast until we arrived at the city of Patani;[25] we anchored there to replenish our supplies of provisions. We set out once again and sailed along the coast, always within sight of land, up to the city of Ligor.[26] The friar and I disembarked and we went to the city to learn news about Siam and to bring refreshments for our companions. Going with the *batel* [carried] aboard a junk that was moored there, which had recently come from Siam, the friar asked for news from there. The owner of the junk told us that Phra Choduk[27]—which was the name of the servant

[20] This is most probably a reference to the group of nine islands, the largest of which is Pulau Redang (Great Redang), which is located off the coast of the present-day Malaysian state of Terengganu. Peter Floris claims there are between 18 and 20 islands of the Redang group. See W.H. Moreland, ed., *Peter Floris, his voyage to the East Indies in the "Globe" 1611–1615* (London: Hakluyt Society, 1934) p. 99, and also the list of place names (*Pula Reidan*).

[21] Ms. *Pula San quixu*. AA: *Pulau Lantinga*. Perhentian Island West. See the list of place names (*Pula Sanquixu*).

[22] Ms. *Pula Reidan*.

[23] Ms. here and subsequently: *ladrones*; lit. thieves.

[24] Ms. *bayus borneos*. See the glossary (*Bayus*).

[25] Port in present-day southern Thailand. See also the list of place names (*Patane*).

[26] Ms. *Lugor*. See the list of place names (*Lugor*).

[27] Ms. *Prachedec*. See the glossary (*Prachidec*).

of the king[28] [and] the friar's friend—was dead, and that the Portuguese who had been taken prisoner had already been released and were walking freely around the city with weapons, and that most of them were killing each other without any punishment from the king, who was indifferent to this. He also said that some Japanese Christians had killed a Dominican friar. The Dominican friars had taken refuge in the church of the Capuchin fathers, but it was to no avail, because some Portuguese killed them at the foot of the altar. Upon being asked who the Portuguese were and what were their names, he said to us: "One of them is called 'somebody De Mota', and the other one is Castilian and he is called Sebastián Cordero."

We went to the city [of Ligor] with this and other news. After having seen everything that there was to see in the city, including very large mosques[29] and temples with gilded bronze idols, we procured some refreshments, fruits and other treats.[30] We returned to the junk the following day when we saw that it was sailing away, fleeing from three junks of pirates who are called *Tutos*.[31] As soon as our men saw us, they made another turn and returned to get us, and the thieves put a brigantine[32] in the water to catch us. In the end we defended ourselves with barrel gun shots and we killed most of the people who were aboard that brigantine. We continued to fight, until we were a barrel gun's[33] shot away from our junk. Then they left us alone; it was already night. We went aboard our junk with the two sailors from our crew who had been wounded. No sooner had we done so when the weather began to turn cool, due to which we lost sight of the enemy, and we reached the mouth of the river of Siam [Chao Phraya River]. We anchored [there] tired and irritated; Friar [Jorge] because of the news that he had heard; and we because of such an arduous journey, which the friar had done so much to facilitate.

---

28 Ms. *moro*. Most probably a corruption of the earlier word *moço*. The corrected expression has been translated as before.

29 Ms. *alcoranes*. In Portuguese the *alcorão* is a minaret belonging to a mosque.

30 Ms. *regalos*.

31 Ms. *tutos*. The exact identity of these maritime raiders remains uncertain. See also the glossary (*Tutos*).

32 A type of sailing craft. See also the glossary (*brigantine*).

33 Ms. *escupeta*.

CHAPTER

VIII

In which the story continues until the point when the embassy arrived; the reception the embassy received[1]

Then, once we were anchored off the coast of Siam, after the friar had received this news, he no longer wished to enter the [Chao Phraya River] and neither did the ambassador; for both of them were of the same opinion, which was[2] to go to Cochinchina.[3] I and the other companions got together as one group and spoke with a unanimous voice, telling the friar and the ambassador that, after having come to Siam with that embassy, we had to enter the river and not to sail to any other land. Finally we entered the river. We then arrived at the first *tabanque*[4]—a city[5] on the river where all vessels that entered the river had to register—which was governed by a mandarin,[6] who, when we dropped anchor, came to the junk to register us and our weapons, so as to inform the king, since this was the custom in that land. The following day I went with the friar—who always took me with him because the others did not wish to be on the forefront if any incidents were to occur—to the governor to request permission for

[1] Ms. fol. 25 recto–27 verso.

[2] Ms. lit. but.

[3] Ms. *Cochin China*. See the list of place names (*Cochinchina*).

[4] Toll station; toll house. This is most probably at Bang Chao Phraya located at the Chao Phraya River estuary. See also the glossary (*tabanque*).

[5] Ms. *ciudad*. Probably present-day Samut Prakan.

[6] An advisor or functionary. See also the glossary (*mandarin*).

the two of us to go to the city of Ayutthaya,[7] the court of the king of Siam, which was situated 40 leguas[8] upriver from there, to describe to the king how our junk and ambassador had come to be there. At this point the governor gave us a *cap*[9]—this is how they call passports—with which we set out upriver in a small, light sloop.[10] There was a lot of security on the river; and warships that did not allow any vessel to pass through, no matter how small, without registering first. We reached the city of Ayutthaya after seven days to the great joy of the Portuguese who were there. They confirmed the news that we had heard in the city of Ligor. We did not find the king, who had gone to hunt elephants. We then went to speak to the governor of Ayutthaya—he was called Okya Wang.[11] After we had briefed him of how our junk and ambassador were at the first *tabanque*, he told us that the king had gone to hunt elephants and that he would return soon. The friar replied that we would like to go to where the king was. He gave us permission, with which we set out aboard a light *perahu*.[12] This was a very long vessel made from a single trunk of wood with 30 oars on each side, which they call *pangaios*.[13] It was beautifully covered with a canopy and we sailed off accompanied by 30 Portuguese who were being held captive there. We sailed upriver for more than four days until we came across two Franciscan friars—one of whom was Castilian, he was called Friar Pedro Ortiz; the other friar [was called] Gregorio da Cruz, he was a Portuguese who had been the vicar of Cambodia—and a Castilian renegade commonly known as Miguel de Pina. They told us that the king had returned to the city. Upon hearing this news we returned with them.

The king had heard the news that we had arrived with an ambassador; he immediately summoned Friar [Jorge] and myself. Then, before we entered the palace, Okya Wang,[14] one of his private staff, gave each of us some flowers made of gold and silver, mixed with other natural

[7] Ms. here and subsequently: *Odia*. A note in the left hand margin reads: "Odia, la corte de Sian" (Ayutthaya, the court of Siam).

[8] Probably about 80 kilometres. See also the glossary (*legua*).

[9] Ms. *thara*. See the glossary (*cop*).

[10] Ms. *chalupilla*.

[11] Ms. *hoya avan*. See the glossary (*Oya Avan*).

[12] Ms. *paro*. See the glossary (*perahu*).

[13] Ms. *pangayos*. A type of longboat or galley. See also the glossary (*pangaio*).

[14] Ms. *hojavangarao*. See the glossary (*Oya, Oya Vangarao*).

flowers—which in India are called *mogra*;[15] they are a type of rose which are as big as a real-of-four [coin]; they smell just like jasmine—for us to present to the king, since it is customary that he does not give an audience unless he is presented with something. When we were about to enter, the friar did not want me to go in with him under any circumstances, even though the king had expressly ordered four or five times that I was to enter, until the friar said that he had some highly confidential matters that he had to discuss with the king and it would not be convenient if I entered. Upon hearing this reply the king ordered that the friar enter alone, with two interpreters, who were brothers. One was called António Hans,[16] the other Miguel Hans, the sons of a Flemish man who had married in the city of Macao, and the two brothers [had settled] in the [main] city of Cambodia.[17] The king of Cambodia had adopted them and sworn them in as princes considering the many services that their father had rendered to him. When the king of Siam[18] captured that kingdom he took them captive but he treated them well, very differently from the other captives. After the friar had concluded his courtesies to the king and presented him with the flowers, the king said to him: "So, Friar Jorge, what do you bring me?" He answered: "Sire, I have brought an ambassador who is a relative of the king of Portugal [Philip I], from whence he has come to serve Your Highness in the wars with Pegu, or wherever you deem fit. He is a very experienced[19] man who is well versed in matters of war. He was the man who conquered the entire island of Ceylon,[20] and similarly I have also brought ten Portuguese whom the king of Portugal has likewise sent to Your Highness to serve you."

The king was extremely happy and he said: "I would not have rejoiced more, Friar Jorge, if you had brought me a white elephant,[21] not as much as I rejoice with this ambassador and these Portuguese, and from this day forth there shall be no poor Portuguese in my kingdoms. Even though I

---

[15] Ms. *Moguris.* See the glossary (*mogra*).

[16] Ms. here and subsequently: *Ans.* Believed by AA to be an Hispanicised form of the Flemish surname "Hans".

[17] Ms. *ciudad de Camboja* (the city of Cambodia); most probably Lovek. See also the list of place names (*Ciudad de Camboja*).

[18] King Naresuan's campaign against Cambodia in 1593.

[19] Ms. *atendido.*

[20] Ms. *Zeilan.*

[21] A Buddhist symbol of kingship and sovereignty. See also the glossary (*white elephant*).

Printed etching of King Philip II/I of Spain and Portugal on horseback taken from Emanuel van Meteren's *Commentariën ofte Memoriën* (Commentaries or Memoirs), 1652. (Private collection, Peter Borschberg).

do not habitually receive any ambassador, but since the king of Portugal is such a great monarch, almost as great as I, I wish to receive him with many honours." Up to this point these were the words of the king. He ordered that the friar and the Phrakhlang,[22] his overseer of the treasury, and Oya Simintoy,[23] his general responsible for the rivers, gather together and agree upon the way that the embassy was to be received, and that it was to be done as per the friar's wishes. At this point he ordered that the junk be sailed to the city, and he bid farewell to the friar, granting[24] him as a royal favour 80 *katis* of silver[25] in coins—each *kati* weighs four marks[26]—and many fabrics woven in gold and silk, laid out on 18 trays filled to the brim that required 18 men to carry them, which was as much as they could carry.

The ambassador arrived a few days later, who, since the friar had played his cards in that fashion, concocted a lie between the two of them that could have cost all of us our lives. That was why the friar had not wanted me to enter the hall when we went to speak with the king, so that nobody would know anything about it.

---

22 Ms. *parabaci.* It is assumed that the "overseer of the treasury" qualifies the title *parabaci* in the same way *Oya Simintoy* is qualified by the explanation "the general responsible for the rivers." The overseer of the treasury in Siam was the Phrakhlang and the chief of the army and navy was the Okya Chakri. See also the glossary (*Parabaci*).

23 Ms. *Oyasimintoy*. See the glossary (*Oyasimintoy*).

24 Ms. adds in the right-hand margin: "sio catis de plata cada cati es 4 Marco, 2 libras." That is: "each kati of silver each kati is 4 marco[s], 2 pounds." See also the glossary (*kati*).

25 About 48 kilograms of coin-grade silver.

26 Ms. *marcos.* A weight to measure precious metals. See also the glossary (*mark*).

CHAPTER

IX

The arrival of the embassy and the reception the embassy received, a continuation of the previous chapter[1]

When the time came for the embassy to disembark, Friar Jorge said to the mandarins—who were the leading men of that kingdom —that he had brought a letter from the embassy in Portuguese which was to be translated into Siamese[2] and read before the king when he received the embassy; and the letter in Malay[3] which had been sent in a golden document tube could be presented in the state in which it had been sent since it was closed and sealed. The mandarins conveyed this to king, who approved and he ordered that the document be translated as the friar had ordered.

To this end, the said mandarins of the committee, the ambassador, the friar and all the Portuguese who had come aboard the junk gathered together in an enclosure that was similar to a hall,[4] which would have been more than 70 or 80 *varas*[5] long, and slightly less in width, inside the king's palace, where all the mandarins and leading figures of the kingdom were seated. After we had taken our seats in due order, they began to present a false embassy, which the friar had concocted and which none of us understood.

[1] Ms. fol. 27 verso–33 recto.

[2] Ms. here and subsequently: [*lengua*] *Siama.*

[3] Ms. here and subsequently: *lengua Malaya.*

[4] Ms. *un theatro hecho a modo de un corridor.*

[5] Ms. *baras.* About 58 to 88 metres. See also the glossary (*vara*).

This was how the events unfolded. The friar knew how to speak Malay and he understood some Siamese. He took with him the aforementioned renegade Miguel de Pina, who could also speak the two languages. In this manner the friar read out a document that he had brought written in his own hand to Miguel de Pina in Malay, and Miguel de Pina relayed it to the mandarins in Siamese, and this was how, during this presentation of the embassy, the friar made us slaves of the king. The mandarins were delighted and asked us what we were called and wrote down our names, calling us *payluan*,[6] which means slaves of the king. The ambassador did not utter a word, he allowed the friar to do everything. The contents of the embassy's presentation were sheer nonsense and stated the following: "The King of Portugal and Spain, Flanders, [the] Algarve, [the] sea of Africa, Lord of Guinea and the conquests, King of the East Indies, [and] the West Indies, etc. I send many greetings to the very powerful king of Siam and Cambodia, conqueror of the neighbouring kingdoms. I am sending to Your Highness [my] ambassador Manuel Pereira de Abreu"—that was his name—"who is a relative of mine, as a symbol of love and friendship, along with ten other Portuguese to serve Your Highness in the wars with Pegu, [along with] an armour set,[7] a barrel gun[8] and a range of [other] armaments,[9] some glass items,[10] and garlands to adorn the heads of your sons, etc."

It went on to state many other lies, only the part about the arms was true. However, the captain of Melaka had sent that embassy in the name of Your Majesty, as the captains of Melaka have been empowered to do. The letter sent by the captain of Melaka was contained in a golden document tube sealed with his seal, and in it, after first stating the titles of the king, our Lord, and then those of the king of Siam, he had requested the king of Siam to release the [Portuguese] captives he was holding in his lands. [The captain affirmed] that Melaka was a friend of Siam and that Siam was a friend of Melaka, and that he was sending him that present in the name of the king, his Lord.

---

[6] Ms. *payluan.* See the glossary (*payluan*).

[7] Ms. *cuerpo de armas.* AO: *Partij wapens.* Possibly a "translation" of the Portuguese *corpo de armas*, a "complete set of armour." Complete sets of armour often featured as formal gifts in this period, as specifically the examples listed in LM, I, p. 351 (20 February 1610) and LM, II p. 161 (13 February 1612). In addition, the Spanish term may also indicate some thing to do with heraldry. AA reads *perro* (dog) throughout.

[8] Ms. *escupeta.*

[9] Ms. *alano de armas.*

[10] Ms. *unos bidrios.*

Once the false embassy had been presented there was no shortage of people who understood what had happened since they were familiar with the language and they went to inform the Capuchin fathers, who wrote a letter to Friar Jorge de Mota telling him that he would soon find himself in trouble and that the truth would soon prevail.

However, none of us dared to utter a word since it would have endangered the lives of all us Christians who were there, and Friar Jorge did not pay the slightest heed [to the Capuchin letter], instead he set about devising and scheming other, even greater imbroglios. Seeing all this, and since the king was so enraptured with the tales he had been told by Friar Jorge, the priest, Friar Pedro Ortiz Castellano, went to ask for his permission to go to Manila, telling King [Naresuan] that he should write a letter to the governor of Manila [Luis Pérez Dasmariñas] since it would be very useful for when His Highness needed something from Manila; and that the governor would be very pleased to serve him, since those lands also belonged to the king of Portugal, and the governor was his vassal. Thus far the king [of Siam] did not know that the Portuguese and the Castilians were both vassals of a [single] monarch.[11] [Naresuan] asked [Castellano] many questions about this and approved of what the Capuchin told him in this regard, since he greatly esteemed this person on account of his virtues and good example. Not only did [Naresuan] give [Castellano] permission to go but also gave him a junk for himself and letters and a piece of jewellery set with rubies for the governor, and told him to take 40 Portuguese with him, and ordered that each [of these] Portuguese was to be given six katis of silver.[12] After the reception that was held for our embassy, these people achieved their business in three days and left, and [Naresuan] sent Miguel Hans, who was being held captive by the said king, as his ambassador.

Having heard the presentation of the embassy, the king ordered that a reception was to be extended to it. On the day of the reception the king sent the ambassador one of his horses, duly caparisoned, and with all the metal tack adorned with beaten gold, with some tassels made from the tails of bush cattle, which are greatly valued there—they are called *combales*—and

[11] This was due to the Union of the Two Crowns of Spain and Portugal between 1580 and 1640 when the king of Spain also ruled as the king of Portugal.
[12] About 3.6–3.75 kilograms. See also the glossary (*kati*).

four very large parasols—the first was made of beaten gold, but was very thin as one might imagine; the second was gilded and painted in various colours; the third was entirely painted in colours; the fourth was made of straw[13] and only the king uses them as royal insignia—for him [the ambassador] to make his entrance. To the friar he sent a palanquin where the seat was covered with a gilded canopy on which he was to make his entrance, and 40 men who were to carry it on their shoulders and another four *sombreros*[14]—parasols—similar to the ones that he had sent to the ambassador. In the same way he sent another palanquin, which was more richly decorated and gilded, and another four parasols for the armour set,[15] and many of his Siamese retainers to carry it on their shoulders, who were perfectly disciplined from their hair to their polished heels and covered in red velvet.

With all this pomp he sent all his guards, trumpeters and drummers, and two richly decorated elephants caparisoned with golden fabrics, on which came the two brothers Miguel Hans[16] and António Hans. Each of them was wearing a golden diadem[17] on their head. After this entire retinue reached the ambassador's house,[18] which was one and a half leguas[19] away from the palace, we arranged ourselves in order to make our entrance.

First of all 1,000 men—musketeers—proceeded in front, walking very silently in two rows, without speaking or making any kind of noise, and none of them carried a lit cord. They were followed by another 1,000 men—archers—walking in two similar rows, and their arrows did not have tips. Then came 1,000 lancers, the tips of whose lances were made of forked iron pieces. Another 1,000 men walked behind them; those on the right side had swords decorated with gold, including the scabbards and everything else; those on the left had swords decorated with silver, and all of them were virtually naked, with only a loincloth to cover their private parts, which they wrapped between their thighs, and their entire bodies were painted

---

13 Ms. *paja*. Probably *atap* rather than straw. See also the glossary (*atap*).

14 See also the image with annotation on p. 8 and the glossary (*sombrero*).

15 Ms. *cuerpo de armas*. See p. 106n7.

16 Ms. here and subsequently: *Ans*. Appears to be a corrupted or Hispanicised spelling.

17 Ms. here and subsequently: *fuente*.

18 Ms. *cassa*.

19 Probably about three kilometres.

with many types of vermin and letters.[20] In the middle of these two rows went the two brothers, each of them on an elephant wearing their golden diadems on their heads; the real embassy document was taken in one of the rows and the false document in the other, placed in the golden document tube; and around these two elephants walked 300 trumpeters, some of the trumpets were made of brass, others of gilded silver, and a similar number of drummers and percussionists. Then followed the ten Portuguese, this number included myself and I was carrying the barrel gun and one of my companions handled the mastiff;[21] each of our other [Portuguese] companions led a tray full of garlands, glass items and vials of perfumed water.[22] After us came the armour set assembled on a richly adorned seat on the palanquin, which was carried on the shoulders of the king's Siamese retainers,[23] along with four royal parasols. Behind the armour set[24] came the friar, Jorge de Mota, on another palanquin, which 40 men carried on their shoulders, along with four parasols; and on his left side came the ambassador [Pereira de Abreu] riding the horse, with his parasols. After the friar and the ambassador came all the Christians and Portuguese who were being held captive.

We walked along in this manner in great silence. Nobody uttered a word, we could only hear the sound of the trumpets and drums, which were producing an infernal din. Not a soul could be seen in all the streets in the city; everyone had locked themselves in their houses. Not even the dogs barked, because they would have killed both the dog and its owner. Nor was there anyone to be seen in the streets through which we passed; the doors and windows of all the houses had been closed, and mats dyed red had been hung along the walls. We arrived at the palace; the king ordered only those who had come with the embassy from Melaka to enter. The ambassador and the friar alighted; all of us took off our shoes. We entered making our bows with great submissiveness and with both our heads and bodies bent very low. In this manner we passed through three large courtyards, each of which would have been as long as a shot of a barrel gun, and just slightly less in width, in which sat all the king's guards who had accompanied us, squatting on their haunches like monkeys; and there

---

[20] Ms. *cuerpo pintado con muchas savandijas y letras.* Probably a reference to tattoos.

[21] Ms. *mastin.*

[22] Ms. *frascos de aguas de flor.*

[23] Ms. *Siamos del Rey.*

[24] Ms. *cuerpo de armas.* See p. 106n7.

were corridors between them, through which we walked. We then arrived, keeping our heads bowed down very low, with both hands together on our shoulders and almost doubled over—it would undoubtedly have been a laughable sight to see us in that posture—at the enclosure where the king was seated with regal majesty at the highest level, on a royal throne made of solid gold—as we learnt later—which was like a bed with a canopy. Instead of curtains it was enclosed with glazed windows, and he was inside, from where he spoke to us through a window that was also rendered in glass. We could barely see him. His brother was seated at the foot of the throne, the White Prince[25]—as they called him—along with a bonzo,[26] who was the head of his priests, the brother of the king of Pegu.[27]

The enclosure[28] would have been about 200 paces long and as many paces wide and around it there were many poles, like columns with little shelters nailed to them, and a mandarin[29] was seated at the base of each pole. The king ordered us to climb up and to sit down at the point or entrance to the theatre. After we had made our bows, the ambassador sat down as did the friar with the two brothers with their two golden diadems who brought the [real] embassy document and the fake transcript, [and] who also served on this occasion as interpreters; and they placed the armour set[30] and the other presents next to the ambassador, and all the ten Portuguese who had come from Melaka sat behind them. There were five rooms[31] of 30 paces each between where we were seated and the king and there was a man at each room. They read the transcript out aloud very slowly, one reading it to the other, who relayed it to the next man, until it reached the king. When the [verbal communication of the] document had reached him he sent the friar and the ambassador a golden box each, which were filled with betel together with his instruments[32] to

---

[25] Ms. *el Rey blanco*; lit. the "White King". The Uparaja (after 1605 King) Ekathotsarot of Siam. Ekathotsaroth was the brother of Naresuan, the "Black King". See also Moreland, *Peter Floris*, pp. xxvii; 52–3, note 4; 55, note 4.

[26] Ms. *bonze*. See the glossary (*bonzo*).

[27] King Nanda Bayin of the Taungoo Dynasty Kingdom. See also the glossary (*Taungoo Dynasty Kingdom, Pegu*).

[28] Ms. *teatro*. This term could also be referring to a stage or a podium.

[29] See the glossary (*mandarin*).

[30] Ms. *cuerpo*; See p. 106n7.

[31] Ms. here and subsequently: *estancias*.

[32] Ms. *petrechos*.

eat[33] with. This is a plant with a very strong fragrance; it soothes the stomach; the natives throughout the Orient eat it and present it during visits as a sign of great honour and courtesy. They are leaves that look like ivy, however, they are larger and more tender; they are eaten with what is called *areca.*[34] It looks a lot like nutmeg, but does not have the same fragrance, [having] a hint of lime. The nobles and leading figures eat it with cardamom,[35] clove and camphor,[36] and with other aromatic substances. Each box was worth 2,000 *escudos.*[37] The ten of us received gilded boxes[38] full of betel;[39] each box was worth 50 escudos;[40] here, as in all of the Orient, this was a very great honour indeed. Then [Naresuan] asked the ambassador with how many men he had conquered the island of Ceylon.[41] He answered that he had done so with 500 Portuguese and 3,000 Indians. With this answer [Naresuan] did not speak for a while—pondering whether it was an incredible lie.

He sent his sword, which was like a falchion,[42] and a kris to the ambassador, which was in a typical Muslim style, with adornments and a sheath made all in gold, embellished with rubies, and the kris was similarly decorated; at the time it would have been worth 8,000 *ducats.*[43] He also ordered, moreover, that he be given a grey Arabian horse with all its tack in silver—which the previous captain of Melaka [Diogo Lobo] had sent to him; along with 60 men to serve him; and [he sent] 40 [men] to the friar for his palanquin, and 200 *marks* of silver;[44] and throughout the entire proceedings nobody spoke except for the friar. With these royal gifts the king bid us farewell.

---

[33] Ms. *corer* (to run). This is probably a transcription error and should read *comer* (to eat).

[34] Nut of the areca palm. See also the glossary (*areca, betel*).

[35] A spice. See also the glossary (*cardamom*).

[36] Tropical or edible camphor. See also the glossary (*camphor*).

[37] Either 7,140 grams of mint-grade gold (Portuguese escudo) or 108.2 kilograms of coin-grade silver (Spanish escudo). See also the glossary (*escudo*).

[38] Ms. here and subsequently: *diadem.*

[39] See the glossary (*betel*).

[40] About 179 grams of gold or 2.7 kilograms of coin-grade silver.

[41] Ms. *Zeilan.*

[42] Ms. *terciado.* See the glossary (*terciado*).

[43] About 28 kilograms of mint-grade gold. See the glossary (*ducat*).

[44] About 30 kilograms of coin-grade silver. See the glossary (*mark*).

C H A P T E R

X

The entourage that accompanied the king when he ventured out and how he wished to send an ambassador to the King, Our Lord, and how the embassy's hoax was discovered, a continuation of the previous chapter[1,2]

When the king ventured out he did so with great pomp and was accompanied by a grand entourage as described herein. He was preceded by the entire royal guard, walking in two rows. He went out [virtually] naked, with just a loincloth that hid his private parts,[3] without any other clothes. On his head he wore a mitre[4] similar to those worn by bishops, slightly closed at the top, made of solid gold with a lot of precious stones and other jewels; he sat on an elephant holding two golden hooks in his hands, with which he controlled the animal. In front walked the friar and the ambassador, [and] us on foot with our hands together on our left shoulder, and behind him followed his brother on another elephant with his hands together on his head and bent very low like someone who is receiving a blessing. He was surrounded by all the trumpeters, horns and drummers. We walked in this fashion at a fast pace so as not to be gored by the tusks of his elephant. He had four very large

[1] Ms. fol. 33 recto–37 verso.

[2] Ms. lit. same material.

[3] Ms. *las partes secretas.*

[4] Ms. *mitra.*

parasols, [on] which were the royal insignia. Everything was very silent and we did not see anybody in the streets; in this manner we went to his gardens. He made us pass through streams fully dressed and wearing our shoes, where the water sometimes came up to our chest, which amused him thoroughly, and was very difficult for us. He used to venture out very often, and the people knew in advance when he was expected to be out and through which streets he would pass; thus, no living soul or even a dog would be seen in the streets, nor would one even hear a dog bark, because it would immediately have been killed along with its owner, with the cruellest tyranny imaginable.

The king constantly bestowed royal favours[5] upon Ambassador [Pereira de Abreu] and Friar [Jorge], giving them many things. The friar went about the city in the palanquin[6] that the king had given him, in much the same manner as the leading *talapois*[7] of that kingdom—the talapois are the priests who administer the rites of those heathen people—which had caused quite a scandal since the friar is a Dominican clergyman. During those days the ambassador allowed the soldiers unlimited access to food supplies and gave many of them clothes. Despite all this they continued to complain saying that we had come to free captives and not to become slaves. Greater deceptions came to light with each passing day. Since the king believed that the embassy was an authentic mission he intended to send to Portugal the friar and two important ambassadors of his kingdom, the sons of a woman who was called Barcaloa.[8] She had been his consort,[9] or perhaps it would be better to describe her as a female friend. She made great pilgrimages to their idols and demons[10] situated outside the city and spent lavishly on distributing food to the talapois, and presented [them] with many jewels and other valuable items as gifts. Amongst other things she gifted a small golden boat, which, at the time, would have been worth more than 12,000 escudos,[11] all of this so that the priests would beseech

---

[5] Ms. *mecedes.*

[6] Ms. *la anda.*

[7] Ms. here and subsequently: *talapois.* Buddhist monks. See also the glossary (*talapoin*).

[8] This name could represent a corruption of Barcalong (Phraklang). See also the glossary (*Barcaloa*).

[9] Ms. *Dama suya.*

[10] Ms. *diablos.*

[11] It is uncertain whether De Coutre has the Portuguese or the Spanish escudo in mind, if the former, it is equivalent to about 42.5 kilograms of mint-grade gold; if the latter it is about 649.7 kilograms of coin-grade silver.

the gods[12] to prevent that journey by her sons because she could not go against the king's wishes.

For the purpose of the journey, the king ordered that the friar was to be given a very large junk that could carry 30,000 quintals;[13] it was much larger than the carracks that sail from Lisbon to India. Aboard this [ship] the ambassadors were to sail [to Portugal]. In addition he also gave him 10,000 quintals[14] of sappanwood[15]—which is a coloured timber. It is used to make dye; [and] it is highly prized in India; it is similar to brazilwood—and [he gave] 400 quintals[16] of white benzoin,[17] a lot of vermilion,[18] large quantities of alum,[19] and many large earthenware jars,[20] all of which were products typical of that land, and many slaves. In effect, everything that he [Naresuan] gave him [the friar] to load onto the junk was worth many ducats. He ordered the friar to take no more than ten Portuguese, and the others would have to stay behind, and the ambassador would be our captain. When the junk was already half-laden and was christened the *Santo Domingo*, the king summoned Friar [Jorge] and Ambassador [Pereira de Abreu]. He showed them a chest of rubies so that they could choose the largest and the finest ruby to take to the king of Portugal. They chose the best, which was a flawless and beautiful cabochon;[21] at that time it was worth 60,000 escudos.[22] I held it in my hands even though I was not present when they chose it and I also held in my hands a very large and perfect sapphire; it weighed 300 carats[23] and at the time it was worth 8,000 ducats.[24] The king ordered that two large pieces of jewellery be made using the said stones, embellished with rough diamonds, all of whose points were perfect, each of

---

[12] Ms. *dioses.*

[13] About 1,380–1,770 metric tons. See the glossary (*quintal*).

[14] About 460–590 metric tons.

[15] Wood used as a red dye. See also the glossary (*sappan*).

[16] About 18–24 metric tons.

[17] Almond-coloured benzoin. See also the glossary (*benzoin*).

[18] Mercuric sulphide. See also the glossary (*vermilion*).

[19] See the glossary (*alum*).

[20] Ms. *sinajas.* Evidently a corruption of *tinajas* (large earthenware jars).

[21] Ms. *cabujon.* A smooth, polished gemstone rather than cut for lustre.

[22] If this is a reference to the Portuguese escudo, this would be equivalent to about 214 kilograms of mint-grade gold; if a reference to the Spanish escudo, this would be about 3,248 kilograms of coin-grade silver.

[23] About 60 grams. See the glossary (*carat*).

[24] Approximately 28 kilograms of mint-grade gold.

which weighed eight carats; at that time both of the jewels [together] were worth 150,000 escudos.[25]

The time to set sail drew ever closer. Ten or twelve days before this the friar called the Portuguese who were his friends and protégés; from amongst them he chose the ten who were to go with him and wrote down their names. Then, when the others saw that they ran the risk of losing their lives they came to seek protection from me and Simão[26] Peres, the factor of the captain of Melaka, saying to us that the king would "fry us all like sardines"[27] if the friar went away and the hoax came to light. [They said that] it would be better if what would inevitably happen at a later time to happen sooner and that it would be best to reveal the truth. Perhaps the king would spare us our lives and set us free. Then Simão Peres and I decided to reveal the vile deception, seeing the peril in which we found ourselves, without paying any heed to the danger that could befall us. We went to find António Hans and we gave him four marks[28] of silver so that he would interpret for us reliably, since he was a friend of the friar. Simão Peres, António Hans and I went to speak with Barcaloa. She bid us to enter a hall[29] that is typical of that land, where they receive visitors. She requested us to be seated, asking António Hans if we were the king's slaves. He replied: "That is why we have come. They are the factors of the captain of Melaka, who is the owner of the ship and [the one who sent] the embassy." In effect, we revealed the entire hoax. She asked us whether what we were saying was the truth. To this we replied that if she wanted to know the truth (and we were not men who would say anything but the truth), the king should order that the letter which had been brought by the embassy—which was still sealed inside its golden document tube and was written in Malay—be translated. [We also said] that with her help we would like to ask the king for permission to return with our junk to describe to the captain of Melaka the hoax that the friar had perpetrated.

---

[25] About 535.5 kilograms of mint-grade gold or 8,121 kilograms of coin-grade silver.

[26] Ms. here and subsequently: *Simon*.

[27] Reference here and subsequently to "frying" refers to a form of torture and execution which is also briefly described in ch. XIV. The expression has been placed here and in all other instances in quotation marks. See also the glossary (*frying*).

[28] About 600 grams.

[29] Ms. *corredor*.

She was very happy with this answer and assured us that she would spare our lives and [obtain] the necessary permission. She ordered that we be given many sweets and fruits, and bid us farewell. At that point she went to describe the entire affair to the king. When the king came to know about the deception he became very angry—and with reason—since he saw that it was an intolerable fraud and hoax. He immediately ordered that junk [the *Santo Domingo*], along with all the wares he had given Friar [Jorge], to be seized and he summoned us the following day. We had already prepared three coloured lac[30] trays, and six feathers of some birds that they call bird of paradise[31]—these can be found only in the Maluku[32] islands in dead trees; they are born in the air and do not have legs;[33] they are highly prized among the peoples of the Indies and some lengths of gold and silk, and some other lengths of very fine taffeta,[34] and 12 bottles of scented water to present to him. When we were on our way to speak to him we ran into the ambassador, accompanied by 15 men, bent on killing us. At this point we took refuge near a small stream and they took up their arms; and we did the same even though there were no more than two of us: myself and Simão Peres. We defended ourselves until we were in the stream, since we were outnumbered. After they had slashed Simão Peres three times with a sword we managed to escape and the ambassador was very badly wounded.

The king came to know of the incident [and] he summoned us the following day. I went with António Hans and we also took Simão Peres along, in his injured state, and our gifts. When we arrived at the palace Okya Wang[35] took us to the king, who was seated in an enclosure within a golden throne that was three varas[36] high and near the enclosure there were two tigers which had been restrained with some chains rolled around them. Near them there were 15 or 16 men with some sticks in their hands; they were the ones who had put the chains around the animals. We

---

[30] A red-coloured gum used as varnish. See also the glossary (*lac*).

[31] Ms. *ormaun*.

[32] The "Spice Islands", sub-group of the Indonesian Archipelago. See also the list of place names (*Maluquo*).

[33] It was a widespread legend in the early modern period that birds of paradise had no legs.

[34] Ms. *bofetan*. Most probably a corruption of *tafetan* (taffeta). An expensive, woven silk fabric. See also the glossary (*taffeta*).

[35] Ms. here and subsequently: *Oyavangarao*. See also the glossary (*Oyavvangarao*).

[36] About 2.5–3.3 metres.

sat down at the foot of the throne on a mat made of rattan[37]—which is a reed that the constables[38] there use as sticks. At this point, after we had presented him the gifts, the men loosened the chains around the tigers to such an extent that they came right up to where I was seated and they almost pounced on me. The king then ordered them to be taken away and he had already been informed about us. He ordered that our junk be laden with sappanwood, he granted it to us as a royal favour, and he gave us permission [to leave] and also to take the Portuguese with us, and in particular Friar Gregorio da Cruz, a Capuchin friar who was held in high regard by the king on account of his virtues. With this he dismissed us and ordered that we immediately be given the [necessary] *cop*[39]—which is similar to a royal warrant.[40] His order was implemented the next day.

After the junk had been laden, even though it was a small vessel, the official in charge of inspecting the ships[41] came to write down all our names and it was necessary for all of us who were [ordered] to stand together in a group, which consisted of the following individuals: Simão Peres, Friar Jorge de Cruz, Luís de Freitas, who was captain of the Tenasserim voyage,[42] and many other Christians we took in place of the sailors, far more than the sailors we had brought with us, most of whom were heathens. When they were about to give us the *cop* and we were about to set sail, the friar [Jorge de Mota] and the ambassador [Pereira de Abreu] with their friends and henchmen came aboard telling the inspector that neither the junk nor Luís de Freitas were to leave for Melaka because they claimed Luís de Freitas had stolen some idols from the king—and this was true, however, he had stolen them before he was taken captive. [The Inspector] said that the junk was to be sunk. They began to act this out; we took up our weapons to defend the junk. When the mandarin who had come to inspect our vessel saw this fracas he was very surprised to see such foolishness and he returned to his perahu[43] and went to describe what had happened to the king. When

---

[37] See the glossary (*rattan*).

[38] Ms. *alguaziles.*

[39] Ms. here and subsequently: *chapa.* Official seal or stamp. See also the glossary (*cop*).

[40] Ms. *cedula real.*

[41] Ms. *baxeles.*

[42] Ms. *viaje de tanacerin.* This means he had tendered for the exclusive right to sail for trade between Melaka and Tenasserim, usually for a period of three years.

[43] Ms. *paro.* See the glossary (*perahu*).

the king heard about the incident he became so angry, he went to hunt elephants and he ordered that his factor[44] and Oya Simintoy[45] (his general of the rivers), and 12 leading mandarins of his kingdom (who had been the ones who translated the embassy documents), to be killed. With these deaths, which had been caused by us, rumours ran rife among the people that the king would order that all the Christians be "fried".

[44] This is probably a reference to the Phrakhlang. See the glossary (*Parabaci*).
[45] Probably Okya Chakri. See the glossary (*Oyasimintoy*).

CHAPTER

XI

How we tried to escape from the kingdom of Siam and how we were again given permission to leave, with which we returned to Melaka[1]

Although Friar [Jorge de Mota] was my enemy, he sent me a message saying that for the love of God I should have a word with him because it was important for all of us. Simão Peres advised me not to go, however, I went just to see what he wanted from me. I found him in a foul mood. He told me, crying uncontrollably, that we had no other remedy than to flee, because it had become common knowledge that the king would order us to be "fried".[2] Even though I had little desire to flee in his company, I asked him how he intended to go about it. He told me, and when I saw that we were not in agreement, because he did not want to take either the Capuchin father or Luís Freitas, who were my friends, along with us, I excused myself and returned to the junk. There I found Simão Peres who was still ill from his wounds, because they had not healed well. When the friar saw that I was refusing to go in his company, he made arrangements with the ambassador and his friends to follow through with his plans.

Simão Peres, myself and the others attempted to do the same thing by means of another route, and to this end we negotiated for three small vessels.

[1] Ms. fol. 37 verso–41 recto.

[2] This refers to a form of torture and execution briefly described in ch. XIV.

We took the sailors from our junk and we went upriver to the place where the king was hunting elephants, pretending that we were going to ask for permission to return to Melaka. We engaged the services of a local pilot who knew a small river that eventually flowed into the sea, through which we had planned to escape. Once we were at sea we intended by the force of arms to seize a junk, which was larger than the sloops[3] on which we were travelling. If we did not find a junk we would have to do whatever was possible to sail to Melaka with the sloops. Our plans never came to pass because three days after we set out we ran into Okya Wang who was accompanied by a large number of perahus.[4] He found us at night and asked us who we were. We told him that we were going to ask for the king's permission to return to Melaka and we showed him a petition that we had brought along to serve as an excuse. The mandarin relaxed upon hearing this explanation, because he thought that we were fleeing—and he was not wrong. He made the Capuchin father, Luís de Freitas, myself and António Hans (who we had taken along as an interpreter) board his perahu. He told us that Friar Jorge and his companions and the ambassador had tried to escape and that he had caught them and had taken them prisoner and that one of the friar's slaves had revealed their plans. He recounted this information and many other things along the way.

After sailing upriver for seven days we arrived at the place where the king was hunting, accompanied by more than 20,000 men and 3,000 perahus, which were longer than a galley.[5] Okya Wang left us there, and as we were unable to speak to the king on that occasion we went to watch the elephant hunt. We reached the hill[6] where there was a very large corral[7] made from large trees indigenous to that area and other very large timbers pillared into the ground. The entrance of the corral would have been about half a legua[8] wide and inside it there were some narrow paths built with trees. We then saw many female elephants enter into the corral, which had been trained for the purpose, and some men covered with branches mounted on top of them, who guided them through the paths. The female elephants had been

---

[3] Ms. here and subsequently: *chalupillas*.

[4] Ms. here and subsequently: *paros*.

[5] A type of rowed vessel. See also the glossary (*galley*).

[6] Ms. here and subsequently: *monte*.

[7] Ms. here and subsequently: *choça*.

[8] Probably about three kilometres.

anointed around their female organs[9] with certain herbs which emitted a smell that bull elephants found irresistible, and as a result they would follow the females in ecstasy. After they had entered the narrow paths one after the other they were surrounded by many men who poked them with pitchforks until they went into the narrowest of all the pathways.[10] They surrounded them in such a way that the male elephants could not back out nor could they turn around. After they had been boxed in as described [the men] put many timbers between one elephant and the next and they tied their feet with green Bengal reeds[11] like fetters. There they chose the good elephants and removed their fetters and tied them to some leafy trees, where they kept them for three or four days without giving them anything to eat or drink. Subsequently, they would feed them with very little food until they grew weak. This was how they were domesticated.

On this hunt the king took some 20 elephants and he ordered the others to be released. He also hunted many deer, of which a very large one could be bought for one real[12] and a wild boar could be bought for the same price. They killed many tigers and other wild animals. When the hunt was over we went to talk to the king. He ordered that we be informed that he was going to the city of Ratchaburi,[13] where he would give us an audience. He came downhill accompanied by more than 3,000 vessels. He took seven perahus that were as large as galleys, which had 60 oars on each side. In the middle of the perahu there was a small cabin made of beaten gold in which he sat. The other perahus [had] similar cabins, some were made of gold and others were gilded, in which sailed his wives and all his guards. They sailed in numerous perahus; the lords and noblemen sailed in other perahus. In this manner we proceeded downstream in complete silence, which was noteworthy. Nobody dared to speak no matter how far away they were from the king, and neither were the trumpets or drums played. As soon as we arrived at the city of Ratchaburi we once again alighted without any delay. We arrived at the city of Suphanburi,[14] which was very large and in ruins.

---

[9] Ms. *untadas las naturas.*

[10] Ms. *callejuelas.*

[11] Ms. *canas de vengala.* AO: *rotanstengels.* This appears to be a type of rattan. See also the glossary (*rattan*).

[12] About 3.75 grams of coin-grade silver.

[13] Ms. here and subsequently: *Repery.* See the list of place names (*Repery*).

[14] Ms. here and subsequently: *Sapampur.* See the list of place names (*Repery, Sapampur*).

In this city the king kept more than 3,000 elephants in some stockades that were half a legua[15] long, where they were kept in very large stables on both sides, as though they were horses; and between one elephant and the next there was a tree trunk pillared into the ground against which the elephants rubbed themselves. The place was populated entirely by mahouts,[16] who looked after the elephants; and these men who are called mahouts used to sleep above ground surrounded by thorns due to tigers, of which there were so many in the area that we were not safe from them even sleeping in our perahus. The king took up residence in a tower[17] or pagoda[18] with his guard around him, and he was surrounded by red cloth panels, and at night they lit large bonfires to protect themselves from the tigers and the flies.

There we gave a memorial to the king written in Siamese[19] asking for permission to return to Melaka. He sent us a message saying that he was going to the city of Ayutthaya, his court, and that he would give us permission there; however, Luís de Freitas was not to go, because he had robbed the king's temples and idols. We arrived there 25 days after setting out from the city of Suphanburi, extremely worn out as during that entire time we had been unable to sleep at night because we were bothered by wretched flies known as elephant flies.[20] They bit us and pierced our clothing like needles. These flies drove the elephants mad, and the men even more so. The worst thing was that at night we could not make any noise or talk loudly. If anyone did so, the king would order that person to be killed. One night when all of us were sleeping, the sailors inadvertently congregated to one side of the perahu and it took on water. We believed it was the current of the river when we found ourselves flooded with water a while later and we had no choice other than to abandon ship. We then held the perahu which was full of water, up with our hands and carried it to land, which was near the said city of Suphanburi. We removed and hid our arms in the forest, running a great risk of being attacked by tigers, because since we were in the process of fleeing we had taken barrel guns, spears, [and] vats of gunpowder; and we did not wish the Siamese to see us because it would have confirmed

15 About one kilometre.

16 Ms. *corneca.* See the glossary (*corneca, mahout*).

17 Ms. *alcoran.*

18 Ms. *pagode.*

19 Ms. *lengua Siama.*

20 Ms. *moscas que se llamavan de Elefantes.*

their suspicions. The king heard the noise and asked what it was; they told him that a tiger had entered our perahu and had capsized it. After bailing out the water we once again hid the arms and we dried them out as best we could. In the city of Ayutthaya[21] the king gave us permission and he sent another junk to accompany us with his ambassadors to the captain of Melaka; and he also allowed our ambassador [Pereira de Abreu] to leave, who sailed aboard the junk sent by the king. We sailed out of the river after having passed a harrowing time over the course of eight months during which we had been held captive there. Friar Jorge was imprisoned along with all the other Portuguese who had been found there in his company.

[21] Ms. *ciudad de Odia*. See the list of place names (*Yudia*).

CHAPTER

XII

What befell me on the voyage from Siam to Melaka and how the ambassador ordered 14 men to treacherously injure me despite his words of friendship, in revenge for the stab wounds I had given him in Siam[1]

The junk aboard which the ambassadors were sailing accompanied us up to the islands of Cambodia,[2] where we became separated. The islands were very green and had many fruit trees. I went ashore on many of them and I killed some snakes and cobras that were as thick as a man and even more. As soon as we came to the Mekong estuary[3] we entered [the river].[4] In the city[5] at that time there was a Castilian[6] and a Portuguese who was called Diogo Veloso,[7] whose wife was still being held captive in

[1] Ms. fol. 41 recto–44 recto.

[2] Ms. *Islas de Camboya.* See the list of place names (*Islas de Camboya*).

[3] Ms. *barra de Camboya.* See the list of place names (*Barra de Camboya*).

[4] Lit: *it.*

[5] The exact location is uncertain, but possibly Lovek as De Coutre mentioned the presence of Veloso in the city. See the list of place names (*ciudad de Camboja*).

[6] He is subsequently identified by name as Blas Ruiz. Morga gives his full name as Blas Ruiz de Hernan González (also spelled Gonçales), see: Morga, *Sucesos*, for example pp. 82, 120; also Subrahmanyam, "Manila, Melaka, Mylapore": 234, where Blas Ruiz is described as "a married settler (*casado*) from Lima, native of la Calzada, which is close to Ciudad Real".

[7] Ms. *Diego Velosso.*

Siam, where he had also been; and the king[8] had sent him to Manila with an embassy and he had not returned with an answer.[9] He went from Manila to the kingdom of Cochinchina accompanied by the said Blas Ruiz—that was the name of the Castilian—from whence they had gone overland to the kingdom of Laos,[10] where a son of the king of Cambodia[11] lived who was married to a daughter of the king of Laos.[12] The two of them advised the king of Laos to send his son-in-law to Cambodia with a very large fleet to seize power in that kingdom, because it was his by right. In effect he followed their advice and sent the prince as a general and Blas Ruiz and Diogo Veloso as captains of the fleet. They arrived in Cambodia, where they found a tyrant who was called Laksamana,[13] who was a rebel and was obeyed as a king.[14] When the tyrant saw such a large fleet he pledged obedience to the prince, albeit with malice. There were many other Portuguese in the city[15] who had escaped from that junk that the king of Siam had sent to Manila, aboard which was the Capuchin father, Friar Pedro Ortiz [Castellano].[16] In the River of Cambodia[17]—where they had been driven by a squall—they had come across a fleet of Laotians,[18] which

[8] King Sâtha I of Cambodia in 1595. Concerning the confusion over the king's identity and that of his father (Barom Racha, Apra Langara Pamararaja) and son (Prauncar, Baroma Racha), see Briggs, "Spanish Intervention", pp. 132–45.

[9] Naresuan sought the neutrality of the Spanish governor in Manila, Don Luis Pérez Dasmariñas, after the 1594 invasion of Cambodia, but Veloso proceeded to Manila on behalf of the King of Cambodia, Sâtha I, see Morga, *Sucesos*, p. 82; Briggs, "Spanish Intervention", pp. 140–1; Subrahmanyam, "Manila, Melaka, Mylapore": 234–5. The appraised date of this Manila incident is June 1595.

[10] Ms. here and subsequently: *Lau*, the kingdom of Lan Xang. See also Bartolomé Leonardo de Argensola's *Conquista de las Islas Molucas* (Conquest of the Maluku Islands, 1609), p. 267; Briggs, "Spanish Intervention", pp. 142–3.

[11] The son was Baroma Racha or King Prauncar, installed after the death of his father Sâtha around 1596–7. Morga reported that Blas Ruiz and Diogo Veloso [Belloso] proceeded to the kingdom of Laos (or Lan Xang) to find the fugitive king and restore him to the Cambodian throne. They found that he had already passed away—and also king Sâtha's eldest son, Chey Chettha—but that several members of the royal family, including the king's second son Prauncar, were still alive. See Morga, *Sucesos*, p. 86; Briggs, "Spanish Intervention", pp. 145–6, 154. See also the list of place names (*Laos*).

[12] King Nokeo Koumanh of Laos. See also Subrahmanyam, "Manila, Melaka, Mylapore": 235.

[13] Ms. here and subsequently: *Laxcemane*. This is a reference to his title or function (admiral) rather than his name.

[14] The Laksamana was earlier mentioned in Chapter VI.

[15] This is most probably a reference to the Cambodian capital Lovek.

[16] Ms. *Ortis*. Friar Ortiz Castellano is previously mentioned in Chapter IX.

[17] Ms. *Rio de Camboja*. The Mekong.

[18] Ms. *armada de laus*.

was the aforesaid fleet; and the junk went up to the fleet to buy benzoin,[19] over which they had some disagreements. The men from the fleet attacked them and killed them all. No more than seven of them managed to escape and ended up in that port after suffering many misfortunes, where they were in the company of Diogo Veloso and Blas Ruiz. All of them came aboard our junk, describing to us what had happened. They told us that they had decided to kill the Laksamana,[20] to be rid of that worry and that we should go to Melaka and tell the captain to send clergymen[21] to administer the sacraments to Christians there and that he should send more Portuguese to reinforce their attempt.

We sailed out of the port, and we would not have gone there if the Capuchin priest, Friar Gregorio da Cruz, had not persuaded us to do so, since he had been the vicar there. We arrived in Melaka and described [all these events] to the captain, Martim Afonso de Melo,[22] who had succeeded Francisco de Silva de Meneses, who had moved to Goa. The captain immediately sent Augustinian clergymen and many Portuguese, who joined Blas Ruiz and the others. They decided to kill the Laksamana, who had suspected that something was afoot. He killed all the Portuguese and the friars, and the prince escaped and fled to his father-in-law, the king of Laos.

By the time I reached Melaka the ambassador from Siam and Manuel Pereira de Abreu, our ambassador, had arrived there many days before. Since Manuel Pereira had come back rich and was thinking of the future, he gifted Martim Afonso [de Melo] the golden box that the king of Siam had given him, and he had become his friend, so that it was now impossible to mention the schemes that had been hatched in Siam. He owed me certain sums of money that I had lent him. I tried to recover them from him there, and we exchanged [harsh] words about the issue. When we wished to settle matters with our swords some friends stepped in and stopped us and so we made our peace and he immediately paid me my money. We then treated each other as friends; he would come to visit me in my home, and I would go

[19] Ms. *mengui.*
[20] Ms. *Laxcemane.* This plot did not succeed, for the Laksamana had most of the Castilians, including Blas Ruiz and Diogo Veloso (sometimes Belloso) killed in a skirmish. The Laksamana himself was eventually driven back into Champa with his Cham and Malay supporters around 1600. Briggs, "Spanish Intervention", p. 158.
[21] Ms. *religiosos.*
[22] See Subrahmanyam, "Manila, Melaka, Mylapore": 238.

to his. However, he still carried a grudge for the stab wounds that I had given him in Siam. But he did not dare take revenge for them, since I was the one who had challenged him, immediately, as soon as I arrived, to resolve matters, and he had not wished to do so. As he was very friendly with the captain, Martim Afonso [de Melo], who was very hostile towards me because of a woman, the two of them connived to kill me under the guise of friendship. Eight soldiers who were friends of Manuel Pereira, and six of the captain's henchmen lay in wait for me at a street intersection near the bridge in Melaka.[23] They sent a man to my house, who told me that he wished to buy an emerald ring that had once belonged to the bishop of Japan, who had been a Jesuit, the bishop who had been present at the martyrdom of the Christians in Japan.[24] The priests had given it to me to sell it. I showed it to him; he told me that he wished to ascertain what it was worth by consulting a friend of his—who was called Manuel de Rocha. Since I did not know him I went with him—it was one in the afternoon, after lunch—by myself, without being accompanied by any slaves—I had three slaves who served as my footmen[25]—but on that occasion I did not find any of them at home. As we drew near the said street he kept my attention by conversing with me and asking me to show him the ring there, when at that very moment one of the men who were lying in wait to ambush me came out from behind him. He struck me in the head with a sword[26] that sliced a significant portion of my skin off. At this point I drew out my sword.[27] Meanwhile he followed up that blow with a second thrust, opening a gash that ran halfway down my back and slashing my arm—I still bear the scar that is two *palmos*[28] long. When he tried to attack me with another thrust of his sword I stabbed him twice with my sword, a rapier. Even though he had a height advantage over me, he fell down at my feet. The others came to assist him and some of them did not leave with a smile on their face since Manuel Pereira and the captain were

[23] Ms. left margin reads: "Bispo del Japon de la Companía de Jesus" (The Bishop of Japan of the Society of Jesus). See the following note.

[24] This is a reference to the martyrdom by crucifixion of 26 Christians at Nagasaki on 5 February 1597. The bishop in question was Luís de Cerqueira, the residential bishop of Japan between 1598 and c.1614.

[25] Ms. *lacayos*.

[26] Ms. *catana*.

[27] Ms. here and subsequently: *espada*.

[28] About 40–44 centimetres. See also the glossary (*palmo*).

witnessing the whole thing from a roof[29] of the fortress on how they were going about killing me. In the end, some bystanders[30] separated us and they took me to the house of one of my friends to heal my wounds. When we passed below the captain's balcony he was standing there and he asked me what had happened. I replied to him saying: "That Jew who is with Your Grace—who was Manuel Pereira—ordered this attack on me".

My wounds healed; even though they were mortal wounds, I escaped because I was still in my youth. Ten days after that fight, Manuel Pereira embarked aboard a vessel along with all those who had lain in wait to ambush me and they sailed to Siam, where, wishing to return to Melaka, they found a Castilian frigate. They joined forces. Since King [Naresuan] did not wish to give them permission to return, they left battling with the entire fleet that was in the [Chao Phraya] River. There were many casualties on both sides. When Manuel Pereira arrived in Melaka he died almost immediately since he was very weak. Friar Jorge de Mota, who was returning in his company, had been shot twice in the back and he, too died a few days later from his wounds.[31] About a month or so after I saw how they had met their end my entire house burnt to the ground, along with a vast quantity of benzoin[32] and all my possessions, with nothing escaping the flames. More than a thousand houses were burnt in that blaze, which comprised the greater part of the outskirts of the city of Melaka. This misfortune I felt was the final blow to befall me after the travails that I had endured in the kingdom of Siam.

---

[29] Ms. *tejado*.

[30] Ms. *vezinos*. This might also be translated as "neighbours".

[31] See also Morga, *Sucesos*, p. 190, concerning the death of Fray Jorge de la Mota.

[32] Benzoin is flammable. See also the glossary (*benzoin*).

CHAPTER

XIII

The barbarities and some things that I saw in the kingdom of Siam over the course of the eight months when I was a captive of that king[1]

I witnessed countless barbaric incidences in the kingdom of Siam that astounded me because they were unbelievable, owing to which I am not writing most of them down.

It is already known that the kingdom is large when compared to its neighbouring kingdoms and is very rich, abounding in everything that is necessary for human life, and it has many lush trees, and elephants, and all kinds of animals. King [Naresuan] has his court in the city of Ayutthaya,[2] which is encircled by brick walls and surrounded by two very broad and deep rivers. It is situated on the bank of a branch of the river Ganges,[3] 40 leguas[4] inland, and even the largest of baxeles can enter and they anchor right beside the city's walls. The medium-sized vessels can enter into the city since it is criss-crossed by rivers, where there are innumerable and very large crocodiles.[5] During the winter[6] everything is flooded and the

[1] Ms. fol. 44 recto–48 verso.

[2] Ms. *Odia.*

[3] There was a widespread belief that rivers in Southeast Asia were connected to the Ganges. Ayutthaya was surrounded by a moat fed principally by the Lopburi and Pasak rivers.

[4] Probably about 80 kilometres.

[5] Ms. *caimanes.*

[6] Ms. *jnvierno.* The monsoon season which corresponds to the months June–September.

water rises by the length of a pike[7] or even more in height, throughout the land, so much so that the hills[8] appear to be islands. These floods last for two and a half months; during this time the people go about and trade in small boats, with which they create markets. The houses are made of planks and reeds[9] built to suit the climate. As the natives are familiar with these conditions they sow the land before the floods arrive; and when the floods arrive the crops grow with the flood water, in such a way that the ears are always above the water—and thus one finds straw that is as long as a pike, and the crops ripen above the surface of the water; and they harvest it in small boats, scything only the ears.[10] During this time, many places that are situated on flat terrain—entire villages—move and retreat towards the mountains; others stay where they are, relocating to high houses where they gather the livestock in corrals built on top of very thick reeds.[11]

Their temples and pagodas[12] are built at the highest areas and [in] cities that the water does not reach. During this period the king goes out to hunt elephants, because that is when all the animals seek refuge in the mountains. Even though the king's palace was built of wood it was surrounded entirely by a brick wall, with five high golden towers, with many steel mirrors[13] on the walls, which were made with wood and planks. He had a royal throne in each tower with a sumptuous pavilion of brocade[14] and many courtyards[15] where his mandarins would observe celebrations from some corridors;[16] and he would also use those royal thrones when he gave audiences to the public; the stables were located nearby[17] in which the

---

[7] Ms. *una pica de alto.* This could be easily three metres or more.

[8] Ms. *montanas.*

[9] Ms. *tablas y canas.*

[10] A similar account by Engelbert Kaempfer dating from around 1690 has been cited in Derick Garnier, *Ayutthaya: Venice of the East* (Bangkok: River Books, 2004), p. 11.

[11] This is probably a reference to bamboo.

[12] Ms. *pagodes.*

[13] Ms. *espejuelos de azero.*

[14] Ms. *pavellon brocado.* See the glossary (*brocado*).

[15] Ms. *patios.*

[16] Ms. *corredores.*

[17] The elephant stables shown on the Vingboons map are outside the palace, which De Coutre mentioned on pp. 133–4. Referring to the stabling for the principal elephants which were in front of the audience halls—marked clearly on Engelbert Kaempfer's map of the palace and described by several 17th-century visitors, were very similar to the description here. See also Chris Baker, Dhiravat na Pombejra, Alfons van der Kraan and David K. Wyatt, *Van Vliet's Siam* (Chiang Mai: Silkworm Books, 2005), p. 11.

Hand-painted bird's-eye view of Lovek, the former royal administrative centre of Cambodia, taken from the Vingboons Atlas, c.1665. (The Hague, NAN, 4.VELH 619, pl. 45).

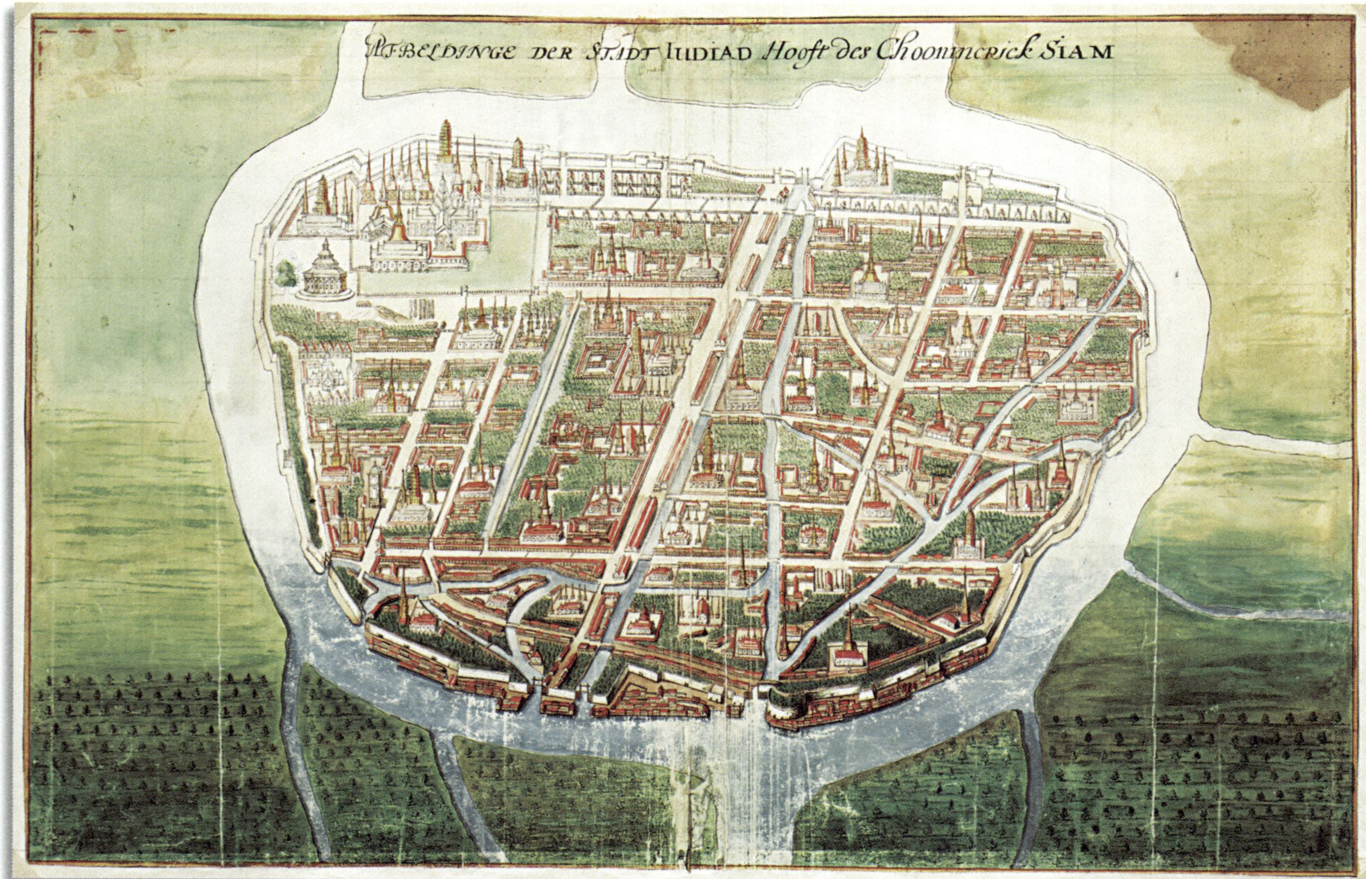

Hand-painted bird's-eye view of Ayutthaya, the capital of Siam, taken from the Vingboons Atlas, c.1665. (The Hague, NAN, 4.VELH 619, pl. 62).

elephants that he used when he ventured out were kept, caparisoned in all their finery.

I went to see the elephants out of curiosity. There were many of them, and among them two were greatly esteemed and pampered.[18] It was an amazing sight to see. Notwithstanding their enormous size, each of them had their own silk mattress and they would sleep on it in much the same manner as a small dog. One can well imagine the size of those mattresses, to accommodate elephants that measured six *varas* tall[19] or even more. They were attached to some chains hanging from above, which were as thick as those used for [city] gates[20] [and] plated in gold. I went closer to them thinking that they were made entirely of gold and I saw that they were in fact plated since the gold had worn away in some places. Even their [restraining] ropes were made of silk and each one of them had six very large golden bowls.[21] One can well imagine how large they must have been; their edges were as thick[22] as a real-of-four coin. Some were filled with oil, which they use to rub down the elephants; others contained water which they use to sprinkle onto the elephants; others were used to feed them, or contained water for them to drink, or were used for the elephants to urinate and defecate in. The elephants were so well trained that, when they wish to urinate or defecate, they would get up from their beds; the mahouts would have already anticipated what they were going to do and they would put forward the bowls. They always ensured that the stables in which [the elephants] were housed were scented and fumigated with benzoin and other fragrant substances. The elephants were kept in this grand style. I would not have believed it had I not seen it with my own eyes.

Apart from this there were four very broad streets in the city where they kept many other elephants in stables on both sides of the pavement;[23] among which there was one small elephant, which was as white as a white buffalo. He was greatly prized and was kept in the same splendid manner as the aforesaid elephants.

---

[18] Ms. *regalados.*

[19] About 4–6.6 metres.

[20] Ms. *portada.*

[21] Ms. *bazos.*

[22] Ms. *gorsura.* Probably copy error for: *grosura.*

[23] Ms. *cera.* Probably a copy error for: *acera.* Concerning the elephant stables, see Baker, *et al.*, ed., *Van Vliet's Siam*, p. 11.

The king was very fond of watching them wrestle with each other. He would often have them brought out to a square precisely for this purpose; there I saw them wrestle each other with their tusks and trunks entwined. While charging at each other they would hit each other with strong blows, trumpeting at each other so loudly that they could be heard half a legua[24] outside the city, and they would gore each other with their tusks that they sometimes broke them; then you could see the tusk fall to the ground as though it were a log of wood—here in this land they do not habitually cut off the tusks as the Muslims do in India. Two or three men would sit on the elephants' necks, one behind the other, with hooks in their hands with which they would control the animals; it was a public spectacle similar to bullfighting in Spain.

In the said city I also saw three of the main pagodas[25]—which is what they call their temples and they use the same word for their idols. Each of them had a very high tower built of stone and bricks held together with mortar, and gilded from the tip to halfway down the tower, with four staircases, each of which was made of gilded lead. The king kept his idols in them, which were made of gold and embellished with precious stones. Nobody is allowed to climb up the tower[26] except for him. The said towers were situated in some very large square courtyards built in brick. There were four ponds in each courtyard, one in each corner, and there were many trees along their banks. Around the tower there was a small wall made of mortar, whose sides were studded with garnets, topazes and many other stones, however, stones of little value. On the inside it was surrounded by many lamps, and many bronze figures arrayed against the wall, as high as a fairly tall man, dressed like the ancient Romans. Some of them held sticks in their hands, others restrained lions tethered on chains, all cast in bronze and very lifelike. These figures had been found 40 years ago[27] in the kingdom of Cambodia,

---

[24] About one kilometre.

[25] It is difficult to identify which three temples come into question here because there were several important *wat* in Ayutthaya. De Coutre probably meant three major temples within the walled island-city, and ones dominated by large central *stupa*. The three most likely temples would be Wat Phra Ram, Wat Mahathat and Wat Ratchaburana, which are three late 14th or early 15th century monasteries dominated by *stupa* in the Khmer-style.

[26] Reference is here most likely to a *chedi*.

[27] The point of reference appears to be the time of writing or compiling the manuscript of De Coutre's (auto-)biography, that was sometime in the mid-1620s. The estimate of four decades would therefore be correct.

in a ruined city that the natives had stumbled across in the mountains;[28] it is not known which nation had inhabited that city. When they discovered it they gave it the name Angkor.[29] It appears to have been populated, judging by the figures, by the Romans.[30]

When King [Naresuan] of Siam captured the kingdom of Cambodia[31] he brought back with him these and many other similar figures made of stone, which he had placed in front of his palace; and there were some cloisters all around the said courtyards and some benches attached to the wall. At the ends of the benches there were many nails on which they would place lit beeswax candles. They would illuminate some idols that were there, made of gilded bronze, of which some were seated, while others were lying down on cushions, and they had long ears,[32] like the native Sinhalese[33] who inhabit the island of Ceylon and the Malabar Coast.

The people from the village would come twice a week on a pilgrimage to these idols, and they visit them in the same manner as us, when we visit altars in a church. They would put candles on the nails, and they would make offerings of small books made of fine gold that were sold at the door, and they would release pigeons and turtledoves in the said cloisters. There were four doors in each courtyard, one in front of the other, through which one entered into some very large halls, where there was a vast number of bronze idols: some of them were standing figures, others were seated, others were mounted on horseback with little flags[34] in their hands and wearing diadems, others had parasols. In my view there would have been more than 3,000 idols in each hall. To leave the courtyard there was another door that led to a much larger courtyard, and in it there was another hall, which was likewise filled with similar idols. However, they were made of stone held together with coloured mortar; only the brocades of the clothes were golden. In this courtyard there was another very large door, which was the main

---

[28] Ms. *los naturales toparon en los montes.*

[29] Likely a reference to Angkor Thom which remained an inhabited and functioning city until the end of the 16th century. The Cambodian court was later transferred to Lovek.

[30] This is very evidently an error.

[31] This is almost certainly a reference to King Naresuan's campaign against Cambodia in 1597.

[32] Evidently Buddha statues with different poses and mudras.

[33] Ms. *chingalas.*

[34] Ms. here and subsequently: *bandellerias.*

entrance to the temple, and in front of it there was an elephant with three heads and a king seated on top made entirely of marble.

I also entered into a hall accompanied by a mandarin who showed me a very large chapel like the chapels we have in our churches. It was entirely filled with idols plated in gold and silver; many of them had diadems on their heads and little flags in their hands, and had various other things. There were many other temples in addition to these three main pagodas.

Outside the city walls I saw a statue that was seated on the ground with its feet crossed, on a cushion, entirely made of stone and brick, held together with coloured mortar, gilded and painted.[35] It had a large parasol over its head made of golden fabrics. The statue was so tall and large that it could be seen four leguas[36] away since it was on flat terrain. Out of curiosity I measured one of the statue's nails, on one of its thumbs: it was five palmos[37] wide and as many palmos broad, on the right hand. The natives said that a king of Pegu had ordered it to be built in a single night when he captured the kingdom of Siam[38] and at the time the king of Arakan[39] had a white elephant. Great wars were fought over this elephant and entire kingdoms were lost fighting over who should keep the elephant, because at the time no other similar animal was to be found in all of India, and many authors wrote about it. However, returning to the matter at hand, it seems to me that it would have been impossible to construct that statue in a single night, since it is a very large structure. I believe that the fact that it was made in a single night was a lie.

Apart from all these things I saw was that amongst the indigenous inhabitants of that kingdom [of Siam] and those of Pegu, all the great gentlemen, whether of medium or small stature wore at the head[40] of their

---

[35] This is possibly a reference to the Buddha at Wat Phanan Cheong, which is located to the south of Ayutthaya outside the city walls. The seated image is about 19 metres tall. The temple, however, predates the founding of Ayutthaya.

[36] About eight kilometres.

[37] About 1–1.1 metre.

[38] This is probably a reference to the campaign of King Bayinnaung, the ruler of the Taungoo Dynasty Kingdom, and his protracted campaign against Ayutthaya between 1563 and 1569.

[39] The King of the Arakan (Mrauk-U Kingdom); see also the list of place names (*Araquão*). This is possibly a reference to King Saw Hla or King Min Setya of Arakan. The kings of Arakan at the time were known as "Lords of the White Elephant". See also the glossary (*white elephant*).

[40] Ms. *en la cabeça*. In the region around the scrotum, or at the tip of the penis. See Teensma, "Literaire, filologische en moralistische bespielingen over de Siamese penisbel", *BKI* 147, 1 (1991): 128–39, esp. 134–5: "op de eikel van de penis". See also the glossary (*bungkal*).

penises, inserted inside the flesh, two bells, which they call bungkals.[41] They are as big as nuts[42] and they tinkle like bells, but quite loudly; and the more noble gentlemen wear two and four more.[43] I went along with five Portuguese to visit a mandarin, who had summoned a surgeon to remove one of his bungkals, because it had been crushed and his penis was swollen; when the surgeon came to visit him he entered as per the custom in that land; without any embarrassment the surgeon removed it from him in front of us after cutting open only one [bungkal] with a razor after which he stitched him up, only to, after the incision had healed, operated on him again to replace the bungkal that he had removed, so that it was just as it had been before. It is amazing how they can procreate with those implants. They told me later that the person who had invented them was a queen of Pegu, because during her time the inhabitants of that kingdom were very inclined towards sodomy,[44] and she made it a law, with very severe punishments for anyone who disobeyed, that the women were to wear their skirts—which are just like petticoats—open from the navel downwards, so that when they walked they revealed all of their thighs. She did this so that the men would desire them and would abjure sodomy.[45] Some bungkals are made of gold and others of silver and of copper; each man has them according to his means and there are innumerable shops in every city and town that sell nothing except

---

[41] Ms. here and subsequently *b(r)unchol(es)*.

[42] Ms. adds in the right margin: "Bruncioles: horroroso martirio para embaratar el vicio nefando" (Bungkals: a most horrendous martyrdom to prevent homosexuality).

[43] W. Foster, ed., *Early Travels in India, 1583–1619* (London: Humphrey Milford and Oxford University Press, 1921), "Journal of Ralph Fitch", p. 40, "The bunches [i.e. bungkals] aforesaid be of divers sorts; the least be as big as a little walnut, and very round; the greatest area as big as a little hennes egge." These "penis bells" were also a curiosity to Chinese travellers as is evidenced by Ma Huan, *Ying-Yai Sheng-Lan. The Overall Survey of the Ocean's Shores, 1433*, tr. and ed. J.V.G. Mills (Cambridge: Cambridge University Press, 1970), p. 104, "… [T]hey use gold to make hollow beads, inside which a grain of sand is placed, and they are inserted [in the membrum virile]; [when the man] walks about, they make a tinkling sound, and this is regarded as beautiful. The men who have no beads inserted are people of the lower classes. This is a most curious thing." See also the editorial comment, ibid., note 4.

[44] Concerning this story on the origin of the bungkals in Pegu, see also Foster, ed., *Early Travels in India*, "Journal of Ralph Fitch", pp. 39–40; Donald Lach, *Asia in the making of Europe*, vol. 1 (Chicago and London: University of Chicago Press, 1965), p. 553.

[45] An almost identical observation was made by Ralph Fitch in Foster, ed., *Early Travels in India*, "Journal of Ralph Fitch", pp. 39–40.

bungkals.[46] Those who do not have them are scorned as sodomites and even though they suffer pain and torment, they all strive to have them. Damsels are not esteemed in this land and nor is their virginity prized, because of the bungkals they cannot penetrate them, and thus from the time they are little girls their mothers break them in with wooden instruments made [specifically] for the purpose.[47]

[46] Ralph Fitch in Foster, ed., *Early Travels in India*, "Journal of Ralph Fitch", p. 40, "Some are of brasse and some of silver; but those of silver be for the king and his noble men. These are gilded and made with great cunning, and ring like a litle bell. There are some made of leade, which they call Selwy because they ring but a litle; and these be of lesser price for the poorer sort."
[47] They rupture the hymen with wooden instruments.

CHAPTER

XIV

The justice meted out by the king of Siam and his tyranny, and how they cremated an elephant that had died, and how they worshipped it, because the king said that it was his father[1]

Since that king of Siam, whose captive I had been, was so capricious and volatile and a tyrant in his governance I thought it opportune to mention certain things about his governance and tyrannies.

All the sentences that he ordered to be implemented were issued verbally and were very often executed in his presence. I saw him in one of the towers, at the foot of which inside his palace could be found a wooden gate, behind which were eight ferocious mountain buffaloes.[2] He ordered that ten men who had been sentenced to death be brought and gave instructions to put them inside the gate, saying that whoever fought the best with those beasts would be allowed to live. Each of the men entered with their lance. In the end no more than one of them managed to escape, but he was very badly wounded and [King Naresuan] ordered him to be removed since he was valiant; and he greatly enjoyed watching the others being mutilated.

I also saw him order people to be "fried" and inflicted various punishments on 28 young girls each of whom was eight years old, as well as on an old woman and a hunchbacked man. It was a pitiful spectacle. They

[1] Ms. fol. 48 verso–53 recto.

[2] Ms. *bufanos*.

first extracted an eye from each of them, then they flayed their hands and pulled out their nails; a little later they cut off a piece of their back and put it in their mouths. Then they "fried"[3] them very slowly, each of them in their own frying pan,[4] so that they suffered for a long time until they died. When I asked why the king had ordered those cruelties they told me that the old hag was a woman who entered the palace as a messenger and she had asked one of the 28 girls for some keys to the treasury, which were lying near the queen's bed. Unaware of what she was doing the girl gave them to her. After the old woman obtained the keys she did not know how to use them and was unable to open the door of the treasury room. She returned the keys to the girl, who left them where she had found them. The old woman, who wished to steal, had described this to the hunchback, who was a wizard and gave her a small pick telling her to use it on the padlock, which would then open. The old woman followed his instructions and removed 150 marks[5] in gold from a safe, which were in the form of spheres sealed with the royal insignia. She locked up the treasury room and broke one of the spheres where she gave a piece of gold to the young girl who had given her the keys to thank her even though she had not used them. A part of the royal insignia was visible on that little piece of gold. As the girl was not aware of the importance of the gold she ran around the house playing with it and that was how the robbery came to light. Soon after, the king ordered that the old woman and the wizard be brought to justice along with the girl and all the girls of the same age who were in his palace. They were guilty of nothing except being of the same age. All of them were the daughters of leading dignitaries and gentlemen of his kingdom.

I saw him implement another, no less cruel, sentence in the presence of our ambassador [Pereira de Abreu] and Friar Jorge [de Mota] along with all the Portuguese who were being held captive. He ordered a pretty young woman to be brought before him. He ordered her to be stripped down to her bare skin and they brought the mastiff[6] that we had brought along with the embassy, which the friar had said was a fierce dog, [but in reality] was more mild mannered than a sheep. They let the dog loose on the woman

---

[3] Ms. *freyeron*. See the glossary (*frying*).

[4] Ms. *sarten*. The description here differs somewhat from the modes of execution involving fire and oil in the *Laws of the Three Seals*. See the glossary (*frying*).

[5] About 22.5 kilograms. See also the glossary (*mark*).

[6] Ms. *mastin*.

so that it could shred her to pieces; the dog did not want to bite her. The boy who had brought the dog then ordered her to throw a stone at it. She followed his instructions. The dog then jumped up at her, leaping onto her breast, and bit her twice, no more. When the tyrant saw this he ordered some tigers to be let loose against her, who played with her like a cat habitually plays with a mouse. After the woman was dead and in pieces he ordered her [body] to be displayed in the square because she had committed adultery and her husband had complained to the king.

I also saw him order that the arms of six men be cut off at the elbows in his presence, and after they had been cut off, he ordered that the arms be tied with a rope and hung around their necks. They were allowed to leave in this state, because he had felt that his elephants had looked weak and the men would now be sure to feed them well and keep them clean.

Apart from these punishments I saw him implement various others against the six mandarins who had been present at the time the embassy letter was being translated[7] and for the same reason he ordered that his factor, who was called Phra Phasi,[8] be hacked in half. It so happened that one of his relatives was nearby, and, after they had cut the factor in half, since he was a gentleman of stature and a leading figure in the kingdom, the relative covered his body with a sheet. The king came to know that he had been covered. He immediately ordered that the person who had covered him up be quartered and that the pieces of his body were to be left on the factor's body instead of the sheet. The sentence was repeated; they found the relative there mourning the death of the factor. Without telling him anything they caught hold of him and cut him in half and covered the factor's quartered body with the pieces of his relative's body. These and many other things were some of the cruelties that were meted out by the tyrant. He was so inhuman that he ordered one of his brothers to be "fried" alive and ordered that 800 men be burnt together at the stake because they had not assisted him at the time when he had gone to wage a war against Pegu, in which he had defeated the maharaja,[9] the son of the king of Pegu.[10] He was wounded

---

[7] Ms. lit. during the translation of the embassy letter. For this episode, see Chapter X.

[8] Ms. *Parabasi*; the Phrakhlang. See also the glossary (*Parabasi*).

[9] Ms. here and subsequently: *Maharraya*. AA, p. 139: *Maha Uparat.*

[10] Most probably a reference to Mingyi Swa, the crown prince and son of King Nanda Bayin.

in one arm by a musket shot, and the maharaja eventually died in the city of Tavoy,[11] having been injured in the neck by a spear.

I cannot fail to describe another barbarity committed by that tyrant, which was worthy of admiration. A year after the said war, the elephant on which he had been mounted when he achieved his victory, died. The day the animal died he was extremely upset, saying that his father had died. He ordered the people and all the leading figures of his kingdom to go and worship the elephant. To this end they took the elephant outside the city to the other side of the river and they placed it before a temple [known as] *Arros*[12]—which was what the idol was called[13]—and all the idols inside the temple were life-sized and were made of bronze, everything was plated in gold as thick as the edge of a real-of-four, to which the king normally went on a pilgrimage. They erected a very large canopy made of blue damask[14] over the elephant and cut open the animal's abdomen. After they had removed its intestines they enbalmed it with many aromatic ointments and placed a large quantity of flowers and roses on top of the animal. They inserted some golden poles into the animal in order to keep its stomach open and four talapois, who are their priests, sat inside the cavity. The priests were dressed in yellow and held some beads in their hands, which they call *gantra*[15] and there were many lit wax candles around them. At times some [monks] would come in and others would leave. After this they built a very large square wooden structure all around the animal, which was entirely gilded and painted, with five steps reaching down to the ground and completely surrounded by balustrades; and they built the entire contraption in less than a day and a half. The stench of the elephant could be smelt over half a legua[16] away. Subsequently, all the leading figures and gentlemen came to worship it in the structure or cloister, where a large number of candles were burning all around, placed on the balustrades; and everyone worshipped the animal on their knees. This barbarity went on for eight days, during which dances were continuously held and infernal music could be heard day and night,

---

[11] Ms. *Tavai*. This is perhaps a reference to Naresuan's campaign against Tavoy in 1593.

[12] Ms. *de Arros*. AA, p. 139, omits "de" before Arros. See the list of place names (*Arros*).

[13] Most temples are named after the principal Buddha image. Judging by the description which follows, it was likely to have been a Buddhist temple.

[14] A reversible fabric. See also the glossary (*damask*).

[15] See the glossary (*gantra*).

[16] About one kilometre.

consisting of rattles, drums, gongs and other instruments like tambourines. There were many men dressed as tigers and devils and white horses made entirely of paper. The wooden horses and birds were painted yellow, [there were] structures shaped like an ostrich in which the talapois were seated, one *talapoin* in each structure, [which] were as large as a horse. Around the elephant they placed many painted pots filled with an assortment of foodstuffs and the openings[17] of these jars were painted and covered. The barbarians said that this was done so that the animal had enough to eat in its next life. At the end of the eight days the talapois covered the elephant with large and small pieces of wood. The king then came and walked around the elephant three times and set the pyre ablaze. After the elephant's carcass had been burnt he ordered the ashes to be collected and put into some golden urns, and they put the urns in the same place as the ashes of his parents and ancestors.

After the urns had been gathered together two men came to the king who were the carers or mahouts of the elephant. They said that since the elephant, their master, was dead they wished to go and serve the animal in its next life. After thanking them profusely for their gesture the king drew out the sword that he was wearing around his waist; he ordered them to be cut in half and then burnt with many honours. To this end they took the said bodies that were placed in some painted coffins to another temple that was situated upriver. More than 3,000 perahus and all the leading figures and gentlemen of the kingdom accompanied the cortege. Amongst the perahus there were four vessels laden with birds and horses fashioned out of paper and many wooden birds, in which the talapois were seated and they were taken along thus, dressed in yellow with shaved beards and moustaches—that was how they habitually went about. It is customary in that land for all the natives in general to remove their beards and moustaches with tweezers. They all look like they have been emasculated; it is rare to see men with beards. Many men dressed as tigers and devils also accompanied the procession and they followed along playing instruments and dancing on the perahus. In addition there were seven perahus laden with painted pots filled with foodstuffs for the deceased. They arrived at the said temple with this entire entourage; they placed the bodies below a very rich canopy that had been

---

[17] Ms. *bocas*.

erected in the middle of a field; they covered them with wood and placed the pots all around. Then, the talapois lit the pyres with many ceremonies and after the bodies had been burnt they threw the ashes into the river and took the pots to their homes. The barbaric festivities for the elephant were concluded in this fashion.

I also saw many men and women—who had died—being burnt in the same manner with all the accompanying rituals. Whenever a man died his wives [and] female relatives would shave their heads as a sign of mourning, so much so that almost all the women had shaven heads. In all the cities and places of that kingdom there are many shops where it is possible to rent birds and buy horses made of paper, devil's masks and painted coffins, and everything that was necessary for the deceased, in keeping with the status of the individual in question. All the men generally keep some small balls in their mouth shaped like a bar of soap, made from garlic and other herbs and betel; they keep one of these things in each cheek, which they call tobacco.[18] When they wish to speak they take them out and hold them in their hands; at the end of the conversation, they put them back in their mouths. It seemed to me to be quite a disgusting[19] habit. They are cowardly people and even though they use artillery when they go to war it is small artillery, which are known locally as *berços*.[20] They have a large number of full warehouses, and they have many elephants and horses; however, the horses are small, like the horses of Galicia. They also use barrel guns but they only have a few, which are short and loaded with iron and small shots. The cannons are richly decorated with silver and gold. When the said king goes to war everybody goes along with him and along all the paths through which they pass the king provides them with supplies of rice. On each journey he orders warehouses to be erected with trays filled with rice, guarded by many men. However, since the king does not value his people, [and because they are] so numerous, and unmotivated, most of them die of want and disease. The land abounds in victuals[21] and everything is extremely cheap, so that prices cannot rise.[22] Also, a very good large deer can be bought for one

---

[18] Ms. *tapaca*.

[19] Ms. *suzia*.

[20] A small artillery piece. See also the glossary (*berço*).

[21] Ms. *mantenimientos*.

[22] Ms. *no se puede encarecer*.

real of silver,[23] and a wild boar can be bought for the same price, and 20 chickens can be bought for a *real*.[24] Fruit, fowl and other game are worth almost nothing. The kingdom has many commodities the principal of which is a wood that is called sappan, [then also] deerskins, rayskin, vermilion, lead, white benzoin,[25] slaves and a lot of silver. The coins are made of silver, shaped like a harquebus bullet, with the insignia of the king of Siam, which consists of an elephant with three [heads]; each coin is worth seven and a half reals. The coin is known as a *tikal*[26] and there is another coin, which they call *emas*;[27] this coin is worth one and a half reals. For currency in smaller denominations, some shells[28] are used, and the products that are worth the most in the said kingdom of Siam are textiles.

I also went overland into the interior up to the kingdom of Pegu and I saw many ruined places and temples along the way, and I witnessed many barbaric things, which I will not describe so as not to be overly verbose.

---

[23] A Spanish currency unit. See also the glossary (*real*).

[24] Ms. adds in the right hand margin: "20 galinas por un R[ea]l." (20 chickens for one real.)

[25] See the glossary (*benzoin*).

[26] Ms. *tical*. This makes it equivalent to about 28.1 grams of coin-grade silver. See also the glossary (*tikal*).

[27] Ms. *mazes*. About 5.6 grams of coin-grade silver. See also the glossary (*emas*).

[28] Cowry, a small, generally white shell that was commonly used as a medium of payment in Asia and Africa. See also the glossary (*cowry shell*).

CHAPTER

XV

How I went from Melaka to Manila in the year 1597. The events that I experienced before I arrived[1]

Nothing affects a man more in his life as not having resources; and I cannot put in words what I felt when my house burnt to the ground with all my possessions.[2] However, the enthusiasm that I always had to improve my circumstances remained undiminished. A few days after that, an opportunity presented itself when a junk captained by Martim Afonso was sailing to Manila. I embarked aboard the vessel. Then, as there is inevitably to be some friction aboard ships, it so happened that as soon as we arrived at a tip of the island of Borneo—which is called Tanjung Baram[3]—there were some differences involving one of my companions. A man who was quick to draw his sword had injured a Castilian[4] in the head. The captain of the junk was a young man. Instead of calming frayed tempers he further fanned the flames of the quarrel and supported the other party. As a result, all the men on board were split into two factions. A great misfortune would have befallen us if we had not managed to call in at port on the said island. We sailed along the coast of the island for 30 leguas[5] until we were in front

---

[1] Ms. fol. 53 recto–58 recto.

[2] See Chapter XII.

[3] Ms. *Tangibaran*. See the list of place names (*Tangibaran*).

[4] Ms. here and subsequently: *Castellano.*

[5] About 165–83 kilometres.

of the port,[6] accompanied by more than 500 perahus of the orang laut,[7] which seemed like a very powerful fleet. They came to sell us refreshments: water, fruit, chickens, fish and other things; however, we traded with them very carefully, always keeping our weapons in our hands. We did not let them come on board to trade except in groups with no more than four individuals at a single time, because they are treacherous people; because they are thieves in the guise of fishermen, and we have learnt our lesson the hard way. When we were five leguas[8] away from the port, a Castilian colleague who was called Gómez Arias and I disembarked into one of those perahus, and we went ashore to charter a Chinese junk,[9] so that I and my companions could go to Manila in it, as a result of the differences that had arisen.

I came across a junk with Chinese and Borneans who were getting ready to set sail. Amongst them there were five Christians from Melaka. I struck a deal with them and hired half the junk from them. When we returned to our vessel we found that the disputing parties had made their peace. Despite all this, Gómez Arias and I unloaded all of our belongings, since our other friends did not wish to disembark. We returned to shore in order to go to Manila on the junk that we had chartered. The Chinese and the owner were extremely happy that we were accompanying them. Our [original] junk then entered the port, because the captain was bringing an embassy that had been sent by the captain of Melaka to the king of that island.[10] He received it with scant ceremony because he did not have many resources. His palace was located on an islet and was made of bamboo—which is a plant that is of the same species as reeds and looks similar to them, but can be as thick as a man; some of them are solid while others are hollow—and he had eight ships beached on the shore equipped with bronze artillery.[11] The islet was encompassed by the city, which was very large, having been founded on the sea between some cliffs that surrounded it like a bay. The houses were

[6] The port of "Borneo" was located in Brunei Bay. See also the list of place names (*Borneo*).

[7] Ms. *paros de Saletes.* The exact identity of these people is unknown. It could possibly be a reference to the Bajau laut. See also the glossary (*Bayus*).

[8] About 27.5–30.9 kilometres.

[9] Ms. *junco de Chinos.*

[10] Variously known from period sources as the king or emperor of Borneo; a forefather of the present Sultan of Brunei.

[11] Ms. *pieças de bronze.*

also built of bamboo and the foundations were made with the trunks of wild palm trees. Each house had its own water channel:[12] water that they funnelled down from the cliffs through some pipes made of hollow bamboos set on forked stakes cut from wild palm trees. This flowed throughout the year, winter or summer; and since the city is large and densely populated there were always many conflicts over the water sources. The market and commercial centres consisted of baxeles[13] and numerous small boats, where it was possible to find all kinds of fabrics, silks and provisions.

The island abounds in precious stones and metals. It has a lot of gold and many diamonds,[14] which can be found in two rivers on the island, one is called Lawai,[15] the other Sukadana,[16] when the water level is low.[17] It is possible to find many bezoar stones[18] in the maws of some red monkeys,[19] which are hunted on that island. Likewise in India, in the kingdom of Vijayanagar,[20] they find bezoar stones in the maws of goats. They are very similar, but the stones from the island of Borneo are more efficacious.[21] Bezoar stones are also available in the kingdom of Persia, which are found in the maws of gazelles, which are animals that are similar to deer, however, they have straight antlers with very prominent neck glands.[22] The stones from these animals are more efficacious than all the others and they are worth more. Very large bezoar stones can also be found in the Indies that comprise New Spain,[23] however, they are [like] pebbles,[24] which are found in

---

[12] Ms. *fuente*.

[13] See the glossary (*baxel*).

[14] Ms. reads in the left margin: "q[ue] se hallan en rios" (which they find in rivers).

[15] Ms. *Lavia*. See the list of place names (*Lava*).

[16] Ms. *Socodavia*. See the list of place names (*Suquedani*).

[17] Ralph Fitch confirmed that the Borneo diamonds were not mined, but panned from the rivers. See the journal of Ralph Fitch in Foster, ed., *Early Travels in India,* "Journal of Ralph Fitch", p. 42, "Laban [i.e. port of Lawai, Borneo], is an iland among the Javas whom whence come the diamants of the new water. And they find them in the rivers; for the king will not suffer them to digge the rocke."

[18] Ms. here and subsequently: *piedras bezares*. See the glossary (*bezoar*).

[19] This is presumably a reference to orangutans. The monkey stone in question would probably be derived from the ape's gall bladder; a gall stone.

[20] Ms. *Bisnaga*. See the list of place names (*Badaga*).

[21] Ms. here and subsequently: *mas virtud*.

[22] Ms. *nudos mui vistozos*; lit. very visible knots or knobs. As this appears to be a reference to the Iranian goitered gazelle, the expression has been translated as "very prominent neck glands".

[23] See the list of place names (*Nueva España*).

[24] Ms. *gijaros*.

the mountains and they are not efficacious even though many people hold them in great esteem. Coming back to the task at hand, apart from gold, diamonds and bezoar stones, the island of Borneo possessed an abundance of good-grade camphor,[25] like the kind that is extracted from the trees from between the bark and the trunk. They sell it unadulterated, without mixing it with anything, unlike the habitual practice in these kingdoms,[26] and it is the best camphor to be found in all of the Orient. Turtle [shells][27] are another abundant product and large quantities of this commodity are traded with India. The arms they use are culverins,[28] small pieces that cannot fire more than three-ounce[29] iron shots. They use blowpipes and poisoned darts, and spears made from wild palms without the use of iron, lances and krisses. They do not use other weapons and they are a treacherous and cowardly people.

Despite all this abundance of riches the king makes a living by thievery. He is more of a pirate than a king. His baxeles sail around as privateers, 50 at one cape [and] 50 at another, in squadrons that are known as the Bajau of Borneo.[30] While we were there, the owner of the junk that I had chartered hosted us in his house. Later, while I was in the square negotiating for what was necessary for the voyage, I was summoned by the king of Jailolo,[31] who was staying with his brother-in-law, the king of Borneo, because he had fled from his kingdom for fear that one of his brothers who had rebelled would kill him. I went to his residence in my little boat. He was very ill and his body was swollen and glistened like a mirror. He made me sit down next to him beside his wife and his mother and two daughters. His knights[32] were standing on either side of him, who they call *orang kaya*.[33] He asked me if I knew any remedy for his ailment because he had heard that I was a doctor. With the best of intentions I pretended that I was. I took his pulse and said to him: "Your Highness can neither eat nor sleep". He answered

---

[25] Ms. *alcanfor*. See the glossary (*camphor*).

[26] Forgery and adulteration were problems merchants of the early modern period frequently complained about, especially when dealing in compact, high-value commodities.

[27] Ms. *tortuga*. Reference here is presumably to the shells of the sea turtle known in Malay as *karet*.

[28] Ms. here and subsequently: *culebrinas*. A type of firearm. See also the glossary (*culebrina*).

[29] Ms. *onças*. About 86 grams. See also the glossary (*onça*).

[30] Ms. *Bajus*. See the glossary (*Bajau*).

[31] Ms. *Gelolo*. The island of Halmahera. See also the list of place names (*Malluquo*).

[32] Ms. *cavalleros*.

[33] Ms. *Orancayas*. Persons of standing. See also the glossary (*orang kaya*).

me impassionately[34] that he could not, and since he complained a lot about other maladies I ordered him to take *radix Chinae*[35] and instructed him on how he should take it. He immediately ordered that it be brought to him. As the natives were not familiar with *radix Chinae*[36] they brought him all the roots that were to be found on the island and they showed them to me. I could not find any root that was *radix Chinae.* I then told him that I was going to Manila, from where I would send him *radix Chinae* and many other good things for the ailment that was plaguing him and that I would be leaving from there [and reach Manila] in 14 days.

He immediately summoned the owner of the junk aboard which I was to sail. He praised me highly before him and gave him money so that I could purchase in Manila whatever was necessary to cure his ailment. He ordered that we should set sail at once, bidding me a contented farewell that was full of hope. His wife offered me betel from the same box that she was using.[37] The following day, when I was leaving, he sent me four perahus[38] laden with numerous chickens and amphorae of wine,[39] along with jars full of sour and sweet preserves, fowl, a cow and a deer, and a large quantity of fruit until there was no space on the vessel to store them. I only took what was necessary; the rest I shared with the owner and sailors of the junk, where everybody obeyed me as though I were its captain. I bade farewell to the king's retainer[40] expressing my thanks and I told him to relay my message that [the king of Jailolo] should take *radix Chinae*[41] while I sent him other remedies from Manila. I did not have any bad intentions because I had decided that I would discuss his ailment in Manila with a doctor and ask him for some remedies to send to him [the king], in exchange for the excellent hospitality that he had extended to me and to repay him for the gifts he had sent me. In the end we left the port accompanied by many other Chinese junks, with great festivities, as is usually the case when

---

[34] Ms. lit. with feeling.

[35] Ms. *salçaparilla.* This medicinal substance is called *palo de la China* just a few lines further down; of the *sarsaparilla* family. See also the glossary (*radix Chinae*).

[36] Ms. here and subsequently: *la çarça.*

[37] Ms. *que ella comia.*

[38] Ms. *paros.*

[39] Ms. *tinajas de vino.* This is most probably a reference to palm wine.

[40] Ms. *criado del rey.*

[41] Ms. *palo de la China.*

they leave a port. They fired their culverins[42] and they set coir[43] torches ablaze and threw them into the sea, along with cooked chickens, rice and other foodstuffs in a ceremony and they bid farewell to each other. With this, each junk then sailed its own respective route.

As soon as we arrived at the island of Palawan,[44] located near some shoals that are known as Alcatifa,[45] we ran into a storm, which we managed to escape by the grace of God. After sailing past the Calamianes[46] islands and within sight of the island of Mindoro[47] we ran into an equally fierce[48] storm, where it appeared inevitable for us to not run aground since there was nothing else that could be done. We were quite afraid because we were not familiar with the island and thought that it was inhabited by some indigenous insurgents, who are known as Zambales.[49] They would not spare the life of any Spaniard. Just when we were about to run aground, by God's grace we came across a deep channel. As we did not know what destiny held in store for us we entered the said channel, trusting our fate and fortune to God and at the end we found a bay where we were able to shelter from the weather and repair the forecastle,[50] which had been washed away by the sea. Nobody dared to go ashore because the pilot was not familiar with the region, neither was my companion Gómez Arias, even though he had been a [tax] collector[51] on that island of Mindoro. After three days it became necessary to resupply our fresh water. I went out in the batel[52] accompanied by ten or twelve Chinese and five indigenous[53] Christians, with spears, blowpipes and poisoned darts, and we took with us the containers for water. While sailing along the beach looking for a stream—when we had just passed a tip of land—we were struck by a wave

[42] A type of firearm. See also the glossary (*culebrina*).

[43] Coconut fibre. See also the glossary (*coir*).

[44] Ms. *Paragua.* See the list of place names (*Paragua*).

[45] This is not to be confused with an identical toponym employed later in the context of the Arabian Peninsula. See also the list of place names (*Alcatifa*).

[46] Ms. *Caliminianos.* See the list of place names (*Caliminianos*).

[47] Island to the southwest of Luzon in the Philippines. See also the list of place names (*Mindoro*).

[48] Ms. *no menor.*

[49] Ms. *Sambales.* See the list of place names (*Sambales*).

[50] Ms. *Castillo de proa.*

[51] Ms. here and subsequently: *cobrador.*

[52] See the glossary for a definition of this type of vessel.

[53] Ms. *indios.*

that smashed the batel into smithereens. We all went ashore entirely soaked, however, we were able to save the gunpowder and kept the barrel guns[54] dry. We stripped down to our bare skin, except for a loincloth that covered our private parts, and we arranged ourselves so as to be able to put up a defence if anyone attacked us, until we could fill the water containers and return to the junk. In the midst of all this, Gómez Arias fired a weapon,[55] warning us that people were marching along the beach. The containers had not yet been filled for us to return, and the people were increasingly drawing closer. They would have been some 500 or so in number. We went in their direction, in order to defend ourselves until we were near the junk so that we could save our lives by swimming to the vessel. When those people saw us they hid themselves. Only four of them came to look at us, since they thought that we were Japanese,[56] because a few days earlier a junk full of Japanese corsairs[57] had sacked that place and had killed the headman of the village, which was situated inland. Even though I had never been to Manila I had heard about the garments and dress of those people. I went out to meet them and drew closer with more confidence. Their captain came out with his sword. He was wearing a large number of very thick gold chains and held a staff in his hand like a vizier.[58] I told him how we had arrived there and that there was a Castilian on the junk who had been the second lieutenant[59] of Don Luis Pérez Dasmariñas,[60] [and] who was returning from the ruins of Cambodia.[61] The captain immediately ordered that a canoe[62] that was in a river nearby be brought to him. Its existence was unknown to us. He boarded it and went to the junk. Meanwhile I remained amongst his people as a hostage. As he recognised Gómez Arias—the [tax] collector in his village and who had imprisoned the captain's brother—he did not utter

---

[54] Ms. *escopetas*. See the glossary (*escupeta*).

[55] Ms. *una pieça*.

[56] Ms. *Japones*.

[57] Ms. *cossarios*.

[58] Ms. *alguazil*.

[59] Ms. *alferez*.

[60] Ms. *de las Marinas*. Luis Pérez Dasmariñas had succeeded Gómez Pérez Dasmariñas.

[61] Ms. *perdicion de Camboya*. This is most likely a reference to the 1594 campaign against Siam by the Spanish-Philippine governor Luis Pérez Dasmariñas in Cambodia. The ruins refer to the temple complex Angkor Wat in Cambodia. A mission from the Cambodian king to Manila requesting help had been earlier mentioned in ch. XII and XIII.

[62] Ms. here and subsequently: *canoa*. Possibly also a type of *sampan*. Elsewhere De Coutre calls it a *batel*. See also the glossary (*batel, sampan*).

Printed map of Asia by Jocodus Hondius, 1615. (Amsterdam, UB, Special Collections, O.K. 157).

a single word to him, nor did he linger. He immediately returned with the canoe and went away with all his men, without allowing us the use of the canoe to enable us to take the water aboard the junk, since our batel had been smashed.

In the end it proved necessary to make a buoy[63] out of the containers which were half filled with fresh water. We took it along the beach until we were in front of the junk. As the vessel was already nearby I sat on the edge of the containers and the others swam, pushing the containers along. After we boarded the junk we left the port, which was called Mamburao[64] and we went to the island of Lubang,[65] where I came across a junk that had set sail from Borneo five days after I had left the island. They told me that the king of Jailolo[66] had died; with this [news] I did not have to worry any longer about sending him medicines. We reached the island of Mariveles;[67] there we found the junk aboard which I had set sail from Melaka, [and] which had run aground. The junk had tried to enter Manila during the storm that we had witnessed in Mamburao and had washed up on the shore after it had lost its main mast. We were quite relieved to have reached Manila.

---

[63] Ms. *boya*.

[64] Ms. here and subsequently: *Manboran*. See the list of place names (*Mindoro*).

[65] Ms. *Lubon*. See the list of place names (*Luban*).

[66] Ms. *gelobo*.

[67] Ms. *Mariboles*. An island in the Bay of Manila. See also the list of place names (*Mariboles*).

CHAPTER

XVI

What happened to me in Manila, and the events that took place with Doctor Antonio de Morga and the Dutch; and what happened to me on the voyage while returning from Manila to Melaka[1]

As soon as I arrived in the city of Manila, Our Lord immediately showered me with bountiful blessings, so much so that in a few days I had many ducats and was received very favourably by Governor [Francisco de Tello de Guzmán], who often used me when an opportunity arose to serve the king, and [this] ensured that I made a great fortune, as did all the gentlemen and citizens, no more no less. I sought to establish myself in that city because of the good fortune I had encountered there and since the land was very prosperous and at the same time efficiently governed.

With regard to the city, its streets are well laid out and it is walled similarly to the best cities in Europe, with beautiful buildings and palaces.[2] On the outskirts of the city there is a village of heathen Chinese [called Parián]. Their houses are made of planks covered with tiles, in which live more than 40,000 Chinese. They are all merchants and professionals of all mechanical trades, very ingenious and hardworking people, as all the Chinese generally are. However, they are treacherous people: the Spaniards do not trust them, because when the governor, Gómez Pérez Dasmariñas[3] took them on board

[1] Ms. fol. 58 recto–63 recto. The chapter number is absent in the manuscript.

[2] Ms. *palacios.*

[3] Ms. *de las Marinas.*

as crew on his galley when he went to the Malukus they rebelled during the voyage and killed him together with the other Spaniards who were sailing aboard the galley.[4] Even during my stay in the said city, the inhabitants of the outskirts revolted against the Spaniards.[5] On that occasion they also killed the son of the governor—Gómez Pérez Dasmariñas[6]—whose name was Don Luis Pérez;[7] however, the Spaniards, accompanied by the indigenous inhabitants[8] of the land who were loyal to them attacked them and killed more than 12,000 Chinese and they took some 6,000 of them prisoner. For this reason there are no Chinese inhabitants inside the city and they only enter the city to get all their necessary supplies.

The indigenous inhabitants are called Luzones;[9] they consist of four different nations. All of them are Christians and they have been taught the doctrine well. They have gold mines but they are lazy and are more inclined to follow an indolent way of life rather than work. They do not wish to extract from the mines more than what they need to pay their tributes. They have a lot of silver, which comes from New Spain, since every year three or four carracks[10] come to Manila from the port of Acapulco[11] laden with silver and many wares.

Many other baxeles come from Melaka and other ports, which ensures that a great deal of bustling trade is carried out by merchants in that city. The indigenous inhabitants are very bellicose: they have proved to be of good military stock for the Spaniards and have been deployed on all occasions.[12]

---

[4] Briggs, "Spanish Intervention", p. 149. It is noted here that these "were Chinese merchants" who had been "impressed into service'. The mutiny took place off Punta del Acufre in 1593.

[5] This is unlikely to be a reference to the Chinese revolt of 1603, as De Coutre would have already left Manila by that time. There were, however, a series of revolts in preceding years, including 1601 and 1602. See also note 7 below.

[6] Ms. *de las Marinas*. Gómez Pérez Dasmariñas y Ribadeneira had served as the Spanish governor of the Philippines between 1590 and 1593. See also note 7 below.

[7] Don Luis Perez Dasmariñas who had served as Governor of the Philippines between July 1596 and his death during the Sangley Rebellion of 1603. Concerning his death near the town of Tondo, see the report by Don Pedro de Acuña and the Audiencia of Manila, dated 12 December 1603, in PI, XII, p. 143. It is most unlikely that De Coutre would have still been in Manila at the time this Spanish governor was killed.

[8] Ms. *los indios naturales*.

[9] Ms. *aduçones*. Portuguese: Luçones; people from the island of Luzon. See also the list of place names (*Luzon*).

[10] Ms. *naos*. See the glossary (*carrack*).

[11] Ms. *Capulero*.

[12] This was especially true of the Pampangos of Luzon. See BOC, III, p. 592; GVOC, p. 85.

Hand-painted bird's-eye view of Manila taken from the Vingboons Atlas, c.1665. (The Hague, NAN, 4.VELH 619, pl. 69).

Apart from the fact that it has been equipped with very sturdy walls, the city also has a very good garrison of Spanish soldiers—very splendid people—and they have always been and are especially important to defend against the enemy, both European as well as from the South.[13] While I was there, it so happened that a Dutch carrack and patache[14] sailed up to the anchorage.[15] They stayed there for some 20 days impeding the entry of the

[13] Ms. *sur.* These were the ships of Olivier van Noort. For the Dutch account of this naval confrontation in the Bay of Manila (with etchings as on p. 159) see "Beschrijvinge van de Schipvaerd by de Hollanders ghedaen onder 't beleydt ende Generaelschap van Olivier van Noort, door de Straet oft Engte van Magallanes ende voorts de gantsche kloot des Aertbodems om", Commelin, I., *Begin ende Voortgang Vande Vereenigde Neerlandsche Geoctroyeerde Oost-Indische Compagnie*, facsimile of the edition printed by Johannes Janssonius in 1646 in 4 vols. (Amsterdam: Facsimile Uitgaven Nederland, 1969), II, pp. 45–6.

[14] Ms. *nao y un patache.* A reference to the *Mauritius* and the *Eendracht* (Unity, Concordia). See Jaap R. de Bruin, Femme S. Gaastra and I. Schöffer, *Dutch-Asiatic Shipping in the 17th and 18th Centuries,* 3 vols. (The Hague: Martinus Nijhoff, 1979–87), II, pp. 4–5 and 6–7, entries nos. 0014.2 and 0024.1; see also the glossary (*nao, patache*).

[15] Off Cavite in the Bay of Manila.

baxeles. While this was taking place, the governor, Don Francisco Tello [de Guzmán],[16] ordered a carrack,[17] a frigate[18] and a patache to be prepared, aboard which 500 Spaniards sailed, most of them were *hidalgos*[19] and leading figures. They were commanded by Doctor Antonio de Morga, who knew more about letters than arms.[20] The admiral [of this fleet] was Captain [Joan de] Alcega,[21] from Biscay, who sailed aboard the frigate.

As soon as they saw these ships set sail, the enemy immediately took up a fighting position and waited with sails raised and the prow pointed to take advantage of the wind.[22] When our ships arrived, they began to fire their cannons until they sailed behind the Isla de la Fortuna,[23] where our commander boarded the Dutch flagship.[24] After they had been aboard the vessel for some five hours the frigate arrived and fired four cannon shots at the enemy, who yelled from under the deck: "We surrender![25] We surrender!" Hearing this the Spaniards who were above the deck ceased to fire their muskets and told Captain Alcega to go with God, because the carrack had been secured for the king [of Spain]. Upon hearing this, Captain Alcega once again turned his attention to the Dutch admiral's patache, which was escaping. He caught up with it and managed to board it after much effort.[26] When the Dutch general[27] saw that Captain Alcega, our admiral, had left, he once again began to fire his cannons, even though our men were aboard his vessel, to such an extent that he managed to create gaping holes in the carrack[28] of our general, Doctor Antonio de Morga. Since the latter

---

[16] Loureiro, "European Encounters and Clashes in the South China Sea", II, *Revista de Cultura,* International Edition 12 (2004): 157, "Governor of the Philippines from 1596 to 1602".

[17] The flagship was the *San António.*

[18] Ms. here and subsequently: *galizabra.* See the glossary (*frigate*).

[19] Members of the lower nobility. See also the glossary (*hidalgo*).

[20] De Morga, *Sucesos*, p. 168, concerning the appointment of De Morga as commander of the fleet.

[21] Ms. here and subsequently: *Arcego*. Admiral Alcega (variously also spelled as *Alzega, Alezega*) is also mentioned on several occasions in Morga, *Sucesos*, pp. 171–81, recounting the attack by Van Noort on Manila.

[22] The naval combat described here took place on 14 December 1600, in the Bay of Manila off Cavite. See also the images on p. 159.

[23] Ms. *del Fortum*. See the list of place names (*Isla de la Fortuna*).

[24] The boarding of the *Mauritius* is also detailed in the account of De Morga, *Sucesos*, pp. 177–81.

[25] Ms. *Buena guerra.*

[26] Alcega chased after the *Eendracht* for several hours before he caught up with it.

[27] Ms. *general de los Olandezes* (Olivier van Noort).

[28] Ms. here and subsequently: *nao*, the *San António* (alias *San Diego*). See also De Morga, *Sucesos*, p. 168.

The sea battle between the Spanish and the Dutch vessels under Olivier van Noort on 14 December 1600. From Isaac Commelin, *Begin ende Voortgang* (Amsterdam: Johannes Jansonius, 1646), vol. II, "Beschrijvinge van de Schipvaerd by de Hollanders gedaen onder 't beleydt ende Generaelschap van Olivier van Noort...." (Description of the Dutch Sea Voyage under the Command of General Olivier van Noort), between fol. 46 and 47. (Leiden, UB, 348 C 9–10).

The sinking of Dr Antonio de Morga's flagship in Manila Bay during a fight against Olivier van Noort and the vessels under his command. From Isaac Commelin, *Begin ende Voortgang* (Amsterdam: Johannes Jansonius, 1646), vol. II, "Beschrijvinge van de Schipvaerd by de Hollanders gedaen onder 't beleydt ende Generaelschap van Olivier van Noort ...." (Description of the Dutch Sea Voyage under the Command of General Olivier van Noort), between fol. 46 and 47. (Leiden, UB, 348 C 9–10).

was not a military man, as soon as he saw that his carrack was taking on water he gave orders to cut the ropes with which the two ships were tied together. When the ropes were cut, the carrack sank and everyone on board drowned;[29] only Doctor Antonio de Morga and six men escaped on a coir[30] mattress, which does not absorb water.[31]

The loss was deeply felt since leading figures of Manila had been killed in this incident. As soon as the Dutch general[32] found his ship had been cut loose and our commander's vessel was sinking, he even stopped to kill those who were swimming to stay afloat; then they raised their sails and went away. Captain Alcega captured the patache [the *Eendracht*] and brought [it in] with 18 Dutchmen, 13 of whom were garrotted;[33] 12 of them converted to the faith and died as good Catholics.[34] Only the admiral, who was called Lambert Biesman,[35] died a heretic.[36] I was present on the occasion and served as interpreter. The remaining five Dutchman were allowed to live since they were very young.[37] The bodies of those who had died as Catholics were buried with much honour, accompanied by all the clergymen and gentlemen,

---

[29] Up to 350 lives were lost when the *San António* went under, though De Morga admits to 50. Morga, *Sucesos*, p. 180. The Dutch were reported to have steered the *Mauritius* through the mass swimming Spaniards, stabbing and shooting as they sailed by. Others drowned because they were wearing armour. Concerning the latter point, see esp. Morga, *Sucesos*, p. 180, "Others perished by drowning for they had not even disarmed themselves ..."

[30] Ms. *yesca.* See the glossary (*coir*).

[31] Compare this with Morga, *Sucesos*, p. 180, "After the ship had sunk, the *oidor* [De Morga], taking with him the enemy's quarter-colours and standard, swam for four hours until he reached a very small unpopulated islet, named Fortuna, two leagues away from where some of the ship's crew who were strong enough to survive in the water, had also found safety." See also the list of place names (*Isla de la Fortuna*).

[32] Ms. *general olandez* (Olivier van Noort).

[33] See also the affidavit filed by Simon Lambertsz. Mau on 10 October 1604, reproduced in this volume as appendix III.

[34] According to PI, XI (Morga's *Sucesos*), p. 166, the Dutch prisoners were executed at the behest of the Spanish governor of Manila, Francisco Tello de Meneses, as well as the prefect of justice "notwithstanding the word that Admiral Joan de Alcega had pledged to them". See also *Sucesos,* pp. 181–2, esp. the editorial note by Cummins, ibid., p. 182, note 1: "... the other twelve crew-members turned Catholics, and as such died most piously."

[35] Ms. *Biseman.* See also appendices I and III.

[36] He died a Protestant and was executed in Manila in 1601. See also the parallel account in PI, XI (Morga's *Sucesos*), p. 200, where it is said that "It pleased the divine goodness to restore all, to the number of thirteen, except the admiral, who was an obstinate heretic was hanged and cast into the sea." See also the editorial comment by Cummins, *Sucesos,* p. 182, note 1.

[37] PI, XI (Morga's *Sucesos*), p. 166, "the rest were boys". See the editorial comment by Cummins, *Sucesos,* p. 182, note 1, "Some young people on board the Dutch ship were spared and put into Manila monasteries to be catechised."

who carried them to the parade ground on their shoulders, where they were buried in the chapel of Santa Potenciana[38] in front of the altar.[39]

After having lived in that city for two and a half years I returned to Melaka sailing aboard a navette[40] belonging to Fernão de Albuquerque,[41] who was governing the city of Melaka at that time, with the intention of going to the city of Goa in order to get married. We set sail from the port of Manila with excellent weather and arrived at the island of Borneo, where we acquired the supplies we needed before setting sail again. On the third day after leaving Borneo, our ship was covered with a large number of birds, some of which the sailors called gannets and mangy birds.[42] They were silly birds; they were so tame that we were even able to pick them up with our hands. Our ship was surrounded with such a large swarm of these birds that we could not get rid of them even when we used sticks to scare them. We saw some shoals that were more than five leguas in width.[43] We sailed around the shoals' edge all through that night and innumerable very large, violet-coloured fish[44] jumped[45] aboard our ship. After we had passed the shoals, at midnight that same night, we ran into a great storm—which the natives call a typhoon[46]—which was so fierce that the sea engulfed our ship from the stern to the prow and washed away all the enclosures and shelters for the crew that were on the deck and at the same time filling the ship with water. We were on the verge of sinking because the gutters were clogged with the discarded skins of the many fruit that we had eaten during the voyage. At this point we all worked to bail the water with cauldrons and we managed to get the water out and unclogged the gutters with sticks and skewers. With the storm we were being blown backwards, all of us were crying, begging God with crucifixes in our hands to show us some land so that we could run aground on it and escape with our lives, making

[38] A girls' school founded in 1589 at the behest of Bishop Domingo de Salazar. According to an editorial comment by Cummins, *Sucesos,* p. 182, note 1, those who had converted and then executed were interred in the *Misericordia.*

[39] See also the affidavit of Simon Lambertsz. Mau reproduced in this volume as appendix III.

[40] Ms. here and subsequently: *naveta.*

[41] Ms. *Fernan d'Albuquerque.*

[42] Ms. *alcatraces y tiñossos.*

[43] About 27.5–30.9 kilometres.

[44] This is probably a species of *ikan tulang.* They are known to jump out of the water on to the deck of vessels before a storm. See also the box insert (bottom left) on p. 162.

[45] Ms. lit. came.

[46] Ms. *tufan.*

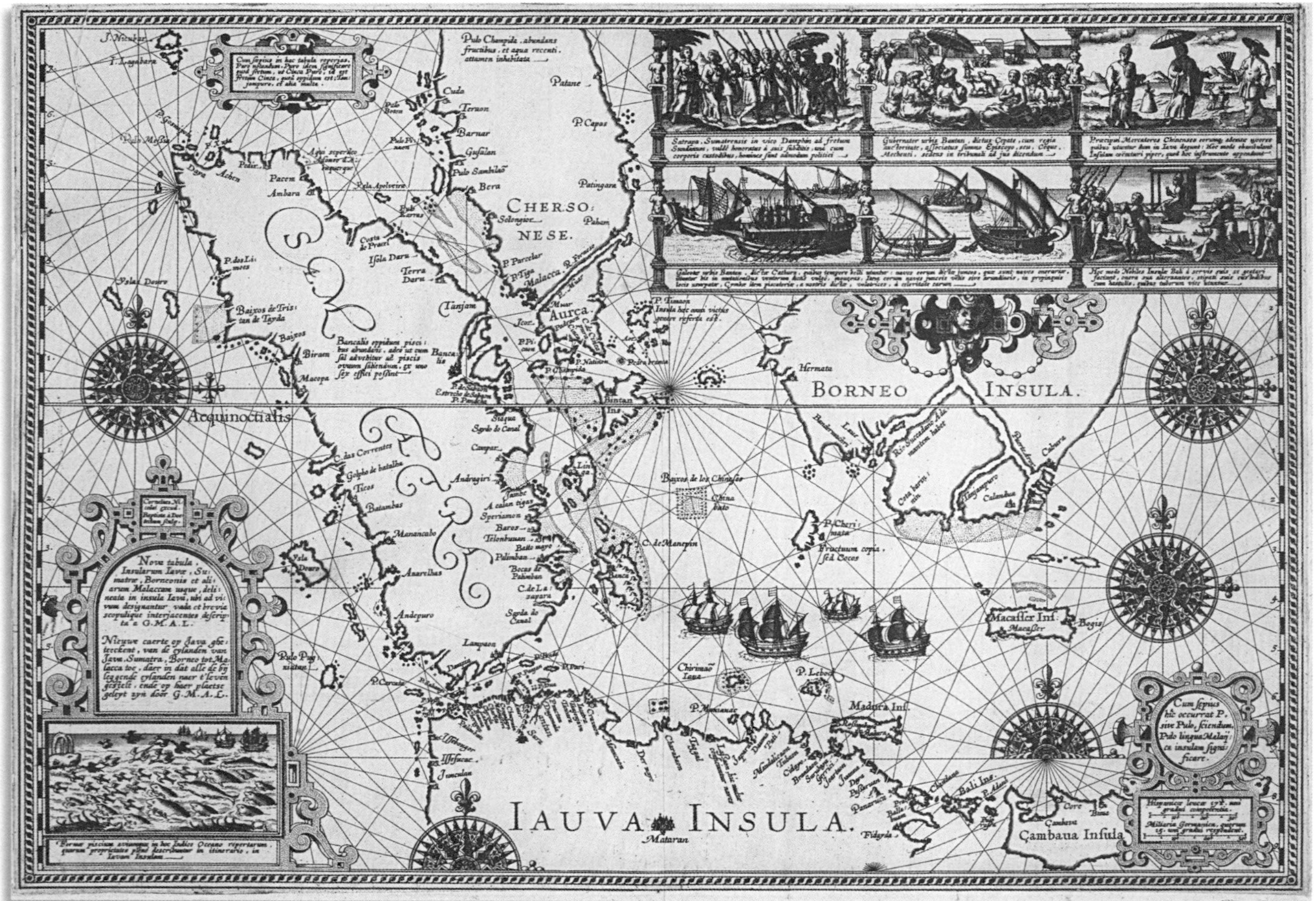

Printed map of Sumatra, the Malay Peninsula, Borneo and Java by Cornelis Claesz, 1598. (Amsterdam, UB, Special Collections, O.K. 130).

great vows—which were not really fulfilled—to carry the foremast on our shoulders in a barefoot procession in honour of Our Lady as soon as we got to Melaka, if God would spare us from that storm.

The storm passed after four days and we sighted land. After having identified the site we found that we were on the opposite coast of the said island of Borneo. We came some five leguas[47] close to it and we saw plenty of nipa palm[48] trunks floating down with the currents of the Lawai[49] River. We dropped anchor closer and behind we saw a canoe[50] filled with natives. They did not wish to come aboard; from far away they just told us that we were in the Lawai River [estuary]. We sailed out of there the following day and we went to some islands that appeared to stretch further than the eye could see. Only two of them were inhabited, by barbarian people. By means of the nautical chart we came to know that they were the islands of Lingga.[51]

Those barbarians spoke the Malay language. Some companions and I went ashore. As soon as they heard us coming they fled towards the mountains. We found some straw huts and in them many local coins and palm hearts from the palm trees. We sailed amongst those islands for a month, completely lost, since we did not know the route [out], and our provisions began to run low. We were always going out in the batel to see if we could find a fisherman to show us the way. We came across many fishermen who were fishing in some small boats,[52] one man in each small boat. They rowed so fast that we were never able to reach them nor could we make them stop with our barrel guns.[53] We forced many of them to run aground. Their boats were so light that they would carry them on their shoulders and escape into the woods. With all of this we only managed to get hold of some small boats that they left behind.

After a few days we returned with the batel to one of the islands to look for water, seafood and fruits to replenish our supplies. As soon as we arrived

---

[47] About 27.5–30.9 kilometres.

[48] Ms. *madera de nisperas*; the trunks of nipa palms.

[49] Ms. here and subsequently: *Lavia.* See the list of place names (*Lava*).

[50] Ms. *canoa*; lit. canoe, here probably a type of *sampan.* Elsewhere De Coutre called the canoe a *batel.* See also the glossary (*batel, sampan*).

[51] Ms. *las islas de Linga.* See the list of place names (*Islas de Linga*).

[52] Ms. *barquillos.* The craft in question here and in subsequent lines appears to be a type of *sampan.*

[53] Ms. *escopetaços.* This is evidently a variant of the earlier term *escupeta.*

at a stream we saw some fishermen go into it. We hid with our weapons, leaving in the batel only the slaves who somehow resembled them and at the same time spoke their language, with the intention of capturing one of the *orang laut*[54]—which was what the fishermen were called. The slaves called out to them in their language, showing them some brightly coloured cloths that they habitually wear. An *orang laut* who had a crooked eye came close to the batel. The slaves said that they wanted to barter the cloths in exchange for fish. He took a tip of a piece of cloth in his hand and began to take out fish to barter. At this point the slaves got into the water as though they were going to see the fish that he had with him. They came closer to him and while he was distracted one of the slaves grabbed him. We then jumped into the water, caught the fisherman and his little boat with the fish and put everything inside the batel, however, always taking great care so that he would not get away and jump into the sea. We returned to the navette feeling very contented, we put some shackles around his feet, [and] we offered him a lot of money and fabrics just so that he would show us the way out of those islands. We promised to give him more money and cloths and to let him go with his little boat as soon as we were out of those islands. In the end, he got us out of the islands in three days and set us on a route that was familiar to us. After that we gave him what we had promised and we let him go with his little boat—off [the coast of] Johor.[55] Even though [the little boat] took on a great deal of water since it was an open vessel and[56] it was so thin that a man could lift it up with one hand, it was nonetheless an amazing sight to see the fisherman so happy and light-hearted, as he pushed the water out of the vessel with one foot and manoeuvred the little boat with the other. With his hands he rowed the boat using an oar with two blades, [in a way] which was quite remarkable. A few days thereafter we reached Melaka.

---

[54] Ms. here and subsequently: *saletes*.

[55] De Coutre and his vessel came through one of the southern tributary waterways leading into the Singapore Straits that was either the Durian or Kundur Straits.

[56] Ms. lit. since; here perhaps "and since".

CHAPTER

XVII

The journey that I made to the kingdom of Patani and what happened to me during [this journey] before the Dutch sank one of my junks laden with wares, an incident in which I lost all the fortune that I had in the year 1602[1]

Owing to a shortage of baxeles I was unable to pursue my intention of going to the city of Goa to get married. When I arrived at the port, there were some ships that were waiting for the fleet from China. They waited so long that they missed their voyage, and the [China] fleet did not arrive that year; they postponed their voyage to the next. When I saw this, I sold all the cloves—that is to say the edible ones:[2] there were equivalent to 82 quintals using the Maluku weight,[3] and other wares that I had brought from Manila. In total these commodities sold for 9,000 ducats.[4] I once again invested the money in printed fabrics with a view of going to the kingdom of Patani. After I had purchased these wares I embarked aboard a Muslim junk[5] that was going to the city of Patani. I could not have chosen a worse voyage in terms of it being filled with misfortunes, even had I wished to do

---

1 Ms. fol. 63 recto–68 verso.

2 Translator's note: The word *clavo* in Spanish can mean either 'clove' or 'nail', just as is the case with word 'nagel' in Dutch.

3 About 3,772–4,838 kilograms.

4 About 31.5 kilograms of mint-grade gold.

5 Ms. *junco de moros*.

so deliberately, since it was fraught with risks and woes. A nephew of the bishop of Melaka[6] and another Portuguese, who had been born in Melaka named Domingos Gonçalves, and some native Christians[7] also sailed on the same junk. We set sail from the port [and] a few days later we arrived at the Strait of Singapore.[8] In this strait we came across the carracks[9] that had set sail from Melaka before us and were on their way to China, they were waiting for a favourable current to sail through the strait. We anchored near them at the mouth of the Old Strait [of Singapore].[10] In the meanwhile, a galliot[11] that was coming from Patani passed by. There was a clergyman aboard this vessel, who was the owner and was named Pero Vaz. He and one of his companions warned us that there were four Dutch carracks in Patani. He also warned the carracks that were sailing to China to proceed cautiously and likewise told us that the Dutch had allowed them to pass in peace and that they were not harming anyone. With this news we reached the Pahang [River] estuary. Six indigenous Christians from Melaka disembarked and apprehensively went ashore; we continued on our journey.

We arrived at Patani; we saw that there were four Dutch carracks anchored in the port. We entered between them, they only asked us from whence we had come. I replied: "From Melaka". We anchored close to the shore. I and Júlio de Barros—that was the name of the bishop's nephew —disembarked; we rented some accommodations. Shortly thereafter a Portuguese man who was a casado in Melaka visited us—his name was António de Saldanha[12]— along with two indigenous Christians from Melaka. We immediately went to hand over a letter that the captain of Melaka[13] had sent to [Raja Hijau], along with a gift of four pieces of fine *cassas* and *beatilhas*;[14] the people present on this occasion were myself and Júlio de Barros. She spoke to us from a distance while seated behind a

---

[6] He is subsequently identified as Júlio de Barros.

[7] Ms. *christianos naturales de la tierra.*

[8] Ms. *Estrecho de Cincapura.*

[9] Ms. here and subsequently: *naos.*

[10] Ms. *Estrecho Viejo.* The carracks were anchored off the western tip of Sentosa at present-day Fort Siloso. They were waiting for the currents to carry them through the Old Strait of Singapore. See also the list of place names (*Estrecho Viejo, Ysla de Arena*).

[11] Ms. *galeota.* See the glossary (*galliot*).

[12] Ms. here and subsequently: *Saldaña.*

[13] The captain-major (*capitão-mór*) of Melaka. He is subsequently identified by De Coutre as Francisco de Silva de Meneses. See also the glossary (*capitão-mór*).

[14] See the glossary for these two types of textiles (*cassa, beatilha*).

Chinese-style reed curtain.[15] However, we were able to see her clearly, along with one of her sisters. She was very pleased to receive the letter, in which the captain had requested her to send many junks to Melaka laden with rice and provisions and had expressed his wish to forge close and friendly ties as before. She immediately ordered junks from her land to be sent to Melaka with provisions and gave instructions that we were to be gifted four cows,[16] many chickens, rice and fruit. I had also been given orders by the captain and factor of Melaka to speak on behalf of His[17] Majesty to other *rajas*[18]—who are lords and [also] vassals of the queen—and to merchants so that they likewise sent provisions to the said city of Melaka.

The arrival of the Queen of Patani during the visit of Admiral Jacob van Neck in Patani, 1602. From Theodore de Bry, *Icones seu Gennuinae et Expressae Delineationes Omnium Memorabilium* (Images or Authentic and Accurate Depiction of all Memorable Events), Frankfurt am Main, 1607. (Leiden, Bibliotheca Thysiana, THYS 874, pl. 4).

---

[15] Ms. *estera de la China.*

[16] Ms. *bacas*. This is probably a reference to (water) buffaloes (*kerbau*).

[17] Ms. *Su.*

[18] Ms. *rayas.*

We came to know that the general[19] of the four Dutch carracks that were there had not been issued orders to fight against the Portuguese even though he had fought in the Malukus against the fortress of Tidore, which belonged to the Portuguese. He had fought to see whether he could recover a patache[20] that a Portuguese man named João[21] Pinto de Morais had taken from him by means of deception and treachery, [and] which had been anchored under the walls of Tidore.[22] When he was unable to recover [the patache] and after having lost many men and his right hand to a bullet wound[23] he withdrew and went to China, to go to Pinal[24]—a port in China—from there. When he arrived at the port of Macao (since he was unfamiliar with the area he thought that it was the port of Pinal)[25] he sent out a reconnaissance team with a *lancha*[26] and his factor,[27] who was called Martin Apius.[28] They went near the shore. Upon going around a tip of land they came across many Portuguese bearing weapons on the beach. When they realised that it was not the right territory[29] and wanted to return to their carracks, the Portuguese called them over, waving a white flag. As they saw the sign of peace, they went ashore and disembarked. The Portuguese received them and hanged them all,[30] leaving only the factor [Apius] alive.[31] This was the reason why Jacob van Neck[32]—that was the name of the Dutch

[19] Ms. here and subsequently: *general.*

[20] A type of sailing vessel. See also the glossary (*patache*).

[21] Ms. *Joan.*

[22] This likely refers to the capture of the pinnace *Trouw*. See Jan Parmentier, Karel Davids and John Everaert, *Peper Plancius en Porselein* (Zutphen: Walburg Pers, 2003), p. 58.

[23] See also Van Foreest and De Booy, ed., *De Vierde Schipvaart*, I, p. 99, where it is reported that Van Neck had lost most of his right hand to a "flying piece of iron"; also Blussé, "Brief Encounter at Macao": 651, "Van Neck had lost several fingers" in a skirmish with the Portuguese in Tidore.

[24] Pinal or El Pinal, a Spanish "port" in China. See also the list of place names (*Pinal*).

[25] Brackets added for clarification.

[26] Ms. here and subsequently *lancha*. A type of vessel. See also the glossary (*lanchara*).

[27] Ms. here and subsequently: *fiscal.* A type of officer dealing with issues of procurement on VOC ships and in factories. See also the glossary (*factor, fiscaal*).

[28] Ms. *Hac.* See P.A. Tiele, "Verklaring van Martinus Apius van hetgeen hem en zijne medegevangenen van de vloot van Jacob van Neck in 1602 te Macao is overkomen" in "Documenten voor de Geschiednis der Nederlanders in het Oosten", *BMH* 6 (1883): 228–42; another copy in Van Foreest and De Booy, ed., *De Vierde Schipvaart*, II, appendix 54, pp. 279–90.

[29] Ms. *que la tierra no era suya.*

[30] This is incorrect. Six mates were hung and eleven were killed by drowning.

[31] This is again technically incorrect. Apius was taken to Goa together with two of the ship's boys. The latter were probably spared because they were very young or under age.

[32] Ms. *Jaquez van Hec.*

The landing of Admiral Jacob van Neck at Patani in 1602. From Theodore de Bry, *Icones seu Gennuinae et Expressae Delineationes Omnium Memorabilium* (Images or Authentic and Accurate Depiction of all Memorable Events), Frankfurt am Main, 1607. (Leiden, Bibliotheca Thysiana, THYS 874, pl. 11).

general—was outraged that the Portuguese had committed such an injustice under the flag of peace.[33]

As the general was a well-intentioned man despite what had happened, he did not in any way harm the Portuguese even though he had the opportunity to do so, and he came to that port of Patani to load pepper, even though no pepper grows around Patani.[34] They convey pepper from Indragiri[35] and Jambi[36] to Patani where it is loaded on to Dutch carracks. I, Júlio de Barros and some other Portuguese approached the general and I apologised on behalf of the Portuguese, saying that the viceroy of India was very upset that the Portuguese in Macao had hung those men under the

[33] Concerning this episode, see also SMS, pp. 71, 76 and GPFT, p. 114.

[34] Ms. lit. there is no pepper in Patani. The translation above derives from the explanation that follows.

[35] Ms. *Andregiri*. In eastern Sumatra. See also the list of place names (*Amdreguiri*).

[36] Ms. *Jamba*. In eastern Sumatra. See also the list of place names (*Jambo*).

flag of peace and that he had ordered the magistrate of the city of Macao to be arrested and brought to him in fetters in order to behead him—we feigned all this so as to soothe the general's feelings.[37] [He] replied saying: "If any one of the 30 men who were aboard the lancha deserved to be hanged it was the factor, because the other poor men who went with him embarked on their carracks without knowing where they were going." Despite all this the general was always very hospitable to us whenever we boarded his carracks to buy crimson cloth[38] and fabrics in other colours, which he had brought in large quantities. On one occasion he asked Júlio de Barros, some other Portuguese and myself to dine with him. He gave us a magnificent banquet accompanied throughout by the music of trumpets and bugles, served in the presence of all the officials of his squadron. He then took us around his carrack and showed us how it was equipped.[39] It had 36 pieces of bronze artillery and 14 pedreros,[40] all arrayed in two rows, and 300 men. He said that he had set out from his homeland with 400 men. At the end he bid us farewell with a great salvo of artillery.

I then took steps to return to Melaka. To this end I sold everything that I had taken there and I bought a junk from António de Saldanha. I had it loaded entirely at my cost with rice and lead as ballast. After eight days another general—who was called Jacob van Heemskerck[41]—entered the port, with two carracks and a patache. This general had captured one of the carracks in the port of Arosbaya,[42] laden with sandalwood—which is an aromatic wood—along with six Portuguese and many sailors. Van Heemskerck[43] came to know personally from Jacob van Neck[44] how the Portuguese had hanged those 30 Dutchmen in Macao. He took the news very badly and wanted to

---

[37] De Coutre's role in conveying this story is confirmed in the "Journaal van Jacob van Neck" in Van Foreest and De Booy, ed., *De Vierde Schipvaart*, I, p. 221. According to W.Ph. Coolhaas, "Een bron van het historische gedeelte van Hugo de Groots De Jure Praedae", *BMH* 79 (1965): 533, note 4, one João Rui do Couto was indeed tried for his role in executing the Dutch sailors at Macao. Concerning De Coutre's lie, see also Blussé, "Brief Encounter at Macao": 662–3.

[38] Ms. *paños de grana*.

[39] The name of Van Neck's flagship was the *Mauritius*, evidently named after Stadholder Prince Maurice of Nassau.

[40] Ms. *pedreras*. A type of artillery piece. See also the glossary (*pedrero*).

[41] Ms. here and subsequently: *Jaquez de Emisquerquen*.

[42] Ms. *Arisbaya*. AA, p. 177, erroneously identified this port as Surabaya. See also the list of place names (*Arisbaia*).

[43] Ms. *Emisquerquen*.

[44] Ms. *Van Hec*.

hang the six Portuguese prisoners that he had brought with him in revenge. Since he seemed set on this [course of action] one of his shipmasters came to warn me of this. Júlio de Barros and I went to speak to Jacob van Neck and we insistently beseeched him to take pity on those poor Portuguese and to ask General Van Heemskerck not to hang them, because those poor men were not to be blame for the incident at Macao. I told him that they were poor men, some of whom were casados in China and others in Melaka, and that they had children. There was no reason to take their lives since they had already suffered the misfortune of losing their liberty and their properties. In effect, I divulged to him a lot of other things, imploring him to be compassionate and likewise asking him to have them released.

Jacob van Neck immediately went to speak to Van Heemskerck and did not wish to give his consent for the Portuguese to be hung. In the end they spared their lives, however, they did not want to release the six Portuguese, but only the Christians from Melaka, who were sailors. Soon after Jacob van Neck had accomplished this good deed his carracks were fully laden with pepper. He departed three days later. Van Heemskerck stayed behind with his ships and a patache. I asked him many times to release the six Portuguese; he never agreed to do so, thinking that there could be some Dutch prisoners in Melaka for whom he could exchange them. He told the Portuguese to write to Melaka concerning this matter and he gave me permission to go aboard his carracks to speak to the prisoners. However, I never wanted to do so because I did not trust him, since he had asked me on many occasions whether I would like to sail with him aboard his ship.

The time for my departure drew ever closer because my junk was already loaded and was anchored outside, near General [Van Heemskerck's] carracks, so that I could leave from there at dawn. I still needed a quantity of rice to finish the loading. I went to buy rice from a junk owned by Malays, who had arrived there from the kingdom of Siam. While I was buying the rice two lanchas full of Dutchmen also came aboard looking for rice that they wanted to buy for themselves. Three *commiesen*[45]—who are similar to factors—had come aboard the lanchas; they asked me if I wanted to go aboard their carracks to talk to the prisoners. I replied in the affirmative, keeping a straight face.[46] I got into their lancha. We arrived at the flagship

[45] Ms. here and subsequently: *comizes*. See the glossary (*commies*).

[46] Ms. *haziendo de ladron fiel*.

carrack.[47] The shipmaster asked the *commiesen*: "How has this man come here?" They replied: "With the general's permission"—and it was a lie; I had been given the permission over a month ago. I went aboard the carrack; they received me very amicably. I made them bring the three Portuguese who were there up onto the deck; they were brought up shackled to each other with iron manacles on their hands. I asked the shipmaster why they were being treated in that manner. He replied: "Two of them had tried to escape; one of them discovered their plans and hence we are holding them in that fashion so that they do not make a mockery[48] of the Dutch." I asked him to issue instructions to free their hands; he did so immediately. The prisoners were very grateful for this good deed. I bid them farewell and went to the captain's ship,[49] accompanied by the shipmaster and the *commiesen*, so as to speak with the other three Portuguese, who were being held prisoner in the same manner. I also made them remove their shackles here and had them brought to the carrack's cabin. They invited us[50] to eat; we all sat down at the table: the prisoners, myself, the shipmaster, the *commiesen* and other officers from the carrack. During this occasion the general and the admiral were on land. One of the prisoners was seated beside me, who, while eating, handed me a note under the table. So that nobody would notice what I was doing, I lifted my handkerchief nonchalantly, as though I was wiping my mouth. I wrapped it around the note and put it into a pocket inside my clothes. The man who gave me the note was named Filipe Lobo.[51] Once we had finished eating I bid all of them farewell and I returned ashore aboard my own lancha. As soon as I reached the beach I came across the general and the admiral, seated near a wooden hut that the general had ordered be built at the edge of the sea to serve as a factory[52] for Flanders,[53] surrounded by water with a drawbridge. They asked me where I was coming from; I replied that I had come from their carracks. When they heard this, their demeanour changed and they were upset because

[47] Ms. *nao almiranta*. The flagship was named *Witte Leeuw* (White Lion).
[48] Ms. *serian*. This appears to be a corruption of *se rían* (they laughed).
[49] Ms. *capitania*.
[50] Ms. *combidaranos*. This appears to be a corruption of *convidáronnos* (they invited us).
[51] Ms. *Felippe Lobo*. This could very well be the same Filipe Lobo mentioned in the letter of Fernão de Albuquerque to Jacob van Heemskerck of March 1603 printed as appendix IV.
[52] A (fortified) warehouse and procurement centre. See also the glossary (*factor*).
[53] Ms. *Flandes*. Read as a Dutch factory.

I had gone to the carracks without informing them, so that they could have extended me even greater hospitality—this was all feigned; they wished to catch me aboard their carracks to hold me prisoner just like they were holding the six Portuguese. I bid them farewell, thanking them for their goodwill. I then went home.[54] I came across my companion Júlio de Barros. I told him: "Let us take a look at this paper that the prisoners gave me", and I described the day's events to him.

The paper stated: "We have received the alms that Your Graces[55] have sent to us; for the love of God. We warn Your Graces that the Dutch and the patache of this squadron are ready to catch Your Graces with your junk as soon as you set sail from the port and they will not spare any of your lives., etc." After reading this warning note I went to the junk and brought it back to where it used to be anchored and moored it even closer to shore. The Christians who had been released by the general had embarked aboard my junk; when they came to know the reason why I had brought the junk back, all of them disembarked that very night, leaving me alone with my slaves. Seeing that I would not be able to defend it by myself in case something untoward happened that night I, too, went to sleep on the shore. I left the junk laden as it was, guarded by just four slaves. When night fell the Dutch came and drilled holes in the prow and the stern. The junk began to fill with water. When the slaves awoke it was already midnight and the junk had almost entirely sunk. One of them came to warn me; I immediately went to see whether I could fix it. When I arrived, the junk was wholly filled with water and had settled onto the bottom of the sea with the low tide. I could only stand there watching it helplessly in impotent fury without being able to salvage anything. The sea began to rise and the junk capsized. At that place I once again lost everything I possessed and whatever I had managed to earn in Manila.

[54] Ms. *a casa*, that is back to the lodgings in Patani.

[55] Ms. lit. Your Graces. The plural is often used in Spanish as a polite form. It is insufficiently clear whether the alms were from one or both individuals, De Coutre and De Barros.

CHAPTER

XVIII

The story continues and how the natives[1] of Patani tried to kill me on the orders of the [Dutch] general; and how they killed António de Saldanha; the reason why and the manner in which they did so. How the Muslims on the junk also tried to kill me during the voyage when I was returning to Melaka[2]

The following night eight men entered the house of António de Saldanha—who had sold me the junk—and they killed him.[3] The same men also went to my house on that same night. As they sensed that I was not asleep and was on my guard and accompanied by some Japanese[4] they did not dare to attack me. They went away to get reinforcements. At this point a heathen woman who I knew came to warn me about how the said men had come to kill me, and since they had not dared to do so they had gone to fetch more men. She took me to her house saying that

---

[1] Ms. *los naturales*.

[2] Ms. fol. 68 verso–72 verso.

[3] This incident is also reported by Jan Pauwelsz., a vice-admiral in the fleet of Van Heemskerck. Van Foreest and De Booy, ed., *De Vierde Schipvaart*, II, p. 311. Without mentioning his name, it is reported that the principal Portuguese in Patani was murdered in his home the previous night, and that all of his goods had been taken.

[4] This is possibly a reference to Japanese (samurai) mercenaries who were commonly hired by both Southeast Asian rulers and Europeans, especially by the Portuguese.

I would be safer there. I went and I made her call all her relatives, who were gentlemen, captains of junks and ships, very well-known people. All their retainers[5] gathered together with arms to defend the house, which was walled all around; and we were some 50 men inside and this was how Cik Tangan[6]—that was the name[7] of that good woman—saved my life that night. She was a very well-known woman in that kingdom and had a lot of influence with [Raja Hijau] in the palace. I later learned that the reason why they had killed António de Saldanha and why they had wanted to kill me on that same night was because Saldanha had advised the governor[8] of the kingdom—in private without the knowledge of the queen who was ruling at the time since there was no king—that he should capture the Dutch carracks, that is the carracks commanded by Van Heemskerck.[9] De Saldanha had indicated to [the governor] a plan and the way he should go about it, telling him that if he did so, then it would result in a firm friendship[10] with the king of Portugal. However, since the governor was on much friendlier terms with the Dutch as a result of the gifts that they used to give him, and because they would buy pepper according to his terms, when he was with General Van Heemskerck during a visit, he informed him about everything that António de Saldanha had advised him to do, in order to strengthen his friendship with the Dutch.

As soon as he learnt of this, the general swore that he would kill António de Saldanha, all the Portuguese and me. At this stage the governor said that he would take care of the matter on his behalf and that he would kill us all in secret, because if we were killed in public it would break the peace with the Portuguese and that there were many junks in the port that were going to set sail for Melaka. They decided that they would kill us all on a single night but they were only able to execute their plan on António de Saldanha because they caught him offguard.[11]

---

[5] Ms. *criados.*

[6] Ms. here and subsequently: *Enchetangan.* See the glossary (*Enchetangan*).

[7] An honorific, not a name. See also the glossary (*Enchetangan*).

[8] Ms. *governador.* In this context probably here and subsequently the *bendahara.* See also the glossary (*bendahara*).

[9] Ms. *Emisquerquen.* Jan Pauwelsz. appears to substantiate this claim in stating that the Portuguese offered for every Dutchman captured one *kati* of gold. See Van Foreest and De Booy, ed., *De Vierde Schipvaart,* II, p. 311.

[10] Ms. *mui amigo.*

[11] Ms. *desprevenido.*

Printed portrait of Admiral Jacob van Heemskerck taken from the 1647 edition of Emanuel van Meteren's *Commentariën ofte Memoriën* (Commentaries or Memoirs). (The Hague, KB, 1790 A 122).

General [Van Heemskerck] always suspected that I had advised Saldanha and had indicated the plan to him and [in his eyes] this was confirmed when I visited his carracks and had brought my junk [closer to shore]. This was also the reason why he had ordered that my junk be sunk and why he wanted to kill me. The following day Júlio de Barros went to inform the general that neither he nor I had advised Saldanha. He stated this in such a way that he made him believe that this was indeed the truth. A few days later I came across the general and he told me that he had been given erroneous information, expressing his remorse at having given orders to sink my junk. He tried to persuade me to go with him to the ship outfitters, [saying] that he would recompensate me for my junk and my properties according to the orders that I placed with the outfitters, and that he would make me a captain, and countless other nonsensical bits, all in a similar vein. To all of this I answered that I was not interested, that I was a casado[12] in the city of Goa, and that I had been raised amongst the Portuguese and that God would provide me with new properties. With these and other words I bid him farewell.

Júlio de Barros and I decided to return to Melaka aboard Muslim junks.[13] We did not dare to do so without the permission of the general,[14] because he used to inspect all the junks that entered and left the port. Júlio de Barros—who was on friendlier terms with him than I was—went to ask him for permission. They gave us permission on the condition that we were to pay 100 *escudos* towards his soldiers' drinks.[15] After we paid, Júlio de Barros went aboard a Muslim junk on which he had loaded his goods; I went aboard another, which was captained by a Muslim called Nakhoda[16] Quevasse, a relative of the same woman who had saved my life. We set sail from Patani that night. After having sailed for many days we reached Pulau Redang,[17] an island, where, since it was very peaceful, I went ashore with two of my slaves to take a bath in a beautiful stream that could be found on that island. Later, when returning, while climbing up a hill I came across a very old kalambak tree[18] that was rotten on the outside but the branches were good and of a large size. I wanted to remove them out of curiosity.[19] While I was starting to do this the slaves called out to me loudly that they were in the batel.[20] I left the kalambak[21] tree and returned to the batel; I saw that the Muslims were sailing away in the junk and that they had wanted to abandon me on the island, which was uninhabited. I got aboard the batel in water up to my chest; I then managed to reach the

---

[12] A married settler. See also the glossary (*casado*).

[13] Ms. *en jucos de moros.*

[14] Of Van Heemskerck, as he might decide to despoil them outside the port.

[15] It is not certain whether De Coutre had the Portuguese or the Spanish escudo in mind. If the former, it is equivalent to about 357 grams of mint-grade gold; if the latter about 5.4 kilograms of coin-grade silver.

[16] Ms. *Nuqueda.* A captain of a vessel. See also the glossary (*nakhoda*).

[17] Ms. here and subsequently: *Pula Ruyden.* See the list of place names (*Pula Reiden*).

[18] Ms. *arbor de clambuco.* A tree that yields odoriferous wood. See also the glossary (*kalambak, gaharu*).

[19] De Coutre was evidently inspecting the dead branches to see whether any of them contained the odoriferous resin.

[20] A small craft. See also the glossary (*batel*).

[21] Ms. *el clambuco.* See the glossary (*aloes, eaglewood, kalambak*).

junk, which was already on its way with its sail fully raised and billowing in the wind. All the merchants and sailors went to tell the captain that they did not wish to go to Melaka unless he killed me and my slaves first. They were all at the ready with their krisses at their belts to carry out their desire, as soon as the captain gave the order. As the captain was my friend and a relative of the aforesaid woman, who had taken me under her wing. When he saw these men so determined and full of resolve, he turned to me and asked them: "Why do you want to kill this man; what harm has he done to you?" The barbarians answered: "Because our people in Patani killed António de Saldanha [and] he will transmit this information in Melaka to the captain,[22] who will then wish to take revenge on us and will deprive us of our lives and properties. If we kill this man and his slaves now he will not come to know of the incident." To this the captain responded: "But what do we know about that death? This man will say no such thing because he is a very good man."

In the end they conferred and decided to invite me to share a meal with them to see what I had to say and [decided that] they could kill me on that occasion depending on what I said. I listened to this entire conversation because I could understand the language. They invited me to eat; at first I did not wish to go. They called me again; since I could not refuse them I put a kris into my breeches. The slaves began to cry, since they thought that they were taking me away to be killed—and they were not wrong—likewise they were also fearful of losing their own lives.[23] In effect, I sat down at the table where the captain was seated, while all the others sat around [it]. They put my slaves near me so that they could serve as interpreters, since they thought that I could not understand their language. They placed a large porcelain dish full of rice on the table along with many cooked chickens. Before we began to eat the captain started to reason things out, telling me: "Now, we can have a safe journey, because we have left the island of Pulau Redang behind us. What will you [all] say in Melaka about the death of António de Saldanha?" Pretending to be oblivious about what I knew, I answered him thus: "Well, what is there to say? Don't you know that António de Saldanha was a drunkard? And that he left the doors to his house open one night, through which entered some thieves, and they killed him in order to rob

---

[22] Ms. *al capitan.*

[23] Ms. *temiendo tambien la muerte.*

him? Aren't there thieves everywhere in the world? If the captain of Melaka asks me, I will tell him how he was drunk and that some thieves killed him in order to rob him. Aren't you all witnesses to the fact that this was what really happened? Won't you all say the same thing if the captain asks you what happened?" They all then responded in the affirmative in a single voice, obviously feeling very happy with what I had just said, and the captain was even more satisfied on account of my answer. They all happily told me to eat, but I could not swallow a single morsel because I was so worried that they would kill me. Concealing my anxiety as much as I could, I ate something, so that they would not notice my fear. After I got up from the table the captain told the others: "Well, didn't I tell you that this man had good intentions?" and the others were very satisfied.

With these perils[24] that endangered my life we reached the Old Strait of Singapore[25] and as soon as we drew up to the Johor River estuary[26] we saw an armada from Melaka, whose captain-major was Francisco de Silva de Meneses.[27] When the Muslims aboard the junk spotted the armada they did not wish to go to Melaka—and they were lucky not to go. They went into the Johor River, telling me that they wanted to cut some trees in the city of Johor Lama,[28] which was in the vicinity, near the estuary. After entering, they sailed upstream along the river to the city of New Johor,[29] which the natives called Batu Sawar[30] where the court of their king was located. They all disembarked, telling me that they did not wish to go to Melaka. I, too, disembarked so as to go from there to Melaka aboard another ship.

[24] Ms. *riesgos.*
[25] Ms. *Estrecho Viejo de Sincapura.*
[26] Ms. *barra de Jor.*
[27] Ms. *Menezes.*
[28] Ms. *Jor Viejo.*
[29] Ms. *Jor Nuevo.*
[30] Ms. *Batalavar.*

CHAPTER
XIX

Why the king of Johor[1] gave orders to kill some 50 Portuguese and many other native Christians from Melaka, from amongst whom two of my slaves and I escaped. A description of the same journey until I reached Melaka[2]

When I disembarked I came across my companion Júlio de Barros and in the city there were some 50 or more Portuguese and many native Christians from Melaka, who told me that the monarch of that kingdom of Johor was very angry ever since the captain-major, Francisco de Silva de Meneses,[3] had seized a junk belonging to the king and had killed an ambassador that he had sent to the king of Perak,[4] his brother-in-law, and everyone who was accompanying the said ambassador. The king had ordered that the captain be asked why he had committed that aggression. The answer was sent two days later; [De Silva de Meneses] replied that His Highness had been misinformed and that he had not done any such thing. With this answer the king and the people calmed down and the following day, the captain-major sent seven or eight women and some barrel guns[5]

[1] Ala'uddin Ri'ayat Shah III.

[2] Ms. fol. 72 verso–76 recto.

[3] Ms. *Menezes*.

[4] Ms. *Pera*. The monarch in question was Ala'uddin Shah Ibni Almarham Raja Kecil Lasa Inu. See also the list of place names (*Pera*).

[5] Ms. *escopetas*.

and some krisses[6] with another message, saying that he had inspected his armada and had found those women and the weapons that he was sending therewith to him—and they had been brought by a captain called Pantaleão Carneiro.[7] They must have been from the missing junk and, he would severely punish the captains who had been accomplices. With the arrival of the women, the people and King [Ala'uddin Ri'ayat Shah III] once again became agitated, so much so that they wanted to kill all the Christians there, saying that the armada had seized all the baxeles[8] that had set sail from that port [Batu Sawar]; and that was why they had not received any news from these [vessels].[9] Upon hearing the noisy commotion, the king's mother emerged and managed to calm the king and the people's wrath, because the captain-major [of the armada, Francisco de Silva de Meneses], had sent a message saying that he guaranteed that henceforth there would not be any more disturbances.

A few days later two Johorese vessels arrived from the kingdom of Pahang.[10] The captain-major issued instructions that they were to be seized and that all the people who were sailing aboard them were to be kept in the holds[11] of his ships. The king and the people became so upset that they apprehended all the Portuguese and the Christians from Melaka who were present in the city and took them to the house of the *shahbandar*[12]—that was what the highest official of justice was called. As soon as I saw this turmoil I went to the house of a Muslim who was a native of Melaka and was the [official] state interpreter for the captain of Melaka who was [in Batu Sawar] at the time as an ambassador—his name was Khoja Ibrahim.[13] He was entrusted with negotiations to unite the armadas of the king of Johor and the Portuguese so as to capture the kingdom of Aceh, since this was something that the king of Johor ardently desired.

---

[6] A Malay dagger. See also the glossary (*keris*).

[7] Ms. *Pantalian Carnero*. This is possibly the same Portuguese named Pantaleão Carneiro, a resident of Manila, who had been a subordinate of Veloso and who was involved in the hearings against the King of Champa in 1593 and accompanied the embassy of King Sâtha of Cambodia to Manila. See Briggs, "Spanish Intervention", pp. 137, 148; also Subrahmanyam, "Manila, Melaka, Mylapore": 234, who claims that Pantaleão Carneiro was a native Portuguese from Lisbon.

[8] A type of vessel. See also the glossary (*baxel*).

[9] Ms. *delles*.

[10] Ms. *Pam*.

[11] Ms. *bombas*.

[12] Ms. *xabandar*.

[13] Ms. *Coya Abraham*.

The king's fleet was making the necessary preparations while the armada commanded by Francisco de Silva [de Meneses] was sailing along the coast creating the aforementioned disturbances. I arrived at the house of Ambassador [Khoja Ibrahim], who lived half a legua[14] away from the city; he was extremely happy to see me. At that time he was conversing with two heathen merchants from Melaka, one of whom was called Nina Gadin[15] and the other was called Nina Aure,[16] about dispatching them to Melaka with a letter for the captain [of Melaka, Fernão de Albuquerque] and letters of complaints about the captain-major of the armada. I told him to send me instead with the letters because in Melaka they would give me more credence than the heathens. He agreed with what I said [and] he wrote the letter immediately. Once the letter had been written, we all went to speak to the king's brother, who was called Raja Bongsu.[17] The ambassador told him how he wished to send me to Melaka and I gifted him some boxes and some glass items imploring him to ask his brother, the king, to give me permission to leave. He promised to do so and was very happy to have received the glass items. He bid me farewell saying that we should wait for him at the king's residence. When I had made it half way there,[18] I was surrounded by many men and they apprehended me and took me to where the other Portuguese and the native, Melaka-born Christians[19] were being held. I was very annoyed with myself because I was fully aware of the fury of those people. I entrusted my soul to God, preparing myself to die along with the others. It is important to note that six or seven days before I was imprisoned, I had adopted the habit of taking a walk along the bank of the [Johor River] every night from eight o'clock to nine o'clock; and on each night I used to hear a voice as though it was emanating from one of the many ships belonging to the local people of that land, which were moored along the river [bank]. The voice used to call out loudly to me in the Flemish language: "Compatriot, go on, go with God [away] from here"; this has left me astounded because I did not know of any Fleming or Dutchman

---

[14] About one kilometre.

[15] The title Nina is an honorific.

[16] Judging by the title they appear to be Tamil merchants from southern India.

[17] Ms. *Raya Bonso*. Raja Bongsu is in fact the younger half-sibling of the ruling monarch, Ala'uddin Ri'ayat Shah III of Johor. See also the glossary (*Raja Bongsu*) and SMS, pp. 112–5.

[18] Ms. *llegue a la mitad del camino*.

[19] Ms. *christianos naturales de Malaca*.

in that place. Nor could I believe that such a person could be there on that occasion. Finally, when I heard this voice I always answered in my [native] Flemish language that this person should tell me where he was, that I would speak with him, and I asked him who he was. He never answered me, he only told me to leave that place. This never ceased to amaze me. What I imagine even today is that it must have been one of the Dutchmen from amongst those who I had met in the kingdom of Patani, who must have been aboard one of those ships, or an angel that was warning me, because I heard these voices [for] six or seven nights; not just once but on many occasions; not in one place but everywhere. I would hear it when I was walking downstream as well as upstream, in such a manner that the voice put me on my guard and made me wary that some very great misfortune was about to befall me. Finally, on the orders of the king, they took my companion Júlio de Barros and me out of prison. The king gave a letter to Júlio de Barros to take to the captain-major [Francisco de Silva de Meneses]. In the letter the king said that if [the captain major] released the people from those two junks that he had seized, with all their belongings[20] and everything, then he would also release all the Christians whom he was holding prisoner along with their belongings; and that if [the captain-major][21] released the people from the junks without their belongings then he would do the same thing with the Christians.[22]

[The king] dismissed me—since I did not have any properties—with another letter for the captain of Melaka [Fernão de Albuquerque]; and Khoja Ibrahim[23]—that was the name of the ambassador—gave me another letter and told me to go in the company of the aforesaid two heathen merchants [Nina Aure and Nina Gadin]. I ordered my two slaves to be brought[24] to me and I set out immediately without bidding any farewells to those who were being held prisoner, because there was no more time to do anything.[25] The following day at three o'clock in the afternoon I went

[20] Ms. here and subsequently: *haziendas.*

[21] Ms. lit. he.

[22] The same or a closely related hostage crisis is mentioned in the letter of Fernão de Albuquerque to Van Heemskerck of March 1603 and published in this volume as appendix IV.

[23] Ms. here and subsequently: *Coyabram.*

[24] Ms. *vir.* This is probably a copying error and should read *venir.*

[25] Ms. *no havia lugar para mas.*

near the estuary. I anchored off the coast of the city of Johor Lama[26] and I came across Júlio de Barros, who was returning with the captain-major's reply and he was bringing an ailing Castilian with him. He told me to wait for him until morning and that he would return in his junk, which was already loaded and had been impounded by the king. I also came across a bantin[27] from the fleet that had brought three Portuguese merchants from Melaka with their goods, to deliver them ashore. I warned them about what was happening and told them that they should not proceed to [Batu Sawar] before gathering some information of what was going on there. Then one of the three merchants, seeing that the captain of the bantin did not wish to go to the city, persuaded his other two companions to disembark there in Johor Lama with their merchandise, saying that the king was a coward[28] and that he would not dare to molest them. In effect, the captain of the bantin left all three of them along with their retainers and goods ashore. After they had disembarked, the bantin moved away from the shore to return to the armada. At that very moment, I swear,[29] the natives[30] jumped on them and killed them, and seized their goods. As soon as Júlio de Barros handed over the reply of Captain-Major [De Silva de Meneses] to the king [of Johor]—as was to be expected—the king[31] immediately ordered that he be killed, along with all the Portuguese and Christians who were being held prisoner; in total they would have numbered some 150 persons. [The Johorese] had already tied Khoja Ibrahim's hands together in order to kill him, however, since he was a Muslim,[32] the king spared his life. If I had been there I would undoubtedly have perished with all the others. When Júlio de Barros told me to wait for him I did not wish to do so. I sailed out of the river proffering heartfelt thanks to Our Lord, who, from amongst all the many people who were being held captive, He saved just myself and two Christian slaves of mine.

Another incident simultaneously happened during this time after our armada had withdrawn to Melaka owing to the deaths that had

---

[26] Ms. *Jor Viejo*.

[27] A type of vessel. See also the glossary (*bantin*).

[28] Ms. *cuitado*.

[29] Ms. *a nuestra vida*.

[30] Ms. *los naturales*.

[31] Ms. lit. he.

[32] Ms. *moro*.

taken place in Johor. In front of the Johor River, the Dutch captured a carrack[33] that was coming from China, which was importing more than two million in gold.[34] The owner of the carrack was Baltasar Serrão.[35] They captured some 500 Christian people along with this carrack—it was said that the king of Johor had warned the Dutch how the [Portuguese] fleet had withdrawn and that the carrack would have to pass through there—in order to take revenge on the Portuguese. I arrived in Melaka and handed over the letters that the king of Johor had given me, along with the letters that the ambassador had sent, to the captain, Fernão de Albuquerque.

---

[33] Ms. *nao*.

[34] Ms. *dos millones de oro*. This is a reference to the seizure of the *Santa Catarina* off Singapore on 25 February 1603. See esp. SMS, pp. 68–75. See also the glossary (*conto de oro*).

[35] Ms. *Baltazar Seran*. In other sources, including his letter to Van Heemskerck written after the seizure of the *Santa Catarina*, he signs his name as Sebastião (Sebastian). See SMS, pp. 75–7, and GPFT, p. 129.

CHAPTER

XX

The vast commerce that used to exist in the city of Melaka at the time when I lived there, and how I returned to India from the South[1] and married in the city of Goa in the year 1603[2]

After I returned from Johor, I took steps to go to the city of Goa to wed, even though I was without a penny in my pocket[3] since I had lost all my goods[4] in Patani, which I had striven so hard to earn, and despite the fact that I was exhausted on account of the many journeys I had made. During the period when I resided in the city of Melaka, apart from the aforesaid [territories] I went to the kingdoms of Indragiri,[5] Jambi,[6] Pariaman,[7] Palembang[8] and those of Siak[9] and Kampar,[10] which are all located on the inside of the Strait of Kundur[11] on the island of Sumatra. In fact,[12] I set sail aboard a patache owned by Álvaro Mendes. However, in this

---

[1] Ms. *sur.* Here broadly used in the sense of Southeast Asia.

[2] Ms. fol. 76 recto–80 recto.

[3] Ms. *un real por haver.*

[4] Ms. *hasienda.*

[5] Ms. here and subsequently: *Andreguiri* or variant spelling.

[6] Ms. here and subsequently: *Jamba.*

[7] Ms. *Priman.* See the list of place names (*Priman*).

[8] Ms. *Pelimbran.* See the list of place names (*Pelibam*).

[9] Ms. here and subsequently: *Çiaca* or variant spelling. See the list of place names (*Siaca*).

[10] See the list of place names (*Canpar*).

[11] Ms. *Estrecho de Saban.* See the list of place names (*Estrecho de Saban*).

[12] Ms. *En effecto.*

context, before describing the events that occurred during my voyage, I will mention the vast trade that used to take place in the city of Melaka during the time when I lived there.

It is important to note that in the past, before the Portuguese captured Melaka, it was a very big city with an equally large population. It was the governing centre[13] of the Malay empire and was where those emperors maintained their court, whose successors are the kings of Johor.[14] Most of the kingdoms of the South belonged to the empire, which disintegrated[15] over time. The kings of Johor were once emperors; but [now] he is the most insignificant king in the South and also the least powerful.

It is easy to see that the city of Melaka used to be a sprawling city in the past because it is still possible to see extremely large orchards measuring two or three leguas[16] in the vicinity, full of sublime fruit, and many fenced-in sections of wild palm trees. At low tide it is possible to see fences that were once part of houses all the way to Cape Rachado.[17] At that time all the houses were built of wood, however, everything has been overwhelmed by very dense jungle.[18] The Portuguese built a wall around what was left of the city. It is located on the coast. It has a small river; large ships cannot enter this river, only bantins, lancharas, balas,[19] sloops[20] and batels can navigate its waters. However, even though it is a rough coast, ships can be anchored in front of the city, no matter how large they are. Then, what can one say about the city's commerce? Years ago it was normal for there to be more than 500 baxeles from the South anchored in that port: carracks, ships, pinnaces, junks, balas, lancharas, all laden with merchandise. The junks used to come from the islands of Banda, Makassar[21] and Java, and from all those kingdoms their vessels would come laden with mace, nutmeg, cloves, benzoin, sugar, rattan, beeswax[22] and other wares. Other junks used to come from

---

13 Ms. *cabeça*.

14 European sources claim that the kings of Johor styled themselves as "Emperor of the Malay Kings" in the late 16th century. See GPFT, pp. 365–6, note 66.

15 Ms. *fue perdiendo*.

16 About four to six kilometres.

17 Ms. *Cabo Rachado*. See the list of place names (*Cabo Rachado*).

18 Ms. *bosques*.

19 A type of small craft. See also the glossary (*balas*).

20 Ms. *chalupas*. A type of vessel. See also the glossary (sloop).

21 Ms. *Macaçal*. Port and polity based in southern Sulawesi. See also the list of place names (*Macasar*).

22 See the glossary (*beeswax*).

the kingdom of Borneo[23] laden with turtle shells,[24] camphor and beeswax, and they used to bring many diamonds, bezoars and gold. Junks from the kingdoms of Johor, Pahang,[25] Patani, Ligor[26] and Siam used to come laden with sappanwood[27]—[which is used] to dye textiles on the Coromandel Coast—civet[28] and a lot of benzoin[29] and gold. More junks would come from the kingdoms of Cambodia, Champa, [and] Cochinchina, laden with eaglewood,[30] kalambak[31] [and] benzoin and they used to bring a lot of gold, all of this was exchanged for textiles. Other junks used to come from the kingdoms of Jambi, Indragiri, Siak, Kampar, Perak and Kedah,[32] all laden with pepper and *calayn*[33]—which is a certain metal similar to tin—and they used to bring a lot of gold. Particularly from the kingdom of Siak they used to bring many porcupine bezoars,[34] which are only found in that kingdom in the maws of porcupines, [and] which are all hunted on behalf of the king of Siak. However, the hunters always purloin some stones and bring them to us to be sold at a cheaper price as compared to those sold by the king. These stones are no bigger than a pigeon's egg[35] or slightly larger. They are very rare; they are similar to jasper[36] in terms of colour. They dissolve in water as though they were soap, and make the water taste very bitter, which is then given to the sick to drink irrespective of what ails them, and these stones have many virtues. They are prized around the world and even more so in the land of their origin: so much so that a stone the size of a small nut is worth 200 ducats or more.[37] Some 35 or 40 baxeles also used

---

[23] A political precursor of present-day Brunei. See also the list of place names (*Borneo*).

[24] Ms. *tortugas*.

[25] Ms. *Pam*.

[26] Ms. *Lugor*. See the list of place names (*Lugor*).

[27] Ms. *sapam*.

[28] Ms. *algalia*. An odoriferious excretion of animal origin. See also the glossary (*civet*).

[29] Ms. here and subsequently: *mengui*.

[30] Ms. *pao de aguila*. An odoriferous wood. See also the glossary (*eaglewood*).

[31] Ms. *clambuco*.

[32] Ms. *Cadha*. See the list of place names (*Cada*).

[33] Ms. *calayn*. Tin. See also the glossary (*calayn*).

[34] Ms. *pierdas* (losses). The word should read *piedras* (stones). Ms. reads in the left margin: "pedra pe Puerco espin se hallá en el Regno de Siaca." (Porcupine stones are collected in the Kingdom of Siak.) See also the glossary (*pedra de porquo-espin*).

[35] Ms. *güevo*.

[36] Ms. *iaspeada*.

[37] This is equivalent to 700 grams of mint-grade gold. Ms. adds in the right margin: "200 D[ucates] y mas" (200 ducats or more).

to come to Melaka, from Goa, Cochin,[38] Chaul,[39] Nagapattinam, Mylapur[40] and the entire Coromandel Coast, as well as from the kingdoms of Bengal, and Pegu, and they used to come laden with textiles from Cambay[41] and from Sindh. They would bring other dyed fabrics from the Coromandel Coast; and coverlets and sumptuous tents[42] from Bengal. From Pegu they would bring lac, beeswax and provisions, and large quantities of all kinds of precious stones, such as rubies, sapphires and other gems. The baxeles that used to come from Goa and other ports used to bring a lot of wheat, wine, olive oil, butter—because the city of Melaka lacks all this. Four or five ships also used to come from Goa, which would then proceed on to China and Japan. The ships from China used to bring large quantities of raw silk, and other silk twisted tightly together and in skeins, and a lot of gold thread, many pieces of taffeta, damask, velvet and satin, and a lot of gold, pearls, alum,[43] sugar, *radix Chinae*,[44] and a large quantity of porcelain, a myriad of very rich tapestries, coverlets and marquees, beds, gilded beds, chairs and immense quantities of other very valuable curiosities. Each of these ships coming both from China as well as from Japan used to render more than 50,000 ducats[45] in duties to Your Majesty's customs house in Goa each year. Two ships used to come from the Malukus every year laden with cloves for the king, our lord, as the contributions that those islands paid. All the aforesaid baxeles would unload their wares to be traded in Melaka, and it was the largest stopover and trading centre in all of the South; and they used to pay duties to Your Majesty, both while entering as well as leaving, which used to be worth a lot of money. All this commerce has been lost after the Dutch went to India; now they reap [the benefits of] this trade since they are the lords of those seas.

Returning to the events that took place during my voyage. We set sail from Melaka. After having sailed for many days we entered Baticaloa,[46] which is a port located on the island of Ceylon, owing to a storm we

---

[38] Ms. *Cochim*. Port in southeastern India. See also the list of place names (*Cochim*).

[39] Port in western India. See also the list of place names (*Chaul*).

[40] Ms. *Meliapor* (São Tomé).

[41] Port in Gujarat. See also the list of place names (*Cambaya*).

[42] Ms. *pavellones*.

[43] Ms. *piedra-hume*. See the glossary (*alum*).

[44] Ms. *palo de China*.

[45] This sum is equivalent to about 175 kilograms of mint-grade gold.

[46] Ms. *Batacalo*. See the list of place names (*Batacalo*).

encountered along the way. However, we did not disembark onto land. Continuing on our journey we arrived at Tuticorin,[47] where there was a college run by the Jesuit fathers, who taught the doctrine to the Saint Thomas Christians[48] who live there. Nonetheless, most of the native inhabitants[49] are heathens, vassals of the *nayak* of Madurai,[50] who is a sovereign lord, but subject to the emperor of Vijayanagar.[51] We once again went ashore in the city of Quilon,[52] one of Your Majesty's fortresses, where I disembarked and stayed for four days until I was able to hire an *enpalega*[53]—which is what some small native boats are called there—with which I went to the city of Cochin. I stayed there for ten days. At that time there were more than 200 ships of the convoy in the port, laden with wares from China, Melaka and the Coromandel Coast, Nagapattinam and Bengal. I embarked on one of the ships, whose owner was called Álvaro Ruiz Negrão.[54] All the ships left the port together but we became separated from each other due to a storm we encountered on the Kunjali Coast[55] and eight ships were washed ashore with the loss of a lot of wealth.[56]

The following day, despite the storm and the fact that the prow of our ship was broken, we entered Mangalore for repairs. Once the storm had passed, we set sail four days later. A few days thereafter we arrived at the island of Salsette,[57] near the island of Goa. I disembarked with another six or seven men in an *almadia*[58]—a vessel similar to a sloop[59]—to go ashore so as to proceed to the city of Goa by land. As the *almadia* was very small and the sea was still tempestuous, when we were nearing the shore a wave rolled over us and we ended up in the sea, and we would undoubtedly have

---

[47] Ms. adds in right margin: "Colegio de la Comp. de Jhs en Tuticorin en la Isla de Ceylan." (The College of the Jesuits at Tuticorin on the Island of Ceylon).

[48] Ms. *christianos del Apostol Sant Thome.* Christians in the south of India. See also the glossary (*Saint Thomas Christians*).

[49] Ms. *los naturales.*

[50] Ms. *naique de madure.* An Indian functionary and ruler. See also the glossary (*nayak*).

[51] Ms. *Emperador de bisnagar.*

[52] Ms. *coulan.* See the list of place names (*Coulão*).

[53] A small coastal craft. See also the glossary (*enpalega*).

[54] Ms. *Albaro Ruis Negran.*

[55] Ms. *costa de cuñale.*

[56] Ms. *riqueza.*

[57] See the list of place names (*Salsette*).

[58] A type of small craft. See also the glossary (*almadia*).

[59] Ms. *chalupa.*

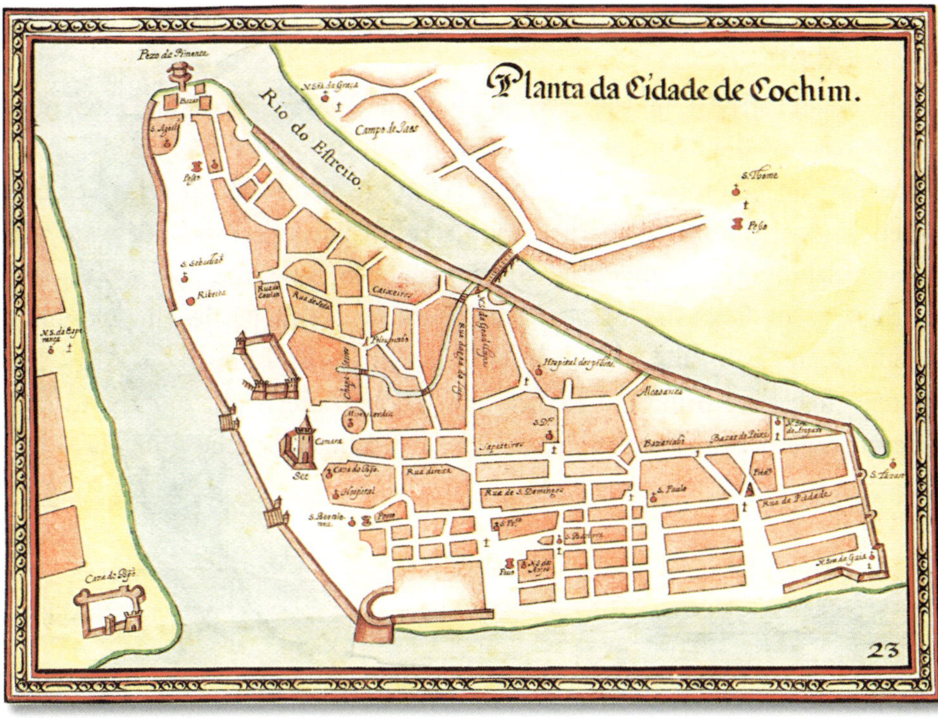

Hand-coloured city plan of Cochin by João Albarnaz I, *Plantas das Cidades, e Fortalezas da Conquista de Índia Oriental* (Maps of the Cities and Fortresses of the Conquest of the East Indies), c.1648. (Munich, BSB, Cod. Icon. 162, pl. 23, fol. 51).

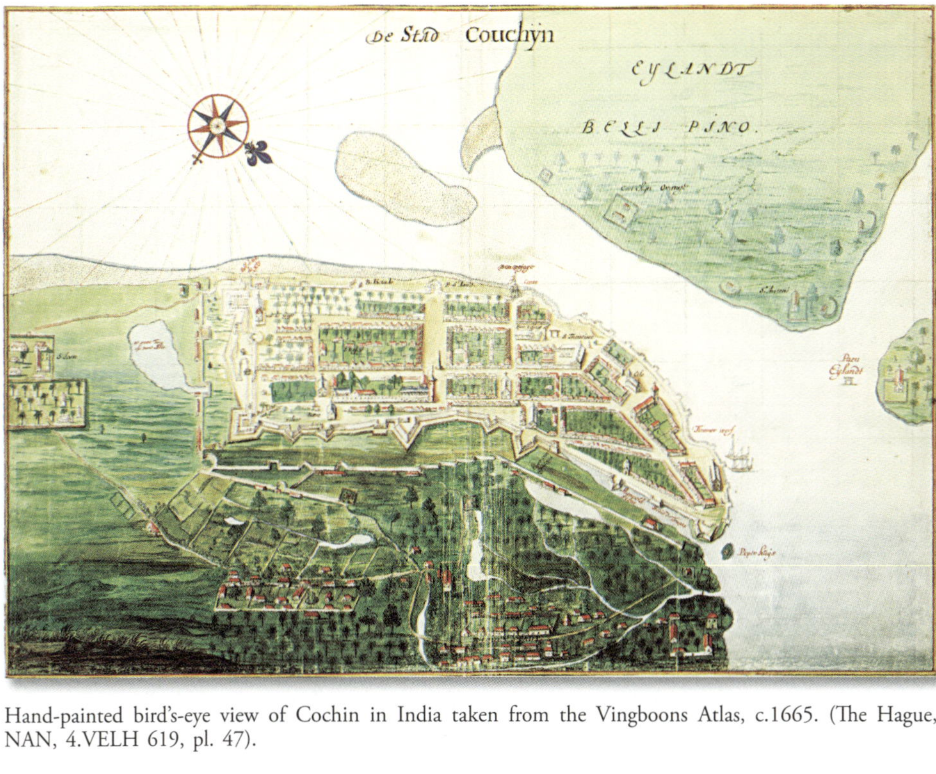

Hand-painted bird's-eye view of Cochin in India taken from the Vingboons Atlas, c.1665. (The Hague, NAN, 4.VELH 619, pl. 47).

drowned if the natives[60] of that island who were on the beach had not come to our aid.

I finally arrived in the city of Goa on 2 May 1603. Six days after having reached the house of my brother, Joseph de Coutre, I married[61] Doña Catarina[62] do Couto, his wife's sister. We wed outside the city in a church called Nossa Senhora de Merces [Our Lady of Mercy]. I did not want any grand celebrations or anything to do with a lot of noise. The Portuguese in the city of Goa and in all of India throw lavish parties and celebrate weddings and baptisms with great fanfare, with processions[63] and rings,[64] as though they were princes. I returned to Cochin after eight months to take care of some personal private business, and I returned home from there one month later.

---

[60] Ms. *los naturales.*

[61] Ms. reads in right margin: *Casan.do, de Jacques de Coutre con D.a. Chataline de Coutre cuñada huia.* (Marriage of Jacques de Coutre with Doña Catarina [Cathalina] de Coutre, his wife.)

[62] Ms. *Doña Cathalina.*

[63] Ms. *carreras*; processions; possibly a distortion of the word *collares* or "necklaces".

[64] Ms. *carreras.* AA, p. 173 suggests the reading should be *collares.*

MEMORIALS OF
JACQUES DE COUTRE
TO THE CROWN AND VICEROY

MEMORIAL

I

How one can do great damage to the Dutch if Your Majesty will give Your vassals, who are merchants, permission to outfit carracks to go to the East Indies, where they can capture booty and trade their wares.[1]

It is necessary, however, that Your Majesty allow the merchants to trade in pepper; with this we[2] will be able to wage great wars on the Dutch, because the carracks will also bring large quantities [of pepper] to Spain, and the rebels will have less profits. This is the main commodity in which they trade.

Firstly, an armada of 12 well-equipped carracks,[3] powerful carracks intermingled with men from Dunkirk,[4] Flanders[5] and Spain;[6] and all the 12 carracks can set sail simultaneously from Seville or Lisbon, and it is important that they do not get separated from each other. It is possible that they might come across rebel carracks when they approach the vicinity of Brazil or Ascension Island.[7] They customarily take on fresh water on Ascension Island and they [also] hunt pigs, which are found in abundance there.

---

[1] BNE Ms. 2780, fol. 252 recto–266 verso.

[2] The term "we" in this context means the subjects of the King of Spain, especially the Castilians.

[3] Ms. here and subsequently: *naos*.

[4] Ms. *Dumquerque*.

[5] Ms. *Flamancos*.

[6] Ms. *Espanholes*.

[7] Ms. *Ilha da Anseisão*. See the list of place names (*Ilha da Anseisão*).

They might [also] come across the rebels off the Cape of Good Hope.[8] They are habitually there in a port that is called Agoada de Saldanha,[9] but it is not recommended that the carracks go to this port when they are sailing from here [Europe] to there, since this port is on this side [western side] of the Cape. It could occur that if they call in at this port they will find it difficult later to sail around the Cape of Good Hope because they will miss the monsoon.[10] It will [then] be necessary to winter in Mozambique.[11] However, whenever it is necessary to winter it is much better to go to the Bab-el-Mandeb Strait[12] [where] they can capture some Turkish vessels, including Dutch or English ships, which very often winter there on certain islands that are located inside the Bab-el-Mandeb Strait.[13]

Dutch ships normally lie in wait for Portuguese carracks in the vicinity of Mozambique, on Madagascar[14] and on the Comoros;[15] and if our carracks are pursued by numerous enemy vessels, they can enter Mozambique and recuperate.[16] If Your Majesty will allow them, they can load a carrack with ebony[17] there and send it to Portugal. It costs no more than just the expenses for cutting and loading the wood. They can also leave their factors there to procure ivory,[18] as the Portuguese do, and send it to Goa and from there it can be sent to Cambay. It is a bountiful trade; ivory is obtained throughout this coast in exchange for dyed cloth from Cambay, and these textiles can also be exchanged for ambergris[19] and gold, and every year more than 4,000 quintals[20] of ivory are brought to Goa. It is a good trade. It is necessary to have factors on the Malindi

---

[8] Ms. here and subsequently with different spellings: *Cabo de Boa Esperanssa*. See the image on p. 70.

[9] Located northwest of Cape Town in South Africa. See also the list of place names (*Agoada de Saldanha*) and the image on p. 70.

[10] Ms. *monsão*. Seasonally-conditioned winds and rain. See also the glossary (*monsoon*).

[11] Ms. here and subsequently with different spellings: *Mossambique*.

[12] Ms. here and subsequently with different spellings: *Estrecho de Mecca*. See the list of place names (*Estreto de Mequa*).

[13] Several groups would come in question here, including the Dalhak Archipelago, the Farasan Islands, the Kamaran group as well as Zuqar and Hanish Islands.

[14] Ms. *Ilha de São Lorenço*; Isle of Saint Laurence. See also the list of place names (*Ilha de São Laurenso*).

[15] Ms. *Ilha do Combro*.

[16] Ms. *refrescar-sse*.

[17] Ms. *pao preto*. A black hardwood. See also the glossary (*ebony*).

[18] Ms. here and subsequently: *marfim*.

[19] Ms. *ambra*. An odoriferous excretion of baleen origin. See also the glossary (*ambergris*).

[20] This is equivalent to about 184–236 metric tons. See also the glossary (*quintal*).

Coast.[21] In order to engage in this commerce it is necessary to have a carrack that loads cargoes of these textiles in Cambay[22] in exchange for ivory and other wares, and send it to Mozambique and Mombasa,[23] to then dispatch the said textiles aboard local vessels[24] to the factors there. They leave from Goa or from Chaul in January for Mombasa or Mozambique.

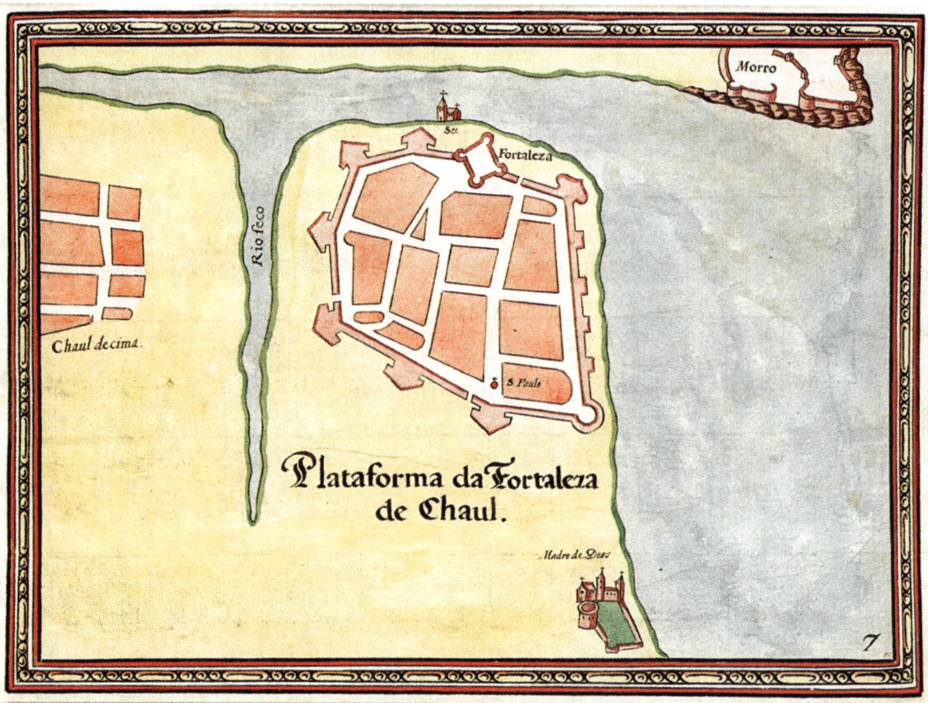

Hand-coloured city plan of Chaul by João Albarnaz I, *Plantas das Cidades, e Fortalezas da Conquista de Índia Oriental* (Maps of the Cities and Fortresses of the Conquest of the East Indies), c.1648. (Munich, BSB, Cod. Icon. 162, pl. 7, fol. 19).

They also take flour and wine from Portugal for the Portuguese who are there, and large quantities of glass beads to exchange for gold in Sofala[25] and in Mwenemutapa.[26] These carracks return to Goa in September during the same monsoon season as the carracks that come from Portugal.

---

[21] Ms. *costa de Melindi*. Around present-day coastal Kenya. See also the list of place names (*Melindi, Mombaça*).

[22] Ms. here and subsequently with different spellings: *Canbaia*.

[23] Ms. here and subsequently: *Bombassa*. See the list of place names (*Mombaça*).

[24] Ms. *barquas de ali*.

[25] Ms. *Sofalla*. See the list of place names (*Sofala*).

[26] Ms. *Monamotapa*. Polity in southern Africa. See also the list of place names (*Monomotapa*).

Hand-coloured plan of Fort Jesus at Mombasa by João Albarnaz I, *Plantas das Cidades, e Fortalezas da Conquista de Índia Oriental* (Maps of the Cities and Fortresses of the Conquest of the East Indies), c.1648. (Munich, BSB, Cod. Icon. 162, pl. 2, fol. 13).

If our ships coming from Portugal should run low on provisions in the vicinity of Mozambique but are unable to call at Mozambique, the pataches[27] can go to Querimba.[28] It is a Portuguese port and here one can find cows and sheep and chickens and clean water and other provisions such as oranges and citrons for the sick. They can also call in at Mombasa, which is a fortress of His Majesty. It is a good land, but a bad port. Few carracks call at Mombasa. Those who call at Mombasa and winter there can only set sail for Goa in April.[29] Those who go there to spend the winter could also, if they wish, winter in the Bab-el-Mandeb Strait, as I mentioned earlier. If the carracks arrive early in the vicinity of Mombasa, such as in July, they could easily go to the Bab-el-Mandeb Strait. This is also the period in which the carracks of the Turks, and of the

[27] Ms. *pataxos*.

[28] Ms. *Querinba*. See the list of place names (*Querinba*).

[29] Ms. lit. … can only set sail for Goa except in April.

Muslims[30] from Aceh, and of the Muslims from Masulipatam,[31] and the Muslims from Cambay, and from all parts of India set sail during this Mecca monsoon[32] from Aden[33] to India. If they [the armada] take this route they will undoubtedly capture many ships and will still be able to catch the monsoon to go to Hormuz[34] and capture [more] ships in Jask.[35]

When one reaches the vicinity of the Strait of Hormuz,[36] some five or six leguas[37] inside the strait near Hormuz there is a port that is called Jask[38] and three or four English carracks always load cargoes of Persian silk there, and they anchor more than two leguas[39] out at sea. Our carracks could easily reach them, even though they are anchored off the coast of Hormuz, which now[40] belongs to the king of Persia; our carracks could get to their carracks. After entering the Strait of Homuz, it is not advisable to call in at Muscat,[41] even though it is a fortress that belongs to Your Majesty, so that the Arabs do not warn the English. They will think [the carracks of the armada] are all English vessels and in this way they [the armada] will be able to go to Jask and catch the English unaware. Later, when they return to Goa from there, they can call at Muscat[42] and take on provisions and identify themselves as vassals of Your Majesty. If they need to take on water, about 30 leguas[43] inside this strait there is the port of Tiwi[44] on the coast of Arabia. It has excellent water and in this area they can also capture many prizes before the enemy takes notice. After the enemy learns of their presence they will trade their trading vessels[45] for more warships and will not make as much profit; they will become more anxious and will suffer more losses.

---

30 Ms. here and subsequently: *Moros*.

31 Ms. *Mosolapatão*.

32 Ms. *Monsão de Mequa*.

33 Ms. here and subsequently: *Ada*.

34 Ms. *Ormus*.

35 Ms. *Yasques*. See the list of place names (*Jasques*).

36 Ms. here and subsequently: *Estreto de Ormus*. See the list of place names (*Estreto de Ormus*).

37 The estimate is about 27.5–37 kilometres but the distance is actually further.

38 Ms. here and subsequently: *Yasques*.

39 Probably about four kilometres or possibly as far as 11–12.3 kilometres.

40 See the list of place names (*Ormus*).

41 Ms. *Mascata*. Port in present-day Oman. See also the list of place names (*Mascata*).

42 Ms. *Masquate*.

43 About 165–85.2 kilometres.

44 Ms. *Teve*. See the list of place names (*Teve*).

45 Ms. *resgates de mercancia*.

Hand-coloured plan of Muscat by João Albarnaz I, *Plantas das Cidades, e Fortalezas da Conquista de Índia Oriental* (Maps of the Cities and Fortresses of the Conquest of the East Indies), c.1648 (Munich, BSB, Cod. Icon. 162, pl. 21, fol. 47).

More than 40 oared ships sail from Muslim lands[46] along the Goa coast into the Strait of Hormuz, laden with pepper, textiles, and lac, and iron and steel, and bamboos for making lances, and planks, and ropes. These ships belong to the Portuguese and are used for smuggling. They take prohibited items and defraud Your Majesty of duties both on the way out as well as on the way back. They are not very powerful ships and carry a small crew, [comprising] Portuguese, blacks and *mestiços*. These ships do great damage to the Estado da Índia.[47] They sail to the Strait of Hormuz to trade with Turks and Arabs and Persians. These ships cannot be caught, unless they use other light vessels from Goa, which are called *sanguicels*.[48] Ships

[46] Ms. *teras de Moros*.

[47] Concerning the damage caused by the smugglers or *pimenteiros*, see specifically also the hitherto unpublished manuscript *Aduertensia de Jaques do Couto ao Conde* ("*Advice by Jacques de Coutre to the Count* [*of Linhares*]"), dated 29 December 1628, in ANTT, Lisbon: Miscelâneas Manuscritas do Convento da Graça, Tomo VI–F, Cx. 3, fol. 52 verso–6 verso and AA, pp. 429–38. See also the glossary (*Estado da Índia*).

[48] Ms. *sanguiseis*. See also the glossary (*sanguicel*).

belonging to Indian Muslims laden with textiles can also be found in the Strait; they are also seized when they are found to be sailing without cartazes.[49]

Sailing from the Strait of Hormuz to Goa the carracks [of the armada] can come directly to Surat,[50] a land which belongs to the Mughal [emperor].[51] There, two or three English ships can always be found loading textiles, indigo,[52] linen[53] and other wares. If [the vessels of the armada] do not find [English] carracks [here] during the month of September they will find them here in October. After having seized some ships there, our carracks can sail along the coast from Surat to Goa; they will undoubtedly find some [more] ships

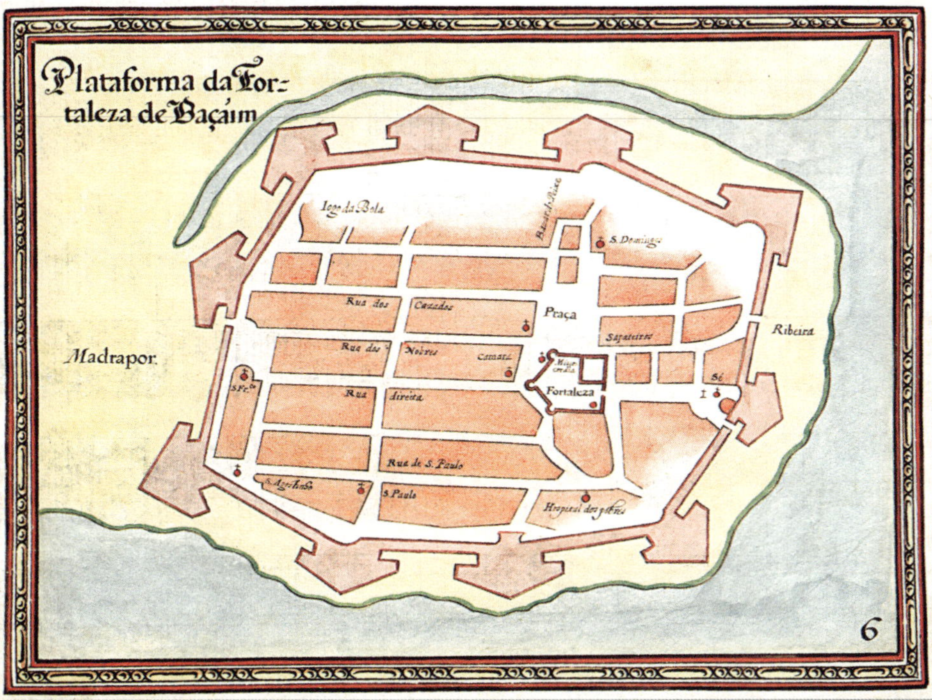

Hand-coloured city plan of Bassein by João Albarnaz I, *Plantas das Cidades, e Fortalezas da Conquista de Índia Oriental* (Maps of the Cities and Fortresses of the Conquest of the East Indies), c.1648. (Munich, BSB, Cod. Icon. 162, pl. 6, fol. 17).

[49] A safe conduct pass. See also the glossary (*cartaz*).

[50] See the list of place names (*Surat*).

[51] Ms. *teras de Mogor*.

[52] A blue dye. See also the glossary (*indigo*).

[53] Ms. *linha*. The term "linen" is commonly employed in early modern literature to designate any piece of cloth or textile of plant origin. See Irwin, "Indian Textile Trade in the Seventeenth Century. II. Coromandel Coast", *Journal of Indian Textile History* 2 (1956): 37–8.

to capture. Your Majesty has fortresses along this coast: Diu,[54] Daman,[55] Bassein[56] and Chaul,[57] where they could take aboard provisions and acquire the latest information of recent events.

There is also Dabul,[58] a land which belongs to King Adil Khan,[59] where there is one of our factors sent on the orders of Your Majesty, who issues cartazes to Adil Khan's vassals so that they can sail safely without our fleets causing them any harm. From there [the carracks of the armada] can sail along the coast up to Goa.

Goa belongs to Your Majesty and is the capital[60] of the Estado da Índia. Two or three carracks could load wares to bring to Spain, taking capital[61] there. The best things to bring are reals-of-eight, reals-of-four,[62] and large and small [pieces of] unprocessed as well as processed coral; full and half-size fabrics dyed red with carmine and scarlet,[63] and everything that is coloured, and other fabrics in the colour of indigo to make shawls[64] and kebayas[65] that the Muslims use. Their factors and merchants of the said company[66] could play an important role in Goa. They could freely send tradable wares to Spain from Goa with the said company such as pepper, cloves, nutmeg, mace, indigo, textiles from Cambay and from Bengal, lac, crude borax,[67] trobito,[68] spikenard,[69] cassia[70] and rubies and diamonds. There will be no shortage of those who do this very well. Also benzoin, eaglewood,[71] kalambak, musk[72] [and] silks from China; everything according to what the

---

[54] Ms. *Dio*. See the list of place names (*Dio*) and the city plan on p. 208.
[55] Ms. *Damão*. See the list of place names (*Damão*).
[56] Ms. *Baçaim*. See the list of place names (*Baçaim*) and the city plan on p. 201.
[57] Ms. *Chaul*.
[58] Ms. *Dabul*. See the list of place names (*Dabul*).
[59] Ms. *Dialquan*. See the glossary (*Dialquan*).
[60] Ms. *cabeça*.
[61] Ms. here and subsequently: *cabedal*.
[62] Coinage from the Spanish Americas. See also the glossary (real-of-eight, real-of-four).
[63] Ms. *panos de gran chochanilhas e mea chochanilas*.
[64] Ms. here and subsequently with variant spelling: *silhas*.
[65] Ms. *cabaias*. A type of woman's dress. See also the glossary (*kebaya*).
[66] Ms. here and subsequently: *dita Companhia*. The term does not appear to refer to a company structure as such, but most likely to the armada or fleet of raiders De Coutre is suggesting to send out.
[67] Ms. *tincal*. See the glossary (*borax*).
[68] Ms. *tinqual*. A root with medicinal properties. See also the glossary (*trobito*).
[69] See the glossary (*spikenard*).
[70] Ms. *canafistula*. See the glossary (*cassia*).
[71] Ms. here and subsequently: *agela*.
[72] Ms. *almiscre*. An odoriferous excretion of animal origin. See also the glossary (*musk*).

merchants feel is best[73] and what is most profitable, after considering the capital that is available.[74]

After the monsoon, around the month of January, the carracks that remain in Goa, which do not take cargoes to Spain, could sail southwards along the coast to capture ships and take Cambay textiles from Goa to trade them in Melaka and in Java, and in the lands of the Malays[75] and in Aceh. If reals-of-eight are available, they can be taken to China [to exchange them] for silks and velvets, and tintinago[76] and copper, and *radix Chinae*,[77] alum stone[78] and benzoin, eaglewood from Cochinchina, lac,[79] camphor, musk and a lot of gold. They will undoubtedly be able to capture ships sailing along this southern coast.

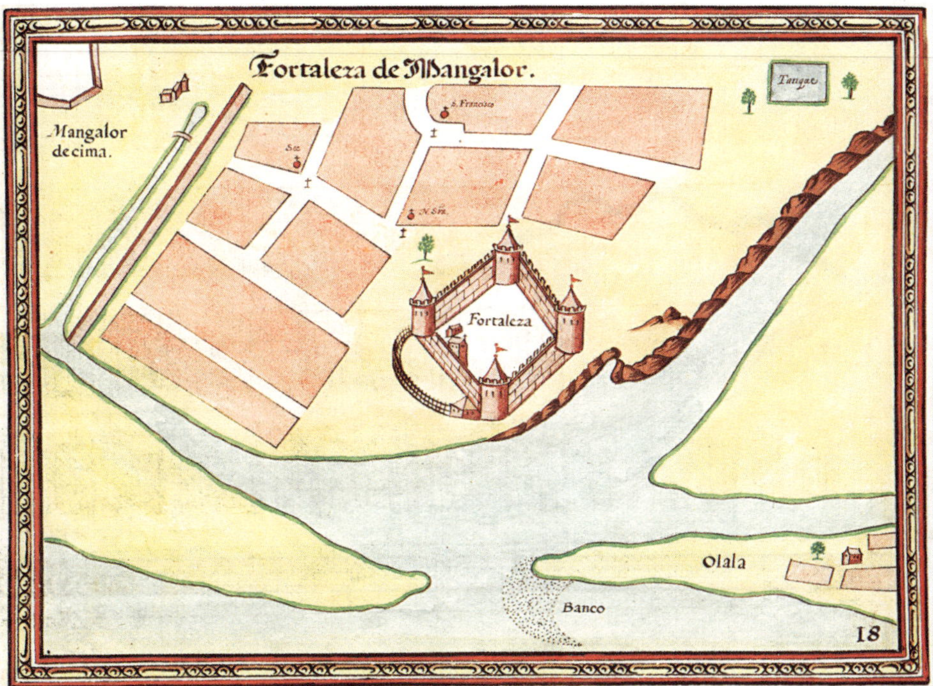

Hand-coloured city plan of Mangalore by João Albarnaz I, *Plantas das Cidades, e Fortalezas da Conquista de Índia Oriental* (Maps of the Cities and Fortresses of the Conquest of the East Indies), c.1648. (Munich, BSB, Cod. Icon. 162, pl. 18, fol. 41).

---

73 Ms. *clanba*.

74 See the glossary for descriptions and definitions of most of these commodities.

75 Ms. *teras de Malaios*.

76 Ms. *tutunaga*. Also *tootnague*, a copper-zinc alloy. See also the glossary (*tintinago*).

77 Ms. *pao da China*.

78 Ms. here and subsequently: *pedra umedo*.

79 Ms. *lanqua*.

If these aforesaid carracks do not have capital to take to China, they can set sail from Goa towards the south. Some 10 or 12 leguas[80] south of Goa, Your Majesty has a fortress, which is called Honawar,[81] where there is abundant pepper, but the carracks cannot anchor there except off the coast. Twenty leguas[82] from Honawar there is another fortress called Mangalore.[83] Pataches[84] can enter the river with the tide. It has pepper and plenty of rice. Then [there is] another fortress—Cananore.[85] All these lands have a lot of pepper and cardamom.[86] Sailing further along this coast there is Cochin,

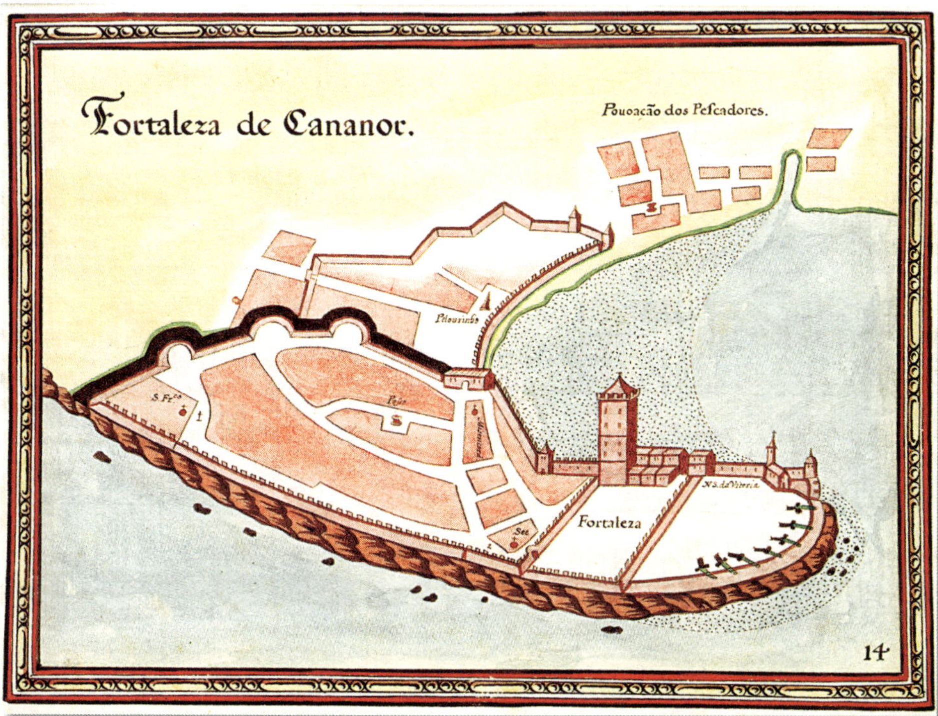

Hand-coloured city plan of Cananore by João Albarnaz I, *Plantas das Cidades, e Fortalezas da Conquista de Índia Oriental* (Maps of the Cities and Fortresses of the Conquest of the East Indies), c.1648. (Munich, BSB, Cod. Icon. 162, pl. 9, fol. 25).

[80] The estimate is 55–75 kilometres but the distance is actually further.

[81] Ms. *Honor*. Port on the Malabar Coast (southwestern coast) of India. See also the list of place names (*Honor*).

[82] About 110–23.5 kilometres.

[83] Ms. *Mangalor*. See the list of place names (*Mangalor*) and the city plan on p. 203.

[84] Ms. *pataxos*.

[85] Port on the Malabar Coast. See also the list of place names (*Cananore*).

[86] Ms. *cardamomo*. A spice. See also the glossary (*cardamom*).

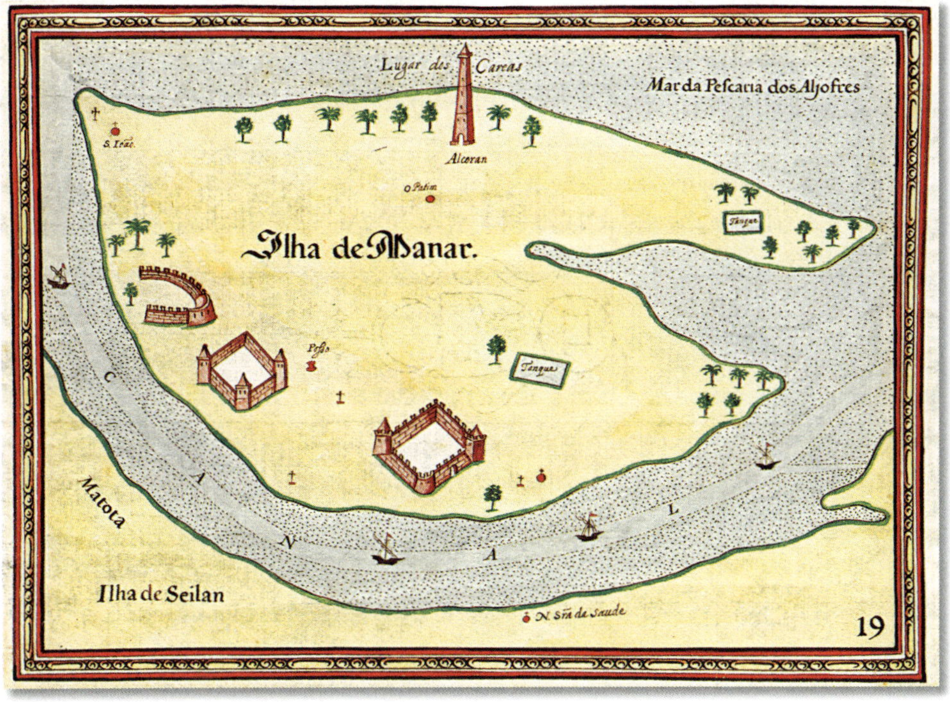

Hand-coloured plan of Mannar by João Albarnaz I, *Plantas das Cidades, e Fortalezas da Conquista de Índia Oriental* (Maps of the Cities and Fortresses of the Conquest of the East Indies), c.1648. (Munich, BSB, Cod. Icon. 162, pl. 19, fol. 43).

a Portuguese city[87] subject to the king of Cochin. This king can load four or five carracks with pepper. He only accepts reals-of-eight and reals-of-four and our carracks can only enter the river if they are not laden, but they can anchor outside in the harbour one legua[88] away from the shore. Cochin is a very fertile land. There is a lot of timber where it is used to build carracks and the keels of carracks, as well as to line carracks with planks. They will find from this king all the assistance they need for their carracks. Here one can also find many wooden chests.

Sailing further south along this coast, we have another fortress called Quilon.[89] It is ruled by a heathen queen who has a large amount of pepper. We could load two carracks, and this could be suggested to her, as also to the king of Cochin, to go and load [our] carracks there in his ports.

[87] Ms. *cidade de Portugueses* (city of the Portuguese).

[88] Probably about two kilometres, possibly further.

[89] Ms. *Coulão*.

From Cochin to Quilon, and from there up to Mannar,[90] there are Theatine fathers[91] all along this coast where they have churches and have converted many [of the natives], who are called Paravas.[92] Our carracks can disembark safely all along this coast, knowing that they are vassals of Your Majesty, and take aboard provisions, but they have to be readily armed with weapons so as to be respected by heathens and Christians alike, and they should not trust them too much. If any of our carracks that might have been lost washes ashore on this coast, even if the wares wash up on land, they are all lost and taken. The local people[93] do this all over India. Tuticorin[94] is a port located south of Cape Comorin.[95] If necessary they can winter there with the carracks. There is a church run by Theatine fathers, but the land belongs to the *nayak* of Madurai.[96] Mannar is also one of our fortresses. [The armada] can take on provisions [here]. Provisions are very inexpensive in this land.

From Mannar they can go to Ceylon,[97] to the city of Colombo.[98] If Your Majesty grant them permission, they could put factors there to buy cinnamon in exchange for textiles and money. From this port they could send carracks to Galle Point[99] to capture ships. There they will find Dutch [vessels] that lie in wait for our carracks sailing from Melaka,[100] and Dutch ships also sail [through there] laden with spices[101] from the South[102] on their way to Pulicat[103] and Masulipatam,[104] and this is the route they take. Then our carracks can sail along the coast of Nagapattinam.[105] One legua[106]

[90] Ms. *Manar*. See the list of place names (*Manar*) and the city plan on p. 205.
[91] Ms. here and subsequently: *Padres Tiatinos*. See the glossary (*Theatines*).
[92] Ms. *pareas*. See the glossary (*Paravas*).
[93] Ms. *gente da terra*.
[94] Ms. *Totoçarin*.
[95] Ms. *Cabo de Comarin*. De Coutre's claim concerning the location of Tuticorin seems incorrect. See also the list of place names (*Cabo de Comarin*).
[96] Ms. *Naique de Madure*. See also the glossary (*nayak*, *Theatines*).
[97] Ms. *Seilão*. See the list of place names (*Seilão*).
[98] Ms. *Colunbo*. See the list of place names (*Colunbo*).
[99] Ms. here and subsequently: *Punto de Gale*. See the list of place names (*Punto de Gale*).
[100] Ms. here and subsequently: *Mallaqua*.
[101] Ms. *drogas*. See the glossary (*drogas*).
[102] Ms. here and subsequently: *sur* (or later also *sul*); from (insular) Southeast Asia. See the glossary (*sur*).
[103] Ms. *Pelicate*.
[104] Ms. *Mosolapatão*.
[105] Ms. here and subsequently: *Neguapatão*.
[106] About 5.5–6.2 kilometres.

Hand-coloured city plan of Colombo by João Albarnaz I, *Plantas das Cidades, e Fortalezas da Conquista de Índia Oriental* (Maps of the Cities and Fortresses of the Conquest of the East Indies), c.1648. (Munich, BSB, Cod. Icon. 162, pl. 13, fol. 31).

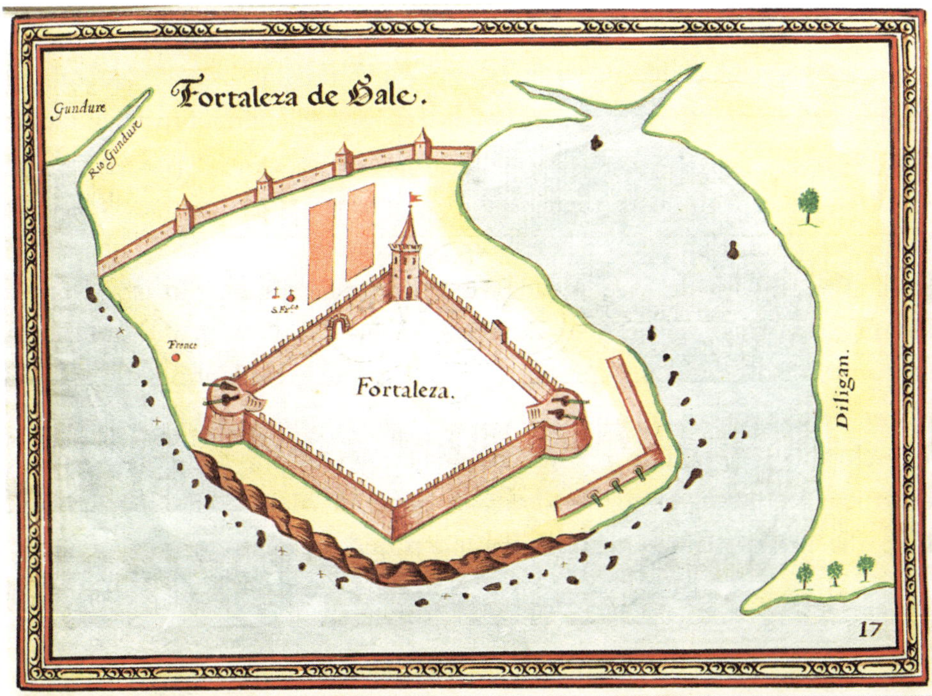

Hand-coloured plan of Galle by João Albarnaz I, *Plantas das Cidades, e Fortalezas da Conquista de Índia Oriental* (Maps of the Cities and Fortresses of the Conquest of the East Indies), c.1648 (Munich, BSB, Cod. Icon. 162, pl. 17, fol. 39).

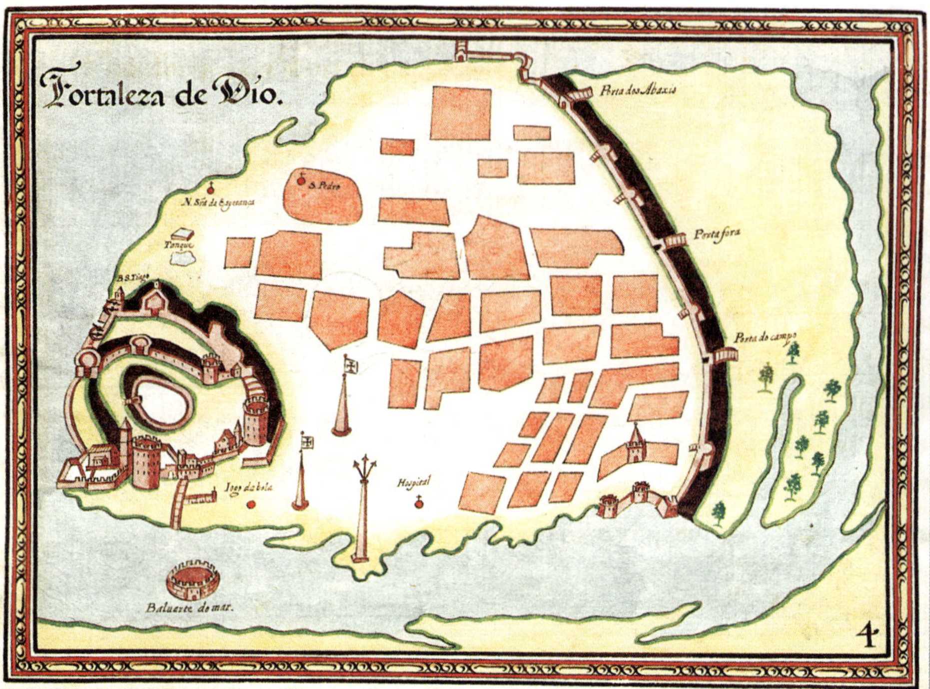

Hand-coloured city plan of Diu by João Albarnaz I, *Plantas das Cidades, e Fortalezas da Conquista de Índia Oriental* (Maps of the Cities and Fortresses of the Conquest of the East Indies), c.1648 (Munich, BSB, Cod. Icon. 162, pl. 14, fol. 33).

before that, in a land that they call Tranquebar,[107] there is a sparsely populated Danish fortress, and the carracks anchor at sea. They will undoubtedly find some ships to seize.

One legua from here there is a Portuguese settlement that is subject to the *nayak* of Thanjur.[108] These Portuguese are virtually rebels; they have nothing to do with the viceroy, nor with Your Majesty's captain, nor do they submit to [Portuguese] justice. Their way of life is based on the survival of the fittest. In this land they produce a lot of printed textiles in every heathen village. But anyone who wishes to purchase these fabrics has to send a man to each village as a factor. This is the manner of the Dutch in Pulicat, and these textiles cater to the needs of those in Melaka and Java, as well as to the Malays. They are [called] *sarassas* and *tapisarassas*[109] and *sahans*[110]

[107] Ms. *Tangebare*. See the list of place names (*Tangebare*).

[108] Ms. *Naique de Tangur*. See the glossary (*nayak*).

[109] A type of skirt; sarong. See also the glossary (*tapisarasa*).

[110] Ms. *sabanes*. A type of textile. See also the glossary (*sahan*).

and *caladaris*[111] and other printed fabrics, popular with those natives in the South. The Dutch cannot do any manner of trade in the South in mace, or nutmeg, or mace,[112] or pepper or other commodities. These fabrics are the most profitable commodity that the Dutch have. As the Dutch took away this commerce from the Portuguese, they have no other choice but to buy these fabrics and order them to be made according to their specifications.[113] When they take these fabrics to the South, they sell them there at whatsoever price they wish, since it is a commodity that can be made and sold at a quick profit.[114]

Setting out from Nagapattinam [the carracks can go to] São Tomé, [which is also] called Mylapur.[115] This is a Portuguese city. It is a vast land with a bishop. These men used to trade in fabrics [taking them] to the South, as I have mentioned above; and they used to load carracks with expensive fabrics and would take them to Melaka and sell them to the Javanese. Now the Dutch take these textiles [there] and impede [Portuguese trade] so that the Javanese and Malays do not come to Melaka to buy textiles. Thus, these men lost this trade in textiles because of the Dutch. Sailing from Mylapur southwards, five leguas[116] away there is a Dutch fortress called Pulicat, where the Dutch procure many textiles in all the villages of that kingdom of Vijayanagar.[117] They have their factors in all the villages. The Dutch bring salt in order to buy these textiles, [including] a lot of cloves, and a lot of nutmeg, and mace, and *calayn* or tin from the South, and lead, and some large cloths from their land, and barrel guns,[118] and tintinago from China, and copper, and Chinese porcelain, and silk and velvet fabrics, and raw silk; they bring all these wares to exchange for textiles. Except for the spices, [the trade in] all the other commodities has been stolen from the Portuguese and the Chinese,[119] who trade illegally there in the South.

---

[111] Ms. *aareiores*. See the glossary (*caladari*).

[112] The original text lists mace twice.

[113] Ms. lit. wishes.

[114] Ms. *vendida por uma mão*.

[115] Ms. *Melapor*.

[116] About 27.5–30.9 kilometres.

[117] Ms. *Badaga*; the commonly employed toponym in Portuguese is Bisnaga.

[118] Ms. *escupetas*.

[119] Ms. *Chincheos*. See the glossary (*Chincheo*).

This fortress of Pulicat is very strong, but does not have a port; it is a rugged coast.[120] The Dutch carracks anchor at sea over a legua and a half away[121] from the fortress; and two or three Dutch carracks are always anchored off this fortress, loading textiles to take to the South or unloading spices they have brought from the South. From there they send their carracks to plunder[122] at Galle Point. Beyond Pulicat, 20 leguas[123] toward Masulipatam, there is a Dutch factory; the settlement is called Trivenipatam.[124] It is on the same coast as Pulicat. There are many commodities at the factory where there is always some Dutch carrack either loading locally made textiles, or unloading goods brought from the South. It is a rugged coast; the Dutch carracks anchor one legua[125] out at sea.

Masulipatam is located more or less 50 leguas[126] further along the same coast. It is a very busy port. It belongs to the Qutb Shah[127] and there are two factories in this port: a Dutch factory and an English factory, with many commodities, spices from the South,[128] and silk from China, and porcelain; commodities[129] they took away from the Portuguese. There are always four English and Dutch carracks in this port, and sometimes there are seven and eight carracks, and they sell these wares. There they buy textiles to take to the South to exchange them for spices and in this land they find all kinds of fabrics that they need, and many small rubies, and bezoars, and diamonds. In this port there are many ships owned by Muslims from Bengal, from Aceh, from Mecca,[130] from Pegu and from other parts of India. All these carracks anchor more than two leguas out at sea,[131] except for smaller vessels that anchor closer to shore. They cannot anchor there during winter, only during summer.

---

120 Ms. here and subsequently: *costa brava.*

121 About three kilometres, possibly further.

122 Ms. *furtar.*

123 About 110–23.5 kilometres.

124 Ms. *Trevenipatão.* See the list of place names (*Trivenipatão*).

125 About 5.5–6.2 kilometres.

126 About 275–308.7 kilometres.

127 Ms. *Rey Catabussa.* See the glossary (*Catabussa*).

128 Lit. South.

129 Ms. lit. trade.

130 Ms. *Mequa*; lit. Mecca. The toponym may possibly represent a corruption of the Arabian port city Mocha. See also Moreland, *Peter Floris*, p. 116.

131 About two kilometres, possibly further.

The Dutch have their factors in all the villages of this land to buy wares to trade in the South.[132] The Dutch are disliked by the local people because they sell their wares for what they demand, all through one man, and they buy in the same manner. These local people used to be more fortunate with the Portuguese merchants, because each one would buy and sell as per their abilities, but now they cannot buy for less. Since their carracks go safely to Bengal, and Pegu, and Mecca,[133] and to other parts of India, the Dutch issue cartazes to the Muslims. The king of that land wanted the Portuguese to expel the Dutch from there and has always shown himself to be a friend of the Portuguese but he finds himself helpless with no other choice but to be an ally of the Dutch owing to the [Dutch] carracks. This settlement [Masulipatam] is very large and there are many merchants here, including Persians as well as Turks, and [people from] other nations. The local people are Telengana and Kanara[134] heathens, and Muslims. This kingdom encompasses more than 300 leguas[135] and all of it comprises a very bountiful land, with many riches.

Further along the same coast there is a land called Gerzelim.[136] In this land there are many provisions to be found and meat, and oil, and butter, [all of] which are very inexpensive. Fifteen years ago Portuguese carracks used to load provisions in these ports to take to Melaka, in exchange for textiles from Mylapur or from Nagapattinam.

Ahead of this land is Bengal, where every year many Portuguese carracks used to go from India, and these carracks used to take from Goa [and] from Cochin to Bengal tintinago, and tin,[137] and cloves, nutmeg, mace, pepper, opium,[138] velvet fabrics from China, coloured taffeta, raw silk, and carved conch shells that they call *shankhas*.[139] These *shankhas* come from Tuticorin; they use them to make handles and play them as instruments. They also used to take seed pearls, which are very small pearls, and emeralds, and wine, and olive oil: things from Portugal.

---

[132] See the glossary (*Sur*).

[133] Mecca does not have a port; here possibly Mocha. See note 130 above.

[134] Ms. *telengas e canaras*.

[135] Probably 600 kilometres, possibly further.

[136] Ms. *Gerzelim*. Port in Bengal. See also the list of place names (*Gerzelim*).

[137] Ms. *calem*.

[138] Ms. *alfião*.

[139] Ms. *chanqua*. See the glossary (*shankha*).

From Bengal 15 or 20 carracks could then go to Melaka laden with rice and beeswax, including an infinite range of textiles: *cassas, saranpuras* and *balachas,* and other textiles, and many *colchas de montaria*, and marquees,[140] and *almoada*[141] (a very expensive product) and *semianas* and fabrics made from plants that look like silk.[142] A similar number of carracks could sail from Bengal to Cochin and Goa, laden with the same wares, and many slaves to sell to men from Portugal. All this commerce has come to an end on account of the Dutch. In Bengal there are towns and cities consisting of Portuguese with their families, but they are like rebels:[143] they appoint captains from amongst themselves, and serve the Muslims, and they kill each other with barrel guns[144] like soulless men. It is a land where the fittest survives.[145] Most of Bengal belongs to the Great Mughal, and his son rules in Bengal, who is called Sultan Traves.[146] The other part of Bengal belongs to the king of Arakan,[147] [which is a kingdom located] along the neighbouring coast bordering Pegu.

Originally many galliots used to go to Pegu from São Tomé and Nagapattinam, laden with textiles from the said land[s], and coloured linen,[148] and silks from China. From Pegu they used to bring a lot of lac with which to dye textiles, and a lot of beeswax, and many small rubies that are used in India, and white almond benzoin.[149] At the entrance to the Pegu River[150] there is a fortress called Syriam,[151] which was built by Filipe de Brito de Nicote,[152] [and] which was populated by Portuguese and locals from Pegu. This man was the lord of this township.[153] He governed for seven or eight

---

[140] Ms. *pavilhãois.*

[141] A cushion.

[142] For all the types of textiles and objects mentioned in this list, see the glossary.

[143] Ms. *levantados.*

[144] Ms. *escupetas.*

[145] Ms. *tera de quem mais pode.*

[146] Prince Parvez, Moghul Emperor Jahangir's second son and governor of Bengal.

[147] Ms. *Raquão.* See the list of place names (*Araquão*).

[148] Ms. *linha.* Here probably cotton or another textile made of plant fibres.

[149] Ms. *benguin de amendoas blanqua.*

[150] Ms. *rio de Pegu.* The present-day Bago River. See also the list of place names (*Pegu*).

[151] Ms. *Serião.* See the list of place names (*Serião*).

[152] Concerning Filipe de Brito de Nicote and his death in 1613, see António Bocarro, *Década XIII da História da Índia*, ed. Rodrigo José de Lima Felner (Lisbon: Typographia da Academia Real das Sciencias, 1876), I, chap. 28–38, pp. 117–64.

[153] Ms. *censo.*

years, until the king of that region descended on him and captured both the fortress and Filipe de Brito, as his people betrayed him. That local king killed Filipe de Brito. Today he is the king of Pegu: he has vast lands; bordering China in the interior and he is the lord of the ruby mines.[154]

Closer to Melaka on the same coast there is a port that is called Tenasserim.[155] It belongs to the king of Siam, [who] is a great king. His lands border the northern sea and the southern sea,[156] and Pegu and Bengal, and the kingdom of Cambodia. In the seas off Melaka many carracks from Mylapur and Nagapattinam used to come to this port of Tenasserim with many textiles from India, and from Tenasserim to Mylapur and Nagapattinam they used to bring many logs of sappanwood,[157] [which is] similar to brazilwood.[158] It is [used] to dye fabrics. This land bustles with an abundance of trade. They also bring a lot of benzoin and beeswax, and lac and lead.

Further in the direction of Melaka there is a port that is called Kedah,[159] and another port that is called Perak;[160] and they belong to different lords. This land has an abundance of tin which they call *calayn*.[161] Carracks upon carracks are laden with this [metal] and they come from Nagapattinam to this land to trade for tin[162] in exchange for textiles. Carracks also come here from Melaka, and small vessels that belong to the captain of Melaka. A lot of tin is also traded in exchange for gold coins they call emas[163] from Pahang and Johor, and some textiles. With this they buy this tin to take to Melaka, and from Melaka they send this tin to India to sell in Cambay and Dhaka.[164] It goes to all parts of India; it is a lucrative business.

Further to the south along the same coast is Melaka, Your Majesty's fortress. It is a good port and a very busy one, but it has nothing apart

[154] King Anaukpetlun (ruler of the restored Taungoo Dynasty Kingdom) overran Syriam in 1613 and, indeed, killed Filipe de Brito.
[155] See the list of place names (*Tenasserim*).
[156] The lands border the Bay of Bengal and the South China Sea.
[157] Ms. *pallo de sapão*.
[158] Ms. *pau de Brazil*.
[159] Ms. *Cada*.
[160] Ms. *Pera*.
[161] It makes more sense to reverse the sequence of *calen* and *estanho* in the English translation.
[162] Ms. here and subsequently with different spellings: *calem*.
[163] Ms. *mazes*.
[164] Ms. *Daquão*. See the list of place names (*Daquão*).

from what is brought from outside. It does not have provisions or meat. It is very fertile and verdant, but neither the Portuguese people nor the inhabitants[165] cultivate the land. Everything is imported, as I have said. Many carracks go there from Goa with textiles from Cambay, and wheat, and wine, and olive oil from Portugal. Other carracks go there from Bengal laden with textiles and rice and other provisions. Carracks go to Melaka from Nagapattinam and São Tomé laden with coloured textiles. Other carracks go to this port of Melaka from Gerzelim and from Pegu. As I have said above, all these carracks sail to Melaka annually. In its heyday[166] more than 400 Malay and Javanese ships laden with mace, and nutmeg, and cloves, and pepper, and [sea] turtle [shells],[167] and camphor, a lot of provisions, and gold [used to go to Melaka]. These[168] Javanese and Malay vessels sold their wares and took textiles back to their lands. All of this has come to an end because of the Dutch. Our carracks used to sell these textiles and used to take loads of spices to Goa, and from there they would be sent throughout the world.

From Melaka the Portuguese used to go to Johor[169] and to the kingdom of Pahang, and to the kingdom of Patani [situated] on the same coast, [and] to Ligor,[170] Bordolong,[171] Siam, and to the city of Ayutthaya,[172] and to the kingdom of Cambodia.[173] There used to be a Portuguese settlement there[174] and monasteries with friars. The lands used to belong to the king of Cambodia. The men from Melaka used to go to all these lands with their ships selling their textiles and other wares, and from there to Melaka they would bring a lot of gold and other wares, as I have mentioned, which were [then] sent to India. The Portuguese from Melaka also used to go to Champa and Cochinchina and they used to take with them textiles and

---

165 Ms. *moradores*.
166 Ms. lit. when it was more prosperous.
167 Ms. *tartugua*.
168 Ms. lit. this.
169 Ms. here and subsequently: *Yor*.
170 Ms. *Lugor*.
171 Ms. *Bordolon*. Today's Phattalung. See also the list of place names (*Bordolon*).
172 Ms. *Yudia*.
173 Ms. here and subsequently: *Canboiia*.
174 Both Cambodia and Ayutthaya had Portuguese "settlements", but De Coutre's employment of the past tense can be taken as a reference to Cambodia only. The Portuguese settlement in Ayutthaya continued well into De Coutre's own time.

Hand-painted bird's-eye view of Macao, taken from the Vingboons Atlas, c.1665. (The Hague, NAN, 4.VELH 619, pl. 65).

reals-of-eight, and coral, and from there they used to bring back carracks laden with eaglewood,[175] kalambak,[176] and benzoin.

From Melaka carracks used to go to China, [and to] Macao, a Portuguese settlement in the land of China. Many carracks from Goa also used to go to these lands and these[177] carracks used to take to China many *pardaos*[178] of reals, which are reals-of-eight, and *catechu*,[179] and coral, and cat's eyes,[180] ambergris,[181] carnelian[182] from Cambay, and wine and olive oil from Portugal. When they [used to] return to Melaka they would pay duties to Your Majesty. If they went to Goa, these carracks would return richly laden with silk, and velvet fabrics, and damask, and taffetas, and silk covers, and domestic silk

---

[175] Ms. *ágela*.

[176] Ms. *calanba*.

[177] Ms. lit. this.

[178] Ms. *pardaos de reales*. A Portuguese currency unit. See also the glossary (*pardao*).

[179] Ms. *pucho*. See the glossary (*pucho*).

[180] Ms. *olhos de gato*.

[181] Ms. *alambre*.

[182] Ms. *laqueca*. See the glossary (*carnelian*).

Hand-painted bird's-eye view of Aceh taken from the Vingboons Atlas, c.1665. (The Hague, NAN, 4.VELH 619, pl. 22).

hangings,[183] marquees,[184] and gilded beds,[185] and also many earrings,[186] and Chinese porcelain, *radix Chinae*,[187] a lot of tintinago, and copper, a lot of alum stone, and *lengkuas*,[188] and a lot of musk, gold, and rubies. Any of these carracks would import a million in gold.[189] They were large carracks and now not even small ships can navigate [these waters] because of the [Dutch] rebels.

From Melaka two or three carracks used to go to Manila every year laden with textiles and many slaves, and from Manila to Melaka they would bring many reals-of-eight, and gold and cloves. From Melaka they also used to go

---

[183] Ms. *armassõis de cazas de seda*.

[184] Ms. *pavilhõis*.

[185] Ms. *esquife dourado*.

[186] Ms. *brinquos*. This could be taken as a reference to jewellery in general.

[187] A medicinal product. See also the glossary (*radix Chinae*).

[188] Ms. *lanquas*. A type of ginger or galangal. See also the glossary (*lanqua*).

[189] This appears to be another term for a *conto de oro*, the equivalent of one million cruzados. See the glossary (*cruzado*).

to Borneo, which is a very large island, and from Melaka to Borneo they would take many textiles, as I have said. From there they would bring back large quantities of camphor, turtle [shells], and beeswax, many slaves, bezoar stones, gold, and diamonds that are found on the said island. This navigational route has since ceased to exist in the Lawai River,[190] since the Dutch are continuously in the Strait of Singapore and [in] the Strait of Kundur,[191] which [are][192] 30 leguas[193] from Melaka. All these carracks from Melaka that I have mentioned must perforce pass through these straits.

Two or three of Your Majesty's carracks also used to go to Melaka each year from Goa, and from there they used to go to the Malukus, to load cloves there on Your Majesty's behalf. From Melaka many Portuguese-owned ships used to go to Java, as well as [to] Palembang,[194] Sunda, Arosbaya,[195] Banten,[196] Penarukan,[197] Makassar, Bima, Solor, [and] Timor.[198] From Melaka they used to take the wares I have mentioned, and from these places to Melaka they used to bring many spices and slaves. All these goods used to pay duties to Your Majesty. They use to go and come through these said straits where the Dutch are now continually present. Since they have their fortresses close by, such as [the] city of Ambon,[199] which used to belong to the Portuguese, and Jayakerta,[200] and other Dutch fortresses and factories such as Johor, Patani, Ayutthaya,[201] Lawai, Sukadana,[202] and Banjarmasin,[203] Makassar, and the Malukus, the Dutch have taken all these estuaries [and natural harbours]. It is very worrying.

---

[190] Ms. *Rio de Lavio.*

[191] Ms. *Estreto de Sinquapura e Estreto de Sabão.*

[192] Ms. lit. is.

[193] About 165–185.2 kilometres.

[194] Ms. *Pelibam.*

[195] Ms. *Arisbaia.* See the list of place names (*Arisbaia*).

[196] See the list of place names (*Bantan*).

[197] Ms. *Paneruqua.* Polity in northeastern Java. See also the list of place names (*Paneruca*).

[198] Locations in the eastern Indonesian Archipelago. See also the list of place names (*Bima, Solor, Timor*).

[199] Ms. *Anbouino.*

[200] Ms. *Yactara.* See the list of place names (*Jaquetera*).

[201] Ms. and subsequently with variant spelling: *Yudea.*

[202] Ms. *Suquedani.*

[203] Ms. *Marmacin.* See the list of place names (*Gamarmasin*).

From Melaka they used to go to Sumatra, which is [across the Strait from] Melaka.[204] They used to go with textiles to Siak[205] and Kampar,[206] and they used to bring from there a lot of gold, and porcupine bezoars, and many provisions. The local people are [called] Minangkabau.[207] From Melaka they also used to go to Aceh with textiles, and silk pieces, and eaglewood, and a lot of golden thread. It is a large port. Many Dutch carracks go there to load pepper, as do Turkish carracks and carracks from Aden, and from Masulipatam, and from Pegu. But these Acehnese are very treacherous: they are undesirable people, you cannot trust them nor any of those that are natives from the South. It is necessary to be very cautious when dealing with them.

On the coast of Sumatra there are also two rivers or ports; one is called Jambi[208] and the other Indragiri.[209] These[210] lands have a lot of pepper and the settlements are along the river. Many ships from Patani, known as junks,[211] go to these lands to load pepper on behalf of the Dutch. The city of Patani is on the same coast of Melaka,[212] some 150 leguas[213] outside the Strait of Singapore, and there are two Dutch factories in this land of Patani. There the [Dutch] carracks load this pepper from Jambi and Indragiri, and from Aceh, and this is the pepper that they take to Holland. No peppercorns are taken from India, and they buy this pepper in exchange for pieces of crimson textile,[214] and other fabrics from Europe, barrel guns, and other small items, and reals-of-eight.

This Patani is a large port frequented by[215] many Muslim and heathen vessels as well as many Dutch carracks. They anchor at sea over a legua and a half[216] away. It is a good place to anchor but it is difficult to disembark

[204] Ms. lit. faces. It is also not clear in this specific context whether De Coutre refers to Melaka as the port city, or perhaps the whole of the Malay Peninsula which was referred to as the Melaka Peninsula. Both interpretations make perfect sense here.

[205] Ms. *Siaqua.*

[206] Ms. *Canpar.*

[207] Ms. *Nanacabos.*

[208] Ms. here and subsequently: *Yanbo.*

[209] Ms. here and subsequently with variant spelling: *Chandreguiri.*

[210] Ms. lit. their.

[211] Ms. *yunquos.*

[212] In this instance this toponym refers to the whole of the Malay Peninsula.

[213] About 825–925 kilometres.

[214] Ms. *panos de gran.*

[215] Ms. lit. with.

[216] Probably about three kilometres, possibly further.

owing to the tides there. It is a land frequented by[217] many Malay, Siamese,[218] Javanese and Cambay merchants and traders from other lands. These vessels belonging to the local people[219] anchor closer to shore. You cannot reach them where they are anchored except when the tide is high, because the sea there is shallow, but the Dutch carracks stay [out] at sea.

Similarly, from the kingdom of Siam, from the city of Ayutthaya, north of the Strait of Singapore, Portuguese ships used to load a wood that is known as sappan in this port, to take to Japan. It is like brazilwood, it is used to make dye. [They take] lead, and deer antler[220] and other animals; and *lixo*,[221] and lead carbonate.[222] They used to sell these wares in Japan, and from there they would bring back nothing less than silver, and they used to go to the port of Macao, and there they would use the silver to trade for [other] commodities, as I have mentioned, which were then sent to India. They used to travel from China to Melaka, and from there to Goa. These voyages from Siam to Japan used to be granted as a royal favour[223] by Your Majesty, sailed by men who had been granted this voyage as a royal favour by Your Majesty for their services.

Men from China from the city of Macao also used to go to Japan and they used to load very large carracks with wares from China. In Japan they used to go selling [these wares] at Nagasaki[224] and when they returned to Macao from Japan, the carracks used to come back laden with silver. The contents of each carrack used to be worth more than 1.5 million cruzados,[225] and Your Majesty grants these voyages as a royal favour, and the individual to whom it is granted is known as the captain of [the] China [voyage]. These carracks are owned by the said individuals or are leased by them, and the said captain is responsible for the cargoes and repairs of these carracks. They are sent with merchants for a percentage, so it is as though this voyage is sailed under the authority of the captain but headed by merchants.

---

[217] Ms. lit. of.

[218] Ms. *siamos.*

[219] Ms. *gentes de terra.*

[220] Ms. *corama de venados.*

[221] Ms. *lixo.* Leather or skin of the stingray. See also the glossary (*lixa*).

[222] Ms. *alvaiade.*

[223] Ms. here and subsequently: *merced.*

[224] Ms. *Nangisaqui.* See the list of place names (*Nangisaqui*).

[225] 1.5 *conto de oro*, equivalent to about 43.65 metric tons of coin-grade silver. See the glossary (*conto de oro, cruzado*).

Hand-coloured city plan of Goa by João Albarnaz I, *Plantas das Cidades, e Fortalezas da Conquista de Índia Oriental* (Maps of the Cities and Fortresses of the Conquest of the East Indies), c.1648. (Munich, BSB, Cod. Icon. 162, pl. 8, fol. 21).

Now the Dutch are in Japan.[226] No more [Portuguese] vessels go from China or from Macao except for galliots, which face many risks at sea, since they are small vessels, and they also face the risk of encountering the Dutch. From Macao they also used to sail to Manila; they [used to] take a lot of silk there and sales were brisk and lucrative for New Spain, and a lot of silver used to be brought to Macao.

All this is no more than a recommendation to do damage to the rebels, and an indication of the ports where we could capture ships and trade, and the wares that are traded between different lands, even though I have not identified the latitude[227] of the ports. I am not a pilot. It will be possible to ascertain the latitude of the ports and where they are positioned by means of a sailing chart.

---

[226] The VOC established trading relations with Japan after 1609, and held a monopoly of foreign trade after 1637.

[227] Ms. here and subsequently: *altura*.

MEMORIAL

II

About the commerce that used to take place in India, especially in Melaka, before the Dutch went to that state.[1]

Your Excellency:

To inform Your Excellency about the commerce that used to take place in India, especially in Melaka, before the Dutch went to that state.

Firstly, with reference to the South: some years ago, in the harbour or port of Melaka, a fortress of His Majesty, there used to be over 500 vessels, some large and others small; namely, ships, junks, balas, lancharas,[2] and all kinds of trading vessels. The junks used to come from the Banda Islands, and from Makassar, and from the island of Java, and from all those kingdoms they used to come laden with mace, nutmeg, cloves, benzoin,[3] sugar, rattan,[4] beeswax, and other commodities. Other junks used to come from the kingdom of Borneo,[5] laden with turtle [shell], camphor, beeswax, and they brought many bezoars, and some diamonds and gold.

[1] BNE, Ms. 2780, fol. 268 recto–269 verso.

[2] See the glossary for a definition and description of these vessel types.

[3] Ms. here and subsequently: *menguín*.

[4] Ms. *rotta*.

[5] The precursor of present-day Brunei. See also the list of place names (*Borneo*).

The king of Aceh receives Dutch guests. From Theodore de Bry, *Icones seu Gennuinae et Expressae Delineationes Omnium Memorabilium* (Images or Authentic and Accurate Depiction of All Memorable Events), Frankfurt am Main, 1607. (Leiden, Bibliotheca Thysiana, THYS 874, pl. 10).

Other junks used to come from the kingdom of Johor,[6] and from that of Pahang, and from the kingdom of Patani, and that of Ligor,[7] and from the kingdom of Siam, which used to come laden with sappanwood.[8] This is used to make dyes to colour fabrics, which are prepared on the Coromandel Coast. They used to bring civet,[9] beeswax, and a lot of benzoin, and a lot of gold to buy textiles.[10] Other junks used to come from the kingdom of Cambodia,[11] and from that of Champa, and from that of Cochinchina; the latter used to come laden with eaglewood,[12] kalambak,[13] benzoin, and they

[6] Ms. *Jor.*

[7] Ms. *Lugor.*

[8] Ms. *sapan.*

[9] Ms. *argalia.*

[10] Ms. here and subsequently: *ropas.*

[11] Ms. *Camboya.*

[12] Ms. *agle.*

[13] Ms. *clanbuco.*

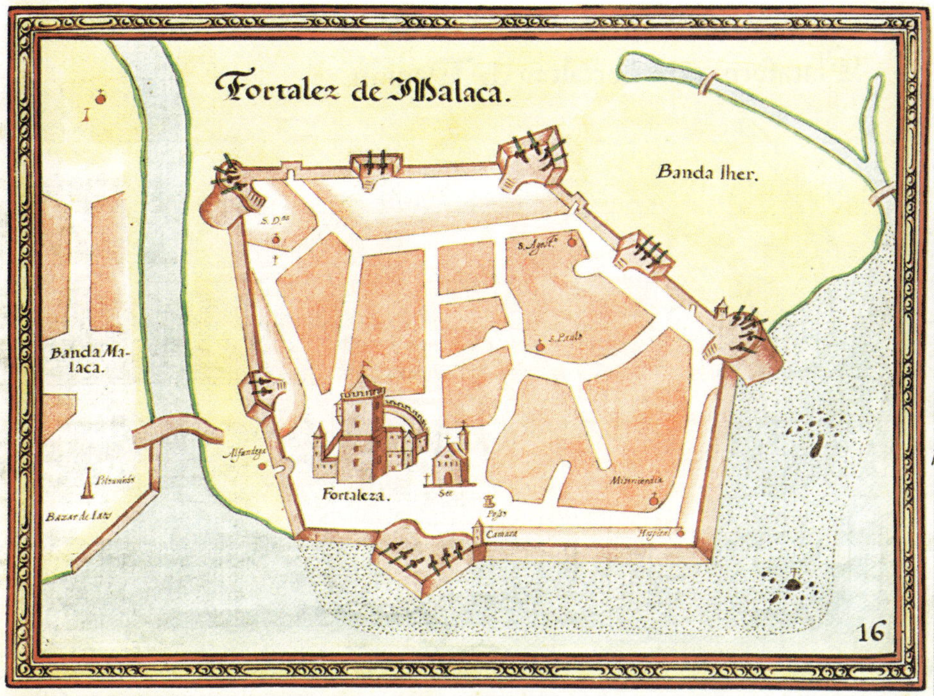

Hand-coloured city plan of Melaka by João Albarnaz I, *Plantas das Cidades, e Fortalezas da Conquista de Índia Oriental* (Maps of the Cities and Fortresses of the Conquest of the East Indies), c.1648 (Munich, BSB, Cod. Icon. 162, pl. 16, fol. 37).

used to bring a lot of gold, all of it to be used in exchange for textiles. Other junks used to come from the kingdom of Jambi, and from that of Indragiri, and from that of Siak, and from that of Kampar, and from that of Perak, and from that of Kedah. These used to bring pepper, tin[14] and gold, to be used [to trade] for textiles.

Furthermore 35 or 40 ships used to come to Melaka from Goa, from Chaul, from Cochin, from Nagapattinam, from Mylapur, and from the entire Coromandel Coast, and from the kingdom of Bengal, and from the kingdom of Pegu. These ships used to come laden with textiles from Cambay[15] and from Sindh;[16] and other ships [used to come laden with] textiles from the Coromandel Coast, and others would come laden with textiles and *colchas*,[17] [and] marquees[18] made of [colcha] de montaria.

[14] Ms. *calayn*.

[15] Ms. *Cambaya*.

[16] Ms. *Sinde*. See the list of place names (*Sinde*).

[17] A fine cotton piece. See also the glossary (*colcha*).

[18] Ms. here and subsequently: *pavellones*.

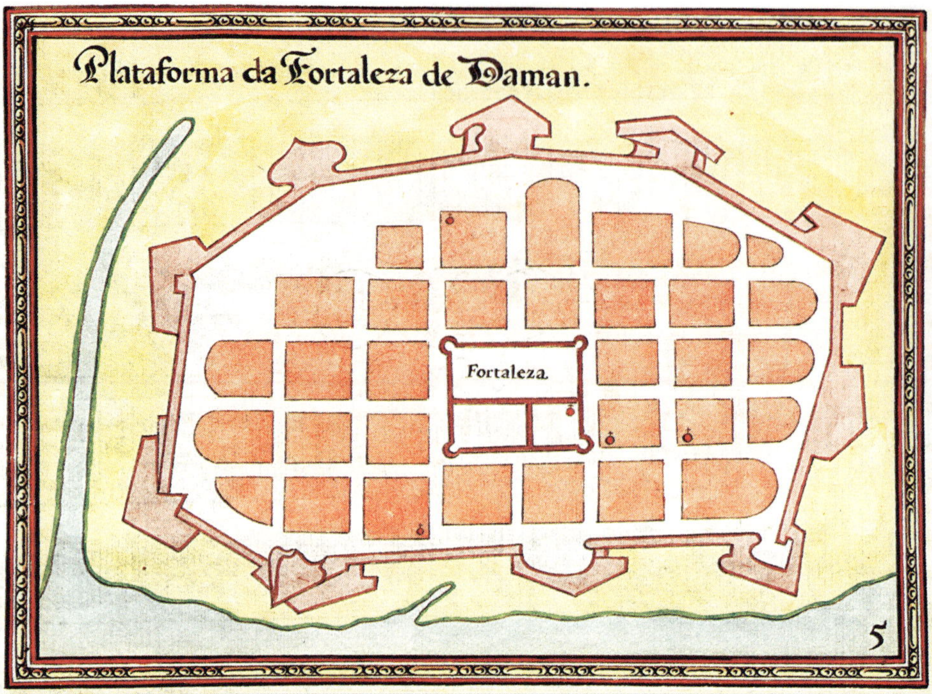

Hand-coloured city plan of Daman by João Albarnaz I, *Plantas das Cidades, e Fortalezas da Conquista de Índia Oriental* (Maps of the Cities and Fortresses of the Conquest of the East Indies), c.1648. (Munich, BSB, Cod. Icon. 162, pl. 5, fol. 15).

From the kingdom of Bengal and from that of Pegu they used to bring a lot of lac, beeswax, and many provisions, and many precious stones such as rubies and sapphires.

The ships that used to come from Goa and other lands used to bring a lot of wheat, wine, olive oil, [and] butter; which the city of Melaka does not have. Four more ships used to go to China and to Japan, and another two ships used to come from the Maluku islands, every year, laden with cloves for His Majesty, which were the taxes[19] that those lands used to pay to His Majesty. All these vessels that I have mentioned used to come to Melaka annually to trade and they used to pay duties[20] to His Majesty.

The Portuguese used to sell their textiles and subsequently buy spices and other commodities. They used to load up their ships and sail to Goa and Cochin; there they once again used to pay duties to His

[19] Ms. *foros*.

[20] Ms. here and subsequently: *derechos*.

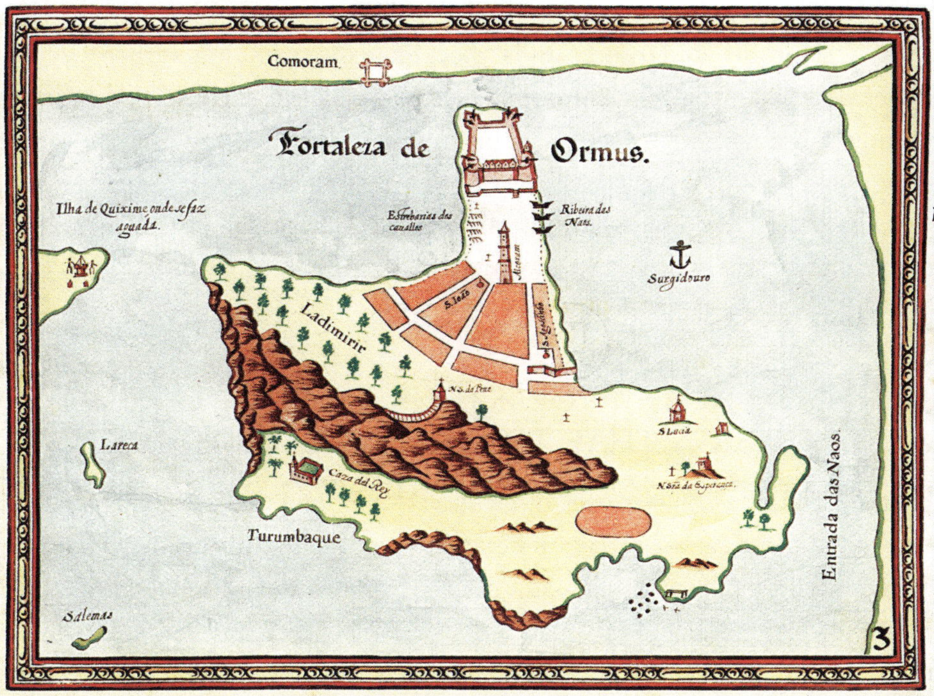

Hand-coloured plan of Hormuz by João Albarnaz I, *Plantas das Cidades, e Fortalezas da Conquista de Índia Oriental* (Maps of the Cities and Fortresses of the Conquest of the East Indies), c.1648. (Munich, BSB, Cod. Icon. 162, pl. 3, fol. 11).

Majesty, apart from the two ships laden with cloves that used to come from the Malukus on behalf of His Majesty, and apart from three or four ships that used to come to Goa every year from China, laden with raw and twisted silks, and many bolts of velvet, damask, satins, taffeta, and many colchas, marquees, decorative silk panels to adorn houses, and large quantities of musk and seed pearls and small pearls, and a lot of gold, and camphor,[21] *radix Chinae*, benzoin, alum, and tintinago, Chinese porcelain, sugar, and other commodities.

Each of these ships from China used to render to His Majesty's customs house in Goa 50,000–60,000[22] pardaos in duties: each pardao is [worth] a real-of-eight.[23] Then they used to take these wares from Goa to the north: [to] Chaul, Cambay, Diu, Daman, Muscat, and Hormuz.

---

[21] Ms. *alcamfor*.

[22] Ms. *and*.

[23] Equivalent to 1.624 metric tons of coin-grade silver.

They used to pay export duties[24] on these wares as well, and in Diu, Muscat, Hormuz and other lands they likewise paid duties there to His Majesty. In addition, the ships that used to sail every year from India to Portugal, brought many spices. This merchandise had to pay an export duty, too.

His Majesty's vassals have lost all of this trade. Now all this trade is in the hands of the Dutch, with which they sustain their fleets, and their thievery.

SO AS TO ALSO INFORM YOUR EXCELLENCY ABOUT THE WARES THAT THE DUTCH TAKE TO INDIA

First of all they take many reals-of-eight, and a lot of gold, but not as much as compared to the carracks that sail between Portugal and India. They take a lot of coral fashioned into rosaries and polished branches, and rough coral. They take a lot of processed and rough amber,[25] which they buy in Danzig. They take many tapestries. They take many pieces of crimson and second grade crimson cloth pieces, cocheneal[26] and second grade cocheneal [cloth],[27] and all kinds of textiles in a spectrum of colours from England. They take a lot of mercury,[28] and vermilion,[29] and a lot of storax,[30] and many sword blades, and many harquebuses,[31] and padlocks, knives, mirrors, lead, and other wares. And [they take] some jewels, but only a few; not as many as the Portuguese.

Jaques de Coutre.

Most Excellent Lord:
Trade that the Portuguese used to have in Melaka before the Dutch went to the East Indies.[32]

---

[24] Ms. here and subsequently: *las salidas*.
[25] This is a reference to Baltic amber. See also the glossary (*amber*).
[26] A red dye of insect origin. See also the glossary (*cocheneal*).
[27] The translation of *media grana* and *media cochunilas* has been taken from M. Léon Diguet, "Histoire de la cochenille au Mexique", *Journal de la Société des Américanistes* 6 (1909): 97, as a "class" or "quality" of textile.
[28] Ms. *azogue*. See the glossary (*mercury*).
[29] Ms. *bermellon*.
[30] Ms. *reçamalla*. See the glossary (*rassamalla*).
[31] Ms. *arcabuces*. See the glossary (*harquebus*).
[32] Ms. *Yndia Oriental*.

MEMORIAL

III

Information about building some castles and fortresses in the Straits of Singapore and other regions of the South, etc.[1]

The coast of Melaka extends to the north and south nearly as far as the Strait of Singapore.[2] Many ships sail to Melaka and return through this strait, these large and small baxeles are from the following kingdoms: from the kingdoms of Johor, Pahang, Patani, Ligor, Siam, Cambodia, Champa, Cochinchina; carracks[3] and junks from China, Zhangzhou,[4] from Manila and Japan; and some baxeles from the Malukus; and from the kingdom of Borneo,[5] Lawai,[6] Banjarmasin,[7] and from all the islands of Borneo. All these vessels pass through the said Straits of Singapore.

When the Javanese come to know that in Melaka there is a captain who mistreats them—as sometimes was the case, though their course is through the Strait of Kundur[8] to Melaka—they go from inside and around the islands

[1] BNE, Ms. 2780, fol. 270 recto–274 recto.
[2] Ms. here and subsequently with variant spelling: *Estrecho de Sincapura*. See the list of place names (*Estrecho de Sincapura*).
[3] Ms. *naos*.
[4] Ms. *de la China, e de Chincheos*.
[5] A precursor of present-day Brunei.
[6] Ms. *Lavio*.
[7] Ms. *Gamarmasin*.
[8] Ms. *Estrecho de Saban*.

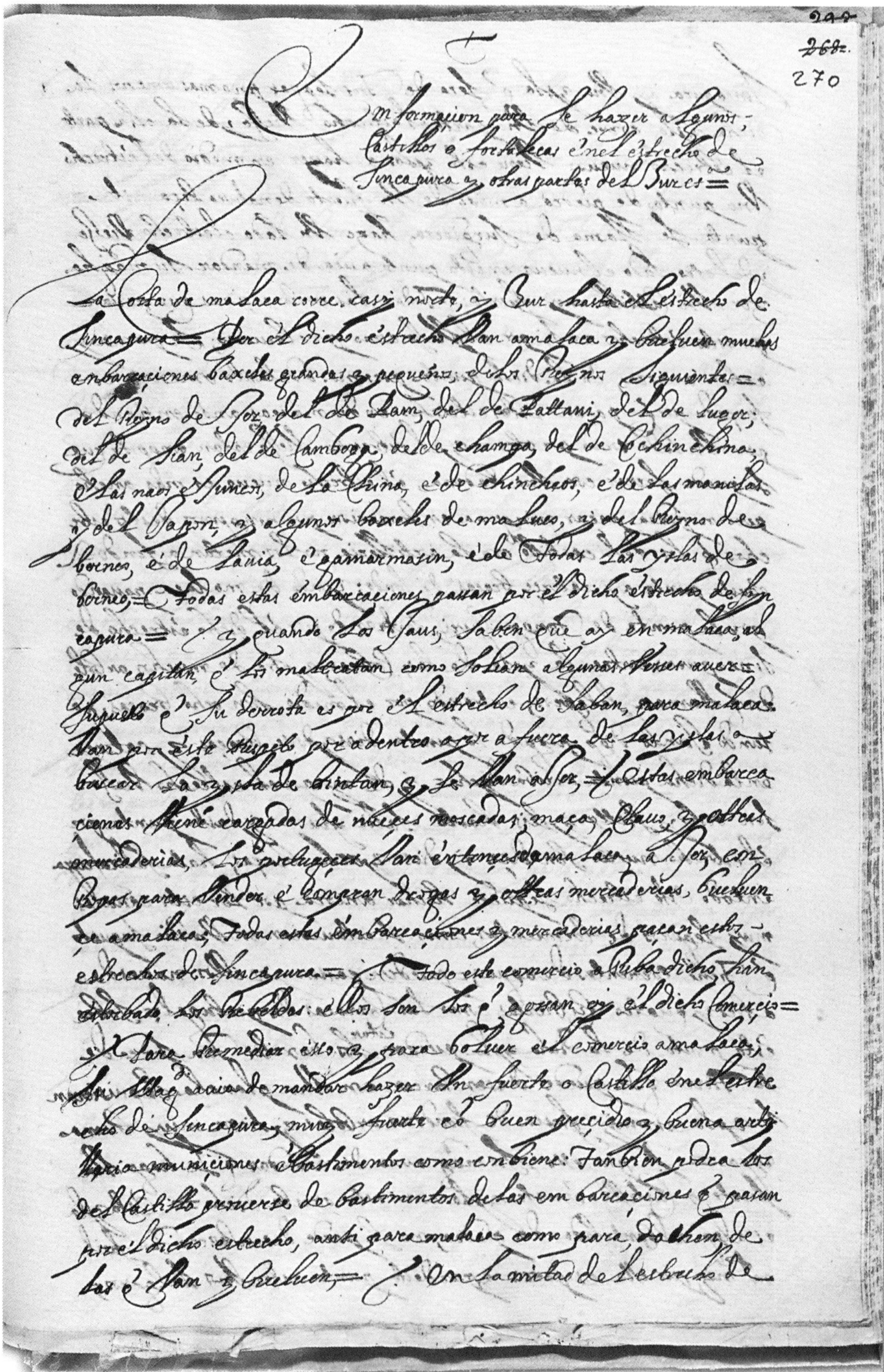

270

Enformacion para se hazer algunos castillos o fortaleças en el estrecho de Sincapura y otras partes del Sur =

La costa de malaca corre casi norte y Sur hasta el estrecho de Sincapura = por el dicho estrecho van a malaca y buelven muchas embarcaciones baxeles grandes y pequeños de los Reynos siguientes = del Reyno de Jor del de Pan del de Pattani del de Sugor del de Sian del de Camboja del de Champa del de Cochinchina

First page of the memorial *Emformación para se hazer algunos castillos o fortaleças en el Estrecho de Sincapura y otras partes del sur, etc.* (Information about Building Some Castles and Fortresses in the Strait of Singapore and Other Locations in the South, etc.) in which Jacques de Coutre advised the king of Spain and Portugal on the construction of fortresses on present-day Sentosa, along the eastern coast of Singapore (around Changi) and at the Muar River estuary. (Madrid, BNE, Ms. 2780, fol. 270 recto.)

in search of the island of Bintan, and they go to Johor.[9] These vessels come laden with nutmeg, mace, cloves and other merchandise. The Portuguese then go from Melaka to Johor, with textiles[10] to sell, and buy spices and other commodities; before returning to Melaka. All these vessels and wares pass through these Straits of Singapore.[11]

All this commerce as described above has been usurped by the rebels. They are the ones who today benefit from the said trade. To remedy this state of affairs and redirect trade to Melaka, Your Majesty must order that a very strong fortress or citadel be built in the Strait of Singapore,[12] with a good garrison[13] and good artillery, munitions and supplies as is advisable. The residents of the citadel could also acquire supplies from the vessels that pass through the said Strait, from those that sail towards Melaka as well as those that are going to Aceh.[14]

In the middle of the Singapore Straits there is an island, which measures more or less three leguas.[15] The Old Strait[16] is [situated] on one side of the aforementioned island, the New Strait[17] on the other. This island forms a stone point [which is located] between the [two] Straits [and] that resembles a fortress created by nature. This point is called *Surgídera*;[18] the Old Strait lies on one side [of it], and the New Strait on the other. Your Majesty should order that a very strong citadel be built on this point; all the vessels that pass through these Straits, through the Old Strait as well as through the New Strait, stop and drop anchor around the said point. It is necessary to do so because two [daily] tides pass through these Straits, entering from one side as well as from the other.

The Old Strait is so narrow that it can be closed off with a chain; the New Strait is wider, but no vessel can pass through either of these straits

---

9 Ms. here and subsequently: *Jor*.

10 Ms. *ropas*.

11 Ms. *Estrechos de Sincapura*. Note the use of the plural here.

12 Ms. *Estrecho de Sincapura*.

13 Ms. *precidio*.

14 Ms. *Achen*.

15 This is a reference to present-day Sentosa. Probably about six kilometres but possibly further. De Coutre's estimate may have included islands located to the southeast of present-day Sentosa.

16 Ms. here and subsequently: *Estrecho Viejo*. See the list of place names (*Estrecho Viejo*).

17 Ms. here and subsequently: *Estrecho Nuevo*. See the list of place names (*Estrecho Nuevo*).

18 *Surgídera* means point of anchorage in this instance. See also the list of place names (*Surgídera*).

Section of an early modern anonymous English map of the Old Strait of Singapore, the narrow passage between present-day Sentosa and Keppel Harbour. The triangular shape of Pulau Hantu is clearly visible. (London, British Library, Add. 15737 fol. 10).

without being in reaching distance from the citadel, which can then sink them with artillery. At [Surgídera] point [the water] is 14 brazas deep.[19] As one comes from Melaka [one passes] the promontory of Tanjung Bulus,[20] and enters the said Strait of Singapore between the Ilha das Cobras[21] and another island[22] that is densely forested with trees that they call *salgeros.*[23] Entering by the middle [the water measures] eight brazas[24] deep; when approaching the aforementioned [Surgídera] point it is 10 and 12 brazas, and 14 next to it.[25] [Passing] through the Old Strait from this point [the water measures] eight, seven and six [brazas] up to the exit;[26] [passing through] the New Strait from [Surgídera] point the water measures twelve, ten and eight brazas until one exits it.[27]

One can drop anchor anywhere in these Straits since these channels are safely sheltered from storms, as though one were in a river, since[28] there are water currents. Ships with three and four decks can pass through these straits, such as the carracks[29] from Portugal. At the tip of the said island[30] the baxeles[31] can come so close to shore that it is possible to disembark on a plank when necessary. The island is very lush with trees with [thick] foliage, and it [also] has very good [fresh] water. This is why Your Majesty should order a fort or citadel to be built on this island, as mentioned above. This island has a number of stone cliffs, [where] it is not easy to disembark, but it is none the worse for this. There are some *salgeros* beside this point.

On the side of the New Strait, one could build a quay here for batels[32] and galleys, [and] ships, and to service the said citadel. The island has flat land as well as cliffs. When our ships come and go to China and Manila[33]

---

[19] Ms. here and subsequently: *braças*. About 23.4–25.6 metres.

[20] Ms. *Tangonburi*. See the list of place names (*Tangonburi*).

[21] Lit. "Island of the Cobras"; present-day Pulau Merambong. See also the list of place names (*Ysla de Cobras*).

[22] This appears to be a reference to the western side of present-day Singapore Island.

[23] The term *salgero* (or *salguero*) refers to a type of willow tree.

[24] About 13.4–14.6 metres. See also the glossary (*braça*).

[25] About 16.7–18.3, 20–22 and 23.4–25.6 metres.

[26] About 13.4–14.6, 11.7–12.8 and 10–11 metres.

[27] About 20–22, 16.7–18.3 and 13.4–14.6 metres.

[28] Ms. *supuesto que*.

[29] Ms. *carracas*.

[30] At the location of the former Fort Siloso built by the British.

[31] A type of vessel. See also the glossary (*baxel*).

[32] A type of vessel. See also the glossary (*batel*).

[33] Ms. *Manilas*. This could also be understood to mean the Philippines in general.

and other parts, they—and other friendly baxeles—can take shelter below the citadel when they hear news of enemies. There are many fishermen called *saletes*[34] in these Straits. They are local people, Malays.[35] If one accompanies and pays them, they will serve that person well. These people visit all the islands around these Straits, and where there are enemies, they come to warn [us] in exchange for [a piece of] cloth worth four reals,[36] which they are given, and it is also for them to remain under our protection.

For the purposes of [maintaining] the said commerce, Your Majesty must maintain in the said Strait five or six well-armed Manila galleys, [that be] placed under [the command of] the citadel to patrol the Strait. These Manila galleys are sufficiently light that they can enter and leave with ease whenever necessary. The enemy will [then] not be in a position to capture as many [vessels] as they now habitually do, nor given the presence of the galleys will they be able to keep one ship at one entrance of the Strait and another at the opposite entrance, as they generally do now, and capture all the junks that pass through these Straits. The enemy will no longer be able to separate their ships, one from the other, because of the lulls and the absence of wind that prevail in this region. This way the [galleys] can patrol the Straits, and the aforementioned vessels would be able to call at this fort and [also] at Melaka, which is presently not possible because the enemy impedes them from doing so. The said galleys can proceed to the Strait of Kundur; from there one [strait] is no more than ten leguas[37] away from the other and there are many channels for the galleys to pass through the said Strait of Kundur. Thus, in a few days they will come to know of all the passageways owing to the knowledge of the fishermen who are known as *orang laut*.[38] These *orang laut* live aboard very small vessels; they sleep there and live and are born on their boats.[39] In short, these vessels are their home.

When our armada arrives at this place to build the said citadel, it will then be necessary to entrench oneself at the aforementioned point with

---

[34] Ms. here and subsequently with different spellings: *saletes*. See the glossary (*orang laut, saletes*).

[35] Ms. *Malayos*.

[36] About 15 grams of coin-grade silver. See also the glossary (*real*).

[37] About 55–62 kilometres.

[38] Ms. here and subsequently with different spellings: *Saletes*.

[39] For a more detailed description of the *orang laut* inhabiting the Old Strait of Singapore, see ch. II and III of the *Vida*.

sacks of earth,[40] and place the artillery in the centre according to the manner and design of the citadel to be built. There is no lack of wood there to entrench oneself while one prepares materials to build the fortification. There is no lack of stone here either and [there are] lots of white stones from the sea that they call [*batu*] *karang*,[41] which is similar to limestone or gypsum. There is also a lot of firewood to burn after having made provisions for materials. [The men of the armada] will then be able to begin constructing the walls and the bulwarks and anything else that is advisable. When they finish a bulwark they can begin to build another, so that they are always entrenched [and prepared] for anything unforeseen. For this and other purposes Your Majesty must dispatch engineers who are well versed in [building] fortifications.

It is advisable that these [proposed] citadels be impregnable, [for] then the rebels will not be able to pass through here, nor the [king of] Aceh with his armadas to sack Johor or the kingdom of Pahang.[42] They would be forced to pass through the Strait of Kundur and bypass the islands, or sail between them; [in any case] it would significantly constrain their movements. When we have galleys stationed there, they can patrol the Strait of Kundur. Although the strait is broad it contains a lot of shoals. Sometimes carracks[43] remain here [at Surgídera point] for seven or eight days without being able to sail through because of contrary winds, even when the tide is in their favour. It is a challenging Strait, and the galleys are thus ideally suited for capturing ships lying at anchor. In this way the [galleys] will be able to inflict a great deal of damage on the enemy.

The rebels come with their ships to load pepper, drop anchor and moor around the said Strait of Kundur outside the Indragiri and Jambi Rivers, where [the water] is not very deep. No more than about 25 leguas[44] separate the aforementioned point from these river estuaries. Meanwhile, our galleys can be on [their heels] night or day, and our enemies will not be able to load pepper, which is the mainstay of their commerce [in these regions]. Since it [would be] in close proximity to our [proposed] fortress, our men would be able to trade

---

[40] It is assumed in this instance that De Coutre actually meant sacks of rock or sand.

[41] Ms. *caran*. This is the Malay word for coral. See also the glossary (*karang*).

[42] Ms. *reyno de Pam*.

[43] Ms. *naos*.

[44] About 138–54 kilometres.

and negotiate. Only small vessels are able to enter this river.[45] Nor would the rebels find refuge in Palembang,[46] which is a kingdom that has always been on friendly terms with us. So, with these galleys and the citadel one could inflict significant damage to the enemy and its trade, and be able to [also] patrol the Straits. When these Straits are patrolled and free [of enemy craft], all the vessels will come from all around to call at the fort and [also] Melaka, because the locals[47] are more than happy to sell their wares to us rather than to the [Dutch] rebels, because the rebels charge levies on all their merchandise, on what they buy as well as what they sell. The [locals][48] evidently do not like the [Dutch] rebels, because they do not sell nor buy like the Portuguese used to.

It is necessary to build a second fortress or citadel in the Johor River estuary[49] at the promontory[50] of the *Isla de la Sabandaría Vieja*.[51] This island is situated in the Johor River estuary and is bordered by the Old Strait and Tebrau Strait.[52] This [second] fortress should be located about three leguas[53] from the [first fortress] at the [Singapore] Straits. The said Isla de la Sabandaria Vieja measures about seven leguas across.[54] The [second] citadel situated at the Johor River estuary and the [first one] at the Singapore Straits can lend each other assistance either by sea or by land. The Old Strait is situated between one island [Singapore] and the other [Sentosa]; it resembles a river that can be sealed off with a chain. At this [second] location Your Majesty must order a citadel to be built in accordance to the first one that has been mentioned [above]. [Your Majesty] should become the lord of this port, which is one of the best that serves the [East] Indies.[55] [Your Majesty]

---

[45] Perhaps De Coutre implied either one, or both, the Jambi and Indragiri Rivers.

[46] Ms. *Polinban*.

[47] Ms. *Yndios*.

[48] Ms. lit. They.

[49] Ms. *barra de Jor*.

[50] Ms. *punta*. A reference to present-day Changi Point, also known from 17th-century Portuguese cartographical specimens (esp. Manoel Godinho de Erédia) as Tanjung Rusa. See the map on p. 76.

[51] Singapore Island. See also the list of place names (*Ysla de la Sabandaria Vieja*).

[52] Ms. *Salet Boru*. See the list of place names (*Salet Boru*).

[53] About 16.5–18.5 kilometres.

[54] About 38.5–43.2 kilometres.

[55] Indication here is that Singapore had a functioning port and that it was in the words of De Coutre "one of the best in the [East] Indies".

could build a city there and become the lord of this kingdom.[56] By constructing this citadel there, no enemy ships would be able to enter without being sunk, even though the Johor River is wide and at the promontory of Johor Lama[57] is a shoal that is surrounded by sea.[58]

When large ships arrive, they move closer to the point where the fortress should be built, and across, [just] a stone's throw away, is a shoal. A small fort[59] could be built on the said shoal to monitor the entire [Johor] River[60] and to prevent both large and small baxeles from entering. The enemy rebels repair and careen their ships in this river estuary. The [Johor] River is very wide and scenic; ships laden with wares can enter and exit without any danger up to 10 or even 12 leguas upstream.[61] There is no lack of wood in these parts to entrench oneself after arriving, nor is there a lack of materials [with which] to build the citadel, nor a dearth of stones with which to make lime and plaster. In this port, near the aforesaid promontory, the Portuguese captured—[or rather] Dom Paulo de Lima[62] captured—Johor Lama, but they did not wish to keep it.

The king of the city of Johor Lama fled and went to live on the island of Bintan, and later returned and built another city, [located] 14 leguas upstream, which is called Batu Sawar,[63] [but which] the Portuguese call New Johor.[64] The king of Aceh[65] captured this port and has kept it occupied, but it could be taken with 1,500 men, as could the city of Pahang,[66] which the said king of Aceh has [also] occupied. For this purpose it would be good to call on the aforementioned king of Johor, since there are four

---

[56] In effect, De Coutre proposed here the establishment of a European-style city on the main island of Singapore two centuries before the British did.

[57] Ms. here and subsequently: *Jor Viejo*. See the list of place names (*Jor, Jor Viejo*).

[58] This is possibly a reference to the area around present-day Pulau Tekong.

[59] De Coutre appears to be suggesting the construction of a third fortification.

[60] Presumably De Coutre meant the river estuary here.

[61] About 55–74 kilometres upstream.

[62] Ms. *Don Pablo de Lima*. Dom Paulo Lima de Pereira launched an attack on Johor Lama and the fortress Kota Batu in the year 1587. See SMS, esp. pp. 209–28.

[63] About 77–85.5 kilometres.

[64] Ms. *Jor Nuevo*.

[65] Iskandar Muda of Aceh. The Acehnese launched a successful attack on the Johor River region and Batu Sawar in 1613. See SMS, pp. 112–5.

[66] Ms. *ciudad de Pam*. The city and "kingdom" of Pahang was previously described by De Coutre in chapter IV of his *Vida*.

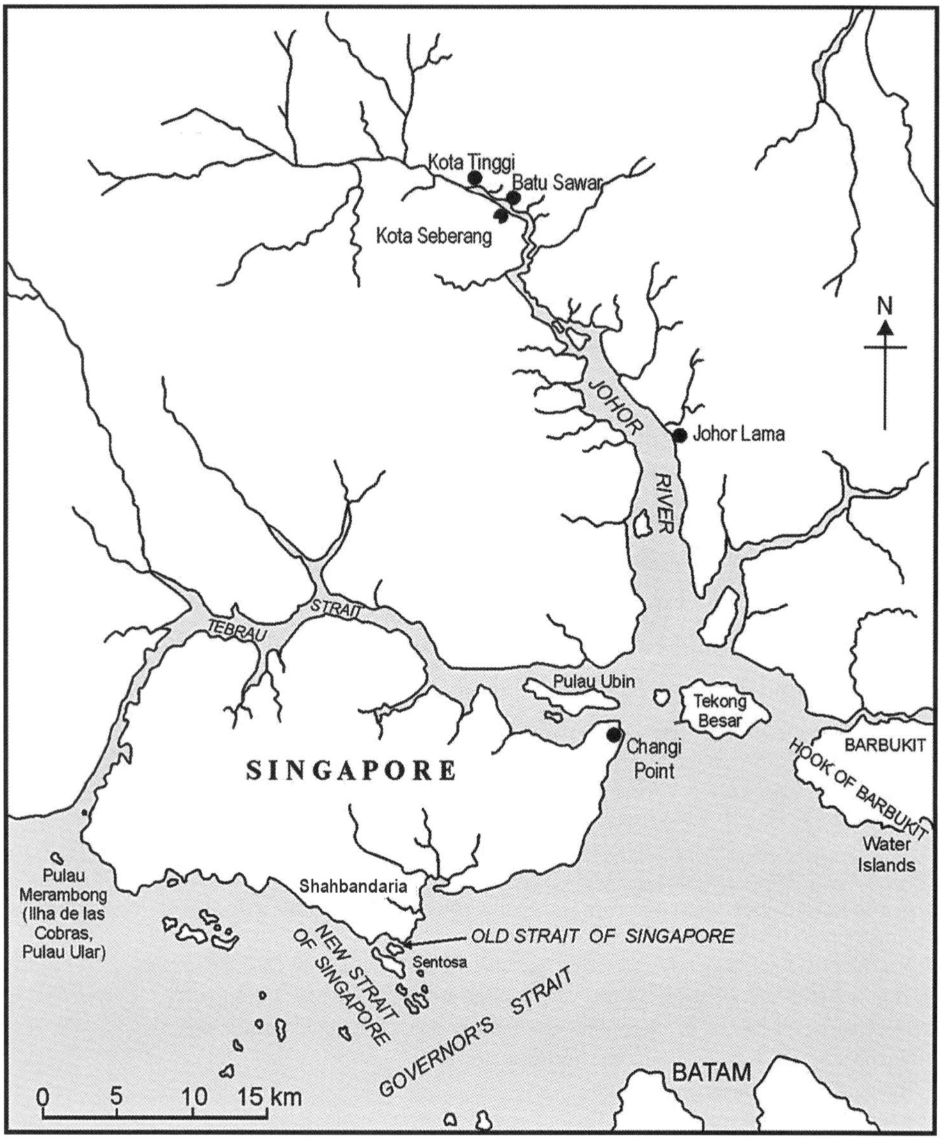

Map of the southern portions of the Malay Peninsula with the Singapore and Melaka Straits and the historic upstream towns of the Johor River region.

brothers,[67] and put one of them in power. Once we have constructed the citadels, we will be safe from the local people,[68] and Your Majesty would have a vassal king [just] like the king of Hormuz[69] used to be. Over time there will be more land, and there will be more provisions for citadels and anything that is necessary, help and assistance for any and all purposes, and the said king of Aceh will no longer be that powerful. When the natives see their monarch and our protection, on the island of Sumatra, Siak,[70] Kampar,[71] Bengkalis[72] and the lands of Aru,[73] all of them will rise up against the [king of] Aceh, for they are Malays.[74]

This land used to belong to the king of Johor, and the island of Sumatra features a kingdom that was governed by Raja Siak,[75] who was a brother of the said king of Johor.[76] Siak is situated at the entrance of the Kundur Strait, [and the raja] controlled more than 60 leguas[77] of coastline. The king of Aceh has now occupied it all. Your Majesty could maintain galleys and galleons in this Johor River. They can enter and exit with the tide and wind. If Your Majesty had six or seven Dunkirk galleons[78] in this port, the rebels would not be safe anywhere in the South, because the [Dutch] rebels drop anchor and moor more than a legua and a half[79] [from the shore] in each and every port in the South.[80] It is possible to get close to them, because they are separated from one another—there is one ship in one port, two in another. As has been said, with the help

---

[67] These four brothers are: Ala'uddin Ri'ayat Shah who ruled as sultan between 1597–1613/5; Raja Bongsu, later Sultan Ma'ayat Shah, who ruled from 1613/5–1623, as well as the Raja Laut and Raja Siak. For a contemporaneous description of these individuals by Dutch Admiral Cornelis Matelieff de Jonge dating from 1606, see GPFT, appendix 13, pp. 211–5.

[68] Ms. *gente de la tierra.*

[69] Ms. *el de Ormus.* See the list of place names (*Ormus*).

[70] Ms. *Çiaca.* See the list of place names (*Siaca*).

[71] Polity and river in central-eastern Sumatra not far from Singapore, linked historically to Melaka and later Johor.

[72] Ms. *Bincales.* Port in central-eastern Sumatra, in the southern reaches of the Melaka Strait.

[73] Ms. *terras d'Aru.* Polity in central-eastern Sumatra. See also the list of place names (*Aru*).

[74] Ms. *Malayos.* Here De Coutre intimated that, while the peoples of Siak, Kampar, Bengkalis and Aru were considered "Malays", the Acehnese (who were their overlords) evidently were not.

[75] Ms. *raxo Siaca.*

[76] See also note 67 above. Concerning the identity of Raja Siak, see GPFT, appendix 13, pp. 213–4.

[77] About 330–70 kilometres.

[78] Ms. here and subsequently: *galeones de Dunquerque.*

[79] Probably about three kilometres, possibly further.

[80] Ms. *en el Sur*; insular and peninsular Southeast Asia.

of the fishermen,[81] our ships can garner information on the whereabouts of the [Dutch] rebels and hence attack them. As they belong to a single people,[82] our men are very often mistaken for the [Dutch] rebels, both by night and by day. In this way one can deprive the rebels of commerce and destroy them.

In order to construct these fortifications, it will be necessary that Your Majesty dispatch 20 galleons with Castilian Spaniards,[83] among them [there should be] about six or seven Dunkirk galleons, which make a total of 20 galleons. [They need to be] well-equipped with artillery and supplies, with each having 250 men and some engineers with the appropriate tools [to build] the fortifications. On arriving in the Strait of Singapore they can inform Manila, [and] should there be an armada [stationed] there, they could come and join them. [In Manila there are] principally the galleys. Your Majesty must dispatch skilled craftsmen to the Johor River who know how to build galleys. There is no lack of [construction] sites or wood to build them, there is [also] no lack of trees to make masts for the galleys, nor [a lack of] cordage, ribs, oars, pitch, [or] oil with which to paint the hull.

As for the crew for the galleys, *kaffirs*[84] can be brought from Goa. They are strong, dark-skinned people like those from Angola. They can be bought in Goa for 20 reals-of-eight[85] per head. From Manila the Spanish go to Goa to buy [them] for their galleys, and they load ships [full] of these people. Our ships could also proceed to the Coromandel Coast[86] and load textiles and take on spices like the Dutch do. Your Majesty has two ports on the Coromandel Coast, one of which is called Nagapattinam[87] and the other São Tomé,[88] where one could dispose of the cargoes. The Portuguese profit greatly from this commerce. From Johor or from the Straits [of Singapore] one can send ships laden with spices to Spain like the Portuguese do, and in this way one will fill Spain, Castile[89] and

[81] Ms. *pescadores*. The orang laut.

[82] Ms. *de una nación*.

[83] Ms. *Españoles castellanos*.

[84] Ms. *Cafres*.

[85] About 541 grams of coin-grade silver.

[86] Ms. here and subsequently: *Costa de Cheramandel*.

[87] Ms. *Negapatan*. Port on the Coromandel Coast. See also the list of place names (*Negapatan*).

[88] Ms. *San Thomé*. See the list of place names (*Melapor*).

[89] See the list of place names (*Castilla*).

Portugal with spices, and Your Majesty's customs houses will yield much more. From there merchants can send [these wares] to France and Germany.

In this way, the Dutch will not be able to reap [much] profits. In this way they and their trade will diminish. As [the VOC] is a company of merchants [and] if there are no profits, each one will withdraw from this company, in view of low profits. Manila and these two citadels or fortresses, [together with] Melaka and Macao, can assist one another, because they are not a [great] distance away from each other. [As for] the two citadels, one in the Straits and the other at the mouth of the Johor River, it is necessary that they both be built in a trice. This will enable them to assist and aid each other by sea and by land, as has been mentioned above. It will be necessary to entrench oneself quickly: there is no absence of safe locations, nor will there be anyone [there] to [stop] them. Before the [Dutch] rebels learn about [the arrival of our men], they will already have established themselves. [Your Majesty] can station ten galleons in the Straits by the fortress and another ten at the mouth of the Johor River, until the said citadels have been secured. After constructing the two citadels, [Your Majesty] can build [a third] at the tip of the Muar River [estuary];[90] then the king of Aceh will not be able to assist Johor in any way, neither by sea nor by land.

[The Muar] River is very beautiful and comparatively much better than the Melaka River. One can enter the Muar River with junks, balas, lancharas[91]—which are vessels of the local people[92]—or [also] laden galliots. [Large] ships cannot enter [the river], but they can drop anchor and moor close by as they do in Melaka. It has a good site to harbour galleys and foists,[93] and there is no lack of secure places to construct them. [Your Majesty] can construct this fortress without hindrance from the local people. There is a very small village nearby. It is not a very important settlement—it is called Muar—but it has a very beautiful beach that is two leguas long.[94] Next to this beach there are some huts of minor

---

[90] A similar proposal to construct a fortification at the Muar River estuary was also mooted (and drawn) by Manoel Godinho de Erédia in his *Declaraçam de Malaca* (Description of Malaca). See SMS, p. 57.

[91] Vessel types. See also the glossary (*balas, lanchara*).

[92] Ms. *gente de la tierra.*

[93] Ms. *fustas.* A small craft. See also the glossary (*foist*).

[94] Probably about 11–12.3 kilometres.

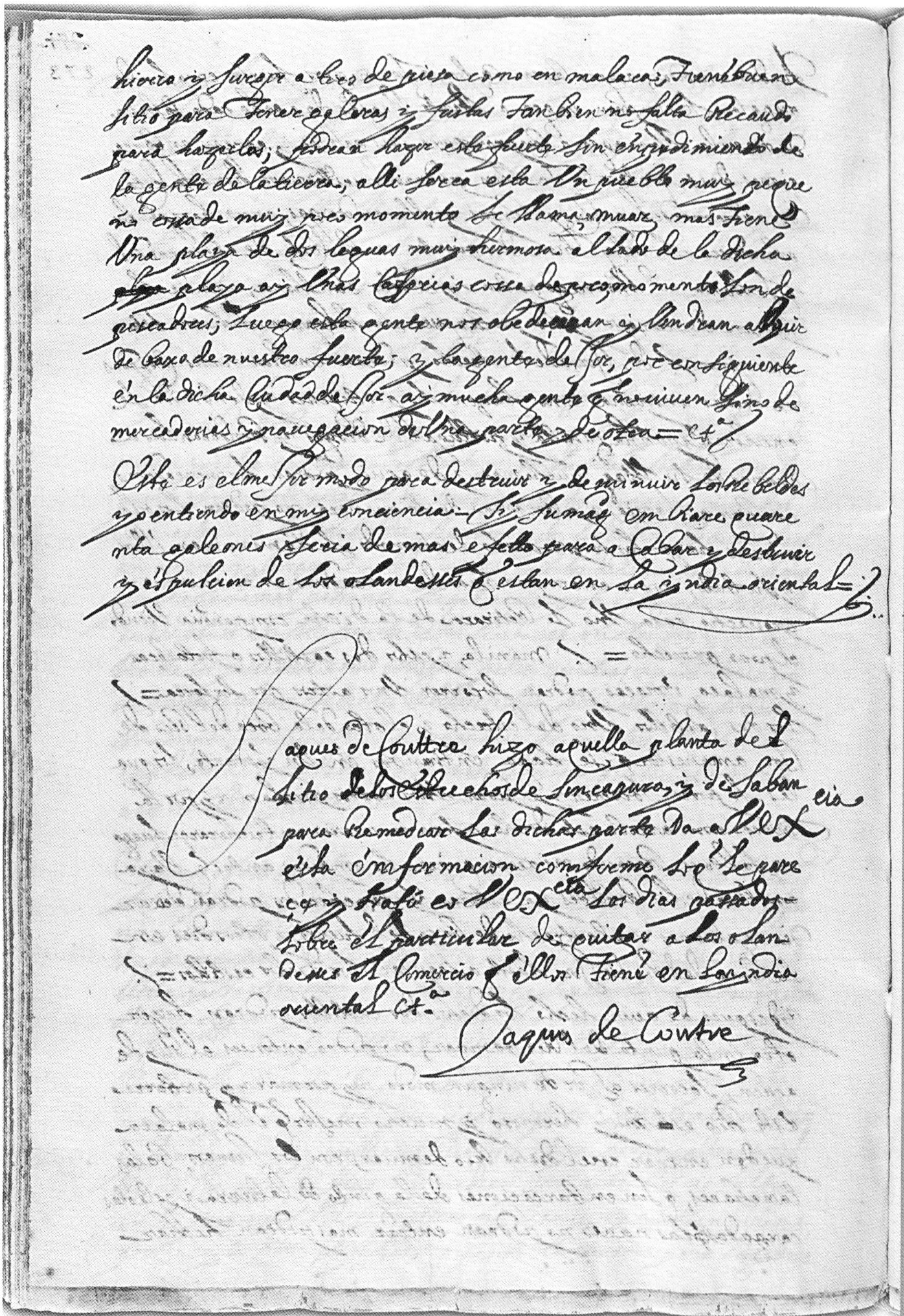

Last page of the signed memorial *Emformación para se hazer algunos castillos o fortaleças en el Estrecho de Sincapura y otras partes del sur, etc.* (Information about Building Some Castles and Fortresses in the Strait of Singapore and Other Locations in the South, etc.) by Jacques de Coutre. (Madrid, BNE, Ms. 2780, fol. 273 verso).

significance; they belong to fishermen. Thereafter, these people will obey us and will come to live around our fort, as will the people of Johor. In the aforementioned city of [Batu Sawar] there are many people who make a living only from merchandise and [from] sailing from one land to another.

This is the best manner to destroy and diminish the [Dutch] rebels as per my understanding done all in good faith. If Your Majesty were to send 40 galleons, it would be more likely to put an end to, destroy, and expel the Dutch who are in the East Indies.

Jaques de Coutre devised this plan of the site of the Straits of Singapore and Kundur. To remedy the said parts he gives to Your Excellency[95] this information according to what appears [to be] and [as] discussed with Your Excellency in the past days, especially about depriving the Dutch of the commerce that they have in the East Indies, etc.

Jaques de Coutre

Information that Jaques de Coutre sends to Your Highness to construct forts in the Straits of Singapore and in the Johor River estuary in the East Indies, etc.

[95] There is a discontinuity in De Coutre's use of honorifics and titles in the present text. The addressee has been consistently addressed as "Your Majesty", but in the present, closing paragraph, De Coutre shifts to "Your Excellency". It would appear that the last paragraph may not form part of the main memorial and instead represents a separate note addressed to a third party. The titles have been translated as they appear in the text and without regard for consistency.

MEMORIAL

IV

Information for Your Majesty to remedy the Estado da Índia.[1]

Most Excellent Lord,

CHAPTER I

If Your Majesty were to dispatch 40 galleons to India with Castilians and Portuguese, like the armada that Your Majesty sent to Brazil,[2] well equipped with men and artillery and good gunners and munitions and sufficient supplies, and if in the next year 20 galleons were sent in the same way, the aforementioned Estado can be remedied in the following manner, because the rebels are firmly entrenched there and have many ships and very strong fortresses.

The following is the order that the armada should maintain to be effective and to expand:

When the armada arrives at the cape that is known as the [Cape of] Good Hope[3] they should sail outside the island of Madagascar[4] and [outside] the

[1] BNE, Ms. 2780, fol. 277 recto–288 recto.

[2] This is a reference to the combined Spanish-Portuguese fleet despatched to Brazil in 1625 under the command of Don Fadrique Álvarez de Toledo y Osorio to oust the Dutch from Bahia.

[3] Ms. *Buena Esperança.*

[4] Ms. *ysla de San Laurenço.*

Carajos Shoals[5] and around all the islands, and they should go to Java, [find] the entrance to the Sunda or Bali Straits,[6] enter through these and sail along the coast of Java. They will undoubtedly come across enemy ships in the port of Palembang,[7] in Tuban,[8] in Penarukan, in Jayakerta,[9] and Banten because it is the same route that the Dutch use when they sail to the South[10] and to Java. The fortress of Jayakerta belongs to the [Dutch] rebels and they trade along this entire coast of Java, and in the Banda Islands, from where they bring large quantities of mace and nutmeg. In all these places, the Javanese, who are the blacks of [that] land,[11] do not get along well with the Dutch owing to the tyrannical manner in which the [latter] trades with them. The Dutch fix the prices[12] of all their wares, whether they are selling or buying. The admiral[13] of our armada should look into establishing friendly ties with the king of Banten to expel the Dutch from Jayakerta.

Once friendly relations are established with the king of Banten there will be no shortage of provisions for our armada, such as rice, meats, many chickens and very good water, including assistance for any purpose. The admiral can send news to Manila to enquire if there is a Spanish armada there, which could then come and join forces with the admiral; in this way it would be possible to perform some good feats. If they cannot immediately capture any prizes at the fortress of Jayakerta, since it is strong or owing to an inconvenience, they can try to capture the city of Ambon,[14] which used to belong to Your Majesty. If our armada cannot go there owing to an absence of or adverse winds or any other inconvenience, they can then go to Melaka and attack Aceh to find out if they can capture that city.

---

[5] Ms. *Baxos de Gargaos.* See the list of place names (*Baxos de Garagaos*).

[6] Ms. here and subsequently: *Bocarron de Sunda o del Valle.* See the list of place names (*Bocarron del Valle, Sunda*).

[7] Ms. *Palinbona.*

[8] See the list of place names (*Tuban*).

[9] Ms. here and subsequently: *Jaquatera.* This is the original name for Batavia.

[10] Ms. *zur.*

[11] Ms. *son negros de la dicha terra,* that is "they are blacks of the said land"; the local population.

[12] Ms. *estanques.*

[13] Ms. here and subsequently: *general,* possibly here to be translated as "commander".

[14] Ms. *Amboino.* Ambon, which had been Portuguese, fell to the Dutch in 1605. See also the list of place names (*Amboino*).

Hand-coloured city plan of Aceh by João Albarnaz I, *Plantas das Cidades, e Fortalezas da Conquista de Índia Oriental* (Maps of the Cities and Fortresses of the Conquest of the East Indies), c.1648. (Munich, BSB, Cod. Icon. 162, pl. 15, fol. 35).

The Dutch also trade there. If they managed to capture [the city of Aceh] they would take a rich prize; that would be good to sustain and expand our armada and to destroy the trade of the rebels. Here, in this port, [the Dutch] load a lot of pepper and it is a port frequented by many vessels, Turkish baxeles from *Meca*[15] and from all the nations of India.

If the said armada cannot proceed through the Straits of Sunda or Bali owing to the absence of wind, or if the wind is contrary, they can then proceed to the Nicobar Islands.[16] This is the route that the carracks which sailed from Lisbon to Melaka[17] used to ply in the past. After our armada reaches the Nicobar Islands they can [then] try [to reach] Aceh and disembark before the [Acehnese authorities] can take any preventive measures. [The armada] could catch [the Acehnese] offguard and take them

[15] Ms. *Meca*; lit. Mecca. Mecca of course has no port. This could also be a reference to Mocha which is located on the Arabian Peninsula near the Bab-el-Mandeb Strait.

[16] Ms. *Nicobares*. Archipelago in the Bay of Bengal region. See also the list of place names (*Nicobares*).

[17] Ms. *Malaca*.

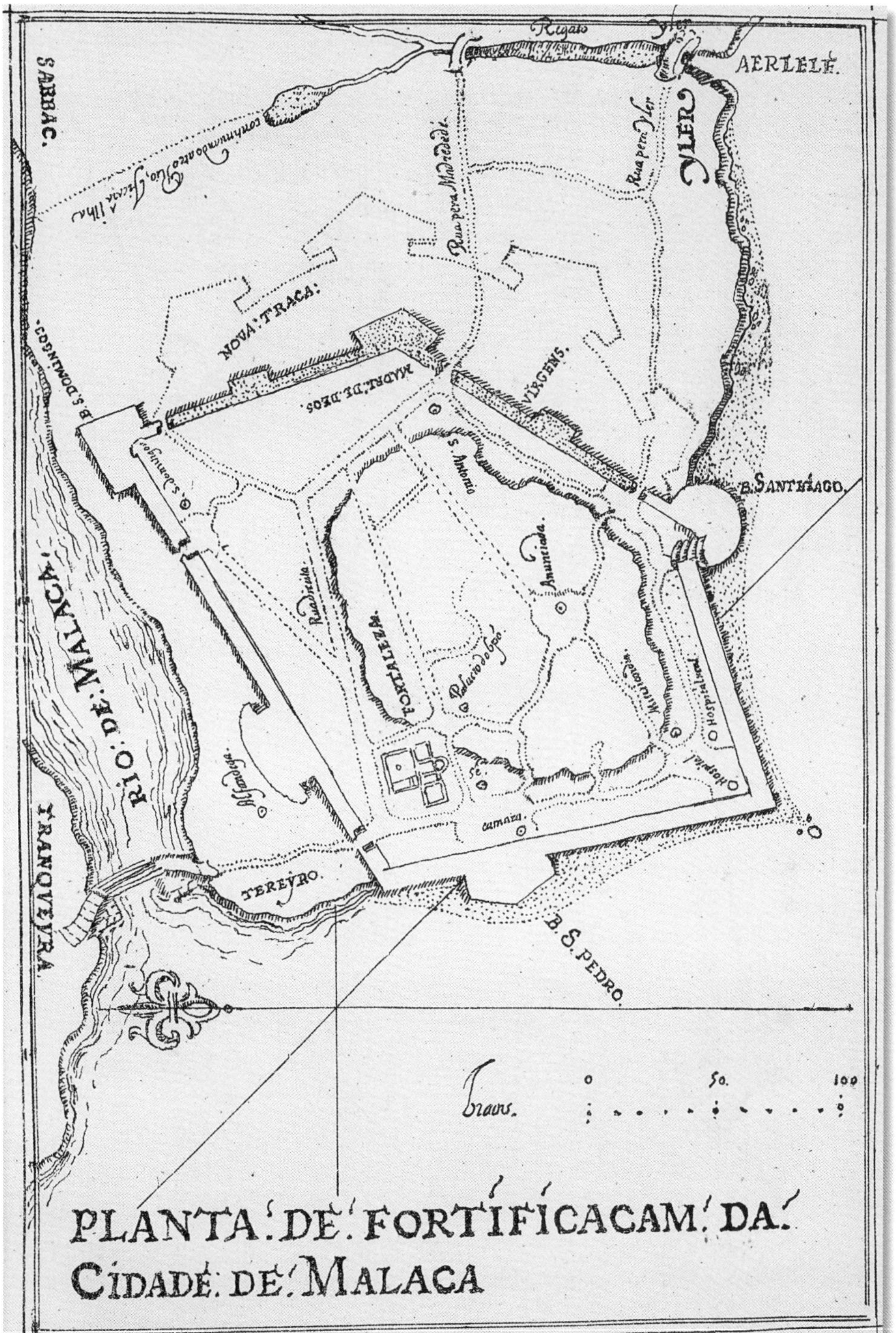

Hand-drawn ground plan of the Portuguese fortress *A Famosa* and the walled city of Melaka by Manoel Godinho de Erédia. The original is found in the manuscript of the *Declaraçam de Malaca* (Description of Melaka), c.1613 (Brussels, Bibliothèque Royale, Ms. 39015A, fol. 8 recto).

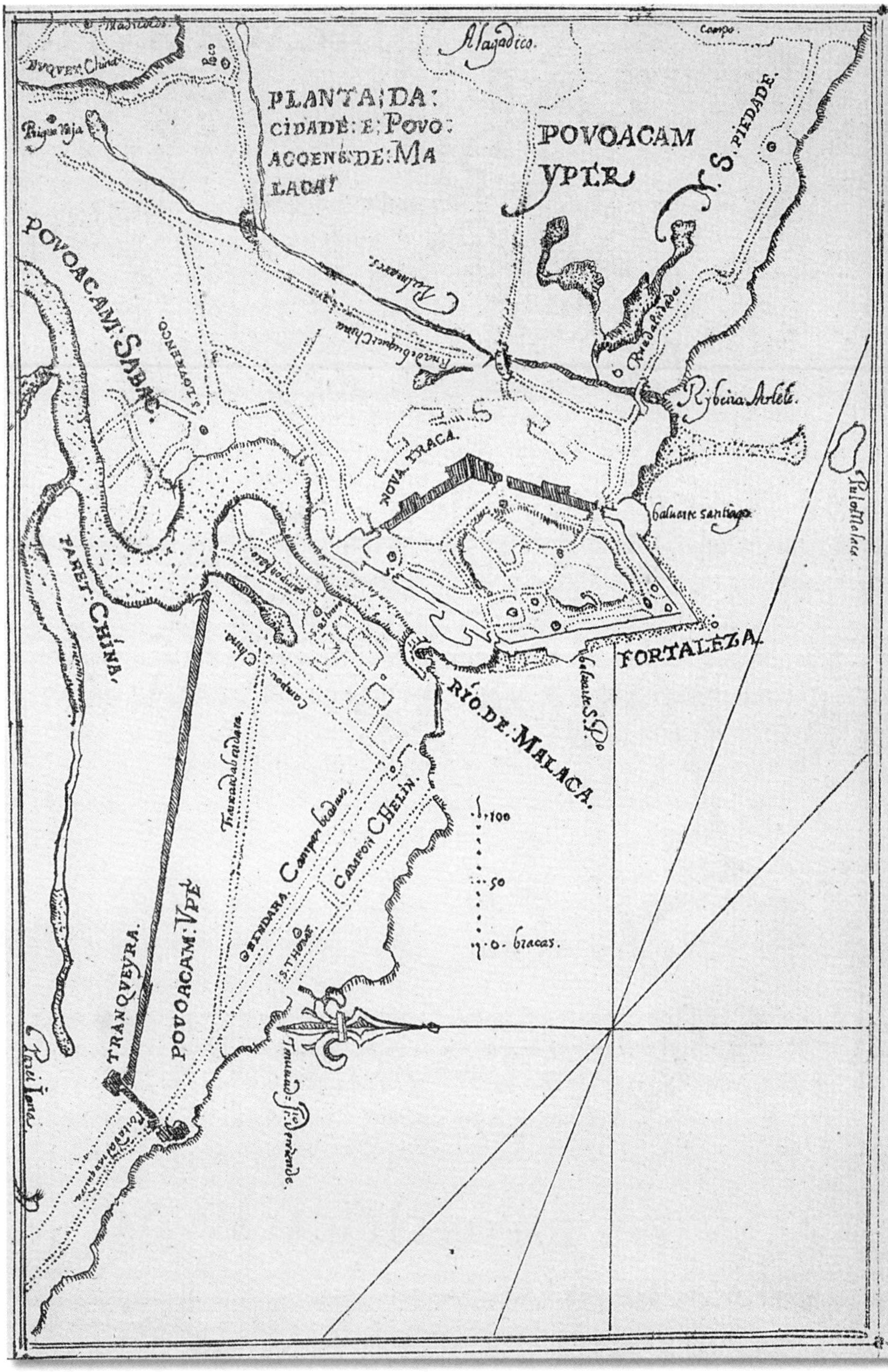

Hand-drawn ground plan of Melaka town and its suburbs by Manoel Godinho de Erédia. The original is found in the manuscript of the *Declaraçam de Malaca* (Description of Melaka), c.1613 (Brussels, Bibliothèque Royale, Ms. 39015A, fol. 9 recto).

unaware, and this will have to be before they arrive at Melaka, so that news does not reach the ears of the king of Aceh that such a large armada has arrived at Melaka. For this it is necessary that the admiral works to have his armada sail together, because this is the main [idea]. They must take some batels, more than what the said ships usually carry, even if they are *quartels*,[18] to disembark the soldiers on land, and unload the good combat artillery;[19] all these could be necessary. From there they can send a message to Melaka requesting for anything that is needed, and [for] small vessels that they call bantins.[20]

If for some reason it is not possible to embark on any of these missions that I have mentioned here, [the ships of the armada] can go to Melaka and sail along the coast of Patani,[21] and determine whether they are able to sack the city of Patani. It is not a difficult task; they would capture great prizes of Dutch carracks and many baxeles, that are called junks.[22] It is a port frequented by numerous baxeles. The Dutch have two factors in the outskirts of the city, and the Dutch carracks[23] anchor far out at sea, a legua and a half away,[24] and the other baxeles [anchor] closer to the shore. Our pataches[25] can go as close to the shore as an artillery shot[26] away. The beach and the shoreline are shallow,[27] and therefore, when one wants to disembark it is necessary to do so only at high tide. The outskirts of the city are much larger than the city itself; all the merchants live in the outskirts. They do not have any defences, neither trenches nor [stone] walls. The city is half a legua[28] away from the shoreline. The city walls are made of thick logs[29] and it has large bronze artillery [pieces], but there are many parts from which it is possible to enter, where the wood has rotted away and the wall is left open. It will be easy to gain entry and one will capture a lot of booty.

---

18 Evidently a vessel type.

19 Ms. *piessas de bater*.

20 Ms. *bantens*. See the glossary (*bantin*).

21 Ms. here and subsequently: *Pattani*. See the list of place names (*Patane*).

22 Ms. here and subsequently: *juncos*.

23 Ms. *naos*. Here the term is employed to designate a sizeable, ocean-going cargo ship.

24 Probably about three kilometres, possibly further.

25 Ms. *pataxos*. A vessel type. See also the glossary (*patache*).

26 Ms. *un tiro de piessa*.

27 Ms. *vaza*.

28 About one kilometre, possibly further.

29 See for example SMS, pp. 97, 124, 215, 224, 280 note 75.

After this enterprise our armada could sail along the coast up to the city of Ligor,[30] a land that belongs to the king of Siam, and sack it. The Dutch also have their factories[31] in this city. [The armada] can sack the city of Ayutthaya,[32] which is the court of the king of Siam, but for this they will need 30 or 25 oared ships, that are called foists[33] in India. With these ships [the armada] will be able to capture the city of Ayutthaya. They are a docile people. It would capture great treasures and riches if it took said city; it is not a difficult task. The [native] people are very cowardly and lack bravery. This city is surrounded by very deep rivers.[34] Our oared vessels can enter right into the city and can sail around it until the ships arrive [our ships] can reach right up to the walls and some [can even enter] the city. This city is located 40 leguas[35] inland, but they can reach there with the tide[36] and [their] sails would not be damaged, since the river is deep. When entering the river it is necessary to enter through the mouth of the harbour with the tide; this is because at that point the water is not very deep, and moreover the river bed consists of soft ground.[37] The ships are in no danger: they will be able to exit with the tide, even if they feel the river bottom passing[38] underneath them, and whether or not these are large baxeles. [The armada] would also capture many junks, which are the baxeles of the natives:[39] they are very large vessels, like carracks, and [carry] a lot of small bronze artillery. The king of Siam has well-stocked warehouses, more for grandeur and status than for defence, and one would find many provisions. The land is fertile here and one will find many villages and settlements along the banks of the river. The people are cowardly. The city could be captured—as I have said—with oared ships; one could easily capture it off-guard.[40]

After our armada has captured some booty, it can leave from Melaka and proceed to India, to the city of Goa. On its way it can go to the port

---

[30] Ms. *Lugor.*

[31] Ms. *facturias.* See the glossary (*factor*).

[32] Ms. *Judia.*

[33] Ms. *fustas.* A vessel type. See also the glossary (*foist*).

[34] Ayutthaya is located at the confluence of the Chao Phraya, Pasak and Lopburi Rivers.

[35] Probably about 80 kilometres, possibly further.

[36] Tidal changes occur in the Chao Phraya River, also affecting the current and water flows of the Pasak and Lopburi Rivers.

[37] Ms. *mas todas es vaza suelta.*

[38] Ms. *aunque se evasen.*

[39] Ms. here and subsequently: *negros.* This and subsequent deployment of this term is to be taken as a reference to the local or indigenous population.

[40] Ms. *descuydo.*

of Masulipatam[41] on the Coromandel Coast. The Dutch have a factory on the outskirts of this city and so do the English. When the armada reaches this port they could capture many Muslim[42] and Dutch and English carracks, which anchor two leguas[43] out at sea, and other vessels closer to the shore. One could capture this city easily, [as] it is completely open without any fortification. The merchants live on the outskirts of the city; it is a large city and there are many merchants here from Persia and from all the nations of India. One would capture a lot of booty. Before the Dutch went to India, Your Majesty used to have in this port of Masulipatam a captain who governed this harbour with the consent of the king of this land, who is titled Qutb Shah.[44] Then the Dutch came and established friendly ties with said king. He allowed their presence in his port so that his ships would be safe from the Dutch. When the armada arrives in this port it will be necessary to try and disembark immediately, before the natives and the rebels can take any preventive measures to defend themselves.

If [the armada] is successful in capturing this stronghold of Masulipatam one can build a strong fort there and sustain it with a equally good garrison,[45] stationed with some oared ships and galleys to patrol that coast during the summer. Because during the winter[46] no baxel can be anchored at this port without running a great risk of being smashed ashore. Our captain can also send an ambassador to the raja of Pulicat,[47] who is like a duke. The fortress of Pulicat belongs to the Dutch. They can reach an agreement with this raja by means of promises and gifts, because these natives are very avaricious. They could agree that the raja could come with his people and soldiers by land and our armada by sea and land. With the Portuguese from Mylapur and Nagapattinam[48] a good company of people could be raised, along with their slaves. Most of them are very good harquebusiers. Even their slaves are skilled at this. In this manner one can observe whether one is able to capture Pulicat by means of starvation or thirst, or [by] the force of arms. On this Coromandel Coast the greatest commerce that

---

[41] Ms. here and subsequently with different spellings: *Mossolepatan*.

[42] Ms. *moros*.

[43] About four kilometres, possibly further.

[44] Ms. *Catabussa*, a corruption of the title of the rulers of Golconda. See also the glossary (*Catabussa*).

[45] Ms. *presidio*.

[46] This is presumably a reference to the monsoon season.

[47] Ms. here and subsequently: *Paliacate*.

[48] Ms. *Meleapor e de Negapatan*. See the list of place names (*Melapor, Negapatan*).

the Dutch have is that of taking textiles to the South[49] and there is a great trade in spices and other merchandise that the Dutch bring in their carracks from the South to this coast.

The raja of these lands of Pulicat is a heathen.[50] All the people along this coast are very discontented with the Dutch, as are the people of the South,[51] owing to the tyrannical manner in which the Dutch trade with them. The Dutch come from the South with their ships to Pulicat and to Masulipatam,[52] and all along the Coromandel Coast, and they bring many spices,[53] porcelain, and other wares from Europe. Their factors sell all the different kinds of wares in all the factories at a single [fixed] price, which [the Dutch] decide. They do not lower this price nor do they bargain. The heathens are forced to comply and are unable to sell their wares as they used to with the Portuguese, where each individual sold for the best price he could get and as he wished. The Dutch do not practise this. The price that the Dutch impose is fixed and [transactions take place] according to Dutch conditions. [The Dutch] have their factors in all the villages and places throughout the Coromandel Coast in order to buy textiles. All the factors buy at the same price, and they all buy each kind of textile for a [single fixed] price. The infelicitous heathens have no choice but to give them the textiles for the price [the Dutch] want. If they are unable to sell they would not be able to pay their tributes to their king nor would they have anything to eat. The Dutch are the ones who take these textiles to the South. They control this trade and when they go to the South with their ships laden with textiles they sell there in the same manner, and they buy spices in the same way. For this reason the natives of the South are also hostile towards the Dutch, because [the Dutch] are paid[54] what they want. India could be saved with this armada. Your Majesty must take steps to conquer [India][55] anew.

The enemy has many ships in India and it will thus be good if our armada does not separate from each other, and I say that the said armada

---

[49] Ms. here and subsequently: *sur.* See the glossary (*sur*).

[50] This is a generic reference to anyone who is not a Christian, Jew or a Muslim.

[51] Ms. *South.*

[52] Ms. *Macelepatan.*

[53] Ms. *drogas.*

[54] Ms. lit. earn.

[55] Ms. lit. it.

should first go to the South before [proceeding to] Goa, to capture some ships, as I have indicated. Because if this armada were to go directly to Goa, to then leave from there to go to the South or to Hormuz, as the Portuguese do not have a banner like the [professional] Spanish soldiers,[56] they do not have that obligation to remain in the infantry.[57] When the Portuguese armada arrives in Goa, and after disembarking on land, [the soldiers] go wherever they wish. Some go to the South, and others to Bengal,[58] and others simply disappear. They do not wish to return aboard the ships; they flee and go to the lands of the Muslims[59] and sail aboard ships engaged in smuggling.[60] When the viceroy wishes to send the armada out again, he will need to pressgang soldiers[61] to put aboard the galleons, as he habitually does. To remedy this, Your Majesty should send orders to Portugal that the soldiers should have their captain and lieutenants with other officials like the Spanish. They should be subject [to serve] not just when they embark, but [also] when they disembark, wherever it may be, on pain of being punished; and each one should be assigned to a banner, and not [go] like they now go to India. Your Majesty pays [for] many men. Upon arriving in India, when they are needed they are nowhere to be found.

For this reason, Your Majesty must not remedy India just with the Portuguese nation, but with Spaniards, just like when they went to the Bahia de Todos os Santos.[62] I say this because the Portuguese had many encounters in India with Dutch armadas, but the enemy always defeated ours. The enemies captured many richly laden carracks and galliots in India, and subsequently enriched themselves. There was a ship that was worth more than two million [cruzados].[63] If the Dutch had not captured so much booty and if they did not have as much trade as they have now and in the

---

[56] Ms. *soldadesca española.*

[57] Ms. *ynfanteria.*

[58] Ms. *Bengala.*

[59] Ms. *tierras de los moros.*

[60] Ms. *navios de contrabando.*

[61] Ms. *avra menester prender.*

[62] The "Bay of All Saints", around Bahia in northeastern Brazil.

[63] Ms. *dos milliones.* Possibly a reference to the *Santa Catarina* incident off Singapore in February 1603 which De Coutre alluded to in ch. XIX of the *Vida.* However, in the *Relação Annual*, the Jesuit fathers estimated the loss at *one conto de oro*, or one million cruzados. See Fernão Guerreiro, *Relação anual das coisas que fizeram os Padres da Companhia de Jesus nas Suas Missões* (Coimbra: Imprensa da Universidade, 1931), II, p. 91. One *conto de oro* is equivalent to about 29,000 kilograms of coin-grade silver. See also the glossary (*cruzado*).

past, they would not be able to sustain such large armadas nor so many ships. Therefore Your Majesty should make great efforts to capture Pulicat and Masulipatam and patrol that entire Coromandel Coast, so that [the Dutch] cannot obtain textiles nor trade along this coast. The textiles represent[64] all the trade that they have with the South, which they exchange for spices, and they then bring many spices to sell along the Coromandel Coast. It would be ideal to send the armada to the Coromandel Coast. If our armada is detained there and [if] winter commences and it cannot proceed to Goa, [the ships] can go and winter in Nagapattinam or in Tuticorin.[65] Other fleets have wintered in these ports. Things are inexpensive in this land, there will be no shortage of provisions for the men.

Your Majesty should order that a Castilian [officer] with a garrison be stationed in all the fortresses of India, so that care is taken to fortify the said fortresses properly. For this purpose it would be advisable to send some engineers who are skilled in fortifications to visit all those fortresses, because there is no one in India who is trained in this profession. Your Majesty grants these fortresses as a royal favour to some men for their services, or for the services of their fathers or brothers, or they buy these captaincies for three years, [for the same period] that Your Majesty habitually attributes them as a royal favour. As soon as these men take up office in these fortresses they do no more than trade and use every means possible to do no more than to profit as much as they can in these three years.[66] If they are obliged to maintain 100 soldiers they do not maintain [even] 15, nor do they try to reinforce[67] [anything] except their own interests. Nor do the viceroys of India verify whether they are suitable men for such jobs, if they can sustain a fortress should an enemy attack it. This is the reason why they lose Your Majesty's fortresses. This is why it is necessary that each fortress should have its [own] castellan and garrison and that the fortresses are looked after.

Your Majesty should reward soldiers like they do in Manila[68] and in all other lands, and not give the fortresses to such men who after nine years of having served Your Majesty, do not want to continue to serve. Many set

---

64 Ms. lit. are.
65 Ms. *Tutucurin.*
66 Officers in the *Estado da Índia* generally held a three-year cycle appointment.
67 Ms. *fortificar.*
68 This toponym could be taken here and subsequently to also refer to the Philippines generally.

Printed map of Asia featuring the historic trading towns from Arabia to the Philippines by Theodore de Bry, dated 1602. This partial section depicts the Indian subcontinent. The original is found in *Neundter Theil der Orientalischen Indien* (Ninth Voyage [of the Dutch] to the East Indies) printed in Frankfurt am Main in 1612. (The Hague, KB, 2112 C4).

sail [for the Indies] at the age of 14 and 15 years old. After having served for nine years, when they are 24 years of age and are still fit to serve they say that they are old soldiers and that their time of service has come to an end. They then send their papers to Portugal to have themselves appointed as captains of fortresses and to other offices by means of royal favours and they no longer wish to sail. Thus, Your Majesty must reward soldiers like they do in Manila and in Flanders and order that men be chosen [appropriately] for offices such as the captains of fortresses and of war galleons. In India they appoint 15-year-old boys as the captains of oared ships, since they have rich fathers or relatives. They are definitely not ready to be soldiers. Your Majesty should remedy this.

To bring to Your Majesty's attention of the fortresses that have been lost in the South: First, the fortress of Ternate,[69] which the Spanish recovered, and the fortress of Tidore in the Malukus,[70] and the city of Ambon in the South, which is in Dutch hands, and the fort in Solor, and the fortress of Syriam[71] in [the kingdom of] Pegu. In the Strait of Hormuz Your Majesty has lost the fortress and island of Bahrain,[72] in the lands of the king of Persia, the fortress of Gombrun,[73] and the fortress of Qeshm,[74] and that of Julfar,[75] and that of Hormuz, which is one of the most important trading ports in India. Your Majesty has also lost all the lands of the king of Hormuz, a vassal of Your Majesty.[76] The Dutch went to the Coromandel Coast where they built a fortress six leguas[77] from the city of Mylapur.[78] When it was half built the bishop of said city of Mylapur went [there] with the Portuguese and local people;[79] he captured the stronghold and they razed it to the ground. They did not wish to maintain the fortress,[80] even though it was so important.

---

[69] Ms. here and subsequently: *Tarnate.*

[70] Ms. *en Maluquo.*

[71] Ms. *Sirian.*

[72] Ms. *Baren.*

[73] Ms. *Gomoron.* Present-day Bandar Abbas. See also the list of place names (*Gomoron*).

[74] Ms. *Quexome.* See the list of place names (*Quexome*).

[75] Ms. *Gulfar.* Present-day Ras al-Khaimah. See also the list of place names (*Gulfar*).

[76] The Portuguese lost the control of Hormuz to the English in 1622. See also the list of place names (*Ormus*).

[77] Probably 33–37 kilometres.

[78] Ms. here and subsequently: *Meleapor.*

[79] Ms. *gente de la tierra.*

[80] Ms. *thing.*

The Dutch once again built the said fortress, which they call Pulicat.[81] The Dutch carry out all their trade in textiles in this place. The reason why they are so firmly entrenched there is due to this and to other lapses that were not prevented from the very beginning in the South.

Your Majesty should assist and remedy [India] with a Spanish and a Portuguese armada and some Dunkirk carracks,[82] as has been mentioned. The Dutch have not managed to capture even an inch of land from the Spanish in Manila nor in all of the Philippines; instead the Spanish have captured Ternate. They had many encounters with [the Dutch] and they defeated them, even though the Dutch had more baxeles.[83] In 32 years not a single Portuguese armada has managed to capture a Dutch or English carrack nor bring [such prizes] to the Goa estuary;[84] instead the Dutch come to the Goa estuary with ten or twelve ships whenever and as often as they feel like doing so. Therefore Your Majesty should assist that state.

CHAPTER II

If Your Majesty cannot immediately despatch such a large armada to India, and would like to assist and sustain it with what is available until further measures are possible, Your Majesty should send annually 20 or 30 large caravels[85] and vessels with sails and crew consisting of Spanish and Portuguese. As these are lightweight vessels, the enemy will find it difficult to capture them, and even if they do capture some, they will not be able to do as much damage [with them] as [with] a large carrack,[86] like the carracks that go from Portugal to India. The men of the caravels can serve in India in garrisons and serve in the armadas of galleys,[87] and oared ships and light galleys can be built in India, as they are in Manila, where the galleys capture Dutch ships. In fact, [the ships] could be built in Portuguese India.[88] Your Majesty should also send some masters from the Levant who know how to build light and sturdy galleys. Your Majesty

---

[81] Ms. *Paleacate.*

[82] Ms. *naos de Dunquerque.*

[83] A vessel type. See also the glossary (*baxel*).

[84] Ms. *barra de Goa.*

[85] Ms. here and subsequently: *caravelas.* A vessel type. See also the glossary (*caravel*).

[86] Ms. here and subsequently: *nao, naos.*

[87] Ms. here and subsequently: *galeras.*

[88] Ms. *Yndia de Portugal.*

will not incur as much expenditure and costs with caravels as compared to galleons. They will defend [India] against the enemy and will serve to obstruct their trade. Some galleys are built in Goa but they are very heavy, like barges.[89]

Your Majesty should order in Portugal and in Castile that all the merchants who wish to sail to India can do so freely with caravels and small vessels, as long as they give a guarantee that they will pay Your Majesty's duties in any Spanish, Portuguese or Castilian port in which their vessels anchor. The merchants can load pepper freely (paying the exit duties[90] in Goa), as well as all other merchandise, so that there is no accumulation[91] of said wares. Reduce the applicable duties for them, to less than what is charged currently in Portugal, since the caravels are small and it is a long voyage, [and] because they will need to take a lot of provisions and water for the journey. On account of this the merchants will have neither the profits or the desire to do the voyage if the duties are not lowered. It would be good to remedy [the situation in] India and Your Majesty's customs houses would generate a lot of revenue, both those of Portugal as well as those of Castile. Your Majesty should not allow [the merchants] to sail with ships that are more than 150 toneladas,[92] or less if possible.

If Your Majesty eases off [the restriction on] the pepper trade[93] for merchants as has been said, a lot of pepper will be sold in Portugal and all of Spain, and from here it will be taken to France and other lands, and the Dutch will not [be able to] sell [pepper], nor will they generate as much profit as they make and have now. They will not be able to capture that many ships, since [the merchant fleet] will consist of only small vessels, lighter than the large ships; and even if they do capture [some], they will not be able to do as much damage as when they capture a carrack like the ones that sail from Portugal to India, which are worth more than ten small ships. That is the scale of their loss. Your Majesty should order the viceroy of India to decree that no merchant is to sail with ocean-going[94] ships, but only with oared vessels. In this way the [Dutch] enemies will not be able to capture as many

[89] Ms. *barcasas.*

[90] Ms. *pagando las salidas.*

[91] Ms. *estanques.*

[92] About 119–38 metric tons. See also the glossary (*tonelada*).

[93] Ms. *largando la pimienta.*

[94] Ms. *naves de alto bordo.*

prizes as they have up until now, thus enriching themselves, nor will they be able to sustain so many ships.

Your Majesty grants royal favours in India to some captains [thus conceding to them] voyages to Mozambique,[95] the Coromandel, and other lands. Your Majesty should order that such captains cease to be appointed, but [instead] merchants should be allowed to sail freely. These captains of the [concession] voyages[96] are merchant captains whom Your Majesty appoints for their services. They make these voyages to Mozambique and to other lands, and nobody can perform those voyages without Your permission, and [thus the merchants] make agreements with the captains [in return] for money. These captains buy ships to take the merchants and their wares, charging freight and duties capriciously. For this reason very often the merchants do not send their merchandise, and Your Majesty's customs houses lose out on revenues. If these voyages were free, they would yield far more.

[If our men] sail in these vessels, as I have said, the enemy will not be able to capture as many prizes. Since the Dutch carracks[97] are outfitted by merchants in Holland, when they see that there are no profits to be made, each one will withdraw and cease to outfit these carracks. For this reason it would be good to sail in the manner I have described until there is sufficient time for Your Majesty to send the blue-water armada[98] comprising 40 galleons, as I have indicated. In this way some remedy can be provided to India and it will be sustained, in my view as a loyal vassal of Your Majesty.

Your Majesty should know that throughout the South in those ports the Dutch ships anchor one and a half leguas, and [even] two leguas,[99] out at sea. Throughout the Coromandel Coast and in the Strait of Hormuz, in Jask,[100] they do not have the [necessary] depth to anchor under the fortresses and under the artillery. We can reach them at night and do them damage since they are so far out at sea. Only in Surat will it be necessary to enter by day with the galleons, owing to the entryway[101] that is

---

[95] Ms. *viages de Mossanbique*.

[96] Ms. *capitanes de viages*. See the glossary (*viagem*).

[97] Ms. here and subsequently: *naos*.

[98] Ms. *armada de alto bordo*.

[99] About three to four kilometres, possibly further.

[100] Ms. *Jasques*.

[101] Ms. *boca*.

Printed map of Asia featuring the historic trading towns from Arabia to the Philippines by Theodore de Bry, dated 1602. This partial section depicts insular and mainland Southeast Asia. The original is found in *Neundter Theil der Orientalischen Indien* (Ninth Voyage [of the Dutch] to the East Indies) printed in Frankfurt am Main in 1612. (The Hague, KB, 2112 C4).

called *El Poço*.[102] Thus, if there are [Spanish] galleys there [in India] as in the Philippines, they could attack [the Dutch vessels] at night, and capture and set them ablaze.

Your Majesty should order that the city of Goa be fortified and send engineers for this purpose, and also to the other fortresses in India. The city of Goa is unenclosed like this town of Madrid;[103] [enemies] can enter through the river and by land at night and by day without anyone being aware of it. The Portuguese have begun to build a wall; it is four times larger than the city and its outskirts; a haphazard thing and without any defences. His Majesty King Philip II, who is with God, sent to Goa and to all the fortresses of India an Italian engineer, a man who was very well-educated in these matters to fortify all Your Majesty's cities and fortresses. This engineer surveyed the city of Goa thoroughly and put large stones on all the bulwarks with their [respective] letters and numbers where the walls were to be built and he did this in all the fortresses of India. But none of these fortresses have been fortified according to the plans and orders of this engineer [made] years ago, when India was at its zenith and could afford to have them built.[104]

At that time there were yet no Dutch ships that could have prevented [these works]; [so] they stopped building [the fortifications]. They began constructing the wall that I have mentioned some seven years ago, a haphazard thing without any defences. The wall that the engineer had drawn is defendable and inexpugnable, and all the outskirts would have been encompassed within it and [the wall had] very beautiful lines and was not grossly big, conforming to the law of the land.[105] This wall that they have now begun to construct is very large. Before the men are able to reach the walls from their houses they would have felt very exhausted, since the climate of the land is very hot and [the walls] are far [away]. It will take half a day to cross from one part to the other, and the Portuguese are far and few in between. Thus Your Majesty should order that the wall that the Italian engineer had drawn should be built instead, so that the city is kept safe.

---

[102] Lit. The Well.

[103] This sentence indicates that this memorial was written by De Coutre while he was in Madrid.

[104] Ms. *pudiendo hacer.*

[105] Ms. *conforme la tierra requeria.*

To further protect the city of Goa Your Majesty should order that the fort situated in the harbour be extended to the tip of Bardez,[106] and at this tip a strong bulwark should be built in the same way as the other that was built up on the hill; they should both be impregnable. One to protect Bardez from the Muslims[107] and [the other] to prevent the Dutch from anchoring there in the estuary.[108] From there one could watch over[109] the entire estuary with artillery, which we currently are unable to do. The existing fortress is very far upriver. By constructing this extension our ships will be much safer. It is necessary [to have] a castellan in the [fortress] with a garrison: this fortification is the key to Goa. Today the captain of this fortress is very often in the city, and no more than seven or eight Indians manage the fortress, and there are no houses for the soldiers, nor provisions, nor enough munitions for even one day.

There is another fortress further upriver, a cannon shot away, which is called Reis Magos[110] in the same hills, and it does not have artillery, nor people, nor does it have doors; it is exposed along the river's edge. The Muslims can come by land in two hours and take it over without even getting their feet wet. Your Majesty should order that this fort either be razed to the ground and demolished or that it be maintained as it should be. It is highly advisable to demolish this fortress and use its stones to build another at the tip of the estuary, on the reef that extends from Nossa Senhora do Cabo[111] to the bank of the channel through which ships and galliots enter. In this manner the Aguada Fortress[112] will end up being the fortress of said reef; both fortresses can watch over the harbour and the entrance to the river. Engineers will be necessary for this and for other things and to fortify all the fortresses situated on the Malabar Coast, where all the forts are exposed and falling into disrepair, and built in the old-fashioned way; they seem to be more like small towers or watch towers. The materials to build said fortresses are very inexpensive in India and [are] very good

[106] Ms. here and subsequently with different spellings: *Bardeus*. See the list of place names (*Bardez*).
[107] Ms. here and subsequently: *moros*.
[108] Ms. here and subsequently: *barra*.
[109] Ms. *franquear*.
[110] Ms. *Los Reyes Magos*. See the list of place names (*Reis Magos*).
[111] Ms. *Nuestra Señora del Cabo*, that is "Our Lady of the Cape", presently home to the chapel at Cabo Fort outside Goa.
[112] See the list of place names (*Aguada*).

for fortifications, and easy to work with, and the labourers work for low wages. You can do more with one ducat there than with 20 ducats here [in Spain];[113] the stones are very cheap. The supervisors of these constructions earn a real[114] every day, and the labourers half of a real, and they sustain themselves with this and work very diligently.

The land of Bardez has 15 or 16 villages; it is almost entirely surrounded by rivers. It has a pass where the river channel is about as wide as two shots of a harquebus[115] away from the mainland, where in the past they had begun to dig a channel so that one river could flow into the other. [This was done] to separate the part attached to the mainland, so that Bardez would become an island, [safeguarding it] from the Muslims. They have not finished digging it nor do they care whether this project is completed, which is very easy to do because it is [located] on a plain. If they did so then this land of Bardez and the Aguada Fortress would be safe from the Muslims. They will not be able to enter with their elephants and horses on the island as they have done in the past. This land that still remains to be excavated sits on low-lying terrain, which is very often flooded with water. Your Majesty should oblige the Indians in the villages to finish excavating this small bit of land; then the São Cristóvão[116] River and the Coluale River will merge into one. They do not have to dig much because the waters [coming down] from the hills would make the channel deeper; and [Your Majesty should] order that a watch-tower be built there with people standing guard to fend off the Indians from the island of Bardez. The Portuguese smuggle a lot of contraband through this place without paying duties, and weapons for the *pimenteiros*,[117] which are Portuguese smuggling ships that are outfitted in Muslim lands to [sail to] the Strait of Hormuz.

Your Majesty should send engineers to Melaka to build a fortress on the *Ilha das Naus*,[118] which is a cannon shot away from the city. This island is small and all the baxeles, junks, galliots and ships anchor beside it. From there they can watch over the harbour and prevent the enemy

---

113 The addition is justified based on note 103 above.

114 Ms. *real*. A Spanish currency unit. See also the glossary (*real*).

115 A type of firearm. See also the glossary (*harquebus*).

116 Ms. *San Cristoban*.

117 Ms. *pimenteros*. Smugglers. See also the glossary (*pimenteiros*).

118 Ms. *Ysla das Naos*. An anchorage off Melaka town. See also the list of place names (*Ysla das Naus*).

from anchoring there. Good [artillery] pieces should be put in this fortress including a garrison and provisions.

Your Majesty should order that four or five Spanish galleys—there are very fine galleys there—go from Manila to Melaka so that they can be used to capture enemy carracks, since the coast of Melaka is calmer than that of Manila.[119] They would capture some enemy carracks in the Strait of Singapore[120] and in the Strait of Kundur,[121] and they could watch over those straits, and it would send a strong message to the enemy. [Dutch][122] ships would not sail that far apart from one another; they would be obliged to sail together owing to the periods when there are no winds, when they are vulnerable and could be easily captured. When their ships sail together they will not be able to capture that many prizes and they will not be able to be at all the entrances[123] of the straits as they are now. A few vessels have already escaped being captured by them, and when the aforementioned straits are free, ships can come from China, and from the coast of Patani,[124] and from Java to Melaka. Your Majesty's customs and excise houses[125] would generate far more revenue. Galleys can be built in Melaka too, if there were master ship builders who can design and construct them, because there is no dearth of carpenters there, and there is a supply of very good timber for the rigging[126] and planks for the oars. There is no shortage of men there to serve as crews on the galleys, dark-skinned like the inhabitants of Angola, they are called kaffirs.[127] They can be bought at a very cheap price in India and are very suitable as galley crew. In Manila the Spanish value them highly and treat them very well; so much so that the Spaniards go from Manila to Goa to buy these slaves for their galleys, and they bring back shiploads of them.

---

[119] De Coutre meant the waters of the Melaka Strait are comparatively calmer to that of the open seas around the coast of Luzon.

[120] Ms. here and subsequently: *Estrecho de Sincapura*.

[121] Ms. *Estrecho de Saban*.

[122] Ms. lit. their.

[123] Ms. *bocas*.

[124] Ms. *costa de Pattani*.

[125] Ms. *alfandegas o aduanas*.

[126] Ms. *liames*.

[127] Ms. *Cafres*.

With regard to[128] the Straits of Singapore, in the middle of these straits there is an island. The New Strait[129] is on one side of this island and the Old Strait[130] is on the other. The island is triangular[131] and all the ships and vessels that pass through these two straits first anchor very closely to the land. Your Majesty should order that a castle or fortress be built on this island, [equipped] with good pieces of artillery. One would then be able to monitor[132] these two straits, and no ship or vessel would be able to pass through the straits that they could not sink. The tip of the aforementioned island is a natural fortification, and the tip is made up of stone.[133] The aforementioned fortress could be built at little cost. The island has a cooling climate surrounded with leafy trees and it has excellent [fresh] water. This fortress would be very useful and could serve as a safe refuge for ships from China, both on the way out as well as on the way back. If our ships are under the protection of the fortress, they would be safe.

One could have bantins,[134] which are types of vessels that one uses there, to go through the straits to spy on the locations of the enemy there, and one can warn our ships coming from China, or those that are on their way to China, and inform them through which strait they can sail safely without fearing the enemy. These vessels are like brigantines;[135] they are called bantins, as aforesaid. They also serve to tow ships and guide ships through the entrances of the straits, and remove them from shoals, and also to tow vessels to escape from the enemy, and for many other things. Your Majesty should order that they do not sail except with oared galliots,[136] as aforementioned. In this manner there will be trade and Your Majesty's customs houses will generate revenue, (even though it will not be as it was previously in the past), and so sustain the lands. When the merchants are able to sail freely, without the hindrance of

---

[128] Ms. lit. in.

[129] Ms. *Estrecho Nuevo*.

[130] Ms. *Estrecho Viejo*.

[131] Ms. *triangulada*. This is a reference to present-day Sentosa. See also the list of place names (*Ysla de Arena*).

[132] Ms. *franquear*.

[133] In Memorial III, this has been named *Surgídera*.

[134] Ms. *bantines*. A vessel type. See also the glossary (*bantin*).

[135] Ms. *bargantines*. A vessel type. See also the glossary (*brigantine*).

[136] Ms. *galeotas de remos*.

the captains of the [concession] voyages, they will be encouraged to face the risks of going to sea and to build ships.

Your Majesty should order that the lands of Melaka[137]—a very fertile and verdant terrain—be populated there with people called *Chincheos,*[138] just like the Spanish have in Manila.[139] These men are very agile and hardworking and[140] cultivate the land, or raise oxen and cows, pigs and chickens, all of which are in short supply. They are great fishermen and are experts at all kinds of crafts: carpenters, bricklayers, blacksmiths, and all the professions that are needed in a city. One should send for other people from their land to populate the aforementioned lands of Melaka, which are entirely surrounded by forests and have no inhabitants, except for a few poor people who live under the walls of the city of Melaka, [as well as] those who live in the outskirts.

When Francisco da Silva de Meneses[141] was the captain of Melaka 30 years ago, 15 vessels came to the city of Melaka that were as big as carracks with[142] Chincheos, who are the aforesaid people. They asked the captain and the city to give them the uninhabited lands of Bandar Ilir,[143] which they wished to cultivate and subsequently supply provisions to Melaka, thus eliminating the need to import anything. Neither the city nor the captain wished to consent to this, nor [did they] allow [the Chincheos] to come there. It would be an extremely wise decision to allow these people to populate these lands. These lands would be very fertile and able to produce an abundance of everything, and with the passage of time they could pay tributes, as the Spanish do in Manila. The *casados*[144] and citizens of [Melaka] did not wish to allow [the Chincheos] to settle there because the citizens bring in all the provisions in Melaka from outside. Then they

---

[137] Ms. *terras de Malaca*. From the context that follows this is a reference to the lands immediately surrounding the city of Melaka, rather than the whole of the Malay Peninsula which in European cartography was also commonly referred to as *Malacca* during the early modern period.

[138] The Chinese in general. See also the list of place names (*Chincheo*).

[139] See also De Coutre's brief discussion of the Chinese of Manila in ch. XVI of the *Vida*.

[140] Ms. lit. to.

[141] See De Coutre's references to Silva de Meneses in ch. III, VI, VII, XII, XVIII and XIX of the *Vida*. These would help date the genesis of this brief around 1628.

[142] Ms. lit. of.

[143] Ms. *banda de Yler*. The corrupted Malay name literally translates as "City on the Other Side" or "on the Opposite Bank".

[144] Married settlers. See also the glossary (*casado*).

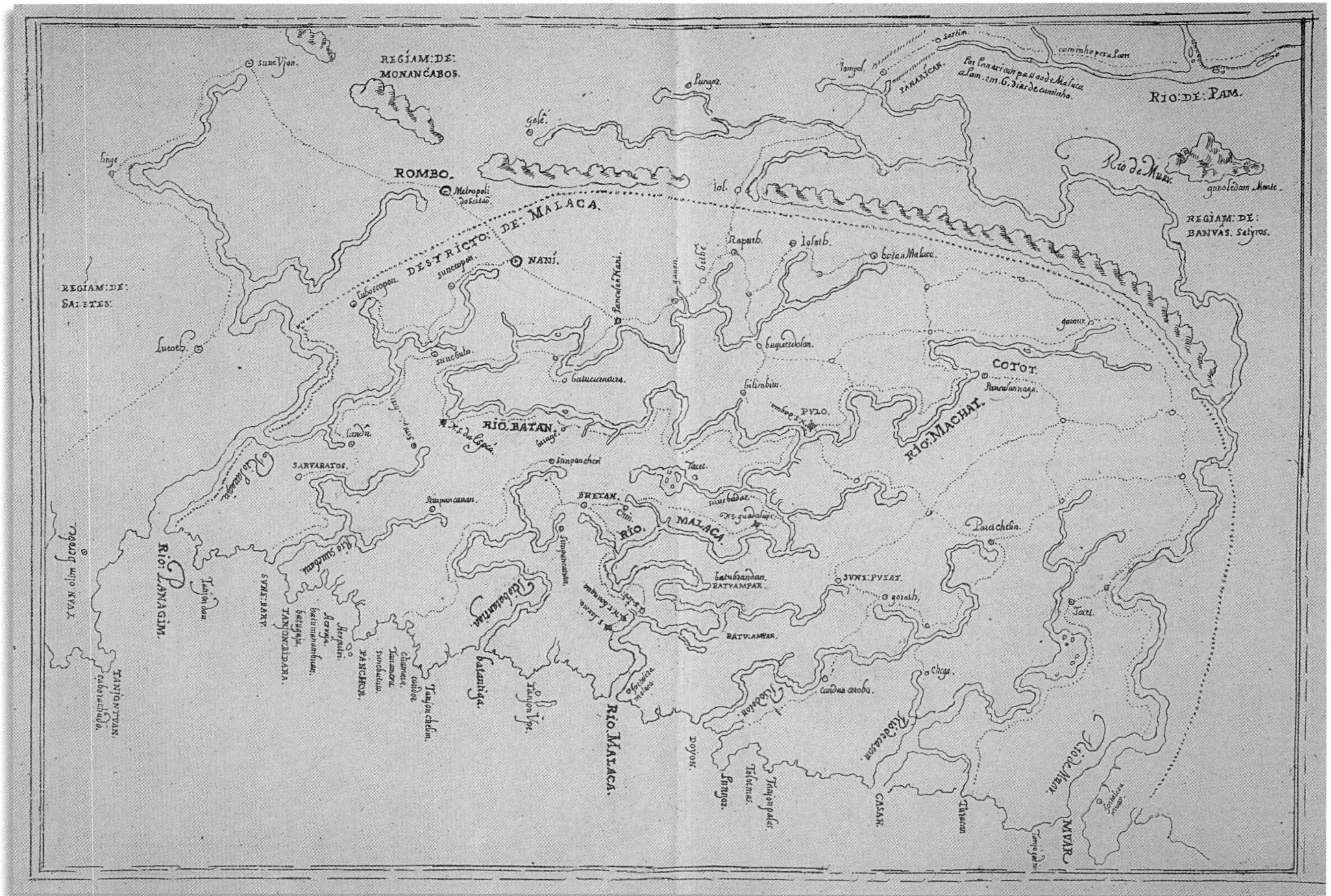

Hand-drawn map of the Portuguese-controlled district around Melaka by Manoel Godinho de Erédia. The original is found in the manuscript of the *Declaraçam de Malaca* (Description of Melaka), c.1613. (Brussels, Bibliothèque Royale, Ms. 39015A, fol. 12 recto).

sell them to the wretched poor, including outsiders, [at prices][145] according to their wishes. All the casados are bakers: they buy a *candil*[146] of wheat—which is equivalent to 10 *fanegas*[147] of wheat—for 15 ducats, and they make bread and sell it for 50 ducats.[148] Nothing is done to bring them to justice; they are all relatives and godparents [to each other's children].

It is necessary to station garrisons at the entrances of the city of Melaka, just like in Manila. I lived for many years in Melaka, and most of the time the entrances were left completely unguarded. This is why Your Majesty should assume control of [the situation] and order that these lands be populated with the [Chincheos], as I have mentioned. It is necessary. I believe that they will go there very willingly. That is also why I have said that Your Majesty should send Spaniards for the garrisons, because they are skilled in guarding anything that is handed over and entrusted to them. They are not negligent.

Your Majesty should be aware that every year more than 40 oared ships, such as galliots, sail annually to the Strait of Hormuz. All these ships go laden with pepper, steel, iron, lances, and bamboo—similar to very strong reeds; they are made into the shafts of lances—and large quantities of textiles, and other prohibited goods. All these ships belong to the Portuguese, [but are] outfitted in the lands of the Muslims.[149] None of them pay duties to Your Majesty. These ships are smuggling vessels.[150] They go very well equipped and armed; that is why the soldiers from Your Majesty's armadas flee and in turn go and serve these men on their ships; they do not wish to serve [on] Your Majesty's armadas.

To remedy this and to remove these [smugglers] from this commerce, and [to ensure that] the soldiers do not defect to serve them, Your Majesty should order that factors be stationed at Muscat, and in Al-Qatif,[151] [on] the coast of Arabia, and in Basra,[152] and in Aveza,[153] [in] the lands of the Arab king Mombarek,[154] and on the shores of Persia, and

[145] Ms. lit. as.

[146] About 550 litres mass or volume equivalent. See also the glossary (*candil*).

[147] See the glossary (*fanega*).

[148] Equivalent to 52.5 and 175 grams of mint-grade gold respectively.

[149] A reference again to the *pimenteiros*.

[150] Ms. here and subsequently: *navios de contrabando*.

[151] Ms. *Alcatife*. See the list of place names (*Alcatifa*).

[152] Ms. *Baçora*. See the list of place names (*Baçora*).

[153] Concerning King Mombarek of Aveza, see the glossary and list of place names (*Aveza, Banbareca*).

[154] Ms. *Banbareca*.

Hand-coloured printed map of Persia and the Persian Gulf by Abraham Ortelius, c.1570 (Private collection, Peter Borschberg).

to also station a factor in Khawr-ash-Shamm,[155] which is in Arabia outside the Strait [of Hormuz]. Your Majesty should order that all these factories be stocked[156] with pepper, steel, iron, and bamboo—used to make the shafts of lances—and textiles. Great profits can be made by selling on Your Majesty's behalf, and this will put an end to the commerce of the ships that smuggle goods from the lands of the Muslims. Your Majesty could send the pepper and the other wares that I have mentioned to these factors[157] through[158] [the] ships from the armada. After having unloaded the merchandise in said factories[159] they could continue sailing in the Strait [of Hormuz] as a fleet, provoking[160] the fortress of Hormuz, impeding trade [there] and in the lands of the king of Persia.

[Engaging] in this trade will incur a great deal of damage to the rebels who also trade here and take the same wares: they will not be able to make as much profit as they do now. [Your Majesty] should also order that all the men who wish to go from Goa or from any other land with pepper and said merchandise should be allowed to go, paying duties to Your Majesty, even though it is contrary to the [papal] bull *De la Cena*.[161] As a matter of fact, this has been done for some time. These ships could do two voyages in a year. Should they find any ships that are committing the act of smuggling, they can seize their goods and punish the sailors.

To inform Your Majesty about the commerce that used to take place in India. Firstly from the South: some years ago more than 500 vessels, large and small, *viz.* ships, junks, balas, lancharas,[162] would frequent the harbour or port of Melaka, a fortress that belongs to Your Majesty, and all these vessels would bring wares to trade. The junks that used to come from the islands of Banda and from Makassar,[163] and from the island of Java and from all those kingdoms, used to come laden with mace, nutmeg, and cloves, benzoin,[164] sugar, rattan, beeswax, and other wares. Other junks that used to come from

---

[155] Ms. *Caxen.*

[156] Ms. lit. filled.

[157] Ms. *alcaldes*; mayors.

[158] Ms. *with.*

[159] Ms. *facturias.*

[160] Ms. *enquietando.* The Portuguese lost Hormuz in 1622, that is before this memorial had been written.

[161] Ms. *De la Seo.* Reference to Pope Paul III's bull of 1536. See also the glossary (*In Coena Domini*).

[162] A vessel type. See also the glossary (*lanchara*).

[163] Ms. *Macaçal.*

[164] Ms. *menguin.*

the kingdom of Borneo were laden with [sea] turtle shell, camphor,[165] [and] beeswax, and they used to bring many bezoar stones,[166] and some diamonds, and gold.[167] Other junks used to come from the kingdom of Johor,[168] and from the kingdom of Pahang,[169] from the kingdom of Patani, and from the kingdom of Ligor, and from the kingdom of Siam. These junks used to bring sappan[wood][170] [that is used] to make dyes to colour [the] textiles that are produced on the Coromandel Coast. They used to bring civet,[171] beeswax, and large quantities of very good benzoin, and a lot of gold to buy textiles. Other junks used to come from the kingdom of Cambodia,[172] and from the kingdom of Champa,[173] and from that of Cochinchina. These junks used to come laden with eaglewood,[174] kalambak,[175] and benzoin, and they used to bring a lot of gold, and all [of this] was used to exchange for textiles. Other junks used to come from the kingdom of Jambi,[176] and that of Indragiri,[177] and that of Siak, and that of Kampar, and that of Perak,[178] and that of Kedah;[179] these junks used to bring pepper, tin and gold to exchange for textiles.

Furthermore, 35 or 40 ships used to come to Melaka from Goa, from Chaul, from Cochin, from Nagapattinam, from Mylapur,[180] and from all [along] the Coromandel Coast, and from the kingdom of Bengal, and from that of Pegu. All these ships used to come laden with textiles from Cambay, and from Sindh,[181] and other textiles from the Coromandel Coast; and other ships [used to come] laden with textiles, and colchas,[182] and very beautiful

---

[165] Ms. *alcanfor.*
[166] Ms. *piedras beçares.*
[167] Similarly, see De Coutre's account of Brunei Bay in chapter XV of the *Vida.*
[168] Ms. *reyno de Jor.*
[169] Ms. *reyno de Pam.*
[170] Ms. *sapan.*
[171] Ms. *argalia.*
[172] Ms. *reyno de Camboya.*
[173] Ms. *reyno de Chanpa.* See the list of place names (*Chanpa*).
[174] Ms. *agle.*
[175] Ms. *clanbuco.*
[176] Ms. *reyno de Jambo.*
[177] Ms. *Andregiri.*
[178] Ms. *Pera.*
[179] Ms. *Cada.*
[180] Ms. *Meleapor.*
[181] Ms. *Sinde.*
[182] A type of textile. See also the glossary *(colcha).*

marquees[183] that can be assembled. From the kingdom of Bengal and from that of Pegu they used to bring a lot of lac,[184] beeswax, provisions, and many precious stones such as rubies and sapphires. From Goa and other lands the ships used to bring a lot of wheat, wine, olive oil, and butter. The city of Melaka does not produce any of this. In the same way four more ships used to go to China and to Japan, and another two used to come from the Maluku islands every year, laden with cloves for Your Majesty, which was [raised] as duties[185] that those lands used to pay to Your Majesty.

All these vessels that I have mentioned used to come to Melaka every year to trade and they used to pay the respective duties[186] to Your Majesty. The Portuguese used to sell their textiles and buy spices and other commodities, and they used to load their ships and sail to Goa and Cochin. Over there they again used to pay their duties to Your Majesty; this apart from the two clove ships that used to come on the account[187] of Your Majesty, and from three or four ships that used to come to Goa every year from China, laden with raw and twisted silk, and many bolts of velvet, damasks, satin, taffetas, and many colchas, marquees,[188] and silk hangings to decorate houses, and large quantities of musk,[189] and seed pearls, and small pearls, and large quantities of gold, and camphor, and *radix Chinae*,[190] and benzoin, and alum stone,[191] and tintinago,[192] Chinese porcelain, and sugar, and various other commodities. Each of these carracks from China used to pay 50,000 to 60,000 pardaos[193] at the customs and[194] excise house in Goa as duties to Your Majesty. They then used to take these wares from Goa to the north: [to] Chaul, Cambay, Diu, Daman, Muscat,[195] [and] Hormuz. They again used to pay exit duties[196]

---

183 Ms. *pavellones*.
184 Ms. *lacre*.
185 Ms. *fueros*.
186 Ms. *derechos*.
187 Ms. *por cuenta de*.
188 Ms. *pavellones*.
189 Ms. *almiscar*.
190 Ms. *palo de la China*.
191 Ms. *piedra-umedo*. See the glossary (*alum*).
192 Ms. *Totunaga*. An alloy of copper, zinc and nickel. See also the glossary (*tintinago*).
193 Equivalent to about 1.355 and 1.625 metric tons of coin-grade silver. See also the glossary (*pardao*).
194 Lit. or.
195 Ms. here and subsequently: *Mascate*.
196 Ms. here and subsequently: *las salidas*.

for these products, and then again more duties to His Majesty in Diu, and Muscat, Hormuz, and other lands, aside from the ships that used to come every year to Portugal from India, which used to bring a lot of spices.[197] They also used to pay the exit duties for this merchandise that they brought.

Your Majesty has lost all this trade; which is now in the hands of the [Dutch] rebels. They have grown rich with this commerce and by means of their robberies, and the Portuguese in India have become impoverished with this significant loss. This is why Your Majesty should help remedy that state in the manner that I have described, so as not to lose these lands and the many Christian communities over there.

LIST[198] OF WHAT THE REBELS TAKE TO THE EAST INDIES.

First of all they take many reals-of-eight, and a lot of gold, but not as much as compared to the quantities that the carracks take from Portugal to India. They take a lot of coral fashioned into rosaries[199] and in polished branches,[200] and rough coral. They also take a lot of processed and rough amber,[201] which they buy in Danzig.[202] They take many tapestries, they take many first and second-grade crimson cloth pieces, and first and second-grade cocheneal cloth pieces,[203] and all kinds of textiles in a spectrum of colours from England. They take a lot of mercury,[204] and vermilion,[205] and a lot of sweetgum,[206] and many sword blades, and many harquebuses, and padlocks, and knives, and mirrors, and lead, and other wares; and some jewels, but only a few, not as many as the Portuguese.

---

[197] Ms. *drogas.*

[198] Ms. *arancel.* The word technically means tariff, duty, or rate; it can also mean tariff ledger. In the present context the term "list" makes more sense.

[199] Ms. *roçarios.* Probably to be used as a necklace or as a rosary used in prayer.

[200] Ms. *ramas polidas.*

[201] Ms. *alambre.* Fossilized resin, not to be confused with *ambergris.* See also the glossary (*amber*).

[202] Ms. *Danzic.* Present-day Gdańsk, Poland.

[203] See the explanation above on p. 226n27.

[204] Ms. *asoge.* See the glossary (*mercury*).

[205] Ms. *bermellon.* See the glossary (*vermilion*).

[206] Ms. *rassamalla.* See the glossary (*rassamalla*).

APPENDICES

APPENDIX I

Affidavit of Admiral Jacob van Neck concerning his dealings in Patani in the year 1602.[1]

Around October 1604, the directors of the VOC in Amsterdam arranged to pass to the famous lawyer Hugo Grotius a bundle of affidavits that touch on the misdeeds of the Portuguese committed against the Dutch in the East Indies. This bundle, which is bound in white vellum and bears the title *Boeck Tracterende vande Wreede, Verradische ende Hostile proceduren der Portugesen In Oost-Indien* (Book Concerning the Evil, Treasonous and Hostile Proceedings of the Portuguese in the East Indies) is presently preserved among the papers of Baron H. van Zuylen van Nyevelt in the Nationaal Archief van Nederland in the Hague. The affidavits contained herein were perused by Grotius when drafting the historical chapters of his famous work *De Jure Praedae Commentarius* (On the Law of Prize and Booty) around that date.

[1] The Hague, Nationaal Archief, Collectie 102, Baron H. van Zuylen van Nyevelt, suppl. 2, no. 13 (2.21.179.01 no. 13), *Boeck Tracterende vande Wreede, Verradische ende Hostile proceduren der Portugesen In Oost-Indien (*Book Concerning the Evil, Treasonous and Hostile Proceedings of the Portuguese in the East Indies), pp. 35–43. A transcript of the original Dutch has also been published in Coolhaas, "Een bron van het historische gedeelte van Hugo de Groots De Jure Praedae", *BMH* 79 (1965): 453–60. Translated from the original Dutch by Dr Corinna Vermeulen, Noctua Taal en tekst, Leiden. Concerning the broader historic importance of this bundle of documents within the context of Grotius studies, see also GPFT, pp. 111–4.

Portrait of the Dutch humanist Hugo Grotius, c.1613. In 1604 he received a set of affidavits from the directors of the Amsterdam Chamber of the VOC as part of a packet of materials to assist him in writing his first major work on the law of war and the law of nations, *De Jure Praedae Commentarius* (Commentary on the Law of Prize and Booty). De Coutre is indirectly mentioned in two of the affidavits contained in this bound bundle. (Leiden, UB, Icones 66).

In chapter XVII of his autobiography, Jacques de Coutre claimed that he had encountered the Dutch Admiral Jacob van Neck while in Patani. The admiral confirmed this incident, reminiscing in his affidavit filed on 10 October 1604 that "in this city [of Patani] came to me a jeweller born from Bruges, residing at Goa". Although not mentioned by name, this reference is made unmistakenly to De Coutre. The following text translates the full affidavit of Van Neck into English.

Affidavit of Jacob Van Neck, Admiral, Concerning the Hostility of the Portuguese

I, Jacob van Neck, hereby declare and testify on my manly integrity, honour, loyalty and piety—instead of a solemn oath—at the behest of the Directors of the East Indian Company[2] in Amsterdam, that it is true that in the year of Our Lord and Saviour Jesus Christ 1600, on the first day of May, I set sail for the East Indies from the province of Holland with six ships, over which I had been appointed admiral. By the Lord's merciful guidance, we arrived before the city of Banten with three of our ships on 30 March 1601. The governor of that place had me welcomed kindly on our ships, requesting me to visit him as soon as possible, which I did the next day. He received me with great joy, saying that he regretted (among other things) that he could not provide cargo for more than one of our ships at that time, and asked where I wanted to send the others. To which I replied that I intended to sail them to Banda in person. Having understood this, he began to advise me against it strongly, saying that the Portuguese had turned all the kings of Java against us with many presents and other cunning pretences and persuaded them to attack our ships by surprise, under the pretext of friendship, and take them from us.

He also told me that a Portuguese captain by the name of Raja[3] Lella had come to him requesting permission in the king of Tuban's name to make a raid on two Dutch ships that had been moored at the roadstead there [Banten] a few months earlier. For that purpose, he had 40 large perahus or rowyachts,[4] well-manned, lying at Jayakerta,[5] a small city not far from there. But he had not wanted to give him that permission in any way. He also said that the Portuguese were equipping ships to drive the Dutch out of the islands of Banda and the Malukus, and earnestly advised me to break off my voyage, for he feared for misfortune on my behalf. But I took my leave from him, leaving one of our ships [the *Delft*] there, and sailed to the Maluku islands with the other two.

---

[2] See the glossary (*VOC*).

[3] Ms. *Rage*.

[4] A vessel that is propelled by breast oars and that can also be sailed. See also the glossary (*rowyacht, yacht*).

[5] Ms. *Jacatra*.

In Ternate,[6] we were received kindly by the king. We discovered there that the Portuguese staying at Tidore (which is the island closest to Ternate) by deceit had very brutally attacked a ship which had come from the Pacific, being one of Admiral [Jacques] Mahu's[7] ships. They had given the captain of that ship a friendly reception and had persuaded him to come ashore with some of his sturdiest men to help tie up a buffalo which they had promised him for provisions. When he was going back on board afterwards, they killed him in the sloop and threw him into the water like a dog. Meanwhile, the Portuguese had come aboard in great numbers under the pretext of friendship; and since the captain had gone ashore, they slew all they found there and thus made themselves masters of the ship and the goods. Now when they heard that we had arrived at Ternate and had been very well received by the king, the Portuguese wrote him a letter, which was translated by our merchant (who was very well versed in the Portuguese language) and another, who understood the Malay language quite well.

In it they said that they were quite surprised that the king allowed us into his country so easily, because we were bad people without law or religion; therefore, they could not but warn him to be on his guard, lest we wrest the fortress from him one day or the other; for once we were inside, he would have trouble driving us out. They further wrote that they advised him all of this because they wished him well and they would feel sorry if any mishap befell him. Therefore, it would be necessary for them to assist him with all their might.

Now when the king heard this letter being translated, he was quite alarmed and asked if we were such people as would treat him like the letter said. But when he had been asked to take into account that the letter had been written by the people who were our greatest enemies and therefore made up these lies, he was reassured a little. Apart from what the Portuguese had written about us in the letter, they had the bearer of the letter say many slanderous things about us: that we were ungodly people and mixed with others like Sodomites, and other indecent stories with which they wanted to discredit our nation throughout the islands of the East. They also

[6] Van Neck reached Ternate in early June 1601.

[7] Ms. *Admirael Mahieu*. The fleet belonged to the Magelhaense Compagnie which had set sail on 27 June 1598. See DAS, II, p. 0018.1.

promise and give lavish gifts to various kings and peoples in order to turn us into enemies in the end, regarded with suspicion and distrust, to and in all of the East Indies. And if one really investigates, one will find that all the murders and raids which our nation has suffered in the Indies were all committed by the Portuguese or through their agency; for instance, the murder of Cornelis de Houtman,[8] that of Captain de Cordes with all his men, the attack of the Javanese on Adriaen van Veen[9] at Banda, and many other nasty episodes.

After we had much discussed and noted these things and found that regardless of where we turned, we would always have these envious, murderous and resentful people as our mortal enemies, we decided among ourselves that we would regard them (who were making attempts on our lives, ships and goods everywhere) as our public enemies as well. And since we had to wait for harvest time there, lying at anchor near Telingami[10] (a town by that name), where we were not safe from enemy attacks (for one cannot leave at will there, so that the enemy could easily have overpowered us with fire ships), in order to prevent such dangers we decided to go and fight them with the permission and good will of the king of Ternate. For we were being told every day that the Portuguese were preparing to come and visit us with two carracks, a ship and two galleys. When we came near their ships,[11] we found that they had brought them so close to the shore that they could walk into and out of them at will, so that we could not come alongside them without running too great a risk, firstly of running ashore and secondly that in burning their own ships, which they could leave when they pleased, they would set fire to ours as well. We therefore took position at a distance of some hundred paces and started firing at them to see if we could make them abandon the ships, but we could not achieve our goal. Like us, they were very well equipped with guns, which they had all brought to one side and fired them vehemently at us. When we saw that we were not making any progress, we let our ships drift off and did not make

---

[8] Cornelis de Houtman was killed in a naval battle off Aceh by Keumalahayati, a female admiral.

[9] According to Coolhaas, "Een bron", p. 520, note 1, Adriaen van Veen arrived on the *Zeeland* and was stationed in Lonthor on Banda to oversee Dutch interests on the island. He departed from Banda with the fleet of Wolfert Hermanszoon on 24 June 1602.

[10] According to an editorial comment by Coolhaas, "Een bron": 456, note 7, Telingami (variously also Telingama, Tilligam) was a town located on the eastern coast of Ternate.

[11] Coolhaas, "Een bron": 457, note 2, dated this as 11 June 1601.

any further attempts, because I had to remain ashore for some time then to heal from an injury I had sustained in the cannonfire.

When we had been lying at anchor at Ternate for about another month and that year's harvest still did not come, we took leave from the king[12] and through the Philippines sailed to the great kingdom of China;[13] in a violent storm we came to an island near the city of Macao.[14] The next day we came within a mile from the city,[15] which we mistook for a village because a large part was hidden out of sight behind a mountain range. I sent a well-manned big sloop there to find out our whereabouts, on the condition that they would be on their guard against surprise attacks—although we had no idea that this was the city of Macao,[16] where the Portuguese resided in great numbers. When they saw our sloop, they flew a peace flag until our men had landed. Then the Portuguese came forward and imprisoned them as rebellious subjects of their king and evil pirates; and that in a country where they have no authority except over their own countrymen. The day after, I sent our helmsman in our biggest cutter to gauge the depth and see if we could come near the city. But because he ventured too close, he was captured as well, together with eight other brave men. Of these crew members, 21 in number altogether, the Portuguese hanged some and drowned the others, with the exception of Martin Apius, who will report more extensively himself.[17]

Then, after we had spent some days there, in great danger because of storm and thunder, we finally sailed for the city of Patani,[18] where we suffered little trouble from the Portuguese because very few venture there (although they used to trade on a large scale there), since because of their willful insolence all the Portuguese living there, numbering no less than a thousand,

---

[12] Coolhaas, "Een bron": 457, note 5, dated this as 31 July 1601.

[13] Ms. *groote Coninckryck van Chyna.*

[14] Ms. *Stat Makau.* Coolhaas, "Een bron": 457, note 6, dated this as 27 September 1601. The subsequent events are also described in detail by Van Neck in his *Journaal.* See Van Foreest and De Booy, ed., *De Vierde Schipvaart*, I, pp. 205–13.

[15] A Dutch sea-mile is about 7.4 kilometres.

[16] Ms. *stadt van Macau.*

[17] A separate copy of this affidavit by Martin van Aap (Latinised "Apius") was sold at the 1864 auction in the Hague of Hugo Grotius' working papers as part I lot 22. A full transcript of Apius' affidavit was published in Pieter Anton Tiele, "Documenten voor de Geschiednis der Nederlanders in het Oosten", *BMH* 6 (1883): 228–42; another copy can be found in Van Foreest and De Booy, *De Vierde Schipvaart*, II, annex 54, pp. 279–90. See also GPFT, p. 340 note 36.

[18] Ms. *Stadt van Patanij.*

were killed by the city's inhabitants at one single time, as we were told. In this city a Fleming came to me, a jeweller born from Bruges,[19] residing at Goa. He was coming from Manila[20] then, where he had seen (so he told me) a certain Lambert Biesman,[21] captain of one of Olivier van Noort's ships,[22] being brought in as a prisoner with some of his men.[23] He had spoken to him in prison,[24] where the man was garrotted eight days later, together with most of his crewmen.[25] However, that was not done by the Portuguese, but by the Spanish.

These were my experiences with the Portuguese during my second voyage to the East Indies. As to my first voyage in the year 1598,[26] I did not have any dealings with the Portuguese that were worth mentioning, because of the brief period of time we spent lying before Banten. But we did hear there that they had come to Banten a year earlier, in 1597, with an armada of three big galleys, three warships and a great number of low ships under the command of a certain Dom Emmanuel, brother of the viceroy of Goa.[27] They intended to overpower Houtman's ships, which had departed from there some time before, and to punish the people of Banten for deceiving the Portuguese. For the governor of Banten had received several thousand reales[28] on the condition that he would deliver Houtman's ships into the hands of the Portuguese, but had failed to do so. Therefore they now came with this armada to vanquish the Dutch and punish and subdue the Bantenese,

---

[19] Ms. *een vlaming, gheboren van Brugghe, synde een Juwelier, die syn residentie hielt in Goa.* This is without doubt a reference to De Coutre who also mentioned that he had met with Admiral Van Neck at Patani. A very similar statement of identity is made in connection with the executed mates at Macao. See the "Journaal van Jacob van Neck" in Van Foreest and De Booy, *De Vierde Schipvaart*, I, p. 221, "... soo ons een Vlaminck seyde, die sijn woonplaetse in Goa hielt, ende in Patani in compangie van eenige Portugeesen was comen handelen." (... as we were told by a Fleming who maintained his residence at Goa, and who had come to Patani to trade in the company of some Portuguese.)

[20] Ms. *Manilies.*

[21] Ms. *Bresman.*

[22] Ms. *Olijvier van Noord.*

[23] De Coutre mentioned this episode in his *Vida*, chapter XVII.

[24] This is confirmed in the affidavit of Lambert Simonsz. Mau in appendix III.

[25] See the affidavit in appendix IV below.

[26] See "Waerachtig verhael van de Schipvaerd op Oost-Indien ... indenjaere 1598 ..." in BV, I.

[27] Coolhaas, "Een bron": 459, note 4, notes that Dom Emmanuel was a commander of a fleet that came from the Malukus. If he was indeed a brother, he was a sibling of Matias de Albuquerque who served as viceroy from 1591–97. Coolhaas does not see him as a brother of Matias' successor, Dom Francisco da Gama, the Conde da Vidigueira (served as viceroy between 1597 and 1600).

[28] See the glossary *(real)*.

although the outcome was very different from what they had expected. For their three big galleys were raided by the Javanese and all on board were killed, and the rest of the armada was put to flight.

Thus this nation had wanted to drive our people—who did not attempt anything against them at first—out of the East Indies from the beginning, and it is possible that they will not stop until they are driven out themselves by those they intended to ruin or destroy. May the good Lord grant that this happens soon, for the good of the fatherland.

Thus declared by me on September 28, 1604, and in token of truth I have signed and confirmed this is my statement with my signature. Signed by Jacob van Neck and Bruyning, notary public.

Having been collated against the original, written and signed as above, the copy was found to accord with it after collation, on this 10th day of October 1604. W. Kick, notary public.

APPENDIX

II

Affidavit of Jacob van Heemskerck concerning the atrocities committed by the Portuguese in the East Indies and the execution of several mates of Jacob van Neck's crew at Macao.[1]

The following document is contained in the same bound bundle titled *Boeck Tracterende vande Wreede, Verradische ende Hostile proceduren der Portugesen In Oost-Indien* (Book Concerning the Evil, Treasonous and Hostile Proceedings of the Portuguese in the East Indies) described in detail under appendix I.

In chapter XVII of his autobiography, Jacques de Coutre explained that he had met Admiral Jacob van Neck in 1602 while conducting business at Patani. The Dutch admiral was joined a little over a week later by his countryman Jacob van Heemskerck. Jacques explained how Van Neck had informed Van Heemskerck of the execution of the members of his crew at the hands of the Portuguese at Macao, and that the fiscaal,[2] Martin Apius, had been spared and brought to Goa for

[1] The Hague, Nationaal Archief, Collectie 102, Baron H. van Zuylen van Nyevelt, suppl. 2, no. 13 (2.21.179.01 no. 13), *Boeck Tracterende vande Wreede, Verradische ende Hostile proceduren der Portugesen In Oost-Indien*, pp. 120–33. A transcript of the Dutch original has also been published in Coolhaas, "Een bron van het historische gedeelte van Hugo de Groots De Jure Praedae", *BMH* 79 (1965): 521–31. Translated from Dutch by Dr Corinna Vermeulen, Noctua Taal en tekst, Leiden.

[2] An officer responsible for judicial issues and discipline. See also the glossary (*fiscaal*).

questioning. Enraged by the events at Macao—so we are informed—Van Heemskerck initially sought to execute some Portuguese prisoners. But the presence of the Johorese Raja of Siak at Patani and the inability to seize Portuguese cargo vessels in the open waters off Tioman in revenge for the Macao massacre led to a series of developments that adminated in the seizure of the carrack *Santa Catarina* on 25 February 1603. Van Heemskerck's attack and plundering of the richly laden cargo vessel—mentioned by De Coutre in chapter XIX—took place off the eastern coast of Singapore.

Statement by Jacob van Heemskerck regarding the hostile proceedings of the Portuguese, with a translation of some Portuguese letters.[3]

I, Jacob van Heemskerck, at the behest of the Directors of the East Indian Company at Amsterdam declare on honour and loyalty, by true Christian words—instead of a solemn oath—that on 23 April 1601,[4] I sailed from Texel with a fleet of eight ships[5] (of which the Directors had made me admiral) in order to pursue our planned voyage to the East Indies.[6] Having sailed for some days and keeping our course straight over the sea, we had passed by the Canary Islands[7] when we were met by a fleet of 13 ships—Spanish, well-equipped and full of men. They attacked us and vehemently hit one of my ships, named the *Rode Leeuw*,[8] with heavy cannon. Then they boarded it and shot dead several people (the skipper and others),

[3] These were letters exchanged between Van Heemskerck and the Portuguese authorities on land in Melaka, specifically with the Portuguese governor Fernão de Albuquerque, the Melaka city council (*câmera*), as well as the captain of the ill-fated carrack *Santa Catarina*, one Sebastião Serrão. See also GPFT, appendices 7–10, pp. 194–207.

[4] Ms. erroneously *1600.*

[5] DAS, II, 0056.1–0063.1, pp. 12–3. The fleet set sail from Texel and Wielingen between 22 and 23 April 1601, and arrived in Banten on 22 February 1602, with the exception of the *Zwarte Leeuw* (Black Lion), which arrived later on 4 April that year. The fleet had been financed and equipped by the *Eerste Verenigde Compagnie op Oost-Indië* (First United Company for the East Indies). Admiral Van Heemskerck sailed aboard the 500-ton *Amsterdam.*

[6] The voyage had been organised by the United Amsterdam Company.

[7] Archipelago off the western coast of Africa which was then, and still remains, a Spanish possession. See also the list of place names (*Canary Islands*).

[8] Ms. *Roode Leeu*; "Red Lion". DAS, II, 0061.1, pp. 12–3. The *Roode Leeuw* has been described as a yacht that was placed under the command of Pieter Klaasz. See also the glossary entry for that type of vessel (*yacht*).

wounding some others, so that the aforementioned ship had to leave the fleet and break off its journey, which caused great damage and detriment to my aforementioned fleet. The ship ran the risk of falling into enemy hands, had it not been relieved by me and the others; as I boarded the enemy with my ships, they shot ten or twelve of my men as well. Five or six of them died,[9] while most of the rest were crippled. To sum it up: we were in great peril of losing our precious ship, men and goods, as combat is subject to that in many various things.

On 23 February 1602,[10] I arrived at Banten with six ships of my fleet. I learned that a month or six weeks earlier a fleet of eight carracks and ships, with another 25 low ships and rowyachts, had arrived and passed by there, headed toward Goa and other destinations in the East Indies under the command of their general André Furtado [de Mendonça],[11] with express orders to destroy and completely exterminate all the Dutch and their ships, as well as all inhabitants of the East Indies who had conducted any trade with us or shown us any friendship. For after said fleet had failed to accomplish its mission at Banten because it was met by the five ships under the command of Admiral Wolfert Hermansz[12]—who forced them to abandon their plans at Banten with considerable damage—said André Furtado[13] sailed to Ambon with his fleet.[14] How badly he treated the people of Hitu[15] and others there who had allowed us to trade and extended their friendship to us, is sufficiently known to all; those poor people were forced to leave their houses and goods to be plundered, fleeing into the jungle and to the mountains, in order to prevent the killings and slaughter by the Portuguese.

After the aforementioned General André Furtado had finished all his business at Ambon, he sailed to the Malukus with his fleet in order to ruin

---

[9] Coolhaas, "Een Bron": 522, note 1: citing Heert Terpstra who revised the casualty figure to three men.

[10] DAS, II, pp. 12–3, registered the date of arrival as 22 February 1602.

[11] Ms. *Andrea Furtado.*

[12] Ms. *Hermansz.* This refers to events in the year 1601. For the broader historical context of this naval campaign, see also Borschberg, "The Seizure of the *Santa Catarina* Revisited: The Portuguese Empire in Asia, VOC Politics and the Origins of the Dutch-Johor Alliance (c.1602–16)", *JSEAS* 33, 1 (2002): 31–62.

[13] Ms. here and subsequently: *Andrea Fortade.*

[14] Tiele, "De Europeërs", BKI, part VI, chapter 5: 198–205.

[15] Ms. *Itu.* One of the Maluku islands. See also the list of place names (*Maluku*).

all of these islands (which fall under the king of Ternate's authority)[16] and tyrannise the said king, as they did earlier with his forebears, and rob him of his kingdom. To this end, said general used all the might, means and help he could muster, also assisted by a ship or two that the Spanish had sent to his aid from Manila—they are each other's natural enemies otherwise, but they concur in their desire to expel us from the East Indies by force, deceit or otherwise. They would not leave untried any evil means one could imagine, if they could reach their goal that way. But their intentions were broken by God's hand and the whole Armada disappeared without achieving anything noteworthy; and as I learned just before I left Banten, General André and the captain from Manila were said to have been killed and would thus have died by God's hand in the middle of their evil plans.

I was also informed of the vile thing which the Portuguese did to 20 people at Macao, having let them come ashore from Admiral Jacob van Neck's ships, in part by giving the sign of peace.[17] They tried to make the Chinese suspicious of these 20 people, accusing them and our nation of all kinds of evil, nasty and unreasonable acts; but the Chinese (despite the fact that they are heathens and without knowledge of Christ) could not believe this and tried to protect our men and get them out of Portuguese hands. As soon as the Portuguese were informed of this, they hastily set up our men's trial for the sake (or rather the sham) of justice and hanged or garrotted 17 men, sending two boys and a man (the *fiscaal*)[18] to Goa as prisoners.[19]

---

[16] With reference to the year 1607, the Dutch Admiral Cornelis Matelieff de Jonge explained the expanse of Ternate in the following words: "For most of Jailolo [Halmahera] is subject to the king of Ternate, Sula, a large part of the island of Celebes [Sulawesi], Makassar indeed fell under him, most of Seram, Mindanao and other parts ..." See J.G. Frederiks, "Cornelis Cornelisz Matelieff de Jonge en zijn geslagt", *Rotterdamsche Historiebladen,* J.H. Scheffer and Fr. D.O. Obreen, eds., 3 afd., 1.1 (1871): 204–357, esp. 273–4.

[17] See also the affidavit by Admiral Van Neck featured as appendix I.

[18] See the glossary (*fiscaal*).

[19] This is a reference to Martin Apius and the two boys whose lives were spared because of their age. Martin Apius had also prepared a sworn affidavit roughly around the same time as Van Heemskerck and others. A transcript has been published in Pieter Anton Tiele, "Documenten voor de Geschiedenis der Nederlanders in het Oosten" in *BMH* 6 (1883), II, "Verklaring van Martinus Apius." (Declaration of Martin Apius): 228–42. This notarised testimony bears the date 18 October 1604 (Tiele, "Documenten": 242). The affidavit is also mentioned in Coolhaas, "Een bron": 416. A Portuguese translation available as M. Apius, "Incidente em Macau, 1601" ed. and tr. Arie Pos, *Revista de Cultura* 12 (2004): 61–7.

I also learned from certain letters from a Portuguese monk (residing in Cochinchina)[20] that this monk, pretending to help and counsel the king of Cochinchina, had persuaded him to attack our people by surprise, (who were lying at anchor there to conduct trade, with two ships under the command of a certain Groosberghen), kill them and take their ships. The king, strengthened by the monk's evil counsel, did the deed, killing 20 or 22 of our men and taking several others prisoner, who were later released in exchange for one or two brass cannons.

I also learned that three of the people I had left at Banda on my previous journey were sent to Ambon by their commander Adriaen van Veen to conduct trade there; they were vehemently pursued by the Portuguese and one of them, a chirurgeon, was caught and pulled asunder by four galleys. The other two fled and with great trouble reached an island, where they took refuge in the jungle.

And while I lay at anchor at Banten, the king of Demak[21] (situated on the coast of Java) sent to me, offering his friendship. I therefore sailed there with four ships, because I was informed that it was a country abundant in rice. Upon my arrival, that king, without having any cause, from the beginning launched several ambushes under the pretence of friendship in order to attack and conquer one or more of my ships by surprise. When he failed at those attempts, he captured 20 of my men who had gone ashore with merchandise to trade. I could not obtain their release by any[22] reasoning, so that I was forced to agree on a ransom after a few days, and eight men were released for half of the agreed sum. But he kept the other 12, using them in the war against his enemies; he did not want to release them on the basis of the preceding agreement or by any other decent means. So I decided to occupy his river and seize everything that went in or got out from there, in order to exchange people for people and goods for goods.

Then among other junks a junk from Johor[23] arrived, which also planned to sail up the river of Demak.[24] We seized the junk with its cargo and held it alongside our ship for a few days; we sent several people from the

---

20 Ms. here and subsequently: *Cochin China*.

21 Ms. *Dauma*. Kingdom in central-east Java. See also the list of place names (*Damão*).

22 Coolhaas erroneously reads: *egene* instead of *geene*.

23 Ms. here and subsequently: *Jor*.

24 Ms. *Damao*.

junk ashore to the king with the request to release our 12 men, stating that we would be willing then to return the loaded junk with its crew immediately, in the same state in which we had obtained it, offering to show him and his people all friendship and honour from then onwards. Nothing came from this, other than the king's intention to take the junk away from our ships by force, which cost him many of his men. And since we feared that he would make another attempt on the junk and [it] would be sunk by our cannons, we decided to unload the goods from it and store them in our ships.

Some days later (because we saw that the king did not care about his people, despite the fact that we had taken prisoner no less than 100 souls) we sent the empty junk ashore with its captain and about 70 souls, having promised the captain that if he could intercede with the king and achieve the release of our imprisoned men, we would restitute all his goods to him, or five kati[25] of gold instead, which he said they had cost. But none of this did us any good, and since time was running out (to our great detriment), because we had many sick on our ships every day and were running out of fresh water, we decided to weigh anchor and sail to Yortan[26] (another port, situated on the east end of Java). We reached it after a few days and from there sent the remaining Javanese we had captured off to Demak[27] with a perahu,[28] and two Malays[29] (whom I had kept with me from the junk from Johor) with letters and gifts to the king of Johor with a junk that was lying ready to depart for Johor. I asked the king not to blame or hold me responsible for what had happened to his subjects in the seizing of the junk; the two Malays would tell him the cause of it. I also wrote that I intended to sail to Johor, if it was possible. I had already hired a pilot for that purpose, and if it was unfeasible, I would sail my ships to Patani[30] without fail; I asked the king to send someone there with power of attorney, to whom I was willing to pay the five kati[31] of gold which the aforementioned captain had said the goods had cost.

---

[25] Ms. *caty*. About three kilograms of gold of unspecified purity.

[26] Ms. *Jurtan*. Present-day Bangil near Pasaruan, eastern Java.

[27] Ms. *Damao*.

[28] Ms. *proa*.

[29] Ms. *malayen*.

[30] Ms. *Patanij*.

[31] Ms. *catij*. About five kilograms.

Then, when I had arrived at Patani, the above-mentioned king [King of Johor] replied to me in two separate letters (which are still being kept) that I had done well. He said that he had never heard that the Dutch had harmed anyone (who acted friendly toward them), that it is praiseworthy to free oneself from damage suffered, and that if he or any of his subjects had sustained damage in the process, he had been sufficiently consoled and did not want any recompense but my friendship and that of the Dutch. Furthermore, he kindly requested that I come to his ports with my ships to take in cargo, saying that they were more suitable for spices than any other ports. He added that I would find him to be a very different man from other kings with whom we sought to conduct trade.

After this, I talked to the king's brother, named Raja Siak[32] (who had come to Patani to take a wife), and I received him well on board our ships. He earnestly recommended the king's friendship to me and complained about the damage they suffered from the Portuguese. He encouraged us to wait for the carrack from Macao, saying that his brother would assist us against the Portuguese; the Patani dignitaries did likewise, such as the *shabandar*[33] and the treasurer,[34] who gave me much information about the carrack from Macao and where I should lie in wait for it. They also told me that we could not do the Portuguese too much harm, as long as we let the ship lie at the roadstead undamaged, and offshore we could take it. That they were no friends of the Portuguese but just tolerated them, because of the pieces of cloth the Portuguese import there from Melaka and which they do not want to go without. As soon as we brought them pieces of cloth, they would cut off the Portuguese; and if we came with a force to conquer Melaka,[35] they would assist us with rice and provisions.

After that, when we were lying at anchor at Pulau Tioman,[36] a bantin (which we call a rowyacht) arrived there with several high-ranking persons

---

[32] Ms. *Rage Syack*. One of the four surviving sons of the Johor king Ali Jalla bin Abdul Jalil and half-brother of Raja Bongsu and the ruler monarch, Ala'uddin Ri'ayat Shah. Concerning his identity, see GPFT, appendix 13, pp. 211–5.

[33] Ms. *sabandar*.

[34] Ms. *Tresorier*. The *bendahari*. See also the glossary (*bendahari*).

[35] The maritime siege and attack on Portuguese Melaka was undertaken not by Van Heemskerck, but by his countryman Admiral Cornelis Matelieff de Jonge in 1606.

[36] Ms. *Pula Tyamao*. Island off the southeastern coast of the Malay Peninsula. See also the list of place names (*Pulatimom*).

Corte ende sekere Beschrijvin-
ghe vant veroveren der rijcke ende ghe weldighe
krake comende uyte Ghewest van China.

Door den Admirael Iacobus Hems-kerck liggende met twee schepen voor de straet
oft Fretum de Malacca, vanden Coninc van Ior een vyant der Portugeser
opgehouden ende ghebeden sy geweest/hy soude met zijn schepen
op een rijcke ende wel geladene Portugaloise krake die
drij jaren tot Makauw ende int gheweste van
China om syne Waren inne te ne-
men gelegẽ hadde/wachten.

Midtsgaders hier noch by ghevoecht het ghene datter tot Oostende gepasseert
is sindert dese twee Maenden Februarius ende Martius.

Ghedruckt na de Copy van Middelborch by Richard
Schilders/ Anno 1604.

Dutch pamphlet titled *Corte ende sekere Beschrijvinghe* (Short and Accurate Description of the Taking of the Rich and Imposing Carrack Coming from the Region of China) published in 1604 announcing the attack on and plunder taken from the Portuguese carrack *Santa Catarina*. The vessel had been seized by Admiral Van Heemskerck off the coast of Singapore on 25 February 1603. (Amsterdam, UB, Special Collections, OTM Pfl. K. 26).

on board. The most important one handed me a golden kris and a sealed letter (which is still at hand). Since neither I nor any of my men could read, much less understand it, I opened the letter and had it read by one of the most prominent among them (a very prudent and wise man). He declared that its content in essence was as follows: that the Portuguese at Yortan[37] had been informed that I had written and sent gifts to the king of Johor, requesting his friendship so that we could conduct trade there. They had passed the information on to the governor of Melaka, who already knew that my letter and gifts had arrived there and that the king of Johor in turn had sent me several letters at Patani, offering his friendship and asking us to come to his ports. This had been grounds for the said governor to send an envoy to the king of Johor, announcing that he had received reliable information about the above and that he was sorry that the king would be thus deceived; that the Dutch were thieves and only wanted to spy in his country under the pretence of friendship, and that later we would come with great force (since we have a country full of ships) to run down the king's entire country. If the king became friends with us, he would then have the Portuguese as hereditary enemies; and the king knew well how difficult it would be for him to have the Portuguese for enemies.

The king allegedly replied that he had never heard that the Dutch were such as the Portuguese said about them, but that they vehemently resist anyone who seeks to harm them; therefore he was not afraid to offer us his country. If the Portuguese had something to settle with the Dutch, that was not his business.[38] And the Portuguese had no ground whatsoever to lay down laws for him in his own country as to what he should do or with whom he should trade. On the contrary, the Portuguese at Melaka ought to live by his laws, since they reside in his (the king of Johor's)[39] country. "For the aforementioned reasons, and to prevent you from coming to Johor with your ships, the Portuguese have positioned three war ships and five low ships at the mouth of my river, doing nothing but harming my

[37] Ms. *Jortan.*

[38] This passage was loosely quoted by Hugo Grotius in his early treatise *De Jure Praedae Commentarius* (Commentary on the Law of Prize and Booty). See Grotius, *Commentary on the Law of Prize and Booty*, ed. and intr. M.J. van Ittersum (Indianapolis: Liberty Fund, 2006), p. 297; *De Jure Praedae Commentarius. Commentary on the Law of Prize and Booty. A Translation of the Original Manuscript of 1604*, tr. G.L. Williams and W.H. Zeydel (Oxford: Clarendon Press, 1950), p. 213.

[39] Ms. *Coninx van Jors.*

subjects every day. And since I have been informed that you are near the island of Tioman[40] to meet the carracks from China, I kindly request you to please leave that position and come and lie at the mouth of my river[41] with your ships, where the carracks have to pass close by to go through the straits and you will have a much better opportunity than at the location where you are now. At the same time you will help me avenge the damage which the Portuguese are causing my people (because of the favour I have shown you), and obtain an everlasting bond of friendship between me and your people."

This and much more was translated for me by the envoy. The truth of it became clear later, when we seized the carrack,[42] as would have been shown more broadly if but one of the king's envoys had been able to come over. But the king of Johor's affection and favourable inclination have been noticed sufficiently from the letter he wrote to His Princely Excellency,[43] to which I further refer.

For the goods that came from the aforementioned junk, I paid the captain (whom we called Raja Duta)[44] when I was at Johor, by the king's permission granted at my request. I counted out 1,200 reals-of-eight instead of five kati of gold,[45] although the goods did not bring in more than 700 reals-of-eight.[46]

Everything expounded above was done to me or my fellow-servants of the Amsterdam Directorate by the Spanish or the Portuguese, during or about this latest voyage of mine to the East Indies. After I had sent five of my ships to Banten for all they needed to get fully loaded, I left Banten with two well-equipped ships on 3 March, taking an eastward course to look for suitable cargo. Thus it happened in the meantime that we received news of everything narrated above. And having considered it well, together with

---

[40] Ms. *Teyama*.

[41] The Johor River estuary, probably somewhere off the eastern coast of Singapore Island near present-day Changi.

[42] The *Santa Catarina*. See also GPFT, pp. 42–7; SMS, pp. 68–75; also Borschberg, "The Seizure of the *Santa Catarina* off Singapore: Dutch Freebooting, the Portuguese Empire and Intra-Asian Trade at the Dawn of the Seventeenth Century", *Revista de Cultura*, International Edition 11 (2004): 11–25.

[43] Prince Maurice of Orange, the Stadholder of Holland and Zeeland.

[44] Ms. *Raga Duta*.

[45] The reals-of-eight are equivalent to about 32.5 kilograms of coin-grade silver. Five *kati* of gold are equivalent to about 3 kilograms.

[46] About 19 kilograms of coin-grade silver.

the council[47] assigned to me, paying close attention to the consequences, we found it very necessary to not only resist the enemy when the situation is critical and the knife is at one's throat, but to oppose them at an early stage so that we were hindered or imperilled as little as possible, causing them all possible damage wherever we could, to the salvation and increase of this our East Indian trade and navigation which we have started, which would inevitably have been lost otherwise, and also for the honour and reputation of our fatherland and His Princely Excellency, stadholder and admiral-general of these United Netherlands, to whose regulations and commission we are sworn. So that we in good conscience are at peace with what we have done, and we did not fear forfeiting all our means, amounting to less than 4,000 Flemish pounds,[48] and our persons at the demand of the Gentlemen Directors, if our case had gone badly. And we still are willing and prepared to give account at any time, to authorities high and low, of how we dealt with things during this voyage of ours.

To clarify the degree of certainty of my testimony, let me say that I myself have seen and heard part of what has been described above, being more or less present during these events, and that I have heard part of it from others. To certify the truth, I have signed this statement with my usual signature, at Amsterdam, on 4 October 1604. Signed by Jacob[49] van Heemskerck and by me who was present, Bruyninck, notary public.

Collated against the original, written and signed as above, this copy was found to accord with it. On this 11th day of October 1604. *Ita attestor*,[50] W. Kick, notary public. 1604.

---

[47] A reference to the Broad Council. See also the glossary (*brede raad*).

[48] About 24,000 guilders, or approximately 256.8 kilograms of coin-grade silver. See also the glossary (*Flemish pound, guilder*).

[49] Ms. *Jaques*.

[50] Lit. This I affirm.

APPENDIX

III

Affidavit of Simon Lambertsz. Mau confirming that the senior merchant Lambert Biesman of Nijmegen was garrotted in prison in Manila, etc.[1]

The following affidavit touches on the execution of Lambert Biesman and his men at Manila and forms part of the bound bundle of affidavits (described under appendix I) collectively titled *Boeck Tracterende vande Wreede, Verradische ende Hostile proceduren der Portugesen In Oost-Indien.* The affidavit by Simon Lambertsz. Mau is dated 10 October 1604. According to chapter XVI of the autobiography, De Coutre arrived in Manila around the time of the naval confrontation between the Spanish and the Dutch in Manila Bay (14 December 1600) and acted as an interpreter during the formal proceedings against Lambert Biesman and 17 of his mates who had been captured. Of the prisoners, 13 were subsequently executed in the city of Manila, the others were set free because they were still young. It is uncertain whether the "person who had lived in the East Indies on a permanent basis" mentioned by Simon Lambertsz. Mau may have been in fact Jacques de Coutre.

[1] The Hague, Nationaal Archief, Collectie 102, Baron H. van Zuylen van Nyevelt, suppl. 2, no. 13 (2.21.179.01 no. 13), *Boeck Tracterende vande Wreede, Verradische ende Hostile proceduren der Portugesen In Oost-Indien*, pp. 84–5. A transcript of the Dutch original has also been published in Coolhaas, "Een bron van het historische gedeelte van Hugo de Groots De Jure Praedae", *BMH* 79 (1965): 493–4. Translated from Dutch by Dr Corinna Vermeulen, Noctua Taal en tekst, Leiden.

Affidavit that the senior merchant Lambert Biesman of Nijmegen was garrotted in prison in Manila, etc.

Before me, Geeraert Vreem,[2] notary public admitted by the Court of Holland[3] upon nomination by the City of Amsterdam, and the witnesses mentioned below, appeared skipper Simon Lambertsz. [Mau], having made three voyages to the East Indies, now 46 years of age, and at the request of the Gentlemen Directors of the East Indian Company of this city declared, gave testimony and attested that it is true that Olivier van Noort, sailing from Rotterdam with his ship and cutter, subsequently arrived at Manila[4] near the Philippines.[5] There two ships or galleons came sailing, intending to come alongside the aforementioned Olivier, so that one ship or galleon was sunk by gunfire from Olivier and his crew, and Olivier's cutter was subsequently taken by the other[6] ships or galleons. Lambert[7] Biesman was captain on this cutter, and was imprisoned in Manila. The witness also declares having spoken with a person[8] who had lived in the East Indies on a permanent basis, declaring that he had visited Lambert Biesman in prison and that Lambert Biesman had been garrotted in prison.

The witness has declared that all this is the truth and is prepared to confirm it under oath at any time as well as in case of a request for further investigation. The witness furthermore consents to the execution of this deed by me, notary. Done formally on 13 September 1604, in the presence of Gilles Michielsen and Mathys Claessen, witnesses requested for this purpose, and signed. *Quod attestor rogatus*,[9] Vreemd, notary public.

---

[2] The name is also variously spelled 'Vreemd' below.

[3] Ms. *Hove van Hollandt*.

[4] Ms. here and subsequently: *Manielges*.

[5] Ms. *ontrent de Phillippinen*.

[6] This meant it was taken by the two aforementioned enemy craft. These were two vessels under the command of Dr Antonio de Morga.

[7] Ms. *Lambrecht*. Biesman, according to an editorial comment by Coolhaas, "Een bron": 493, note 3, was the son of a burgomaster of Nijmegen. He was originally hired as an *oppercommies* (similar to a factor) and in the course of Van Noort's expedition became skipper of the *Eendracht* (Unity, Concordia). See also Morga, *Sucesos*, pp. 165, 181, "Lamberto Viesman of Rotterdam".

[8] This is almost certainly De Coutre, who is known to have acted as a translator during the formal proceedings against Biesman and his men. In his affidavit, reproduced as appendix I, Van Neck confirmed that De Coutre had spoken to Biesman in prison about a week before he was executed.

[9] Ms. erroneously reads *ragatus*. The phrase means: "To which I bear witness, having been requested to do so."

Having been collated against the original, written and signed as above, this copy was found to accord with it after collation, on this 10th day of October 1604. W. Kick, notary public, 1604.

APPENDIX

IV

Second letter by Fernão de Albuquerque, Governor of Melaka, to the Dutch Admiral Jacob van Heemskerck, dated 26 March 1603[1]

Having earlier left Patani where he had met with Admiral Van Neck, Jacob van Heemskerck proceeded to the waters around Tioman and later plundered the Portuguese carrack *Santa Catarina* in the Singapore Strait on 25 February 1603. After a fierce battle off the coast of Changi which reportedly lasted for most of the daylight hours, the carrack's captain, Sebastião Serrão, the crew, soldiers (*soldados*)[2] and passengers aboard the vessel surrendered. As a condition of their surrender, they were all brought safely by Van Heemskerck to the Portuguese port and colony of Melaka. A series of letters were exchanged between Van Heemskerck and the authorities on land, including the city council of Melaka as well as the colony's captain (governor), Fernão de Albuquerque. The following represents a second letter of the Portuguese governor to

[1] This English translation of the German text was earlier published in GPFT, appendix 10, pp. 206–7. The original Dutch text can be found in the Hague, Nationaal Archief, Collectie 102, Baron H. van Zuylen van Nyevelt, suppl. 2, no. 13 (2.21.179.01 no. 13), *Boeck Tracterende vande Wreede, Verradische ende Hostile proceduren der Portugesen In Oost-Indien*, pp. 136–38. A transcript of the Dutch translation has been published in Coolhaas, "Een bron van het historische gedeelte van Hugo de Groots De Jure Praedae", *BMH* 79 (1965): 533–4. A partial transcript is found in another copy in Van Foreest and De Booy, *De Vierde Schipvaart*, II, appendix 53, p. 279.

[2] Soldiers. See also the glossary (*soldado*).

Van Heemskerck. The original in Portuguese is lost, but translations survive, including a Dutch translation found in the *Boeck Tracterende vande Wreede, Verradische ende Hostile proceduren der Portugesen In Oost-Indien.* The letter mentions one Philip (Filipe) Lobo of Melaka, who is also mentioned by Jacques de Coutre in chapter XVII of the *Vida* as a prisoner aboard the vessel of Van Heemskerck at Patani. Lobo had been dispatched by Fernão de Albuquerque to negotiate (via the good services and mediation of Van Heemskerck) with Johor's Raja Bongsu for the release of certain unspecified Christian hostages.

I received Your Honour's[3] letter with great joy, as I can sense from its contents the great affection You have shown toward the crew and passengers of the captured vessel. Such can be readily expected from a captain and admiral, and I am also willing to enter into correspondence with such a man, for it may happen [in future], that one of the Dutchmen is brought into this fortress [of Melaka]. What concerns the crew, however, that Your Honour reports to be in Japan in the East Indies, the Viceroy is accustomed to treating them well, and is not at all satisfied with the course of the hearings in China. He has also imprisoned one of the administrators,[4] and threatens to severely punish him, and for this reason Your Honour should not be angry at the Portuguese collectively, as they regard the miscarriage of justice in China as evil and unrightful. Concerning this effort, Your Honour shall do Your best for the captured Christians who are in a state of misery and sadness, [and] this instills me with hope, that Your Honour will render this favour of friendship and treat with the King of Johor [Ala'uddin Ri'ayat Shah III] and his brother [Raja Bongsu], for the release of the Portuguese and the Christians which he holds captive under the pretext of peace.[5] What concerns the goods from the junk or the ship, on which he had taken the [said] Portuguese captives, I do not demand to have these returned, because I know well, that they have been distributed among the [said king's] warriors. I only desire and request that they release

[3] Jacob van Heemskerck's letter, see also appendix II.

[4] According to Coolhaas, "Een bron": 533, note 4, one João Rui do Couto was indeed tried for his role in killing the 17 Dutch sailors at Macao. Several translated documents of this incident survive in Dutch, including a justification of Portuguese actions at Macao by the oidor Jouan Ruy de Souto. See Van Foreest and De Booy, *De Vierde Schipvaart*, II, pp. 296–9.

[5] It is possible that these are some or all of the Christian captives mentioned in Book I, Chapter XIX of De Coutre's *Vida*.

the Portuguese and the Christians who enjoy no dignity among the Malays. For this purpose I dispatch Filipe Lobo and Pero Mascarenhas and ask Your Honour to render this act of friendship and take them under Your protection, so that they may arrive safely with the Portuguese [prisoners], and hope this meets Your Honour's approval and good will. May God protect You and may he fulfill your wish and desire to bring you back to Holland in good health. From Melaka, the 26 March, in the year 1603.[6]

Fernao dal Buquerque

[6] The Dutch translation correctly dates the letter as 26 March on p. 138. The printed German translation of 1606 indicated the date of this letter as 6 March 1603.

GLOSSARY OF NON-GEOGRAPHIC NAMES, CURRENCIES, MEASURES AND COMMODITIES

aguardente — (Spanish: *aguardiente*). A fermented or distilled alcoholic beverage which is usually clear. The term has been employed to designate various forms of hard liquor, such as "brandy". In the context used by De Coutre, it is certainly known in Malay as *arak*.

almadia — This term appears to be of Arabic origin. It is used to designate a small craft such as a canoe or a "small native boat". Leitão and Lopes describe it as a light craft made of a single tree trunk. De Coutre claims it is a small craft similar to a sloop.[1]

almiranta — The ship under the command of an admiral.

almoada — (Also: *almohada*). A type of cushion or pillow.

aloes — (Also: *aloeswood*). An odoriferous wood. See also the separate entries for eaglewood, gaharu, and kalambak.[2]

alum — (Also: *pedra-humida, alum stone*). A natural cosmetic containing potassium and alum crystal. It tightens the skin and is often used as a deodorant and antiseptic. Alum was also used as an ingredient in dye to make the colour adhere to the cloth fibres.[3]

---

[1] BOC, II.3, p. 600; DLM, p. 31; GVOC, p. 11; HJ, p. 15; MNI, p. 205.

[2] HJ, p. 16; IMM, I, pp. 120–1; SMS, pp. 336–7.

[3] EFS, II, p. 1392; GVOC, p. 12; IMM, I, pp. 2–6.

amber A fossilised resin featuring a range of colours from saffron-yellow to red. Contrary to some popular myths, amber is flammable and floats on water. Expensive pieces contain curious objects, impurities or small insects in the fossilised resin. Yellow amber originates chiefly in the Baltic region where it was often picked up along the shores as it was washed up or retrieved in fishing nets. It was, and remains, very popular as jewellery in China. In Southeast Asia, Burma is a source of amber, but here its hue ranges from pinkish to wine red in colour. The fossilised resin amber should not be confused with ambergris, which is a natural, odoriferous and very costly baleen product. See also the separate entry for that product.[4]

ambergris (Also: *ambar* and other spellings). Not to be confused with amber (a fossilised resin, see the entry above), ambergris is a baleen or whale product. The term is of Arabic origin. Ambergris appears to be a natural excretion of the indigestible parts of the whale's diet. Freshly excreted, ambergris is dark and coloured by the melanin it has ingested from the whale's diet of octopus. When floating on the sea, and exposed to the sun, the melanin washes out and the ambergris appears whitish in colour. Ambergris was commonly collected along beaches near the migration routes of whales. It contains an odoriferous substance which is uniquely sweet and pleasant. Ambergris was believed to possess certain pharmacological properties and was commonly used in medicine, perfumery as well as an ingredient for cooking and confectionary.[5]

arak A term employed in Arabic and Malay for an alcoholic beverage, usually made from the leaf sap of various types

---

[4] BUR, I, p. 130.

[5] BOC, I.2, p. 692; BOC, II.3, p. 600; BUR, I, pp. 130–1; GVOC, p. 12; IMM, I, pp. 138–9; SMS, p. 337; Dunlop, *Bronnen*, p. 792; Borschberg, "O comércio de âmbar asiático no início da época moderna (séculos XV–XVIII)—The Asiatic Ambergris trade in the early modern period (15th to 18th century)" *Revista Oriente* 8 (2004): 3–25. Borschberg, "Der Asiatische Ambra-Handel während der frühen Neuzeit", *Mirabilia Asiatica II*, ed. Jorge Alves, Claude Guillot and Roderich Ptak (Wiesbaden and Lisbon: Harrassowitz-Fundação Oriente, 2004), pp. 167–201.

of palm trees.[6] The term is often used to designate local types of Asian fermented juices (such as nipa palm wine and various forms of toddy) and at times as a reference to rice wine and hard liquor.[7]

areca — (Also: *catechu*). A type of palm (Malay: *pinang*) that grows in the tropical regions of India and Southeast Asia. As confirmed by the description of De Coutre, the "nuts" of the areca palm are usually chewed with betel leaf and lime. See also the separate entry for *betel*.[8]

arroba — A unit to measure the mass or weight of liquids commonly used on the Iberian Peninsula. As a rule of thumb it is equivalent in Spain to about 16.2 litres, but there are noteworthy variations depending on the region as well as the actual liquid measured (for example wine, oil, honey, etc.). The *arroba* was also sometimes used to measure certain bulk solids, mainly foodstuffs, such as flour, rice, or sugar. In Portugal, the *arroba* was subdivided into 32 *arratéis* (singular: *arrátel*) and equivalent to 14.7 kilograms. In Portugal 54 *arrobas* and in Spain 80 *arrobas* make a *tonelada*; and 4 *arrobas* make a *quintal*. See also the separate entries for these measurements.

Arros — This is the name of a temple attributed by De Coutre to be the place where King Naresuan's favourite war elephant was given an elaborate cremation outside Ayutthaya. The name does not immediately appear to represent a corrupted Thai word, the name could represent a corruption of the honorific "Phra". Nevertheless "*arros*" means "rice" in Spanish. As there were many rice fields around Ayutthaya, this temple conceivably may have been associated with rice growing or the rice harvest, with storing harvested rice, or it may have been a place where people came to worship

[6] EFS, II, p. 1392.

[7] GVOC, p. 13; HJ, p. 36; MNI, p. 205.

[8] BOC, II.1, p. 813; BUR, I, pp. 225–31; ENI, I, p. 59; GLA, I, pp. 51–2; GVOC, pp. 13, 105; HJ, p. 35; IMM, I, pp. 130–3; MNI, p. 205.

or make offerings to the rice deity. Neither the location nor the temple could be identified.

atap — (Also: *attap*). This term refers to the (dried) leaves of the nipa palm used across the Malay Archipelago and some parts of mainland Southeast Asia as roofing. Other materials include the leaves of the sago-palm and *alang-alang* (a type of grass). European observers often refer to atap roofs as a "straw" or "thatched roof". See also the separate entry for *nipa palm*.[9]

Bajau (*laut*) — (Also: *Bayos Borneos*). This name refers to a seaborne tribe of nomads especially active in the area around Borneo and Sulawesi, but reports had them moving across most of insular Southeast Asia. The Bajau are sometimes called *Bujus* in early Portuguese chronicles of the 16th century, but they generally fall under the category of "celates", "saletes", "orang laut" or "to-ridjene" (as they were called in Makassar).[10]

baju — (Also: *bajoo* and other spellings). A Malay word to describe "clothing", "jacket", "dress", "skirt". Pedro Teixeira described it as a "light, short skirt".[11]

balacha — (Also: *alacha*, *halacha*, *alleja* and other variants). A textile made of cotton and silk, commonly produced and sold along the Coromandel Coast, featuring red and white or blue and white stripes; occasionally with flower motifs and adorned with gold or silver thread. De Coutre interchanged the letter "b" for the "h". He did the same in the case of *sabanes* for sahans. See also the separate entry below for that type of textile.[12]

---

[9] ENI, I, pp. 67–8; GVOC, p. 14; HJ, pp. 39–40, 780–1.

[10] ENI, I, pp. 100–1; GVOC, p. 117.

[11] GLA, I, pp. 81–3; GVOC, p. 15; HJ, p. 46–7; Sinclair, ed., *The Travels of Pedro Teixeira*, p. 4.

[12] EFS, II, p. 1392; CTCB, pp. 253–54; MNI, p. 205; Irwin, "Indian Textile Trade in the Seventeenth Century. I. Western India", *Journal of Indian Textile History* 1 (1955): 25; "Indian Textile Trade in the Seventeenth Century, III. Bengal", *Journal of Indian Textile History* 3 (1957): 66; Irwin and Schwarz, *Studies in Indo-European Textile History* (Ahmedabad: Calico Museum of Textile, 1966), p. 57.

balas — (Also: *balão*, *bâlos*). This term referred to a small Asian type vessel that was propelled by breast oars and could also be sailed. Moreland claimed it is equivalent to the Malay *balyan*, a kind of "rowing-boat".[13]

Banbareca — (Also: *Bombareca*, *Mombarek*). Name of the ruling king of *Aveza*. According to Pedro Teixeira, the area controlled by *Mombarek* was located in a region "three days journey" upstream from Basra. The "northern Persian plains are in the possession of Mombarek, son of Motelob, an Arab chief who holds them against the Turk, and is at war with him pretending a right to these and to the territory of Basra. In his territories are Magdom, Oëza and Soreka, cities of importance." See also the separate entry for *Aveza*.[14]

bantin — (Also: *banteen* and other spellings). According to J.V. Mills' notes to chapter 13 of Manoel Godinho de Erédia's *Declaraçam de Malaca* (Description of Melaka), a *bantis* was a Malay craft used in naval warfare in the 16th and 17th centuries. It was "propelled by breast oars" and featured "two rudders and two masts".[15] Monsignor Dalgado's *Glossário Luso-Asiático* traces the word to the Malay name *banting* and defined it as a commercial vessel with two masts.[16]

Barcaloa — This appears to be a corruption of Barcalong or Phraklang, the minister of the treasury, trade and foreign affairs. The name and spelling *Barcalon,* for example, is found in the memoirs of the Jesuit Father de Bèze whose account of his dealings at the royal court at Lopburi ranks

---

[13] EFS, II, p. 1393; Moreland, *Peter Floris*, p. 70, note 3; Loureiro, "European Encounters and Clashes in the South China Sea", II, *Revista de Cultura,* International Edition 12 (2004): 155.

[14] W.F. Sinclair and D. Ferguson, ed., *The Travels of Pedro Teixeira with this "Kings of Harmuz" and Extracts from his "Kings of Persia"* (Nendeln: Kraus Reprint, 1967), pp. 25–6. See esp. also the editor's note 1 on p. 26.

[15] Brussels, Bibliothèque Royale, Ms. 39015A, fol. 61 recto. Manoel Godinho de Erédia, *Declaraçam de Malaca*, c.1613.

[16] GLA, I, p. 97.

among one of the most important testimonies of early modern Siam.[17] De Coutre's *Barcaloa* may have been the wife or daughter of the Phraklang.

batel — (Also: *batelo*, *botella*). A small vessel used in northwestern India and Bengal. The term was used by De Coutre to designate a small craft propelled by breast oars.[18]

baxel — (Also: *baixel*). A generic Portuguese term that referred to a cargo ship or barge. In the Malay Archipelago, the term was commonly applied as a synonym for *perahu*, but sometimes it could also be referred to as a junk. In one instance De Coutre claimed it is similar to a *lanchara.* See the separate glossary entries for *lanchara* and *perahu.*

beatilha — (Also: *beatilla*, *betille*, *bettelas*, *beteelahs* and other spellings). A word of Portuguese origin meaning "veil". The term *beatilha* refers to a lightly woven, semi-transparent cotton textile (muslin) from Golconda. This was commonly used by women as veils and by men as turbans, and in some instances the fabrics were decorated with floral patterns, gold or silver thread. See also the separate entry for *cassa.*[19]

beeswax — Beeswax was widely used in the design and preparation of traditional cloth wares in Southeast Asia, especially in the production of batik fabrics. The wax is melted and put in a canting, an instrument that resembles a pen. It features a small tub at the top that contains the liquid wax.

bendahara — (Also: *bendara*). A high-ranking official in a Malay polity who in more recent times has become almost synonymous to the "minister of interior" or "prime minister".

---

[17] E.W. Hutchinson, ed. and tr., *1688. Revolution in Siam, The Memoir of Father de Bèze, S.J.*, 3rd impression (Bangkok: White Lotus Press, 2002), p. 10, note 2.

[18] HJ, p. 71.

[19] BOC, I.1, pp. 735, 737; GVOC, p. 20; HJ, p. 90; MNI, p. 206; Irwin, "Indian Textile Trade in the Seventeenth Century. II. Coromandel Coast", *Journal of Indian Textile History* 2 (1956): 35; Irwin and Schwarz, *Studies in Indo-European Textile History*, p. 59; Moreland, *Peter Floris*, p. 66, note 3; also EFS, II, p. 1394.

Early modern Dutch sources sometimes translate the term bendahara as *Rijksbestierder* ("governor of the empire"). The bendahara's role is important. He also served as the master of ceremonies and legitimised activities at the court through ritual.[20]

bendahari — A high-ranking official in a Malay polity often called treasurer (or *tresorier* in certain 17th-century Dutch sources) and in more recent times "minister of finance".

benzoin — (Also: *benjuim, menjuin* and other spellings in De Coutre, sometimes also *benjamin*). An (odoriferous) resin of the *styrax benzoin* known among Arab traders as *luban Jawi* (Javanese frankincense). The substance was widely used in medicine of the early modern period, and also in the production of incense. Traders differentiated benzoin by provenance or quality. The most expensive was the so-called "almond benzoin" (*benguin de amêndoas*). This was of an off-white or egg-shell colour and was chiefly sourced in Siam, Pegu (Burma), Lan Xang (part of present-day Laos) and other regions of mainland Southeast Asia.[21]

berço — A breech-loading swivel gun (often made of wood) that had developed since the late Middle Ages and evolved during the early modern period. They were widely used in Europe and Asia, including specifically in China and Southeast Asia of the late 16th and early 17th centuries. These small-calibre swivel guns were common in naval warfare and usually mounted on the decks of ships.[22]

betel — The leaf of a creeping vine related to pepper (scientific name: *piper betle*) and commonly grown for chewing in South and Southeast Asia. The betel leaf is used to wrap around areca and is sometimes mixed with lime or tobacco, hence the (erroneous) reference to "betel nut". The mix is chewed as a stimulant and as a breath freshener. Offering

---

[20] GLA I, pp. 115–6; GVOC, p. 18; HJ, p. 84; SMS, p. 334.
[21] BOC, I.1, p. 727; EFS, II, p. 1394; BUR, II, pp. 2139–46; GLA, I, pp. 112–3; GVOC, p. 19; HJ, pp. 86–7; IMM, II, pp. 1182–3; SMS, p. 337.
[22] DLM, p. 93.

betel to guests and at special occasions was an important aspect of Southeast Asian court rituals and among most strata of society, especially with the rich and the nobles. As Farrington and Dhiravat na Pombejra explain, "elaborate boxes, receptacles and cutters evolved as part of the ceremonial". See also the separate entry for *areca.*[23]

bezoar (Also: *piedras de bazares, beçares*; Malay: *guliga*). Bezoars are concrements found in different parts of the intestinal tracts of mammals, especially in ruminants. When harvested from monkeys (so-called monkey stones), they are generally the gall stone found in the ape. Bezoar stones are not exactly the most sightly of objects to look upon, but their potential value as a life-saving medication and their deployment as a panacea in almost all medication in Europe of the early modern period rendered bezoars more costly than diamonds. For this reason, jewellers—such as De Coutre who appears to have been very knowledgeable about bezoars—dealt in this rare and most costly of Asian commodities. In traditional cultures of Arabia, Europe, India, as well as in the Indianised cultures of Southeast Asia, bezoars are also believed to possess magical or mystical properties to ward off spells and many forms of evil. For this reason they were also mounted in jewellery and headpieces of royalty and religious leaders. Among the most expensive of all were the porcupine bezoars which were harvested on the Malay Peninsula, Sumatra, in Riau and on Borneo. Johor (specifically the capital Batu Sawar), Pahang and Banjarmasin were among the most important trading centres of this extremely rare and very costly product. Porcupine bezoars were widely considered the sovereign remedy against cholera, dysentry and other life-threatening diseases and most important of all, they were considered a reliable cure against (arsenic) poisoning.

---

[23] BUR, II, pp. 1767–72; EFS, II, p. 1394; GLA, I, pp. 121–4; HJ, pp. 89–90; IMM, I, pp. 960–4; MNI, p. 206.

In the early modern period, bezoars were often treated like precious stones. They were sold by the carat, and the price per carat rose exponentionally, just as was the case with diamonds and other cut or polished gems. The prices cited for average-quality pieces during the early modern period range between 20 and 200 cruzados at cost—and even went well upwards of that.[24] For this reason—and especially also for the bezoar's alleged life-saving properties—jewellers generally dealt in these concrements on behalf of their wealthy clients. See also the separate entries for *carat* and *cruzado.*[25]

bonzo A word of Iberian origin which refers to a Buddhist monk of unspecified rank.

borax This term of Arabic (or perhaps Persian) origin refers to a salt that forms along lakes in India, China, Tibet and Japan. In the Spanish Americas it was mined at Potosí together with silver. Borax was used for the cleaning and welding of gold, for curing leather, and also as a medicinal substance. It is also an essential ingredient for the production of gun powder.[26]

braça A unit for measuring the depth of water. The *braça* (Portuguese), *braza* (Castilian, Spanish) or *brasse* (French) traces its origins to the full span of two human arms. The Portuguese *braça* generally measures about 1.76–1.83 metres and the Spanish *braza* about 1.67 metres. The French *brasse* is about 1.60 metres. The *braça* is subdivided into 8 *palmos*

---

[24] Equivalent to between about 600 to 6,000 grams of coin-grade silver.

[25] BOC, I.1, p. 728; BOC, III, p. 587; BUR, I, pp. 324–6; EFS, II, p. 1395; GLA, I, pp. 107–9; GVOC, p. 20; HJ, pp. 90–1; Borschberg, "The Trade, Forgery and Medicinal Use of Porcupine Bezoars in the Early Modern Period (c.1500–1750)" (bilingual article, Portuguese-English), *Revista Oriente* 14 (2006): 60–78; "The Euro-Asian Trade in Bezoar Stones (approx. 1500–1700)", *Artistic and Cultural Exchanges between Europe and Asia, 1400–1900: Rethinking Markets, Workshops and Collections*, ed. Thomas DaCosta Kaufmann and Michael North (Aldershot: Ashgate, 2010), pp. 29–43; P.G. Leupe, "The Siege and Capture of Malacca from the Portuguese in 1640–1641. Extracts from the Archives of the Dutch East India Company", tr. by Mac Hacobian, *JMBRAS* 14, 1 (1936): 142.

[26] BOC, II.3, p. 602; GVOC, p. 22.

(see the separate entry for *palmos*). It is not clear which *braça* De Coutre had in mind when he spoke about the depth of water, and therefore an approximate metric range is provided.[27]

brede raad — (Also: *breede raad*; broad council). The broad council fulfilled the function as both an advisory and decision-making body on important commercial and military issues as well as major offences committed aboard Dutch ships. It was composed of senior officers (usually the commanders of each of the vessels of the fleet) and also of senior commercial representatives.

brigantine — A small sailing vessel that can also be propelled by breast oars and usually featuring one or two masts. De Coutre claimed they are similar to *bantins*. See also the separate entry for that term.

brocado — A thick or heavy cloth featuring interwoven threads of gold, silver, or both.

buah duku — (Scientific name: *Lansium domesticum*). This fruit is variously known as *langsat* (spelling varies) in different parts of Southeast Asia. The Hokkien name is *bah luku*. Growing in clusters sometimes resembling grapes, this fruit has a thick, egg-shell coloured skin that is frequently covered with small brown speckles. The flesh of the fruit is white with greenish-brown seeds.[28]

bungkal — A Malay term for a penis bell or penis insert. Bungkals are inserted into the shaft or head of the penis. It is also noteworthy from the text of the *Vida* when we read the words: *en la cabeça de la natura*. Esteban de Coutre who edited his father's texts may have been unsure about the exact reference and may have confused two very similar (Portuguese) words: *cabaça* and *cabeça*. The latter term would mean the "head", but the former means "gourd",

[27] DLM, p. 108; MNI, p. 206; SMS, p. 331.

[28] BUR, II, pp. 1335–7.

"waterer" or "hose" and implicitly therefore, the penis shaft. As shall be seen below, both interpretations are valid. The best and probably most reliable description of the bungkals from Pegu, Ava, Lanna and Siam of the late 16th and early 17th century—contemporaneous with De Coutre in other words—is the account by Ralph Fitch. Many of the observations made by De Coutre are in fact identical to those of Fitch, which may raise some additional questions about (common) sources or authenticity.[29] Fitch wrote on the occasion of his visit to Chiang Mai in 1587: "In Pegu, and in all of the countreys of Ava, Langeiannes [Lan Xang], Siam and the Bramas [Burma], the men weare bunches [i.e. bungkals] or little round balles in their privy members: some of them weare two and some three. They cut the skin and so put them in, one into one side and another into the other side; which they do when they be 25 or 30 yeeres olde, and at their pleasure they take one or more of them out as they thinke good. ... The bunches aforesaid be of divers sorts; the least be as big as a little walnut, and very round; the greatest are as big as a little hennes egge." According to the study of Donald Brown, James Edwards and Ruth Moore, "The bells, balls, and irregular objects inserted under the skin were sometimes under the surface of the glans, sometimes under the skin around the shaft of the penis, and sometimes in or under the foreskin."[30]

caladari A plain, closely woven but light cotton cloth (calico, see also the separate entry for that type of textile) from the Indian subcontinent, and chiefly from Bengal, featuring

---

[29] Fitch acknowledged António Galvão's work, first published in 1563, as a known parallel discussion on these bungkals. See A. Galvão, *Tratado dos Descobrimentos* (Porto: Livraria Civilização Editoria, 1944); and its English translation as *The Discoveries of the World from their First Original until the Year of Our Lord 1555*, tr. Richard Hakluyt and ed. Admiral Bethume (London: Hakluyt Society, 1862), p. 113.

[30] EFS, I, p. 70; Foster, ed., *Early Travels in India*, "Journal of Ralph Fitch", pp. 39–40; D.E. Brown, J.E. Edwards and R.P. Moore, *The Penis Inserts of Southeast Asia: A Bibliography, Overview and Comparative Perspective* (Santa Barbara: Department of Anthropology, University of California Santa Barbara, 1988), esp. p. 5.

black or red stripes. This was generally used for clothing. De Coutre refers to this textile by the name *aareiores.*[31]

calayn (Also: *calem*, *callen*). The Portuguese term for tin from Asia (*estanho Oriental*).[32]

calico According to Villiers, a calico is a "type of fine cotton cloth woven along the Malabar Coast and shipped from Calicut". It formed part of the larger Luso-Indian trade in textiles.[33]

camphor The early modern merchant had to distinguish carefully between at least two types of camphor: first, tropical camphor that was harvested between the bark and the trunk of the camphor tree (scientific name: *Dryobalanops aromatica*). It was chiefly found on Sumatra and Borneo and is non-toxic to the human body when ingested. For this reason, it is also referred to in early modern medical literature as *camphora edibilis* (edible camphor). Tropical or edible camphor was in Asian (including Arab) and European pharmacology thought to be the sovereign remedy against intestinal parasites. Second, Japanese laurel (or cinnamon) camphor (scientific name: *Cinnamonum camphora*) was produced synthetically in both China and Japan. It is toxic to the human body if ingested, but can be applied externally on the skin to reduce an itching sensation and offer symptomatic treatment for rashes. In early modern trade, tropical or edible camphor typically cost about ten times more than its synthetic counterpart.[34]

candil A unit for measuring the mass or volume of bulk commodities such as rice or grain. It is roughly the weight that can be transported by an ox cart. Monsignor Dalgado believed the term to be of Malayalam origin, other authors traced its etymological roots in the Sanskrit word *khand*

[31] GLA, I, p. 178.

[32] GLA, I, pp. 178–9 and II, p. 475.

[33] EFS, II, p. 1395; GVOC, p. 25; HJ, pp. 147–8; Villiers, "Review": 455.

[34] BUR, I, pp. 886–7; EFS, II, p. 1396; HJ, pp. 151–2.

	(divide) and recognise more immediate linguistic links to either Telegu or Hindi. One *candil* is equivalent to about 280 litres or 0.28 cubic metres if used to measure volume. Leitão and Lopes claim it is equivalent to 220 kilograms, but Dalgado's estimate is substantially higher at 460 kilograms. According to De Coutre, a *candil* can be subdivided into ten *fanegas*. See also the separate entry for *fanegas*.[35]
capitana	The ship of the captain-general, the commander-in-chief of a fleet; flagship.
capitão-mór	A Portuguese term that translates into English as "captain-major". The commander of a fleet comprising several large vessels; the headman of an unofficial Portuguese settlement.[36]
carat	A word of Greek and later also of Arabic origin, representing a unit to measure the weight of precious metals and precious stones. In the diamond trade, one carat is equivalent to approximately 0.2 grams.[37]
caravel	A sailing ship based on Arab and Mediterranean precursors commonly used during the 15th and 16th centuries. The caravel features a shallow draft, and either two or three masts with lateen (triangular-shaped) sails. The caravel is a highly maneuverable vessel that was favoured by the Portuguese and Spanish in the early phase of European expansion and exploration.[38]
cardamom	(Also: *cordamonium* and other orthographical variants; scientific name *Zingiberacea*). As a member of the ginger family, early modern spice traders distinguished importantly between green (scientific name: *Elettaria cardamomum*) and black cardamom (scientific name: *Amonum cardamomum*),

[35] BOC, II.2, p. 449; BOC, II.3, p. 602; DLM, p. 132; GLA, I, pp. 199–200; GVOC, p. 59; MNI, p. 206.
[36] SMS, p. 335.
[37] BOC, II.1, p. 823; GVOC, p. 59; MNI, p. 206.
[38] BOC, I.1, p. 730; DLM, pp. 137–40; SMS, p. 332.

the latter of which was, and still is, far more costly. Cardamom was one of the most expensive spices found in the early modern ledger books of the East India companies, far surpassing the price of cloves or nutmeg. Even today cardamom remains one of the most costly spices, ranking third after saffron and vanilla. Apart from its use as a spice in the preparation of food, it is also seen to possess certain medicinal properties. It was used to stimulate digestion and strengthen a weak stomach.[39]

carnelian A reddish and sometimes reddish-brown variant of the mineral chalcedony. In the early modern period it was commonly mounted in jewellery and likewise carved into beads and used in prayer such as for rosaries. Carnelian also goes under a variety of other names including "Mecca stone" and "pigeon blood agate".

carrack (Also: *nao*, plural *naus*). Generic term of Arabic origin for a large and generally lightly-armed Portuguese trading ship used mainly in the 16th and early 17th centuries. The design characteristically features a forecastle and an elevated poop deck. It is evident that De Coutre employed the term "carrack" to designate any large ocean-going vessel, and like many of his contemporaries, employed it as a synonym for galleon. See also the separate entry for *galleon*.[40]

cartaz A safe conduct pass issued by the Portuguese or Spanish crowns granting the owner license to navigate the (high) seas claimed by them. The term derives from the Arabic word *qirtas* meaning "paper" or "document". The Portuguese first introduced the cartaz in 1502 to protect the commercial interests of their allies Cananore, Cochin and Quilon. In its origin, therefore, the cartaz was geographically limited to the waters around the Indian subcontinent. It subsequently evolved into a means of enforcing a monopoly of maritime

---

[39] EFS, II, p. 1396; GLA, I, p. 215; GVOC, p. 25; Dunlop, *Bronnen*, p. 794.

[40] BOC, I.1, p. 739; DLM, pp. 368–9; HJ, pp. 165–6; SMS, p. 332; Dunlop, *Bronnen*, p. 794.

traffic claimed and asserted by Portugal (and Spain) over the high seas, including the Atlantic, Pacific and Indian Oceans, usually for a fee or a share in the profits generated by a specific maritime venture. If a vessel was intercepted and found to be without a valid cartaz, the captain and crew were imprisoned and the ship and cargo confiscated. In Asia, local merchants could obtain a cartaz fairly easily and at a modest fee, but in Europe cartazes were generally restricted to natural-born subjects of the crowns of Portugal or Spain respectively. In Asia, specifically in coastal areas of the Western Indian Ocean, cartazes functioned similarly to safe conduct passes known in Arabic as a *qawl* (lit. declaration, report, pronoucement), and permitted "to land … men and make an agreement to trade …"[41]

casado — A Portuguese term meaning "married" or "resident". This refers to a Portuguese subject who married and settled in a given colony and was no longer liable for military service. Often the Portuguese *casados* were soldiers-turned-traders. Specifically in the context of the Estado da Índia, the *casados* were usually separately listed from the *soldados* (soldiers).[42]

cassa — (Also: *cossaes*). A term of Persian and Urdu origin meaning "special" or "select". As a textile it refers to a high-quality, loosely-woven, semi-transparent cotton fabric (muslin) from Bengal. This fabric was commonly used by (Muslim) women as veils and by men as turbans. See also the separate entry for *beatilha*.[43]

---

[41] DLM, p. 145; GLA, I, p. 220; K.S. Mathew, "Trade in the Indian Ocean and the Portuguese System of Cartazes", *The First Portuguese Colonial Empire,* ed. Malyn Newitt (Exeter: Department of History and Archaeology, University of Exeter, 1986), pp. 69–84, esp. p. 73; Moreland, *Peter Floris,* p. 10, esp. also note 1.

[42] GVOC, p. 28; Loureiro, "European Encounters": 155.

[43] BOC, I.1, p. 737; BOC, II.1, p. 816; BOC, II.2, p. 449; EFS, II, p. 1398; GLA, I, p. 223; GVOC, p. 28; HJ, p. 707; MNI, p. 206; Irwin and Schwarz, *Studies in Indo-European Textile History,* p. 62; Moreland, *Peter Floris,* p. 66, note 3.

cassia (Also: *canafistula, cassia fistula*). A plant native to India cultivated for ornamental purposes and also for its medicinal properties. It is used as a laxative, to purge bile, reduce body temperature, subdue inflammation and as an expectorant. Cassia is also effective against mouth ulcers. Subspecies of cassia are used in cases of rheumatic fevers, jaundice, syphilitic sores, and in the treatment of ringworm.[44]

Catabussa This appears to be a Portuguese corruption of Qutb Shah which is the title carried by the rulers of Golconda.[45]

cebadera A sail that was unfurled on a crossed hook below the bowsprit, outside the boat or ship. De Coutre was probably referring in this single instance to the bowsprit yard.

celamine (Also: *celemin, selemin* and other spellings). A Spanish unit to measure the volume or mass of foodstuffs and equivalent to about 4.6 litres. Twelve celamines are equivalent to one *fanega* (see also the separate entry for that term). De Coutre mentioned this unit in the context of purchasing rice and other provisions on the markets in Siam where he claimed that one *chupo* is worth half a celamine. See also the separate entry for *chupo.*

Chincheo The name commonly employed by the Portuguese and especially the Spanish to generically refer to people from China, and specifically from the coastal region of Fujian (which is sometimes also referred to as the Amoy Coast). The name is thought to represent a corruption of the toponym Zhangzhou, a port on the Fujian coast of China. It was home to many peddlars and merchants who sailed to Southeast Asia to trade. Certain sources such as the travelogue of Zeygert de Rechteren (1632) also mention the "Chincheo River" (present-day Jiulong River).[46]

---

44 BOC, I.2, p. 694; BUR, I, pp. 478–88; GLA, I, pp. 195–6, 224; GVOC, p. 28; IMM, I, pp. 290–1.

45 GVOC, p. 95; Moreland, *Peter Floris*, p. 18, note 1.

46 Loureiro, "European Encounters": 156; "Journael ende Verhael Vande Oost-Indische Reyse by den Heer Admirael Wybrant Schram .... Item Oost-Indische Reyse ghedaen by Seyger de Rechteren" ... in BV, III, unfoliated map inserted between pp. 44 and 45.

chupo	A unit to measure mass or weight. De Coutre mentioned it in the context of Siam where he claimed people buy "rice, vegetables and other provisions" measured in chupos. He explained it is equivalent to half a celamine, or approximately 2.3 litres. See also the separate entry for *celamine.*
civet	(Also: *algalia, argalia*). A word of Arabic origin referring to the odoriferous, oily excretion, similar to black musk, of the so-called "civet cat", which is more closely related to the mongoose than to felines. Civet was widely used in perfumery and also as a medicinal substance, but its high price invited many forgeries, imitations and adulterations.[47]
cocheneal	This is a water-soluble, red dye of insect origin from Central America. During the early modern period it had been used to colour and even flavour other substances, such as tobacco.[48]
coir	(Also: *Cairo, cayro*). A fibre made from the rind or husk of a coconut. This fibre was water- and rot-resistant and used across monsoon Asia for the making of ropes, as a thatch for roofing or as a stuffing for pillows and mattresses.[49]
colchas (*de Montaria*)	A *colcha* is a fine cotton (and more specifically cotton and silk) embroidered cloth produced in Bengal and used by the Portuguese as wall hangings or bedspreads. Montaria appears to be the provenance or place of origin.
commies	A commercial officer or agent aboard VOC ships. De Coutre explained that they were similar to a factor.
conto de oro	One conto de oro is equivalent to one million cruzados. See also the separate entry for *cruzado.*

[47] BOC, I.1, p. 730; EFS, II, p. 1398; GVOC, p. 32.

[48] GVOC, p. 33.

[49] HJ, pp. 233–4.

cop (Also: *cap*, *chop*, as in the former's pronunciation). A word of Urdu or Hindi origin (*chāp*) adopted into Malay. It refers to an (engraved) official seal or stamp, or in some instances to the whole document bearing the official seal. De Coutre also called it a "royal warrant".[50]

corneca Probably a corruption of the Sinhala word *kuruneka.* This refers to the chief of a herd of elephants, or to an elephant tamer; a driver or keeper of elephants; a mahout. See also the separate entry for *mahout.*

cowry shell A word of Indian origin (*kauri*) referring to small, white, marine shells. Cowries were used as currency (small change) in parts of Southeast Asia and Africa. The 15th-century Chinese author Ma Huan noted: "In trading they [the Siamese] use cowries as money for current use." The Maldives were reportedly the largest source of cowries.[51]

cruzado A Portuguese silver coin. In the period under review, the cruzado of 400 reis was worth about 10 per cent more than the Spanish-American real-of-eight, but in practice the two were often used interchangeably on a one-for-one parity. The silver content was thus just over 29 grams. Four cruzados made a Portuguese escudo. See also the separate entries below for these other currency units and coins (*escudo, real-of-eight*).

culebrina (Also: *culverin* and other spellings). A class of firearms of Medieval origin ranging from a light, long-barrelled gun (precursor of the musket) to an artillery field piece. Characteristic of the larger culverins was that they could load the weapon from the back. This rendered them easy to load and were thus ideal artillery pieces for ships.

---

[50] BOC, II.1, p. 817; EFS, II, p. 1397; GLA, I, pp. 260–1; MNI, p. 206.

[51] BOC, II.1, p. 817; EFS, II, p. 1399; GVOC, p. 29; HJ, pp. 269–71; MNI, p. 206; Ma Huan, *Ying-Yai Sheng-Lan*, p. 107.

damask — Reversible woven-pattern Chinese fabric that is usually made of cotton, silk or both.[52]

Dialquan — (Also: *Idalquan*). Adil Khan, the title of the Muslim rulers of Bijapur.

Don — (Portuguese: *Dom*). From the Latin *dominus* (lord, master). Don or Dom is used as an honorific especially for addressing members of the nobility, in Spain and Portugal, respectively. The female equivalent is Doña (Portuguese: *Dona*).

drogas — Spanish and Portuguese for spices and also medicinal produce. The boundaries between the two are not always clear.

ducat — A currency name of Italian origin (*ducca*) widely minted in Western Europe in the early modern period. It was generally equivalent to about 3.5 grams of gold.[53]

eaglewood — A literal translation of the Portuguese *pao d'aguila*, eaglewood or *aquilaria* in Latin is a type of odoriferous aloeswood drenched in its own resin that, when burned, releases a sweet, pleasant odour. In the early modern period traders divided it into three qualities or grades: *cabeza* (the highest quality), *bariga* and *pee.* Eaglewood was, and remains, much sought after in the Arab world as well as in Japan and greater China, where it was (and still is) used in aromatherapy or burned as an offering in temples. See also the entries for *aloes, gaharu* and *kalambak.*[54]

ebony — A black hardwood from Africa. Ebony was used for carving effigies, as well as for prayer and rosary beads.

emas — (Also: *mas, mazes* and other variants). A unit to measure weight as well as a coin commonly used in Southeast Asia. The emas is generally equivalent to 0.1 *tael* or about 3.75 grams, but in early modern Aceh it was considerably

[52] BOC, II.3, p. 603; EFS, II, p. 1399.
[53] MNI, p. 207.
[54] BOC, II.1, p. 813; BUR, I, pp. 198–206; GVOC, pp. 10–1; HJ, pp. 335–6; MNI, p. 206; SMS, pp. 336–7; Leupe, "The Siege and Capture of Malacca", p. 142.

less at about 0.58 to 0.61 grams. Moreland claims that the emas was equivalent to 0.25 *tikal*, or 0.0625 *tael* (see the separate entries for these units of measurement). De Coutre claimed that an emas (probably the *salung*) in Siam was worth 1.5 reals (*reales*) or the equivalent of 5.6 grams of coin-grade silver.[55]

Enchetangan — De Coutre explained that *Enchetangan* was a powerful woman in Patani who saved his life and apparently had (an extended) family with interests in commerce and shipping. The word appears to be composed of the Malay (or Cham) words *Cei* or (*En-*) *Cik* (an honorific, a salutation, in this instance: "Madam") and *tangan* which has several connotations, including "hand" or in an extended sense "power" or "authority". Taken as a whole, the term expresses an honorific or a title rather than a personal name, something along the lines of "Powerful Madam" or "Madam with Authority"; or implicitly also the head of an organisation. De Coutre himself appeared to have translated the "title" when he explained that *Enchetangan* was a "powerful woman", a "woman in authority". She may even have been vested with authority similar to a high-ranking Malay official (*bendahara*, *shahbandar*, *temenggong*). AA has erroneously identified this person as Raja Hijau (*Hidio Raya*). See also the separate entries for *bendahara* and *mandarin.*[56]

enpalega — According to De Coutre, this was a small type of coastal vessel used in southeastern India (Coromandel Coast). Leitão and Lopes described it as a small craft used along the Malabar Coast.[57]

escudo — In the context of De Coutre's writings, there are two escudos to bear in mind. First is the Portuguese escudo which is a gold coin with a face value equivalent to 4 cruzados or about 3.57 grams of gold. In terms of gold weight,

[55] BOC, II.1, pp. 834–5; GVOC, p. 70; WMSA, I, p. 102; Moreland, *Peter Floris*, p. lxix.

[56] AA, p. 161.

[57] DLM, p. 224.

this makes it roughly equivalent to the ducat. Second, the Spanish escudo which has a face value of 16 reals (or equivalent to two reals-of-eight), that is 54.14 grams of coin-grade silver. As it is insufficiently clear which *escudo* De Coutre had in mind when he appraised the given value of an object, calculations will be made in metric weight for both gold and silver equivalents. See also the separate entries for *cruzado, ducat* and *real-of-eight.*

escupeta — The term appears to be a corruption from the Italian *schiopetto,* being the name for a hand-held barrel gun of the late Middle Ages and early modern period. These firearms were relatively simple to produce and operate because they only featured a pipe or barrel with a vent hole. The escupetas were notoriously inaccurate firearms.

espadela — A large oar, usually kept on deck, that fulfilled a number of functions, including substituting a broken rudder on ships.[58]

Estado da Índia — Lit. translates as the "State of India". This term collectively refers to the patchwork of Portuguese colonial dependencies around the Indian Ocean and the Western Pacific that were administered from Goa. The Estado da Índia was made up of a string of forts and ports and at times larger territories that were subject to different degrees of authority, ranging from outright sovereign possessions to forts and ports under contract with neighbouring Asian or African rulers. The expression is often used interchangeably with "Portuguese India", *Ásia Portuguesa,* as well as its colonial administration and bureaucracy.

factor — Resident head of a so-called factory (sometimes called "lodge" or "house" in VOC sources). The term is of Italian or Portuguese origin and in earliest times referred to a commercial agent or the head of a collection and billing station. In the context of East Indian trade, however, the *feitoria* or "factory" was often a heavily fortified structure

---

[58] DLM, p. 242.

with a resident population rendering support services to the factory as well as its broader activities. These settlements were usually beyond, or specifically exempted from, the jurisdiction of the local overlord by treaty. The factor was in charge of the entire operation within a given compound, and in the case of larger settlements also oversaw public works. In VOC ranks, those associated with the name "factor" included *oppercoopman* (senior merchant), *coopman* (merchant), *fiscaal*, and *commies*. See also the separate entries for *commies* and *fiscaal*.[59]

factory See the entry for *factor*.

fanega A Spanish unit for measuring the mass or volume of certain bulk commodities. One fanega is equivalent to about 55 litres. It can be subdivided into 12 celemines. According to the information provided by De Coutre, ten fanegas make a candil. See also the separate entries for *candil* and *celamine*.

fiscaal The *fiscaal* is normally associated with a judicial officer, including the public prosecutor. In the context of the VOC and its predecessor companies, it refers to an officer who was responsible for investigating and prosecuting company servants.[60]

Flemish pound The Flemish pound was equivalent to about 6 guilders in the late 16th and early 17th century. This would render it equivalent to about 2.4 reals-of-eight or 2.2 Portuguese cruzados. As the latter were silver coins, this would render the Flemish pound equivalent to about 64 grams of coin-grade silver. See also the separate entries for *cruzado*, *guilder* and *real-of-eight*.[61]

foist (Also: *fusta*). A category of vessel that, as a rule, features a single row of oars and a single mast. Foists were lightly armed and often deployed for patrolling the coast.[62]

---

59 GVOC, p. 42; HJ, pp. 345–7.
60 GVOC, p. 44.
61 SMS, p. 340.
62 DLM, p. 279; SMS, p. 332.

frigate — The term originally refers to an open Portuguese naval craft that was often rowed and in the 16th and 17th century deployed in the East Indies. By the 18th century the term referred to a naval sailing vessel featuring three masts and armed with up to 50 cannons. Frigates were usually deployed as vessels of war on account of their speed and excellent handling abilities.[63]

frying — There are several instances in the text of the *Vida* that make reference to a mode of execution in Siam that De Coutre called "frying". As stipulated in the *Law of the Three Seals* (the *Kotmai Tra Sam Duang*, compiled in 1805 under the rule of King Rama I from older legal sources), there were different modes of execution involving fire and boiling oil. Among these were: 1) wiping the condemned man with a cloth dripping with oil, then setting him alight; 2) doing the same, but this time tying the oily cloth around the man's fingers alone (he would have burnt to death anyway); and 3) setting a kettle of oil to boil, then pouring its contents over the condemned.[64]

gaharu — Name of the wood or tree of the *Aquilaria* family which, when infected with a fungus, produces an odoriferous resin to defend itself. Gaharu wood by itself is not valuable, but when the tree produces this resin (in which case it is no longer called gaharu but aloeswood, eaglewood or kalambak, depending on grade and quality) it emits a sweet odour when burnt. See also the separate entries for *aloes*, *eaglewood* and *kalambak*.

galleon — (Also: *gallion*, *galeón* and other spellings). A type of ocean-going sailing ship of the late 16th to 18th century that was deployed either as a vessel of burden or in naval wars. Galleons feature an elongated hull, multiple decks (especially if designed to house artillery) and three to five

[63] GVOC, p. 45; Dunlop, *Bronnen*, p. 798.

[64] A special thanks to Dhiravat na Pombejra for researching these Siamese methods of punishment and execution.

masts. Galleons supplanted the carracks as commercial ships not least because they could sail faster and were easier to handle under various wind and sea conditions. The term galleon was often used as a synonym for carrack during the early 17th century. See also the separate entry for *carrack*.[65]

galley (Also: *galés*, *galea*, *galeia* and other spellings). A type of rowed vessel that traces its origins to ancient Greece and Rome. In later centuries, galleys were widely deployed in the Mediterranean and around parts of West Asia, such as the Red Sea and the Persian Gulf. Galleys served chiefly as warships and feature several rows of oars on each side of the vessels and they usually had one or two masts.[66]

galliot (Also: *galeota*, *galiota* and other spellings). A type of vessel featuring one or two masts and a shallow draft. The vessel could be sailed or propelled by breast oars. It also refers to a smaller type of galley. See also the separate entry for *galley*.[67]

gantra (Also: *ginetra*). According to De Coutre, this term referred to the prayer beads of Buddhist monks. This means the *gantra* is equivalent to the wrist or hand *mala* which are normally carved from wood and sometimes made of semi-precious stones, especially jade.[68]

guilder Also known colloquially as the *florin*, the guilder was the accounting currency of the province of Holland as well as the VOC. In the early 17th century, the guilder was a notional or an imagined currency unit, and actual coins with a face value of one guilder were only minted after 1681. The silver equivalence of the guilder was linked to

[65] BOC, I.1, p. 732; DLM, p. 283; GVOC, pp. 45–6; SMS, pp. 332–3; Dunlop, *Bronnen*, p. 799.
[66] BOC, I.1, p. 732; DLM, p. 284; SMS, p. 333.
[67] BOC, I.1, p. 732; DLM, p. 284; GVOC, p. 46; SMS, p. 333.
[68] W.H. Moreland, ed., *Relations of Golconda in the Early Seventeenth Century* (London: Hakluyt Society, 1931), p. 27.

its value against the *stuiver*. As a rule of thumb and with reference to the period 1608–10, the guilder was equivalent to about 10.7 grams of coin-grade silver. Generally, 2.5 guilders were equivalent to about one Spanish-American real-of-eight. See also the separate entries for *real-of-eight* and *stuiver*.[69]

halberd — A weapon mounted on a long pole that can serve either two or three functions in war. The tip is formed as a spear for stabbing the enemy. There is an axe for hitting or chopping off limbs. On the opposite side of the axe there is often a hook-shaped instrument which can be used to pierce the armour or headpiece of the enemy and pull him down from a horse. Rui Manuel Loureiro described the halberd as a "pole arm with a sharp, long metal head crossed by an iron crescent-shaped blade".[70] For a depiction of the halberd, see the image on page 9.

harquebus — (Also: *arquebus*, *harkbus*). A muzzle-loaded firearm common in the 16th and 17th centuries. The *VOC Glossarium* describes it as a "heavy type of gun; a small cannon". Harquebuses were based on a German-manufactured precursor and resembled later firearms such as the musket and the rifle. They were far more accurate firearms than the simpler *schiopetto* or *escupeta*. See the separate entry above for that type of weapon.[71]

hidalgo — (Portuguese: *fidalgo*). A member of the lower nobility; "gentleman".

ilha — Portuguese word for island. See also under the entries in List of Place Names for the Spanish words *isla* and as well as its older orthographical variant *ysla*.

in coena Domini — (Also: *De la cena* bull). The opening Latin words of a papal bull promulgated by Pope Paul III in 1536. It forms part

[69] SMS, p. 340.
[70] Loureiro, "European Encounters": 154, see the entry: *alabarda*.
[71] GVOC, p. 51.

of a long list of papal edicts, promulgated between the 14th and 18th centuries, that address issues of heresy, excommunication, and punishments to be meted out on believers who assisted the enemies of Christ. Like its predecessors, the bull of Paul III prohibited, under the pain of excommunication, the sale of weapons, metals or any other goods to Muslims, especially since they could in turn be used in warfare against Christians.

indigo Plants belonging to the *Indigoferae* family grown in many parts of India and Southeast Asia that yield a dark blue dye. Different types (and implicit qualities) of indigo were usually named after their more precise place of origin, such as indigo Agra, Biana, etc.[72]

junk A type of ship used across Asia, but most frequently associated today with Chinese-type vessels of burden used during the age of sail. Deriving from the Malay word *jong,* these ships featured a shallow draft, watertight compartments, leeboards for stabilising the craft at sea, and sails made of either cloth or reeds. Junks are very versatile and easy to handle in all wind conditions with a comparatively small crew. De Coutre has used the term *baxel* as a synonym for junk. See also the separate entry for *baxel.*

kaffir Term of Arabic origin used to designate a person who is not a Muslim. The Spanish and the Portuguese adopted this expression during the early modern period and often employed it as a pejorative. It generically referred to persons of colour, especially Africans, South Indians, and the peoples of the Malukus, the Bandas, Irian Jaya (New Guinea), Flores, Solor and Timor. The equivalent Dutch or Flemish term of the period is "swarten" (lit. blacks).

kalambak (Also: *calambac*, *clanba*, *clanbuco* and other spellings). Highest-grade aloeswood, usually from Champa (present-

[72] BUR, II, pp. 1252–60; EFS, II, p. 1402; GVOC, p. 55; Dunlop, *Bronnen*, p. 801.

day southern Vietnam) and widely deployed in early modern medicine in Europe and in Asia. Kalambak was also used in the production of incense. See also the entries for *aloes, eaglewood* and *gaharu*.[73]

kati (Also: *cattee, catty* and other spellings). Widely-used unit for measuring weight in Asia. As a rule of thumb, a kati is equivalent to about 600–625 grams and represents 16 taels or 1/100 of a *pikul* (being 60–62.5 kilograms). See also the separate entries for these measurements (*pikul, tael*).[74]

karang (Also: *batu karang*). This is the Malay word for coral. When ground up or pounded, coral served as mortar in the construction of stone buildings.

kebaya (Also: *cabaia, kabaya* and other spellings). A type of long-sleeve jacket used by Malay (Muslim) women. Kebayas can range from the simple to the ornate. Monsignor Dalgado described the kebaya as a dress or tunic worn by the rich.[75]

keris (Also: *creese, cris, kris* and other spellings). A highly esteemed weapon widely found in maritime Southeast Asia that was utilised in both traditional ceremonies as well as in combat. However the use, function and the associated symbolism of this weapon should be understood against the broader canvass of specific cultural, geographical and historical contexts, that is the role and place of the *kris* in the history and culture of Malay, Javanese and Filipino societies. Limited references to the *kris* also apply to certain parts of the western Indian Ocean region, including Ceylon.[76]

Khoja (Also: *Coya, Godia* and other spellings). Khoja or Khwaja derives from the Persian language, and in the 17th

[73] BOC, II.1, p. 816; EFS, II, p. 1395; GVOC, p. 58; HJ, pp. 144–5; SMS, p. 337.

[74] EFS, II, p. 1396; HJ, p. 175; GVOC, p. 60; SMS, p. 339.

[75] GLA, I, pp. 158–60; GVOC, p. 57; HJ, pp. 137–8; MNI, p. 206.

[76] HJ, p. 274; SMS, p. 337.

century the term was sometimes used as an equivalent or counterpart to the Portuguese *Senhor* or Dutch *Heer*. Khoja was broadly employed as an honorific meaning such as "opulent merchant" or "eunuch". The honorific was attributed to, or used by, merchants of specifically Armenian (Christian) origin. According to Moreland the title was "assumed by merchants among other classes".[77]

lac (Also: *gommelack*, *gomlak*, *gumlac*, *gum Malacca*; also *schellak*). A term of Sanskrit origin which refers to a red-coloured gum used as a varnish; red lac. Lac is the resin-like, red excretion of a beetle-sized insect (Latin: *Laccifer*) that lives on certain trees in Assam, Bengal, Myanmar and Thailand. In Arabic and Persian the word is also applied more loosely to a range of substances that are used as a red dye.[78]

laksamana (Also: *lassamane*, *lacamane* and other spellings). A Malay title or official corresponding approximately to the commander of the fleet or "admiral". In Aceh, the *laksamana* was reportedly also responsible for dealing with foreign merchants, similar to the *shahbandar* in other ports of the Malay Archipelago. The Portuguese chronicler João de Barros called this Malay official the *capitão-mór do mar* (captain-major of the sea). See also the entry for *shahbandar*.[79]

lanchara (Also: *lancha*, *lancharan*, *lancharã*, launch and other spellings). The Portuguese name for a small commercial sailing craft widely used in the Malay Archipelago during the early modern period. The expression is thought to be of Malay origin, deriving from the word *lancar*, meaning "fluent", "quick" or "swift". See also the separate entry for *baxel*.[80]

---

77 GLA, I, pp. 295–6; EFS, II, p. 1403; Dunlop, *Bronnen*, p. 800; Moreland, *Peter Floris*, p. 43, note 1.

78 BUR, II, pp. 1311–5; HJ, pp. 499–500; GVOC, p. 49; Dunlop, *Bronnen*, p. 800.

79 GLA, I, pp. 516–7, II, p. 502; GVOC, p. 67; SMS, p. 335.

80 HJ, pp. 502–3; SMS, p 333.

lanqua (Also: *langua, lankua*). A type of galangal or ginger and a member of the *Zingiberaceae*. The specific name here is of Arabic origin (*khalanjan*). This root was used either fresh or in dried form as a condiment, in baked goods or as herbal medicine. Among the Arabs it was also known as an aphrodisiac.[81]

legua (In Portuguese also: *legoa,* sometimes loosely translated into English as league). An Iberian unit to measure distance at sea. It is not clear which *legua* De Coutre had in mind when estimating distances. A Spanish *legua* measures about 5,567 metres but the Portuguese unit measures about 6,174 metres. Overland distances seem to be expressed in *leguas* of 1,964 metres. For this reason metric equivalents will be provided in approximate ranges.[82]

lixo (Also: *lixa*). De Coutre explained that this is the skin or leather of the sting ray. On page 84, the term has been employed as a leather or paper with rough surface, "sandpaper".

mahout (Also: *mohawat*). The permanent caretaker and rider of an elephant. See also the separate entry for *corneca.*[83]

manchua A Portuguese corruption of the Malayalam word *manji.* This is a large cargo-boat featuring a single mast with square sails. It was prevalently found along the Malabar Coast.[84]

mandarin This is generally believed to be either a corruption of the Sanskrit-derived term *mantrin* (councillor, minister) or a derivative of the Portuguese verb *mandar* (hold authority, command, govern). Although the title *mantri* (or *menteri*) is also widely employed across the Malay Archipelago and on mainland Southeast Asia, the term *mandarin* is most often

[81] BUR, II, pp. 1323–35; Dunlop, *Bronnen*, p. 798.
[82] SMS, p. 333.
[83] GVOC, p. 77.
[84] DLM, p. 336; GLA, II, pp. 19–20; HJ, pp. 549–50.

associated today with officials of a Confucian state, such as those from China, Korea, Vietnam, etc. These mandarins were often drawn from humble social backgrounds and had reached their status by passing rigid state examinations. In the early modern period the term was used more flexibly and was also applied to officials from other polities, notably from Cochinchina and Siam.[85]

mark (Also: *marco* and other spellings). A unit for measuring the weight of precious stones and precious metals (gold, silver). The mark (or *mark fijn* in Dutch) is equivalent to 24 carats for weighing gemstones; about 230 grams when weighing gold and silver, and up to 244.5 grams in certain other instances. The mark is also equivalent to eight Dutch *ons* (ounces). De Coutre claims that four marks make a *kati* (meaning the mark is equivalent to about 150 grams). See the separate entry for *kati*.[86]

mercury (Also: *asoge*, *azogue*; *quicksilver*; Malay: *raksa*). Mercury was widely used in Europe—and is still used in China today as a medicinal substance—especially in the treatment of skin disorders, syphillis and other ailments. A residue of mercury was also used to extract gold from rocks and ores.[87]

mogra Colloquially known as Indian Jasmine, mogra is commonly worn by women in their hair. Its essential oils are also deployed as ingredients for cosmetics, perfumes, and in the preparation of herbal medicine.

monsoon (Also: *trade winds*). This term of Arabic origin (*mausin*, "season") refers to the strong, seasonally conditioned winds which were used by traders in the age of sail. In Asia there are two monsoon seasons, the northeast monsoon (October–February) and the southwest monsoon (May–September). Depending on the monsoon season and the

[85] GVOC, p. 73.

[86] BOC, II.1, p. 825; GVOC, p. 73; MNI, p. 208; Dunlop, *Bronnen*, p. 800.

[87] BUR, II, p. 1479; EFS, II, p. 1408; IMM, II, pp. 67–83.

	geographic location in Asia, the winds are responsible for bringing rainfall, hence their frequent association with heavy precipitation.[88]
musk	(Also: *almizcle, almíscar, almiçre, mizcle, black musk*). Today, the term "musk" is used to designate many types of odoriferous substances, of both animal and plant origin. In the early modern period, however, the expression was employed almost exclusively to signify the natural excretion of the Asian musk deer which is found mainly in China, Siberia and the Himalayan range. In the early modern period, musk was used in perfumes, as a medicine, and sometimes as an ingredient for baked goods and confectionery.[89]
musket	A muzzle-loaded long gun developed in the 16th and 17th centuries. It is fired—like the modern rifle—from the shoulder and is technologically more advanced than the *escupeta* or even the *harquebus*. See also the separate entries for these two weapon categories.
nakhoda	(Also: *nacoda*, *nacoder* and other spellings). A word of Persian origin meaning "captain"; master or owner of a ship.[90]
navette	A term of Portuguese origin (*naveta*) meaning "small boat"; a small sailing craft often used as a vessel of burden.[91]
nayak	This title derives from the Sanskrit *nāyaka* (leader, chief, general) that originally refers to a cavalry captain under the Hindu rulers of Southern India and in the Vijayanagar Empire. It became synonymous for a governor of a province who sometimes exercised power and authority similar to an independent overlord.[92]

---

[88] GVOC, p. 77; HJ, pp. 577–8.

[89] BUR, I, p. 787; EFS, II, p. 1405; GLA, I, p. 27; SMS, p. 337; Borschberg, "O comércio europeu de almíscar com a Ásia no inicio da edad moderna—The European Musk Trade with Asia in the Early Modern Period", *Revista Oriente* 5 (2003): 90–9.

[90] EFS, II, p. 1406; HJ, pp. 612–3.

[91] GVOC, p. 80; SMS, p. 333.

[92] GVOC, p. 79; HJ, pp. 614–5.

nipera — The Spanish or Portuguese word for "nipa palm" (scientific name: *Nypa fruticans*). The juice or water of the nipa palm, when left to ferment, produces arak. Its leaves are used for roofing and is called *atap* in Malay. See also the separate entries for *arak* and *atap*.[93]

onça — A Portuguese ounce, equivalent to 1/16 of an arrátel or about 28.7 grams. See the separate entries for *arroba* and *quintal*.

orang kaya — (Also: *arangkaio, orangcay* and other spellings). A Malay term that means "wealthy" or "powerful person". In certain parts of the Malay Archipelago, the expression, however, does not refer so much to wealth as to status or power. An *orang kaya* is, therefore, also a person of authority and good standing, and the term is often used as an honorific. Moreland described the *orang kaya* as a "general title for persons of high position".[94]

Oya — (Also: *Okya* or *Phraya*). A Siamese title of nobility ranking second in precedence. Moreland simply defined the bearer of the title as a "mandarin of the highest grade".[95]

Oya Avan — (Also: *Oyavangarao*). De Coutre mentioned this functionary only once and described him as the "Governor of Ayutthaya". This is very likely a reference to Okya Wang, who was the minister in charge of palace affairs at Ayutthaya. Subsequent employment of *Oyavangarao* in the context of De Coutre's visit to the royal palace at Ayutthaya appears to confirm this reading.

Oyasimintoy — This name is evidently composed of the Siamese honorific *Oya* or *Okya* and another as of yet unidentified, corrupted Thai word. (See the separate entry for *Parabaci* that raises a similar problem). From the context in which the name

---

[93] BUR, II, pp. 1583–8.

[94] BOC, II.3, p. 613; EFS, II, p. 1406; GVOC, p. 83; HJ, pp. 644–5; SMS, p. 335; Moreland, *Peter Floris*, p. 34, note 2.

[95] GVOC, p. 82; Moreland, *Peter Floris*, p. 56, note 1.

or title is used by De Coutre, *Oyasimintoy* is the "general of the rivers". This broadly conforms to the Okya Chakri who according to Chris Baker *et al.* was the "chief of the army and the navy and minister of interior … Chief over the political, military, ecclesiastical and civil affairs. He was kind of a chief minister, with jurisdiction over both civil and military affairs, and also held the title of *onkharak,* head of the royal bodyguard".[96] The *VOC Glossarium* described the Chakra as the "Siamese minister of the interior" and the "governor of the southern provinces in Siam". He was, among others, responsible for "receiving embassies and maintained relations with foreigners". The actual term employed by De Coutre could also represent a corruption of Si Mahatthani, after the name of the ministry.[97]

palmo — An Iberian unit to measure length. It originally referred to the full span of a spread hand. As a rule of thumb, the *palmo* corresponds to about 20–22 centimetres. Eight *palmos* make a *braça.* See also the separate entry for *braça.*[98]

pangaio — (Also: *pangara*, *pangaia*). A small craft similar to a longboat that is propelled by breast oars or paddles and is deployed as a vessel of burden. According to Monsignor Dalgado, the term etymologically traces its roots to the Malay word *pinggang* (hip, waist). De Coutre employed this expression in two separate contexts: once to describe a small craft in the region of southeastern Africa (especially Mozambique), and once in the context of longboats or galleys found on the "River of Siam" (Chao Phraya River). He claimed that the galley (*pangaio*) he saw featured 30 oars on each side and was made from a single tree trunk.[99]

Parabaci — (Also: *Parabasi*). According to De Coutre the *Parabaci* is the royal treasurer of Siam. This appears to represent a

---

[96] Baker, *et al.*, ed., *Van Vliet's Siam*, appendix I, p. 324.

[97] GVOC, p. 30.

[98] DLM, p. 389.

[99] GLA, II, pp. 157–8; HJ, p. 668; *Commentaries of the Great Afonso Dalboquerque, Second Viceroy of India*, ed. and tr. Walter de Gray Birch, 4 vols. (London: Hakluyt Society, 1880), vol. III, pp. 60–1, note 1.

corruption of the Siamese honorific title *Phra* and the Thai word *phasi* meaning "taxes". The official in question corresponds to the Phraklang.[100] At the end of chapter X of the *Vida*, De Coutre alluded to him again by describing him as a "factor", a chief of trade. Baker and Van der Kraan explained his functions as follows: "chief of the king's warehouses, keeper of the great seal, and intermediary for the foreigners who are in the country ... counsel and leader of all foreign affairs at the court and keeper of the great seal. Head of the Khlang (treasury) department".[101] AA, by contrast, treats the title *Parabaci* as a possible Portuguese corruption of the Javanese word *jurubahasa* (*jurubaça*; "translator").[102]

Paravas — A seafaring warrior caste from southern India that lived along the Malabar and Coromandel Coasts of present-day Kerala and Tamil Nadu in India. Monsignor Dalgado described them as fishermen from a low caste who lived between Cape Comorin (*Cabo de Comarin*; today's Kanyakumari) and Mannar.[103] Other sources associate them exclusively with pearl fishing in southern India.[104] The Paravas are known to have been among the first peoples in the Indian subcontinent to convert to Christianity. See also the separate entries in the List of Place Names for *Cabo de Comarin* and *Manar*.

pardao — (Also: *pardau*). The name *pardao* generally refers to one of two coins. The gold pardao (*pardau d'ouro*) in India varied in value, but as a rule of thumb it was equivalent to one gold *pagoda*. The value of the pagoda, depending on location, fluctuated between 75 and 120 stuivers (3.75 and 6 Dutch guilders). The Portuguese minted silver pardaos in Goa with a face value of five *tangas* (of 60 *reis*

---

100 Baker, *et al.*, ed., *Van Vliet's Siam*, appendix I, p. 324; GVOC, p. 91.
101 Ibid., p. 324.
102 GLA, I, pp. 499–500.
103 GLA, II, pp. 172–3, 511.
104 BOC, II.2, p. 459.

each) or 300 reis. For this reason the silver pardao was often interchangeable with the Spanish-American real-of-eight. The VOC minted its own version of the silver pardao for conducting trade along the Malabar Coast. See also the separate entries for *guilder*, *real-of-eight* and *stuiver*.[105]

patache — The name is of Arabic origin and refers to a small, lightly-built commercial vessel with a shallow draft commonly used around the Iberian Peninsula and France. As a rule the *patache* features two masts. They generally served as vessels of burden and also as support vessels for larger ships such as carracks or galleons. See also the separate entries for *carrack* and *galleon*.[106]

payluan — This appears to be most likely a corruption of the Thai expression *phrai luang* which means "manpower under royal control". De Coutre has translated it as "slave" which represents a very loose, but not an exactly accurate translation of that expression. AA has changed the reading to fit the Persian term *paidar* which, according to Monsignor Dalgado, means "courtier". This word is definitely not a corruption of the Malay word *palawan* (hero) as suggested by AA.[107]

pedra de porquo-espin — Porcupine stone or porcupine bezoar. For details see especially the separate entry for *bezoar*.

pedrero — (Also: *pedreiro*). A cannon of a small calibre that shoots stones or stone pellets. Pedreros were commonly deployed in naval warfare during the 16th and early 17th centuries.[108]

perahu — (Also: *prao*, *proa*, *parau*, *paro*, *prahu* and other spellings). A type of small craft that can be either sailed or rowed. The term is very flexible in its application, and the types of vessels covered by this category range from coastal cargo

---

105 BOC, II.1, p. 829; GVOC, pp. 84–5, 87; HJ, pp. 672–8; SMS, p. 340.

106 GVOC, p. 88.

107 GLA, II, p. 139.

108 DLM, p. 404.

ships (that are chiefly sailed) to longboats on a river. Perahus were—and still are—common in the Malay Archipelago and the Indian subcontinent. They were generally used as vessels of burden or in naval combat.[109]

pikul (Also: *picol* and other spellings). A unit of weight commonly used in early modern trade, the *pikul* is equivalent to 1/3 of a *bahar,* ten *gantang* or 100 *kati*; or approximately 60–62.5 kilograms. In VOC ports the weight of a *pikul* ranged from 120–122 Dutch *pond* (about 494 grams).[110]

pies A Spanish unit to measure length. As the name suggests, the *pies* is the Spanish equivalent of a foot, measuring about 28 centimetres.

pimenteiros A type of vessel used around the Indian subcontinent. According to De Coutre, the *pimenteiros* were Portuguese smuggling ships that are equipped in Muslim lands to conduct trade and business in the Strait of Hormuz and the Persian Gulf region. John Villiers underscored that the pimenteiros were instrumental in weakening and eventually bringing down Portuguese rule in Hormuz.[111]

pinnace A light boat with shallow draft propelled by sail and sometimes by oars. Pinnaces were commonly used as vessels of burden and at times in naval combat.[112]

Prachidec (Also: *Prachidech*). De Coutre mentioned this Siamese official on two occasions. Little is known about him other than the fact that he was a "personal servant of the king". This is possibly a reference to Phra Choduk, the head of the Port Department of the Left Prasadet, or the governor of Ayutthaya and factor of the king.

pucho According to the Portuguese medic García da Orta, *pucho* is the term used in Melaka for cate or catechu. He described how it was mixed with betel and areca for chewing.

---

[109] EFS, II, p. 1408; HJ, pp. 733–4; SMS, p. 334.

[110] BOC, II.1, p. 829; EFS, II, p. 1407; GVOC, p. 91; SMS, p. 339; Dunlop, *Bronnen*, p. 799.

[111] Villiers, "Review": 455.

[112] GVOC, p. 70.

Orta also claimed that catechu was abundant in the region around Bassein, Mannar and Daman. Similarly, Duarte Barbosa explained that *pucho* is a drug which he claimed came from Cambay and was much valued in Java. Catechu was commonly used in Indian (Ayurvedic) medicine where it has several applications, including as a breath freshener. See also the separate entries for *betel* and *areca.*[113]

quintal — An Iberian unit for measuring the weight of bulk commodities. It is uncertain whether De Coutre has the Portuguese or the Spanish *quintal* in mind. The Spanish quintal (pl. *quintales*) is equivalent to about 46 kilograms and the Portuguese quintal (pl. *quintais*) to about 59 kilograms. In Portugal, four *arrobas* or 128 *arratéis* (singular: *arrátel*) make a *quintal.* In Spain, 20 *quintals* make a *tonelada.* For this reason all estimates involving *quintals* will be converted into metric and given as an approximate range. See also the separate entries for *arroba*, *tonelada* and *onça*.

radix Chinae — Also known as "China root" and in Malay as *obat raja* (royal medicine) and in Latin as *smilax China*, this is a knotty rhizome of the Sarsaparilla family. *Radix Chinae* was widely procured by both Dutch and Portuguese traders in China as it found widespread application in the treatment of gout, skin disorders and, infamously, the advanced symptoms of syphilis. In the Arab and Persian world, *radix Chinae* was also used in herbal cooking. It is said to lend a rosy complexion to those who consume it.[114]

raja — (Also: *raya*, *raia* and other spellings). A term of Sanskrit origin meaning "king". Historically the term was used in a very flexible manner, spanning from the title of a great king in India (maharaja) to a petty prince in Southeast

---

[113] GVOC, p. 28.

[114] BUR, II, pp. 2073–5; BOC, I.1, p. 745; BOC, II.1, p. 831; EFS, II, p. 1397; GLA, II, p. 196; GVOC, p. 95; HJ, p. 199; IMM, II, pp. 1143–4; SMS, p. 338; Borschberg, "The Euro-Asian Trade and Medicinal Usage of Radix Chinae": 102–15; Dunlop, *Bronnen*, p. 808.

Asia. The title of raja was commonly used on the Indian subcontinent as well as in the Indianised regions of insular and peninsular Southeast Asia, and remained in use well after the advent (beginning of the 13th century) of Islam across the region. Dutch and Portuguese sources of the 16th and 17th centuries commonly referred to the Malay sultans as "rajas" or translate the title into their own language, as for example *raya*, *rayale* or *koninck*.

Raja Bongsu Malay title literally meaning the "Young King". Although there have been other Raja Bongsu in the early modern history of the Malay Archipelago, the individual mentioned by De Coutre is the younger half-sibling of Ala'uddin Ri'ayat Shah III of Johor. Raja Bongsu is also known from other sources as Raja Sabrang and Raja di Ilir and he appeared to have maintained his own settlement (Kota Sabrang, opposite the capital city Batu Sawar on the Johor River) and his own client-subjects. Raja Bongsu always played a major role in forging Johor's relations with external powers, and thus could be seen in modern terms, among other functions, as the "foreign minister". He succeeded Ala'uddin as the crowned ruler after the Acehnese invasion of Johor in 1613. For a problematisation of his geneology, see also the excellent study of Paulo Pinto.[115]

Raja Mudaliar The title *Mudaliar* is of Sinhalese origin and means as much as "great governor". The Raja Mudaliar was the wealthiest merchant in the Melaka Sultanate at the time of its fall to the Portuguese in 1511. The Raja Mudaliar was said to have been of Chettiar (South Indian) origin.[116]

rassamalla (Also*: reçamalla*, *roçamalha*, *rasamala* and other spellings; scientific name: *liquidambar* (*orientalis*), *Altingia*, *styrax officinalis*). *Storax* (also sweetgum) is a liquid resin derived from *styracaceae*. It is used in the production of incense, in

[115] PMS, pp. 238–55; Leupe, "The Siege and Capture of Malacca", p. 149, letter by Cornelis Simonsz van der Veer to Governor-General Antonio van Diemen dated 12 December 1637.

[116] GVOC, p. 78.

perfumery and as a medicinal substance to stop the itching caused by scabies. In Arabia and India it is used in the production of *liquidambar orientalis.*[117]

rattan — (Malay: *rotan(g)*; Latin: *Daemonorhops*; *calamus rotang*; Portuguese: *rota*). A strong cane-like vine harvested across Southeast Asia from the creeping stems of a climbing palm. Rattan is "more pliable than bamboo" and could be "split and twisted to make thick cables for ships or woven into sails for junks." Rattan was used in numerous ways in the household. *Cana de Bengala* or "Bengal cane" (Latin: *Arundinaria Wightiana*) has been described as a plant reminiscient of a rose bush with pliable stems or branches.[118]

real — (Also: *ryal*). A currency unit in Spain and the Spanish Americas. The best known coins are the ones struck in present-day Mexico and Bolivia with a face value of eight (reals-of-eight, pieces-of-eight) as well as in face value of four reales. See also the separate entries for these coins and currency units (*real-of-eight*, *real-of-four*, *stuiver*).[119]

real-of-eight — (Also: *peso de a ocho*, *real de a ocho*; ryal-of-eight, piece of eight, Spanish dollar). Spanish-American coin of eight *reales* face value minted in present-day Mexico and Bolivia. This coin was ranked among the first globally traded and recognised "currencies" and was widely accepted not only in the Americas but also in East and Southeast Asia. Period documents refer to the real-of-eight by a host of other names, including "piece of eight" and later as the "Spanish dollar". In the early years of the VOC's activities in Asia, prices and inventory were often expressed in reals-of-eight or their equivalent value. For the period under review, the Spanish-American real-of-eight was roughly equivalent in

[117] BUR, I, pp. 117–21; GVOC, p. 96.

[118] BUR, I, pp. 758–64; EFS, II, p. 1408; GLA, I, pp. 116–7 (Bengala) and II, pp. 260–1 (rota); HJ, pp. 757–8.

[119] GVOC, p. 96.

the Dutch Republic to a *Rijksdaalder* (or Reichsthaler in Germany), which is 2.5 Holland guilders or 48 stuiver (later in the 17th century it was 60 stuiver). The silver content of the real-of-eight remained stable at about 27.07 grams.[120] See also the entry for *real-of-four.*

real-of-four (Also: ryal-of-four). Spanish coin of four *reales* face value, a half of a real-of-eight. See also the entry for *real-of-eight.*

rodela A type of shield. The term derives from the Italian word *rotella*. The *rodela* or *rotella* is similar, but not identical, to a buckler.[121]

rowyacht (Also: *rowing yacht*). A yacht that is predominantly propelled by breast oars rather than sailed. See also the separate entry for *yacht.*

rutter (Portuguese: *roteiro*). A handbook, manual, or document giving some detailed instructions for sailing from port to port, and describing main navigational landmarks. Rutters often provided details about winds, currents and topographical features of the maritime routes described, conditions of trade, taxes and dues to be paid, or the list of commodities that are best bought and sold in a given port.[122]

sahan (Also: *sahans*). A higher quality calico from northeast India and particularly from Orissa. According to Irwin and Schwarz, the term may etymologically be derived from the Hindi *sahan* (enduring).[123] De Coutre spelt the name as *sabanes* interchanging the letter "b" for the "h". He has done this in another instance with *balacha* for *halacha* or *alacha.*

---

120 GVOC, pp. 96, 98; SMS, pp. 340–1.

121 DLM, p. 464.

122 DLM, p. 466; SMS, p. 334.

123 Irwin and Schwarz, *Indo-European Textile History*, p. 70; Irwin, "Indian Textile Trade in the Seventeenth Century, III. Bengal", *Journal of Indian Textile History* 3 (1957): 71.

See also the separate entries for *calico* and *balacha.*

salet(es): (Also: *selates*; *orang laut*; *sea nomads*; sometimes also *sea gypsies*). The origin of the term appears to be the Malay word *selat* which means the strait (as opposed to *laut* which means the open sea). The term *saletes* was commonly used to designate nomadic fishermen known today as the *orang laut* and in British colonial times as sea nomads or sea gypsies. It is widely believed that political control over the *orang laut* was a crucial factor in establishing maritime dominance in the Malay Archipelago, including especially the kingdom of Johor, where they acted as the naval force to the Johor rulers. Economically the *orang laut* played an important role in harvesting marine products, including pearls; acting as pilots in the Singapore and Melaka Straits, and according to some sources served as and "flying vendors" to passing ships of all nationalities. See also the entry under *Bajau* (*laut*).[124]

saliga: (Portuguese: *saligue*; Malay: *saligi*). The late 16th and 17th century traveller Pedro Teixeira (cited in Dalgado's *Glossário Luso-Asiático*) defined the saliga or saligi as follows: "But the commonest [weapons] are salikhes, which are charred stakes, so hard as to pierce like iron; and easily broken, whereupon they have the wound full of a thousand splinters that make it almost incurable".[125]

sampan: (Also: *sampão, champan* and other spellings). A small craft that was generally used across the Malay Archipelago and Southeast Asia at large. They were, and still remain today, a vessel commonly used by fishermen and petty traders

---

[124] SMS, pp. 335–6; Tomé Pires, *The Suma Oriental of Tome Pires. An Account of the East from the Red Sea to Japan. Written in Malacca and India in 1512–1515*, ed. Armando Cortesão, 2 vols. (London: Hakluyt Society, 1944), II, p. 264; Meilink-Roelofsz, *Asian Trade and European Influence in the Indonesian Archipelago between 1500 and about 1630* (The Hague: Martinus Nijhoff, 1962), p. 29; Oliver W. Wolters, *Early Indonesian Commerce: A Study of the Origins of Srivijaya* (Ithaca: Cornell University Press, 1967), pp. 223–4; David E. Sopher, *The Sea Nomads, a Study Based on Literature of the Maritime Boat People of Southeast Asia* (Singapore: Lim Bian Han, 1965).

[125] GLA, II, p. 277.

(peddlars). Sampans were commonly rowed with a single-bladed paddle and often feature a short mast and one (small) lateen sail.[126]

sanguisel (Also: *Sanguicel*). Leitão and Lopes described this as a small craft used along the western coast of India. It was a versatile and light vessel that was also deployed in naval warfare. According to De Coutre sanguisels were commonly found around Goa.[127]

sappan (wood) (Scientific name: *Caesalpina sappan*). A prized tree native to Southeast Asia that yields a red-coloured dye and is also used as a medicinal substance. It was and still is often compared to brazilwood. The term derives from the ancient Javanese term *sapang* (red). The 15th-century Chinese author Ma Huan claimed that in Siam sappanwood was "as abundant as firewood, and for colour decidedly superior to the product of other countries". It was presented by the Siamese as a tributary gift to China. De Coutre claimed that most of the sappanwood harvested in Siam was exported either to Japan or to the Coromandel Coast of India. Apart from its use as a dye, sappanwood was known to have medicinal value. Today it is known, among other things, for its antibacterial properties.[128]

saranpura (Also: *sarampuri, salempouris* and other variants). A type of white or coloured cotton textile that was produced in the city of Sarampur (Serampore) in western Bengal. Saranpuras were used to make clothing, or as upholstery and blankets. Sarampur was a city famous in the early modern textile trade. It was acquired by Denmark in 1755 and renamed Frederiksnagore. Sarampura cloth was traded chiefly on the eastern coast of India (for example the Coromandel).[129]

---

126 BOC, II.1, p. 817; GVOC, pp. 100–1.

127 DLM, p. 474; HJ, p. 791.

128 BOC, II.2, p. 461; BOC, II.3, p. 616; BUR, I, pp. 394–7; GLA, II, pp. 290–1; GVOC, p. 101; HJ, pp. 794–5; MNI, p. 206; Ma Huan, *Ying-Yai Sheng-Lan*, p. 107.

129 BOC, I.1, pp. 735, 738; BOC, I.2, p. 700; BOC, III, p. 593; EFS, II, p. 1409; GLA, II, pp. 293–4; MNI, p. 209.

sarasa — (Also *sarassa*, *serasah*, *saraça* and other spellings). The term possibly derives etymologically from the Hindi *sarasa* (superior) or alternatively from the Malay word *serasah* (colourful). A cotton cloth that is decorated with hand-painting or printing (*pintado*) and used as clothing (skirts, sarongs). These textiles were among the luxury items of Portuguese trade in India and were mostly exported to the Malay Archipelago. See also the separate entry for *tapisarasa.*[130]

semiana — (Also: *samina*, *semiano*). A type of fine cotton textile produced in Samana (Patiala) and Girhind in northern India. It has also been described as a type of striped calico. This textile was popular on account of its size and especially its breadth. See also the separate entry for *calico.*[131]

shahbandar — (Also: *chiabandaer*, *shahbunder*, *xabandar* and other spellings). A term of Persian origin meaning "king of the port", used loosely as "port master" or "harbour master" in the Malay Archipelago, the Indian subcontinent and around the western Indian Ocean. In Malay polities, the term denoted a high-ranking official of state who issued maritime passes (*licentmeester*; license master) and as a rule acted as an intermediary between the ruler and foreign merchants. (The notable exception is in Aceh; see the separate entry for *laksamana*). The shahbandar was often also a foreigner who enjoyed the trust and confidence of a local ruler, and for this reason he is reported to have supervised imports and warehousing of imported goods, as well as investments of the ruler or members of the royal family. The shahbandar wielded considerable power in arbitrating disputes involving foreign merchants and exercising judicial and policing

---

[130] BOC, I.1, p. 737; BOC, II.1, p. 832; GLA, II, p. 293; GVOC, p. 104; CTCB, p. 267; Irwin, "Indian Textile Trade in the Seventeenth Century. II. Coromandel Coast", *Journal of Indian Textile History* 2 (1956): 42, Irwin and Schwarz, *Studies in Indo-European Textile History*, p. 70; John Guy, *Woven Cargoes. Indian Textiles in the East* (London: Thames and Hodson, 1988), p. 187; Moreland, *Peter Floris*, p. 28, note 4.

[131] CTCB, p. 267; Irwin, "Indian Textile Trade in the Seventeenth Century", *Journal of Indian Textile History* 1 (1955): 30; "A glossary of terms used in the textile trade", Irwin and Schwarz, *Studies in Indo-European Textile History*, p. 71.

powers over foreigners. In the Melaka Sultanate there were a total of four shahbandars who held jurisdiction over the principal ethnic communities that were active in the city's commerce. The title was equally applied to the port masters of towns situated inland along major rivers, such as for example in Batu Sawar and Johor Lama.[132]

shankha De Coutre claimed that these are carved conch shells that were commonly used as handles and sometimes as musical instruments. They were made in or around Tuticorin. See also the entry for *Totoçarin.*

sloop A single-masted sailing boat featuring a lateen mainsail and a headsail. The sloop is similar in design to a yacht. Smaller types resemble a skiff. De Coutre also used the term to describe the craft of the *orang laut.* See also the separate entry for *yacht.*[133]

soldado Portuguese and Spanish term for "soldier". In the context of the Estado da Índia, the *soldados* were usually listed separately from the *casados,* the latter being married Portuguese settlers. See also the separate entry for *casado.*

sombrero (Portuguese: *sumbreiro*) A parasol; a hand-held construction that blocks direct exposure to the sun. In contemporary usage it refers to a broad-brimmed sun hat. See also the image on p. 8.[134]

spikenard (Also: *espiquenardo*, *nardo*; scientific name: *Nardostachys jatamansi*). Spikenard (variously also muskroot, nard) is a flowering plant that grows in India and the Himalayas. It has been used for centuries in Ayurvedic medicine as a cure for insomnia, and in the preparation of perfumes and incense.[135]

---

132 BOC, III, p. 593; EFS, II, p. 1409; GLA, II, pp. 419–20; GVOC, pp. 69, 106; HJ, p. 816; SMS, p. 336; Dunlop, *Bronnen*, p. 795.

133 SMS, p. 334.

134 HJ, p. 851.

135 GLA, II, p. 101; GVOC, p. 109.

Saint Thomas Christians — Christians of the so-called Syrian rite who lived chiefly along the Malabar Coast of India. They were brought into the Roman Catholic fold around 1599. The Saint Thomas Christians are thought to be descendants of believers who had been originally converted by Saint Thomas the Apostle.[136]

stuiver — A Dutch currency unit also used by the VOC in Asia. In Europe there were 20 stuivers to one guilder (see the separate entry for *guilder*). According to Willem Wolters, the silver content of the stuiver amounted to 0.535 grams during the years 1608–10, which was subsequently reduced to 0.509 grams during the period 1614–20.[137]

tabanque — (Also: *tollhouse*). According to Monsignor Dalgado, this is a term derived from the Malay word *tabing* (margin or end of the river).[138] The word could also represent a corruption of the Thai expression *tha ban;* with *tha* meaning "landing" and *ban* meaning "port". De Coutre claimed it is a settlement in the Chao Phraya estuary where ships had to register before proceeding upstream. This was located at Ban Chao Phraya. Derick Garnier explained: "At Samut Prakarn there lived an official who was responsible for the security of the lower reaches of the Chao Phraya, and so held in his hands, as it were, the keys of the kingdom .... His official residence was up a small river on the east bank, near the mouth, probably at Samut Prakarn, where the 'changwat' [i.e. district] harbour master has his office to this day. The area thus became known as Ban Chao Phraya." On a map entry of 1729 depicting the course of the Chao Phraya, Engelbert Kaempfer made an entry which is located just south of Ayutthaya: "Tolhuys; Douane" (Toll house, customs). On a similar map of 1762

---

[136] GLA, I, p. 324.

[137] See Willem G. Wolters, "Heavy and light money in the Netherlands Indies and the Dutch Republic: dilemmas of monetary management with unit of account systems", *Financial History Review* 15, 1 (2008): 37–53; see esp. p. 42.

[138] GLA, II, p. 333.

by the French royal cartographer Jacques Nicolas Bellin the same location features the entry *"Tabanque ou Douane"* (Tabanque or customs house).[139]

tael — (Also: *tayel*, *tayl* and other spellings). A unit to measure weight commonly used across East and Southeast Asia. A *tael* is equivalent to 1/16 of a *kati* (about 37.5 grams) and can be subdivided into 10 *(e)mas*. In Siam, the *tael* was equivalent to 1/20 of a *kati* or about 30 grams.[140]

taffeta — A term of Persian origin that refers to an expensive, top-quality type of woven silk.[141]

talapoin — (Plural in Portuguese: *talapois*). A term used to refer to Buddhist monks by early Portuguese authors writing on the East Indies. See also the separate entry for *bonzo.*[142]

tapisarasa — (Also: *tapisarassa*) According to Irwin and Schwartz (who appear to follow Moreland) the term *tapih* (sometimes also *tapé*) is of Javanese origin and means "skirt" or "sarong" with reference specifically to the Malay Archipelago. John Guy described the *tapi* or *tape* as "inexpensive painted cottons produced for the Indonesian, Malay and Thai markets". The fabric often featured bird and floral patterns. The term therefore refers to a type of ladies garment rather than to a specific type of textile. Moreland defined the *tapih* as "a piece of cloth of the correct size and pattern, worn by both sexes wrapped around the waist". See also the separate entry for *sarasa.*[143]

terciado — It is not exactly certain what De Coutre had in mind. It might refer to a sword that is one third of the normal

---

139 Garnier, *Ayutthaya: Venice of the East*, p. 37, Kaempfer: "Carte du cours de la Rivière de Meinam depuis Judia jusqu' à son embouchure"; also p. 22, Bellin: "Carte du Cours du Menam Depuis Siam Jusqu' à la Mer"; citation from ibid., p. 25.

140 BOC, II.2, pp. 834–5, GVOC, p. 112; HJ, p. 888; SMS, p. 341.

141 GLA, II, pp. 336–7; HJ, p. 708; MNI, p. 209.

142 GLA, II, pp. 341–3, 517.

143 BOC, I.1, pp. 738–9; BOC, II.1, p. 834; BOC, II.2, p. 464; EFS, II, p. 1409; GVOC, p. 113; CTCB, p. 267; Irwin and Schwarz, *Studies in Indo-European Textile History*, p. 72; Guy, *Woven Cargoes. Indian Textiles in the East*, p. 187; Moreland, *Peter Floris*, pp. xix, 27, note 3.

length, for example a falchion or a broadsword. It might possibly also refer to the three-bladed *trisura* commonly associated with Lord Shiva and Siamese royalty.

Theatines — Monastic order of the Roman Catholic church founded in the 16th century and bound by strict laws of poverty. The Theatines were among the first to establish missions in Asia, including southern India, Burma (present-day Myanmar) and Southeast Asia. However, the name Teatinos was employed by De Coutre to refer to the Jesuits, in a slightly derisional manner.

tikal — A unit of weight and also of coinage in Siam (where it is known as a *bat*; sometimes also spelled *baht*). In the Taungoo Dynasty Kingdom (Pegu) it is known as *ta-kyat* or *kyat*. The tikal is equivalent to eight *fuang* or *fanam* or four *salung* (Siamese *emas*); four *tikals* make one tael or one *tamlung*. De Coutre claimed the tikal in Siam was worth the equivalent of 7.5 reals—just short of a real-of-eight (see also the separate entry for *real-of-eight*). Information from historic materials differ when alluding to the weight of the Siamese *tikal*. Sources cited in Henry Yule's *Hobson-Jobson* claim 80 *tikal* make one *kati*—implying here that one *tikal* is equivalent to about 7.5 grams.[144]

tintinago — (Also: *tootnague*, *tutanego* and other spellings). A term of Persian or possibly Tamil origin. It refers to a copper-zinc-nickel alloy used across different metallurgical industries, including the casting of cannonballs, musket shots or (church) bells. Sometimes it was also used as a substitute for silver. The term was often used as a synonym for spelter. Commercial vessels departing from China often loaded *tintinago* as part of the ship's ballast. At the port of destination this ballast was then sold off at a handsome profit.[145]

---

[144] BOC, II.2, p. 464; EFS, II, p. 1411; GLA, II, pp. 371–2; GVOC, p. 116; HJ, p. 918, WMSA, II, pp. 580, 586.

[145] BOC, I.2, p. 702; BOC, II.3, p. 618; EFS, II, p. 1412; GLA, II, pp. 394–5; GVOC, p. 119: HJ, pp. 932–3; MNI, p. 210; SMS, p. 338.

tonelada A unit commonly used on the Iberian Peninsula to measure the weight of ships' cargoes as well as the mass of liquids. In Spain the *tonelada* was equivalent to 20 *quintal*, 80 *arrobas* or about 920 kilograms. In Portugal, the tonelada was equivalent to 54 arrobas or 794 kilograms. See also the separate entries for *arroba* and *quintal.*

trobito (Also: *turbito*; scientific name: *Ipomoea thurpethum*). A root vegetable used in cooking and in Ayurvedic medicine as a purgative.

Tutos According to De Coutre they were maritime raiders or pirates who operated off the coast of Siam. Their more precise identity remains uncertain.

vara An Iberian unit for measuring length. It is not certain which *vara* De Coutre had in mind when employing this term. The Spanish *vara*, which is shorter, measures approximately 83 centimetres. The Portuguese *vara*, by contrast, is substantially longer at about 110 centimetres. For this reason a range will be given in metric as an approximate guide.[146]

vermilion A red mercuric sulphide found naturally as cinnabar. Cinnabar or vermilion was most commonly used in Europe in the preparation of paint. In Asian cultures it was—and still is—widely deployed in religious and funerary rites. During the early modern period, vermilion was also produced artificially in China.

viagem (Plural: *viagens*; lit. voyage). This term refers to the exclusive concession by the Portuguese crown to organise voyages between two specific ports for a limited and specified period, generally between one and three years. The *viagens* were conceded for voyages starting and terminating in Goa, Melaka and later also Macao for destinations across maritime Southeast Asia (notably the Malukus), China, Japan and Africa. The *viagens* were sometimes sold and at

[146] DLM, p. 527.

other times granted by royal favour as a reward for past services to the crown.[147]

vientos generales (Lit. general winds). This is another term used to imply the monsoon or trade winds. For additional information, see also the separate entry above for *monsoon*.

VOC *Vereenigde Oostindische Compagnie* (*VOC*) or the United Netherlands Chartered East India Company, was established in 1602. The company was formed by merging six regional trading companies (so-called fore-companies or pioneer companies), and it was given a wide range of powers through its charter from the Dutch States General. These included the right to enter into treaties and alliances, wage war, levy troops, build forts, appoint governors, and pronounce justice. After 1619 its administrative centre in Asia was centred in Batavia (formerly known as Jayakerta or Jacatra) on the northern coast of Java.

white elephant White elephants are highly revered in Buddhist culture and are considered to be an auspicious hallmark of Buddhist kingship. White elephants are believed to symbolise one of Lord Buddha's earlier incarnations.

yacht (Dutch: *jacht*). A sailing vessel favoured by the VOC in the early 17th century that as a rule features a single mast with lateen sails, more than one (lateen) headsail, and is usually equipped with oars. It is similar in design to a sloop or a cutter. A rowyacht is a boat of this design that is propelled by oars and can also be sailed. See also the separate entries for *rowyacht* and *sloop*.

ysla (Also: *Isla*). Spanish word for island, here in a premodern spelling variant.

[147] PMS, p. 340.

LIST OF PLACE NAMES AND GEOGRAPHIC TERMS

The following list of geographic place names, or toponyms, is designed to help the reader navigate through the various place names across Asia and eastern Africa mentioned in book I of the *Vida de Jaques de Coutre* as well as his memorials. As readers may not be familiar with old or obscure place names, the following list features the modern equivalent and offers also short explanations. The entry follows the original spelling used by De Coutre. Readers can also find the modern place names with the help of the general index.

Abrolhos — (Also: *Abrollos*). The *Abrolhos* are a group of five islands located off the coast of northeastern Brazil approximately at the latitude of Bahia. They are not to be confused with the Houtman Abrolhos, a string of reefs and islets located off the coast of Western Australia.

Achem — (Also: *Achen*, Aceh). River, port and polity located near the northern tip of Sumatra in present-day Indonesia. In the 16th century, Aceh and the Estado da Índia were economic and religious competitors. There had been sporadic attacks by Aceh on Portuguese Melaka, and the most significant took place on 20 January 1568. According to the early-17th century memorial *Informatie van diversche landen en eylanden naer de Oost-Indien gelegen* (Information concerning different lands and islands in the East Indies) by Stalpaert van der Wiele, Aceh was best known in the context of the pepper trade with sourcing networks spanning south to Indragiri, Jambi and Pariaman (all on Sumatra), as well as Kedah on the western coast of the Malay Peninsula. The Gujaratis were singled out as the foremost customers of Acehnese pepper, and by the end of the 16th century the Portuguese sold more pepper and spices in this port than they shipped back to Europe. Other commodities commonly sold in Aceh included nutmeg, mace and cloves, cotton pieces as well as opium. See also the images on pp. 62, 216 and 244.[1]

Ada — (Present-day Aden). Leading port city located of the southern coast of the Arabian Peninsula in present-day Yemen. Aden marks the confluence of key maritime trading routes that connect the Red Sea with Egypt, the eastern coast of Africa, and the Malabar Coast.

Agoada de Saldanha — (Also: *Aguada de Saldanha*). Port and bay located up the southwestern coast of Africa from present-day Cape Town, South Africa. De Coutre cautioned that ships should not call here on their eastbound journeys to take on fresh water and provisions, as prevailing winds and tides would make it almost impossible to continue sailing on to Asia. This was thus a point of call for westbound journeys. See also the reproduction of the historic chart on p. 70.

Alcatifa — (Also: *Alcatife*; *Al-Qatif*). A coastal region in the Persian Gulf, presently located in Saudi Arabia. It was a hotly contested area in the 16th century, and finally fell under Ottoman rule in 1549. According to information provided in the *Glossário Toponímico* (Glossary of Toponyms), a Portuguese fortress, was located ten leguas or about 60 kilometres from the island of Bahrein.[2] This location should not be confused with a second *Alcatifa* which De Coutre mentioned and is located off the island of Palawan in the Philippines.

---

[1] JO, III, pp. 152–3.

[2] GVOC, p. 11; LGT, I, p. 204.

Aguada — Portuguese fortress outside Goa constructed in 1612 with the intention of providing security to the port and town from land and sea attacks. It is located in the Bardez district on the banks of the Mandovi River and overlooks the sea. See also the separate entry for *Bardez.*

Amboino — (Also: *Anbouino*; Ambon, *Amboina*). Island and port city located in the Maluku group, and a trading post of importance for the spice trade (cloves, nutmeg, mace). The town of Ambon traces its origin to a settlement located outside the walls of the fortress *Nossa Senhora da Anunciada* built by the Portuguese in 1576. The town and island of Ambon fell to the Dutch in 1605 after a bloodless takeover. See also the separate entry for *Maluquo.*

Amdreguiri — (Also: *Andregiri, Chandregiri*; *Indragiri*). Name of a river, port and polity located in central-eastern Sumatra. Indragiri was an important port in the early modern pepper trade.

Araquão — (Also: *Raquão*; *Arakan*). A coastal kingdom in present-day Myanmar (Burma) centred around the capital Mrauk-U. Arakan remained independent until 1784.

Arisbaia — Arosbaya, a port located on the northwestern coast of Madura. Arosbaya was one of the earliest ports visited by the Dutch in 1596. It served as an outlet for trade along the northern coast of Java, as well as a marketplace for spices from the Maluku and Banda Islands.[3]

Aru — In the early 16th century, Aru is widely considered in Portuguese sources to be a nation of sea-raiding plunderers. There can be little doubt that it represented a political competitor to both Melaka and later Johor. Denys Lombard reported that Aru had been taken by Aceh in 1564, but the exact status of Aru after this is vague. It would appear that the ruler of Aru refused submission to Aceh or briefly freed himself of it. By the early 17th century it was described as an ally of Johor. Aru was again attacked in 1613 (the same

[3] ENI, I, p. 62.

year as Aceh's offensive against Batu Sawar) and it would appear that hereafter a vanquished Aru finally accepted submission to Aceh and was subsequently known as Deli.[4]

Aveza — (Also: *Aiveza*). A kingdom in the present-day border region between Iran and Iraq and said to be ruled by an Arab king named Mombarek (Banbareca). *See* also the separate glossary entry for *Banbareca.*

Baçaim — (Also: *Basain*, *Bassain*; Bassein; Vasai). A port situated on the western coast of India located in present-day Maharashtra State. Bassein or Vasai was taken by the Portuguese from the sultan of Gujarat in 1534 and controlled it until 1739 when the Marathas captured it. Bassein was famous, among others, for its shipyards. See also the image on p. 201.

Baçora — (Also*: Basora*, *Basura*). Present-day Basra, a port in Iraq in the Persian Gulf region.

Badaga — (Also: *Bisnaga*; *Vijayanagara*). Founded in the early 14th century, and sacked by Muslims in 1565, Vijayanagara was the capital of the wealthiest and most powerful Hindu empire in southern India. Its rulers resisted Islamic expansion for more than two centuries while maintaining Hindu religion and cultural practices.

Bantan — (Also: *Bantam*; present-day Banten). A port city in north-western Java at the Sunda Strait. Banten's significance rose after the Portuguese captured Melaka in 1511. It had long served as an important centre for both regional and long distance trade, not least because the Strait of Sunda was easily accessible to traders under any monsoon conditions.

Bardez — A region and settlement located to the north of Goa. See also the separate entry for *Aguada.*

---

[4] Denys Lombard, *Le Sultanat d'Atjéh au temps d'Iskandar Muda 1607–1636* (Paris: École français d'Extrême-Orient, 1967), pp. 37, 83, 92. Also Anthony Milner, *The Malays* (Oxford: Wiley-Blackwell, 2008), p. 50. With reference to Aru in general, see also A. Milner, E. Edwards McKinnon and Tengku Luckman Sinar, "Aru and Kota Cina", *Indonesia* 26 (1978): 1–42, esp. pp. 13–9.

Baroas	This represents most probably a corruption of the Malay name "Beruas" or "Bruas" which means as much as "wild mango". A Kampung Beruas is today still located close to the sea at the Pahang River estuary and forms a suburb of the royal capital Pekan. De Coutre claimed that he landed here on a trip from Melaka in 1594, and that its inhabitants were subjects of the king of Pahang.
Barra de Camboya	This geographic expression means the "Estuary of Cambodia", which is the estuary of the Mekong in present-day southern Vietnam.
Batacalo	(Present-day Batticaloa). A port located on the central-eastern coast of Ceylon in present-day Sri Lanka. Ships plying their way between Ceylon and the northern coast of Aceh would routinely call here to take on food and fresh water and sometimes also to trade.
Batusavar	(Also: *Batellamar*; Batu Sawar). The administrative centre and capital of Johor in the final years of the 16th and early 17th centuries. Located in the upper reaches of the Johor River it is described by De Coutre as a key trading centre and a home to many merchants. Batu Sawar was important not only in the pepper trade, but also in the trade of bezoars and diamonds. On account of the latter, the jeweller De Coutre traded in Batu Sawar. See also the separate entries for *Johor* and *Jor Nuevo* as well as the maps on pp. 62 and 93.
Baxos de Garagaos	(Also: *Carajos Shoals*, *Cargados Carajos Shoals*, *Saint Brandon's Rocks* or *Islets*). A shoal comprising several islets located off the northeastern coast of Mauritius in the Indian Ocean.
Bima	Port city located on the eastern coast of Sumbawa, in the eastern section of the Indonesian Archipelago (West Nusa Tenggara province). Bima became a separate polity in the early 17th century after its ruler embraced Islam.
Bocarron del Valle	Name commonly applied in early modern Portuguese cartography to the Strait of Bali. It separates the island of Bali (east) from Java (west).

Bombasa	(Also: *Bombassa*; Mombasa). Port located in present-day Kenya. Mombasa was controlled for the first time by the Portuguese between the years 1593 and 1631. Home to the Portuguese *Fort Jesus*, Mombasa was famous for its trade in gold, ivory, animal skins and slaves. See also the image on p. 198.
Bordolon	(Also: *Bordolong*). Port on the Isthmus of Kra. In early modern cartography it is often situated north of Kedah bordering two big swamps or estuaries. It is possible that it corresponds to Phattalung located near Trang in the far south of present-day Thailand. See also the separate entry for *Cada*.[5]
Borneo	In the early modern period, this name was used to refer to the island of Borneo, a polity (a precursor of present-day Brunei), or a port (in present-day Brunei Bay). De Coutre visited the port of Borneo and described the settlement and the palace of the ruler who in contemporaneous 17th-century sources was sometimes titled the "Emperor of Borneo". The port was an important trading centre for jungle produce and mainly for tropical camphor, diamonds and bezoars. See especially also the separate entries in the glossary for *camphor* and *bezoar*.
Cabo de Boa Esperansa	(Also: *Cabo de Buena Esparanza*; Cape of Good Hope). Also known as the Cape of Storms, the Cape of Good Hope is located near the southernmost tip of the African continent. It marks the meeting point between the Atlantic and Indian Oceans and was a crucial nodal point for shipping in the age of sail, linking Asia, Europe and the Americas. Ships and crew arriving at different times of the year often had to camp in this region to await the change in weather and the winds. Cape Town was founded in 1652 chiefly as a stopping point and provisioning station for vessels of the VOC on their way to or from Asia.

[5] EFS, II, p. 1395.

Cabo de Comarin	(Present-day Kanyakumari). Cape Comorin is located at the southernmost tip of the mainland Indian subcontinent.
Cabo Rachado	(Present-day Tanjung Tuan; lit. The Master's Cape). The Portuguese name which means "broken cape" is located to the northwest of Melaka along the western coast of peninsular Malaysia. It was considered a strategic point in the early modern period because it marks a narrow point in the Melaka Strait where all ships passing through can be easily monitored.
Cada	(Also: *Cadha*; Kedah). River, port, settlement and polity in the northwestern regions of the Malay Peninsula. In the 16th and 17th centuries, the Portuguese regarded Kedah as a vassal or client state of Siam. It was attacked and overrun by Aceh in 1619.
Caliminianos	(Present-day Calamianes). An island group located to the southwest of the Philippine island of Mindoro. On certain map specimens, such as those by the Dutch cartographer Pieter Plancius (1594), the present-day island of Palawan carried the name Calamianes as well.[6]
Cambaya	(Also: *Canbaia*, *Cambay*; present-day Khambhat). Port and city of the Gujarat sultanate on the Gulf of Cambay (present-day Gulf of Khambhat). Cambay was a major trading city linking the Indian subcontinent with the Arab world and beyond. It was renowned for a number of goods, especially cotton textiles.
Camboya	(Also: *Canboiia*; Cambodia). Polity on mainland South-east Asia, corresponding approximately to the present-day country by the same name (Cambodia).
Campar	(Also: *Canpar*; Kampar). Name of a river, port and polity in central-eastern Sumatra. In the early modern period Kampar was important for the pepper trade and also as a

[6] A. de Booy, ed., *De derde reis van de V.O.C. naar Oost–Indië onder het beleid van Admiraal Paulus van Caerden, uitgezeild in 1606*, 2 vols. (The Hague: Martinus Nijhoff, 1970), II, p. 67, note 2.

source of gold dust panned either in the great river or one of its many tributaries.[7]

Cananore (Also: *Cananor*, *Cannanore*; present-day Kannur). Port and city located on the Malabar Coast of India. The Portuguese maintained a fort there between the years 1505 and 1663, after which control over *Cananore* fell to the VOC. See also the image on p. 204.

Canary Islands Archipelago located off the western coast of Africa around the border between Morocco and Western Sahara (formerly Spanish Morocco). The Canary Islands, acquired by Portugal (1448–79/80) and later taken over by Spain (1479–80) as a result of the Treaty of Alcáçovas, acted as a provisioning station for ships bound for the Americas and at times, Asia.

Castilla (Also: *Castilha* and other spellings; Castile). This refers to the Kingdom of Castile and León, one of the two principal units with Aragon which formed *Hispania* (Spain) through the marriage of the so-called "Catholic Kings", Ferdinand (Aragon) and Isabella (Castile) in 1469. This marriage laid the foundation for the creation of "Spain", but during the early modern period the territories continued to be ruled as an agglomeration of separate and legally distinct political entities that were linked through the person of the ruler. During the period of colonial expansion in the Americas and Asia, the newly-acquired colonies technically came under the immediate rule of Castile.

Chanpa (Also: *Champa*). A polity in the central-southern coastal region of Indochina in present-day Vietnam. *Champa* was one of the most important centres in the trade of aloeswood, eaglewood[8] and kalambak. In the late 16th century, Champa was notorious for piracy and acts of

[7] Leupe, "The Siege and Capture of Malacca", p. 142.
[8] GLA, I, pp. 17–8.

violence committed along its coast, with the royal family evidently having a major hand in these coastal plundering operations. By the dawn of the 17th century, Champa forged closer links with the kingdom of Johor. See also the separate entries in the glossary for *aloes*, *eaglewood*, *kalambak* and in the list of place names for *Johor.*

Chaul — Port and city located on the western coast of India. Originally ruled by the sultan of Gujarat, *Chaul* was taken over by the Portuguese in 1521. A fort was constructed at the nearby promontory in 1613. The Portuguese lost the port city in 1740 in a war against the Marathas. See also the image on p. 197.

Cheramandel — (Also: *Costa de Cheramandel*). The Coromandel Coast is located along the southeastern shores of the Indian subcontinent stretching from Cape Comorin (present-day Kanyakumari) in the south to approximately where False Divi Point is. This broadly covers the coast of the contemporary Indian State of Tamil Nadu. The Coromandel Coast—or sometimes just Coromandel for short—was home to several key ports where cottons and textiles from the hinterland were brought for trading and export. It was also a production area and market for other produce such as dye, spices, pepper, rice and coconut fibre. Concerning the latter, see the separate entry in the glossary for *coir* and in the list of place names for *Cabo de Comarin.*

Chincheo — In Iberian and some Dutch sources of the 16th and 17th centuries, it is used as a generic term for the "Chinese". The name actually represents a corruption of the Chinese toponym Zhangzhou, which is a port near Xiamen located on the coast of Fujian Province (Amoy Coast).

Ciudad de Camboja — (Lit. the city of Cambodia). After Siam-Ayutthaya had attacked and destroyed Angkor in the year 1431, the kings of Cambodia moved their capital city to *Lovek* (variously also *Longvek*, *Eauweck* and other spellings) which is located roughly mid-way between the Tonlé Sap and Phnom Penh. Longvek was attacked in a campaign by King Naresuan of Siam in 1593, and the royal administrative centre was moved in 1618 to Udong, located to the northwest of Phnom Phenh. See also the image on p. 131.

Cochim (Also: *Cochim*, *Cochin*; present-day Kochi). Port located along the southwestern or Malabar Coast. Cochin had emerged as a powerful, independent polity after the 15th century and had become the meeting ground of traders from China, eastern Africa and the Middle East. It remained under Portuguese rule from 1503 to 1663, after which Cochin was ceded to the VOC. See also the images on p. 191.

Cochinchina (Also: *Cochin-China*). Name of a kingdom and also of a geographical name applied to the central regions of present-day Vietnam. Trade in Cochinchina was brisk, and was considered to represent a "back door" to Ming China. Musk, aloeswood and silver were among the most important commodities traded during the early modern period. See also the separate entries in the glossary for *aloes* and *musk.*

Coluale River This is the present-day Chapora River located to the north of Goa.[9]

Colunbo (Also: Colombo). Port and city located in southwestern Ceylon (present-day Sri Lanka). Colombo was controlled by the Portuguese between 1505 and 1656 and was a major destination in the trade of cinnamon, the highest quality of which was (and arguably still is) harvested on the island. See also the image on p. 207.

Costa de Malavar (Also: Malabar Coast). Coast of southwestern India facing the Arabian Sea, stretching from Cape Comorin in the south to the Kerala coast in the north. This broadly covers the coastal regions of the present-day Indian States of Kerala and Karnataka. See the separate entry for *Cabo de Comarin.*

[9] LGT, I, p. 260.

Coulão (Also: *Coulan*; *Quilon*; present-day Kollam). An historically significant port and settlement located on the Malabar Coast in present-day Kerala State, India. By the 15th century, *Quilon* had developed strong maritime trading contacts with China.

Dabul (Also: *Dabhol*; *Dabhul*). A port located to the south of Mumbai (Bombay) on the western coast of India. According to the early-17th century memorial *Informatie van diversche landen en eylanden naer de Oost-Indien gelegen* (Information concerning different lands and islands in the East Indies) by Stalpaert van der Wiele, Dabul was an important centre in the trade of textiles and opium with important sourcing connections reaching up the coast to *Cambay* (see also the entry for *Cambaya*) and the interior of Gujarat. As destinations for the port's textile exports the *Informatie* singles out Java, the Bandas and the Malukus. At the end of the 16th century, Dabul's ruler was reportedly an enemy of the Portuguese.[10]

Damão (Also: *Daman*). Port located on the northwest coast of India. Daman was seized by the Portuguese from the sultan of Gujarat in 1523 and remained a Portuguese possession until 1961. Administered by Portugal as a union territory together with Goa and Diu (see the separate entry for *Dio*). De Coutre employed the same Portuguese name for Demak which he sometimes also refers to as *Dauma* or *Dama*. The latter is a port and polity situated on the north-central coast of Java. See also the image on p. 224.

Daquão (Also: *Dacca*; Dhaka). Former capital city of Moghul-ruled Bengal between the 16th and 18th centuries as well as a port and trading centre in present-day Bangladesh. After the Battle of Plassey in 1765, Bengal, and implicitly also Dhaka as its capital, was ceded to the British.

---

[10] JO, III, pp. 149–50.

Dio — (Also: *Diu*). Port located on an island off the Kathiawar Peninsula in northwest India. The Portuguese took the port from the Sultan of Gujarat in 1535 and Diu remained a Portuguese possession until 1961. See also the separate entry for *Damão* as well as the image on p. 208.

España Nueva, Nueva España — (Also: *New Spain*, Mexico). Major administrative unit in central-northern Spanish America governed by a viceroy based in Mexico City. Though more expansive than present-day Mexico, it is not uncommon to use New Spain and Mexico interchangeably.

Estrecho de Sabam — (Portuguese: *Estreito de Sabam*; present-day Strait of Kundur). In the early modern period, this was an important maritime artery that connected the southern reaches of the Melaka Strait with maritime routes to Palembang, Banten, key ports along the northern coast of Java, and additional destinations in the Nusa Tenggara. The Strait of Sabam (or Kundur) extends from south to north between the eastern shores of Sumatra and the western shore of Kundur and later Karimun Besar (Great Carimon). On some cartographical specimens, the *Estrecho de Sabam* is taken to refer to the maritime artery running along the eastern coast of Sumatra between Karimun, Kundur and as far south as Bangka. See also the separate entry for *Sabam* and the image on p. 76.

Estrecho de Sincapura — (Portuguese: *Estreito de Sincapura*; also: *Syncapura, Sinquapura* and other spellings; present-day Straits of Singapore). The Straits of Singapore refer to a series of maritime passages that connect the Melaka Strait with the South China Sea along or near the shores of Singapore Island. In the early modern period there were three main passages, the best known being the Old Strait of Singapore. See the separate entries for *Estrecho Nuevo* and *Estrecho Viejo* and the image on p. 76.

Estrecho Nuevo — (Portuguese: *Estreito Novo*; New Strait of Singapore). The New Strait of Singapore was a maritime route that, according to the testimony of João de Barros, opened up after the 1580s when Johor had blockaded the Old Strait (see the separate entry below) with logs, debris and sunken vessels. This route, also known in Portuguese as the *Estreito de Santa Bárbara*, or Strait of Santa Barbara, brought vessels during the age of sail along the southwestern coast of present-day Sentosa and then either through the Buran Channel or around the southern islands and on to the region of the Johor River estuary. See also the images on pp. 76 and 230.[11]

Estrecho Viejo — (Portuguese: *Estreito Velho*; Old Strait of Singapore). The western entrance to the Old Strait of Singapore begins at the site of present-day Fort Siloso (on the Sentosa side) and the *Varella* (also Longyamen, Sail Rock, Batu Belayer, Batu Blair, Lot's Wife) that was situated in today's Labrador Park. It continued through the narrow maritime passage between present-day Sentosa and the Keppel Harbour area and ended after Pulau Brani. Detailed instructions for sailing this strait were provided, among others, by Jan Huyghen van Linschoten in his *Reysgeschrift* of 1595. Ships sailing east would have to drop anchor and wait around the area of Fort Siloso for a favourable tide, current and wind conditions. The *orang laut* who frequented the nearby shores often acted as paid pilots to guide ships through the treacherous waters of the Old Strait. If ships had to pass during the hours of darkness, the *orang laut* would place lights to mark dangerous spots and outcroppings.[12] See also the separate entry in the glossary for *orang laut* as well as the images on pp. 76, 230 and 236.

Estreto de Mequa — (Also: *Estrecho de Mecca* and other spellings; lit. Strait of Mecca, possibly also Strait of Mocha). This is a name commonly employed in early modern cartography to the Bab-el-Mandeb strait, the entrance to the Red Sea from the Indian Ocean.

---

[11] SMS, pp. 31–2

[12] SMS, pp. 26–35; The translated text of Van Linschoten is found ibid., pp. 32–4.

Estreto de Ormus The Strait of Hormuz represents the eastern entrance into the Persian Gulf, located between present-day Iran and Oman. See also the separate entry for *Ormus.*

Gamarmasin (Also: *Marmacin*; Banjarmasin). Polity, settlement and port situated at the estuary of the Barito River in southern Borneo (Kalimantan). In the 17th century it was famous for its bezoars, gold dust, pepper and rattan. See also the separate entries in the glossary for *bezoar* and *rattan.*

Gerzelim (Also: *Gerzelin*, *Gergelim*, *Angelim*). According to the Visconde de Lagoa's *Glossário Toponímico* (Glossary of Toponyms), this is the Hijili region in Bengal not far from Hugli.[13] Monsignor Dalgado's *Glossário Luso-Asiático* features the terms *zerzelim* and *gergelim* which means sesame (*sesamum orientale*).[14] The etymological origin of this name may have a connection with, or represent a corruption of, *gergelim.* De Coutre noted that Gerzelim was an inexpensive place to procure meat and other foodstuffs. He also claimed that it had direct maritime traffic with Portuguese Melaka, which had relied heavily on the importation of foodstuffs.

Gomoron (Also: *Gombrun*; present-day Bandar Abbas). Port in the Persian Gulf to the west of Hormuz in Iran. The Portuguese controlled *Gombrun* as part of their Gulf possessions that included Hormuz and Bahrain. *Gombrun* was famous among its wares for its ceramics. See also the separate entry for *Ormus.*

Gulfar (*Julfar*; present-day Ras al-Khaimah). Port and settlement located in the present-day United Arab Emirates inside the Persian Gulf. It is located southwest of the Strait of Hormuz. Benjamin Teensma erroneously identified this as a town in the Hadhramaut region of Yemen.[15]

---

[13] LGT, I, p. 31. Also Loureiro, "European Encounters and Clashes in the South China Sea", II, *Revista de Cultura*, International Edition 12 (2004): 158, where Gergelim is directly identified as Hugli.

[14] GLA, I, pp. 430–1.

[15] CRE, p. 54.

Honor	(Also: *Onor*, *Honawar*, Honnavar; present-day Hanavar). A port located along the western coast of India and located in present-day North Karnataka.
Ilha de Anseisão	(Also: Ascencion Island). Located in the South Atlantic, this island was sometimes used as a watering hole for westbound ships. Mariners used to hunt here for sea turtles. Farm animals were left on the island to roam and graze freely. These animals multiplied and thus offered a source of food for future visitors.
Ilha de São Lourenso	(Also: *Ilha de São Laurenço*). The Isle of Saint Laurence is the old (Portuguese) name for present-day Madagascar.
Insulíndia	Portuguese geographical term that literally translates into "Island India". It generally refers to the island world of the Indonesian and Philippine Archipelagos. The geographic scope covered by this term roughly coincides with the contemporary expression "insular Southeast Asia".
Isla de la Fortuna	(Lit. Fortune Island; Island of Fortune). According to António de Morga, this islet is located about 18 leguas (99–108 kilometres) from Manila. In an editorial note, Cummins explained that it is "near Nasugbu, off the Batangas coast".[16]
Islas de Camboya	This probably refers to one or group of islets near present-day Sihanoukville, Cambodia. Early modern European cartography usually depicted the area with a maze of islets located off the Cambodian coast.
Islas de Linga	(Lit. the islands of Lingga; the Riau Archipelago). Archipelago located off the eastern coast of central Sumatra and due south of Singapore and the Malay Peninsula. It comprises significantly the islands of Bintan, Batam, Bulan, Galang, Karimun, Kundur, Lingga, Rempang and Singkep. From the 16th to the 19th centuries the inhabitants of these islands fell under the rule of the Johor Sultanate,

[16] Morga, *Sucesos*, p. 180, note 3.

and after the Anglo-Dutch Treaty of 1824 to the Sultan of Riau. Lingga was one of the main bases of the *orang laut* and served periodically in early modern times as the seat of the royal Johor administration. Today, the island group forms part of the Indonesian province of Kepulauan Riau. See also the separate entries for *Batusavar* and *Jor*, and in the glossary for *orang laut* and *saletes.*

Jambo (Also: *Janbi*, *Yanbo*; Jambi). River, polity, and settlement located in central-eastern Sumatra. Jambi was second to Aceh as a trading centre for pepper during the late 16th and early 17th centuries.

Jaquetera (Also: *Yactara*; *Jayakerta*, *Jacatra*, renamed *Batavia*; present-day Jakarta). Before Jayakerta became the base for the VOC's Asian operations in the second decade of the 17th century, it was known as Sunda Kelapa and after 1527 as Jayakerta ("Complete Victory"). Historically it had close ties to the kingdom of Sunda and in the 16th century fell under the suzerainty of Banten. The city rose in the late 16th and early 17th century under Prince Jeyawikarta who was loyal to Banten and had established his residence near the Ciliwung River estuary. In 1610, the prince granted permission to the Dutch to establish a wooden warehouse along the right (eastern) bank of the Ciliwung River. Five years later, the Honourable East India Company of London (EIC) was granted the same privilege for the left (western) river bank. The prince's political manoeuvring with the English and the Dutch, eventually led to his downfall. The city was taken by the VOC and renamed Batavia in 1619.

Jasques (Also: *Yasques*; present-day Jask). A peninsula and port located to the southeast of Hormuz in the Persian Gulf.

Jor (Also: *Yor*; Johor). This toponym can refer to a river, a settlement or a polity that straddled the Malay Peninsula and its adjacent islands. After 1511, Johor was widely seen as the moral, spiritual (via the *daulat* or mystical authority to rule) and also legal successor of the fallen

Melaka Sultanate. For this reason its rulers by the late 16th century carried the title "Emperor of the Malay Kings". According to sources of the 17th and 18th centuries, the Johor monarch or sultan commanded the loyalty of subjects in the southern portions of the Malay Peninsula (including the offshore islands located south of Tioman), the Anambas, Tambelan and Natuna Island groups, the Riau Archipelago, Siak in central-eastern Sumatra, and also the region around the Sambas River on the island of Borneo. A Dutch treaty signed in 1610 also acknowledged Mempawah and Landak to fall under the authority of Sambas, reportedly a fiefdom of Johor. De Coutre alluded to a political connection with Lawai. At the beginning of the 17th century, Johor stood in close political and commercial relationship with Aru on the island of Sumatra, as well as with Champa in present-day southern Vietnam. See also the separate entries for *Batusavar*, *Islas de Linga*, *Jor Nuevo*, *Jor Viejo*, *Lava* and *Siaca.*

Jor Nuevo (Lit. New Johor). See the entry for *Batusavar* (Batu Sawar).

Jor Viejo (Also: *Yor Viejo*; lit. Old Johor; Johor Lama). Johor Lama or Old Johor is located on the left bank in the lower reaches of the Johor River. Johor Lama served as the royal residence and capital until it was sacked during a military campaign led by Dom Paulo Lima de Pereira in 1587. Documents of the 17th century reported that the city was rebuilt, destroyed around 1604, and rebuilt again. When the Johor court moved upstream, Johor Lama continued to be used as a port where larger, ocean-going vessels would anchor and transfer their cargo to smaller craft (for example *perahus* or *sampans*). From here the goods were brought to the upstream towns such as the royal administrative centre of Batu Sawar and the nearby settlement of Kota Seberang on the opposite bank of the Johor River. See also the maps on pp. 76, 93 and 236.[17]

[17] SMS, p. 343.

Lao(s)	A landlocked kingdom located in the central reaches of the Mekong. Some 16th and 17th century sources call it *Lan Xang* ("Land of a Million Elephants"). The name "Lao", according to Hobson-Jobson, was liberally applied by the Portuguese to "many people who occupied in the inland frontier of Burma and Siam, between those countries on the one hand and China and Tongking on the other".[18]
Lava	(Also: *Lave*, *Lavio*, *Lawe*; *Lawai*). River and port along the southern coast of Borneo in the present-day Malaysian state of Sarawak. Its exact location is not known, but the port may have been at or around the Kapuas River estuary. Another possibility is the *Bay of Lavio* (sometimes also *Laio*) between Sukadana and present-day Pontianak on the island of Borneo, and yet another explanation identifies it as Sukadana. According to the early 17th century *Informatie van diversche landen en eylanden* (Information concerning different lands and islands) by Stalpaert van der Wiele, Banjarmasin and Lawai were reportedly among the most important ports on the island of Borneo at the turn of the 16th and 17th centuries. De Coutre mentioned a political connection with Johor. See also the separate entries for *Jor* and *Suquedani.*[19]
Luban	(Also: Lubang). An island (present-day Lubang) of the Philippine Archipelago, located to the northwest of Mindoro and southwest of Luzon.
Lugor	(Also: *Ligor*). Port and polity situated on the Isthmus of Kra along the Gulf of Siam. The town of *Ligor* is present-day Nakhon Si Thammarat in Thailand.[20]
Luzon	Main island of the Philippines located in the north of the archipelago. Home to the capital city Manila and the nearby port of Cavite in Manila Bay.

[18] HJ, pp. 504–5.

[19] JO, III, p. 158.

[20] EFS, II, pp. 1403–4.

Macasar (Also: *Macaçar, Macaçal*; Makassar). Name of a port (between the years of 1971 to 1999 it was known as *Ujung Pandang*) and polity in the south of the island of Sulawesi (Celebes). Makassar was important in the context of the seaborne trade, in the bulk trade in spices (especially cloves and nutmeg from the Malukus) as well as rice.[21] In 1605 the ruler of Makassar converted to Islam and began a series of campaigns to control the region, conquering its main rival, Bone, in a campaign from 1608 to 1611. This was followed by campaigns against Sumbawa, Buru, Seram, Banten and eastern Borneo. In the early 17th century, Makassar became a base for many European traders and trading companies, including the English, Danes, and Portuguese, who sought to break the stranglehold on spices held by the VOC. Makassar was defeated in a war against the Dutch in 1667.

Malaca (Also: *Mallaqua*; Melaka, Malacca). Name variously given to the river, the town or city of Melaka, a polity centred around the city (Melaka Sultanate), as well as the entire Malay Peninsula. The name has also been applied to the nearby maritime strait (the Malacca or Melaka Strait). Believed by the Portuguese to be one of the most—some might contend the most—important centres of trade in the East Indies by the early 15th century, the Portuguese attacked and seized the city and some surrounding lands in 1511. Although Portuguese rule over Melaka was contested by Asian and other European parties such as Aceh, the Dutch, and also Johor, the Portuguese held on to the city until January 1641 when it succumbed to famine, pestilence and a protracted military campaign. See also the images on pp. 223, 245 and 246.[22]

---

[21] JO, III, pp. 156–7.

[22] SMS; also Borschberg, "Ethnicity, Language and Culture in Melaka during the Transition from Portuguese to Dutch Rule", *JMBRAS* 83, 2 (2010): 93–117.

Maluquo — (Also: *Maluco*; Maluku, Moluccas, Spice Islands). Subgroup of the Indonesian Archipelago located between the two great islands of Sulawesi (Celebes) and Papua New Guinea (Irian Jaya), comprising among others the clove and nutmeg producing islands of Ambon, Aru, Banda, Buru, Halmahera, Seram, Ternate, Tidore and others. The region is ethnically and culturally diverse, featuring among others Malay and Papuan influences. The islands were contested by the Portuguese and the Spanish, who sought to claim and extend their influence over the islands. In the early 17th century the contest for the Malukus involved the Dutch, who eventually came to dominate the entire archipelago and monopolised the trade in nutmeg, mace (a by-product of nutmeg) and cloves. See the separate entry in the glossary for *mace.*

Manar — (Also: Mannar). An islet located between the south Indian mainland and northwest Ceylon in present-day Sri Lanka. Mannar used to be famous for its seed pearls. See also the image on p. 205.

Manecabo — (Also: *Nanacabo*; Minangkabau). Name of a polity and people in the central-western highlands of Sumatra. The Minangkabau were known for their gold (mined or panned from the river beds) and especially also for their pepper.

Mangalor — Port and city located on the southwest coast of India (Malabar Coast) in the present-day State of Karnataka. Mangalore fell under Portuguese control between 1568 and 1695, and again between 1714 and 1763. See also the image on p. 203.

Mar de sur — Literally the "Ocean of the South" or "Southern Sea[s]". This is a flexible geographical expression to designate large spaces of the Indian and Pacific Oceans. Insular Southeast Asia is surrounded by the *mar del sur* and significantly includes the Java and South China Seas. See also the entry for *Sur.*

Mariboles According to the toponyms used today, Mariveles is not an island, but the southern tip of a peninsula in the present-day province of Bataan on the island of Luzon. There is an island now known as San José which is located to the south of Mariveles, and close-by to the southeast there is also another smaller one called Caballo Island. Both are located almost in the middle of the entrance to Manila Bay. The *Historisch Journael* recounting the voyage of Joris van Spilbergen to the East Indies (1615–17) also mentioned the island "Maribella" and pictorially located it at the entrance of Manila Bay *"I[sla] Maribela alias de Verne"*.[23] De Coutre was almost certainly referring to this.

Mascata (Also: *Masquate*; Muscat). Trading port in present-day northern Oman on the Arabian Peninsula. Muscat was controlled by the Portuguese between 1507 and 1650. See also the image on p. 200.

Melapor (Also: *Melapor, Mellapor*; *Mylapur*; *Meliapore*; present-day Mylapore). The full name in Portuguese is *São Tomé de Meliapore* and is situated on the Coromandel Coast close to Chennai (Madras) in the present-day Indian State of Tamil Nadu. In 1522, the Portuguese discovered here what they believed was the grave of Saint Thomas the Apostle, and his relics were transferred from here to Goa. As De Coutre underscored, this city is commonly known by two different names: *São Tomé* or *Mylapur*. See also the separate entry in the glossary for *Saint Thomas Christians*.

Melindi Eastern coast of Africa, around present-day Kenya. See also the separate entry for *Bombaça* (Mombasa).

Mindoro One of the largest islands of the Philippine Archipelago located to the southwest of Luzon. The town of Mamburao is located on the northwestern side of the island.

23 "Historisch Journael vande Voyagie ghedaen … door de Strate Magallanees naer de Moluques … Onder 't gebied van Joris van Spilbergen", in BV, III, p. 60 as well as the unfoliated map inserted between pp. 60 and 61.

Monamotapa (Also: *Mwenemutapa* and other spellings). Polity in southeastern Africa that straddled regions of present-day Mozambique and Zambia. It had reached its zenith of power between the 13th and 15th centuries. By the time the Portuguese successfully circumnavigated Africa for the first time, the polity was already in an advanced state of decline and had broken into several smaller polities around regional centres. The Portuguese traded primarily with the coastal port and capital which was located in the north and was dominated by the Shona tribe.

Monsanbique (Also: *Mosãobique*, *Mossambique*, *Mossãobique*). Today the toponym Mozambique refers to a country and the region of southeastern Africa. In the early modern period, however, the name was flexible, and in the context of De Coutre's writings referred first and foremost to an island by that name which was occupied by the Portuguese and home to the fort *São Sebastião* (Saint Sebastian). The neighbouring Portuguese settlement on the island was also known as "Stone Town". The name was also applied to the nearby region of southeastern Africa, hence the country of Mozambique. See also the image of the Portuguese fort and settlement on p. 70 as well as the entry for *Monamotapa*.

Mosolopatão (Also: *Macelepatan*, *Mossolapatan*, *Mossolapatão* and other spellings; Masulipatam). Port on the southeastern (Coromandel) coast of India. According to the early-17th century memorial *Informatie van diversche landen en eylanden naer de Oost-Indien gelegen* (Information concerning different lands and islands in the East Indies) by Stalpaert van der Wiele, Masulipatam maintained close trading connections in textiles with Bengal and was known for its cloth pieces and finished clothing. It possessed an excellent port, was abundant in foodstuffs such as meat and butter, and had a genteel population.[24]

---

[24] JO, III, p. 151.

Nangisaqui (Nagasaki). Port and city located on the southern Japanese island of Kyushu. The first Europeans—the Portuguese—arrived in Nagasaki in 1543. It became the home of a Jesuit mission and colony in the late 16th and early 17th century. The Portuguese and the Jesuit missionaries were formally evicted from the Japanese islands after the Shimabara rebellion of 1637. This marked the beginning of Japan's policy of isolation that lasted well into the second half of the 19th century.

Natal This region covers the border regions of present-day South Africa and Mozambique in southeast Africa. A province of South Africa today bears the same name.

Negapatan (Also: *Negapattan*, *Neguapatão* and other spellings; Negapatam, Nagapatam, Nagapattinam). A port located on the Coromandel Coast and technically subject to the ruler of Vijayanagar. It competed in the sale of textiles directly with Pulicat, and in the early 17th century exported cotton pieces to Banda, Ambon, Seram and other parts of Southeast Asia. In the words of Moreland, however it was "controlled by a resident Portuguese community." According to Moreland (who in turn based his insights on Diogo do Couto): "Negapatam, now in the Tanjore district, was de facto in the possession of the Portuguese, but was not Portuguese territory".[25] The port and city were taken by the VOC in 1660.[26]

Nicobares (Also: Nicobar Islands). An archipelago located north of the great island of Sumatra (Aceh) in the Andaman Sea (greater Bay of Bengal). The Nicobar Islands feature prominently in early modern travel literature, especially as a place to take on fresh water and sometimes also food for ships plying the waters between the Indian subcontinent, Sumatra and the Melaka Strait. The islands were also a known source of ambergris which the locals collected

[25] See Moreland, *Relations of Golconda*, p. 2.

[26] EFS, II, p. 1406; JO, III, p. 151; Moreland, *Peter Floris*, p. 8, note 1.

	along the beaches. The islands became a Danish possession in 1754/6 and were renamed *Frederiksøerne* ("Frederick Islands"). The Nicobar Islands and the two Danish colonies Tranquebar and Serampore (see the separate entry for *Tangebare*) were sold to the British in 1845. The islands now belong to India. See also the separate entry in the glossary for *ambergris.*
Ormus	(Also: Hormuz). Port located in the south of present-day Iran near the entrance to the Persian Gulf. Hormuz was ruled by a king who was subservient to the Portuguese between 1507 and 1620. The English took the city in 1622. Hormuz was an important nodal point linking maritime networks with the overland trade routes connecting sub-continental India, China, Central Asia and Persia. See also the image on p. 225.
Paleacate	(Also: *Paliacate, Pelicate,* and other spellings; Pulicat, *Pazhaverkadu*). The port city located on the southeastern coast of India, not far to the north of modern Chennai (Madras) in the present Indian State of Tamil Nadu. In 1502 Pulicat became a Portuguese trading post with the assistance of the Vijayanagar kings, but was subsequently lost to the VOC in 1609. In the early modern period Pulicat was—like most ports along the Coromandel Coast —famous for its cotton textiles. According to the early-17th century memorial *Informatie van diversche landen en eylanden naer de Oost-Indien gelegen* (Information concerning different lands and islands in the East Indies) by Stalpaert van der Wiele, the cloth business also thrived in the surrounding towns, but Van der Wiele also emphasised that cloth pieces in Pulicat were not as abundant as in *Mylapur* or Masulipatam.[27]
Pam	(Also: *Pão*; Pahang). Polity, port and river located in south-eastern Peninsular Malaysia. In the late 16th and early 17th centuries, Pahang was considered as a vassal or client state

[27] JO, III, p. 151.

of Johor. It was famous chiefly for its pepper, gold dust (panned from the river beds) and bezoar stones. It was also important on account of the riverine trading network that linked two coastal towns of Pahang (east) and Muar (west) via the *Penarikan* (portage). According to early-17th century sources, Pahang was a political dependency of Johor and assumed an important position in the pepper trade. See also the map on p. 93.[28]

Paneruca (Also: *Paneruqua*; Panarukan). Port and polity located on the north-eastern coast of the island of Java near the Strait of Madura. See also the separate entry for *Arisbaia.*

Paragua This is the old name for the Philippine island of Palawan which is located to the northeast of Borneo. It is reported that at the turn of the 16th and 17th centuries its inhabitants were loyal to the king (sometimes emperor) of Borneo, a precursor of the present-day Sultanate of Brunei.

Patane (Also: Patani, Pattani). Port and polity located on the Isthmus of Kra at the Gulf of Siam in present-day Thailand. Descriptions of the polity dating from the late 16th and early 17th centuries claimed that most of the eastern coast of the Malay Peninsula fell under the control of Patani, being chiefly the present-day Malaysian states of Kelantan and Terengganu. In the early 17th century, the ruler of Pahang was married to a daughter of the queen of Patani. According to the early-17th century memorial *Informatie van diversche landen en eylanden naer de Oost-Indien gelegen* (Information concerning different lands and islands in the East Indies) by Stalpaert van der Wiele, many Chinese came to trade in Patani—comparatively more than in Banda—and brought a range of trading goods such as silks, copperware and porcelain. The town manufactured among other things neat clothing which were exported to Banda and the Maluku islands.[29] See also the images on pp. 167 and 169.

---

[28] JO, III, pp. 153–4.
[29] JO, III, p. 154.

Pegu (Also: *Peguu*; present-day Bago). Home in earlier centuries to a Mon kingdom, *Pegu* served in the early 17th century as the capital of the Taungoo Dynasty Kingdom that spanned parts of today's Myanmar, Thailand and Laos. Pegu ceased to be the royal administrative centre in 1635 when the capital was moved to Ava (Inwe) in the upper reaches of the Irrawaddy River. According to the early-17th century memorial *Informatie van diversche landen en eylanden naer de Oost-Indien gelegen* (Information concerning different lands and islands in the East Indies) by Stalpaert van der Wiele, Pegu was a source of food supplies for the Portuguese as well as many things that were valuable and highly-priced, especially gemstones (rubies).[30]

Pelibam (Also: *Pelimbran*, *Polinban*; Palembang and other spellings). Port and polity located in central-eastern Sumatra. According to early modern sources, Palembang also commanded the loyalty of the inhabitants of Bangka and Belitung (Billiton). Though chiefly famous in the context of the pepper trade, Palembang was also a centre for eaglewood, beeswax, and lakawood. See also the separate entries in the glossary for *aloes*, *eaglewood*, and *kalambak*.

Pera (Also: Perak). River, port and polity situated in the central-western region of the Malay Peninsula. The royal family of Perak traces its lineage back to the Melaka Sultanate (which had fallen to the Portuguese in 1511), though it is noteworthy that outside interference in Perak also came from the Acehnese in the 17th and the Bugis in the 18th centuries. Perak was chiefly known in the early modern period as a supplier of tin. See also the entry in the glossary for *calayn*.

Pinal (Also: *El Pinal*). This is a port located along the south coast of China. According to Antonio de Morga's *Sucesos de las*

[30] JO, III, p. 152; Tun Aung Chain, "Pegu in Politics and Trade, Ninth to Seventeenth Centuries", Sunait Chutintaranond and Chris Baker ed., *Recalling Local Pasts: Autonomous History in Southeast Asia* (Chiang Mai: Silkworm Books, 2002), pp. 25–52.

Islas Filipinas, written at the advent of the 17th century and thus broadly contemporaneous to De Coutre's life in Southeast Asia, the "Spanish" port of *El Pinal* was located in the region of Macao and Guangdong (Canton).[31] Some historians opine that it was located in, or very close to, the present-day Hong Kong Special Administrative Region of China. In 1593, King Philip II of Spain passed an edict prohibiting Spaniards from trading directly in China. By the time this damaging law was overturned in 1609, however, the fortunes of *El Pinal* had already eclipsed.[32]

Priman — (Also: *Priamon*; Pariaman). A port and polity on Sumatra. Pariaman was absorbed by Aceh in the early 17th century. According to a map sketched by Manoel Godinho de Erédia and featured in his *Declaraçam de Malaca* (Description of Melaka, c.1613),[33] Pariaman is located on the western coast of Sumatra to the south of Barus (which was also under Acehnese control at the time) but north of the Minangkabau coast (which is around present-day Padang). The late 17th-century VOC historian Pieter van Dam reported that Pariaman had once been the most important port along the western coast of Sumatra. The editors of AA erroneously identified Pariaman as Rokan.[34]

Pula — A corruption of the Malay word *pulau* (island).

Pula Pisan — (Also: Pulau Pisang). An islet and navigational landmark located off the southwestern coast of the Malay Peninsula in the present-day Malaysian state of Johor. In 16th-century Portuguese cartography it is often named *Pula Piçâo*, but actual spellings can vary considerably from source to source. This is not to be confused with an islet with an almost identical name (in early modern European

---

[31] Morga, *Sucesos*, p. 137n3.

[32] Morga, *Sucesos*; Boxer, *Fildagos in the Far East*, pp. 46–7.

[33] Brussels, Bibliothèque Royale, Ms. 39015A, fol. 61 recto. Manoel Godinho de Erédia, *Declaraçam de Malaca*, c.1613.

[34] Erédia, *Malaca L'Inde Méridionale e le Cathay*, p. 24 recto; BOC, II.1, p. 271; AA, p. 169.

navigational literature) which is located off the coast of Pahang. See also the separate entries for *Jor* and *Pam.*

Pula Quiliman (Also: Pulau Karimun). There are technically two Karimuns, Karimun Besar (Great Carimon) and the far smaller and uninhabited Karimun Kecil (Carimon Minor). The Karimuns are located between the great island of Sumatra and the Malay Peninsula. The islands are strategically located, as several major shipping routes converge around the islands, including significantly the Singapore, Melaka, Durian and Kundur Straits (the latter being known as the Strait of Sabam or Sabão from Portuguese source materials). See also the separate entry for *estrecho de Sabam* and *Saban* and the map on p. 76.

Pula Reidan (Also: *Pula Ruyen*, *Pula Reydan*; present-day Pulau Redang). A group of islands consisting of the main island Redang (sometimes also Great Redang) together with nine other islets nearby. Peter Floris, a contemporary of De Coutre, wrote: "Wee cam by a greate many ilands lying at about 6 degrees [northern latitude] and are from Patanie about 26 leagues, and are called Redange." Later he noted: "These Ilands of Ridangh are aboute 18 or 20 in number ...."[35]

Pula Sanquixu This appears to be a corruption of *San chio hsü*, the Chinese name for Perhentian Island West. AA falsely identified this without further explanation as *Pulau Lantinga*.[36]

Pulatimom (Also: *Pula Timam* and other spellings; Tioman). An island located off the southeastern coast of the Malay Peninsula. For centuries Tioman was a navigational landmark for ships sailing to or from the Vietnam Coast, China and Japan. Tioman reportedly had a thriving provisioning industry and ships took on food and fresh water before setting across the Gulf of Siam (or vice versa) to Pulau

[35] Moreland, *Peter Floris*, pp. 32, 99.
[36] J.V. Mills, "Malaya in the Wu-pei-chih Charts" in *Southeast Asia-China Interactions*, ed. and intr. Geoff Wade (Kuala Lumpur: MBRAS, 2007), p. 391.

Condor (Vietnamese: Côn Sợn), the largest of a small group of islands located off the southeastern coast of Vietnam. See also the map on p. 93.

Pulatinga (Also: *Pulau Tinggi*). One of the islands located off the eastern coast of the state of Johor in Malaysia, located to the south of Tioman. See also the separate entry for *Pulatimom*, *Pula Sanquixu*.

Pulau Butom A small archipelago (present-day Mu Ko A Dang-Ra Wi) located to the northwest of Langkawi (Malaysia) in present-day Tarutao National Park, Satun Province, Thailand. In the age of sail, these islands were known as a safe place to fetch fresh water and collect firewood. The two principal islands A Dang and Ra Wi form a protected, bay-like entryway that is open toward the south.

Punto de Gale (Also: *Point de Galle*, Galle Point). Rocky promontory located on the southwestern coast of Ceylon (present-day Sri Lanka). The nearby port and settlement, which is sheltered by the promontory, is also named Galle. The town was controlled by the Portuguese between 1505 and 1640. See also the image on p. 207.

Querinba (Also: *Querimba*). Port and archipelago situated off the eastern coast of Africa near today's border region of Mozambique and Tanzania.

Quexome (Also: *Keshm*, Kish, Kishm, Qeshm). Island in the Strait of Hormuz, located to the southwest of the present-day port of Bandar Abbas in Iran. It is also the site of a Portuguese fortress. The name Qeshm referred to the town and the eastern extremity of the island where the Portuguese fort was located. According to information provided by John Villiers, Qeshm was under the sultanate of Hormuz. See also the separate entry for *Ormus.*[37]

[37] HJ, p. 485; Villiers, "Review": 456.

Reis Magos — Settlement on the Mandovi River not far from Goa. The town and surrounding region derives its name from a Portuguese citadel, the fortress *Reis Magos* (Three Kings).

Repery — (Also: Ratchaburi or *Ratburi*). A town in central-western Thailand. In Western sources, including especially early modern European cartography, it is often named *Rapri* or *Repri,* which is very close to De Coutre's *Repery.*

Rio Fermoso — (Also: *Rio Fremoso*). The old Portuguese name for the Batu Pahat River, which spills into the sea at the south-western coast of the Malay Peninsula. See also the map on p. 93.

Ryukyu — (Also: *Liu Kiu* and other spellings). An archipelago situated to the south of the main Japanese Islands and now part of Japan. In the early modern period the Ryukyus were subject to the Daimyo of Satsuma but also engaged in tributary trade with China. Merchants and traders from these islands also called at many ports in Southeast Asia.

Sabam — (Also: *Saban, Sabão*). This is the Portuguese name for island of Kundur in the Riau Archipelago of Indonesia. See also the separate entries for *Estrecho de Sabam* and *Islas de Linga* as well as the maps on pp. 76 and 93.

Sabandaria — (*Shabandaria, Xabandaria* and other spellings). This is the name given by Jacques de Coutre to the principal settlement on what he called the *Isla de la Sabandaria Vieja* (present-day Singapore Island). According to his information, the settlement was located near the eastern entrance of the *Estrecho Viejo* (Old Strait of Singapore). He claimed that its inhabitants paid allegiance to the king of Johor. He also underscored that *Shabandaria*'s harbour was one of the best in all of the East Indies. The exact location of the settlement is unclear but it would have most likely been either at the site of Raffles' Landing Place or possibly around the Kallang River estuary. See also the map on p. 76.

Salet Boru — (Also: Selat Tebrau). The Tebrau or Johor Strait separates the main island of Singapore from the present-day state of

Johor in Malaysia. It forms the modern national borders of Singapore and Malaysia. See also the map on p. 236.

Salsette (Also: *Salsete*). Island located off the western coast of India in the present-day state of Maharashtra. Salsette is home to the city of Mumbai (Bombay). The island was taken by the Portuguese from the Sultan of Gujarat in 1534. It was donated to England as part of a dowry for the marriage of Catherine of Braganza to Charles II of England in 1668.

São Cristóvão River A small river located in the Bardez region near Goa. See also the separate entry for *Bardez*.

São Tomé For a more detailed explanation, see the separate entry for *Mylapur*.

Sambales Reference could be to the original inhabitants of the present-day province of Zambales in northwestern Luzon. As toponyms were very flexible in the early modern period, this name probably once referred to a much wider region in western Luzon as compared to today.

Sapampur (Most probably: *Suphanburi*). De Coutre mentioned it on three occasions, noting that it was a large city in ruins and that it was not far from Ratchaburi (*Repery*). See also the separate entry for *Repery*.

Seilão The island of Ceylon, corresponds to present-day Sri Lanka.

Serião (Also: *Sirian*; *Syriam*; present-day Thanlyin). Port and settlement in the Irawaddy Delta. Syriam is best remembered for its association with the Portuguese adventurer Filipe de Brito de Nicote. De Brito, who as a mercenary had entered the services of the king of Arakan, was appointed governor of Syriam in 1600. His efforts to secure the port in the long term for the Estado da Índia did not succeed, and in 1613 Syriam was attacked, overrun and taken by the Taungoo Dynasty Kingdom.

Siaca (Also: *Siaqua*, *Ciaca*; Siak). A polity and river located in central-eastern Sumatra. Siak is historically associated with

	Johor in the early 17th century. See also the separate entry for *Jor.*
Sião	(Also: *Sian*; *Siam*). The precursor of present-day Thailand. See especially also the entry for *Yudia.*
Sinde	(Also: *Sindh*). An area in the coastal region, and a province of, present-day Pakistan. Sindh was controlled by the Moghuls after 1524.
Sofala	(Also: *Sofalla*). A trading port situated along the south-eastern coast of Africa in present-day Mozambique. It is known today as Nova Sofala and is located just a few kilometres south of the present-day city of Beira.
Solor	An island of the eastern Indonesian Archipelago (Nusa Tenggara) located to the east of Flores and north of Timor. Acquired by the Portuguese in 1520, the island became an important post for the trade in sandalwood with Timor. The Dutch overran the Portuguese settlement and fort in 1613.
Sunda (*Strait*)	Body of water separating Sumatra and the western coast of Java. Due to the strait's orientation (east-west), it could be accessed all year round. This determined why the Europeans (and especially later the Dutch) decided to base their Asian operations here or at nearby *Jayakerta* (now Jakarta). See also the separate entries for *Bantan* and *Jayakerta.*
Suquedani	(Also: *Sukadana*). River, port and polity on the island of Borneo in the present-day state of Sarawak, Malaysia. Sukadana was most famous for the diamonds that were panned in the rivers. It competed with neighbouring Sambas for primacy in the diamond and bezoar trade during the early modern period, especially in the inland regions known as Landak and Mempawah. Other exports included iron ore. The Sukadana River was reportedly navigable for about 40 Dutch sea miles (about 240 kilometres) from the sea. Both Sukadana and Sambas sought to extend their respective authority over the diamond-yielding regions of the interior. Sources reported that in the early 17th

century, Sukadana came under the authority of the Adipati of Surabaya and was conquered by the central Javanese kingdom of Mataram in 1622.[38] See also the separate entry for *Lava*.

Sur (Also: *Sul*; lit. South). The Portuguese commonly employed this term to refer to what today would be Southeast Asia, especially the insular portions of Indonesia and the Philippines. From the vantage point of the Portuguese administration in Goa, this region was located in the "South". Contemporary historians have variously translated this term into English either as "the South" (corresponding literally to the Portuguese), "the East Indies", or occasionally as Southeast Asia. See also the separate entries for *Insulíndia* and *Mar de sur.*

Surat Port and city located on the northwest coast of India. As De Coutre confirmed, Surat was controlled by the Great Moghul and for this reason the port came to host many European players. The Portuguese constructed a fortification in 1540; the English East India Company set up a factory there in 1608, closely followed by the VOC, their Dutch competitors. From the 16th century onward, Surat expanded at the expense of Dabul and itself entered a state of protracted decline after the English factory was founded in Mumbai (Bombay) in 1662. See also the separate entries for *Dabul* and *Salsette.*

Surgídera The etymological origin of this name is uncertain. It might derive from the Portuguese term *surgidoiro*, meaning "roadstead" or "anchorage" (see images on pp. 207 and 225). It could also be derived directly from the verb *surgir*, which means "to rise up" or "emerge". According to De Coutre, either interpretation makes perfect sense: it is a place of anchorage and was also characterised by a hill that rose steeply from the waters of the Old Strait of Singapore. *Surgídera* is

[38] ENI, III, pp. 815–6; M.E. van Opstall, ed., *De reis van de vloot van Pieter Willemszoon Verhoeff naar Azië, 1607–1612*, 2 vols. (The Hague: Martinus Nijhoff, 1972), I, p. 260.

understood and translated in the context of De Coutre's writings as a place of anchorage located at the northwestern tip of present-day Sentosa, which is also the home of the former British Fort Siloso. The nearby hill (which was admittedly flattened by the British during the construction of Fort Siloso) was evidently referred to by the identical name.

Tangebare — (Also: *Tranquebar*; present-day Tharangambadi). Port and city located on the southeastern coast of India (Coromandel) guarded by Fort Dansborg. *Tranquebar* became a Danish colony in 1620 and was sold in 1845 to Britain together with the Nicobar Islands and another Danish colony in western Bengal, known as *Frederiksnagore*. The latter had been acquired by Denmark in 1755, and was better known as Serampur or Serampore. See also the separate entry for *Nicobares.*

Tangibaran — Tanjung Baram is located in the Miri District of the present-day Malaysian state of Sarawak. It is formed by the Sungai Baram, or Baram River located just south and which also marks the national border between present-day Malaysia and Brunei.

Tangonburi — (Also: Tanjung Bulus). The southernmost tip of Peninsular Malaysia, located in the state of Johor due west of present-day Singapore. See also the map on p. 76.

Taungoo Dynasty Kingdom — Often referred to in sources of the late 16th and 17th century as *Brema, Bama* or Burma, or very commonly also *Pegu* (after the capital city), these names all referred collectively to the territory on mainland Southeast Asia controlled by the Taungoo dynasty between the 16th and 18th centuries. In the period of its greatest expanse during the late 16th century (c.1580), the kingdom covered most of today's Myanmar (the kingdom of *Ava* in the north, but not the coastal polity of *Arakan*), Laos (*Lan Xang* in the north), and Thailand (*Lanna, Siam-Ayutthaya*). Pegu ceased to be the royal administrative centre in 1635 when the capital was moved to Ava (Inwe) along the upper reaches of the Irrawaddy River. See also the separate entry for *Pegu*.[39]

Tenasserim (Also: *Tanasserin*; *Tenasserin*; present-day Tanintharyi). Port located along the southwestern shores of present-day Myanmar, but then still considered part of the "Malay Coast". De Coutre correctly noted that Tenasserim was Siamese. Tenasserim and its seaport *Mergui* (an important maritime outlet to the Bay of Bengal) fell under Siamese control from the reign of Naresuan until the fall of Ayutthaya in 1767. See also the separate entry for *Yudia.*

Teve (Also: *Tiwi*). Based on the testimony of De Coutre, this appears to be a place currently known as Wadi Tiwi, an oasis and port located to the southeast of Muscat in present-day northern Oman and facing the Arabian Sea.

Timor An island in the eastern region of the Indonesian Archipelago (Nusa Tenggara). Timor was an important region linked to the trade in white odoriferous sandalwood and also beeswax (used in the production of batik). After the fall of Solor in 1613, competition between the Dutch and Portuguese for control over the forest products intensified, and the island came under the control of the two European colonial powers. See also the entry in the glossary for *beeswax.*

Totoçarin (Also: *Tuticorin*; present-day Thoothukudi). A port and city located on the southeastern coast of India between Cape Comorin and Adam's Bridge (also known as Rama's Bridge; Rama Setu). Tuticorin was especially famous as a centre of the (seed) pearl trade. See also the separate entry for *Cabo de Comarin.*

Trevenipatão (*Trivenipatam*; present-day Thirumalairayan Pattinam). Port located on the Coromandel Coast between Karaikkal and Nagapattinam. It is located on the Arasalar River. See also the separate entry for *Negapatan.*

---

[39] Tun Aung Chain, "Pegu in Politics and Trade, Ninth to Seventeenth Centuries", pp. 25–52.

Tuban — A port and polity located along the northern coast of Java east of Surabaya. In the period of De Coutre, Tuban was a fierce rival of nearby Gresik. See also the separate entry for *Yava.*

Yapão — (Also: Japan, Japanese Archipelago). Since the first half of the 16th century the Portuguese had built up a strategic commercial stronghold in southern Japan and also engaged in the missionisation of the archipelago's inhabitants. After the Shimabara Uprising (of Christian Japanese) in 1637, the Tokugawa shogunate closed Japan to all outside trading relations except with the Dutch, whose presence was confined to the islet of Deshima.

Yava — (Also: Java). In the early 17th century, Java was home to several historically important polities, including significantly, but not limited to Banten, Demak, Gresik, Panarukan, Tuban and the kingdom of Mataram.

Ysla das Naus — (Also: *Ilha das Naus*). An island and point of anchorage for large ocean-going vessels off the coast of Melaka. Due to the shallow waters of the Melaka port, large ships had to load and unload here with the assistance of smaller craft. Literally translating from Portuguese as "island of the carracks", the *Ilha das Naus* has been variously identified as present-day Pulau Melaka. According to surviving Portuguese sources, this islet was regularly patrolled by naval squadrons of the Melakan authorities. In 1606, VOC Admiral Cornelis Matelieff de Jonge secured the islet with an artillery battery and shelled the city from this location, causing great damage. Subsequently, the Portuguese decided to construct a fortification here, and according to the testimony of John Villiers, such a fortification was in place by 1615.[40] De Coutre may not have been aware of this at the time of writing his memorials, as he had already left Melaka by 1603.

---

[40] Villiers, "Review": 456.

Ysla de Arena (Also: Sentosa). Known in British colonial times as *Pulau Belakang Mati*, this island off the southern coast of Singapore was renamed Sentosa in 1972. *Ysla de Arena* is the name used by De Coutre both in his autobiography as well as in the memorials. See also the separate entry for *Estrecho Viejo.*

Ysla de Cobras (Also: *Ilha de Cobras*; lit. Cobra Island; Island of the Cobras). This corresponds to present-day Pulau Merambong located at the western entrance of the Tebrau or Johor Strait. On the 1604 map of the southern Malay Peninsula penned by Manoel Godinho de Erédia in 1604, this island is named *Pulau Ular* (Snake Island). It should not to be confused with the present-day Pulau Ular which is located nearby in the territorial waters of Singapore. See also the maps on pp. 76 and 236.

Ysla de la Sabandaria Vieja (Also: Singapore Island). This is the name for the main island of Singapore used by De Coutre both in his autobiography as well as in the memorials. See also the separate entry for *Sabandaria*. See also the map on p. 76.

Yudia (Also: *Odia*; Ayutthaya). Royal administrative centre or capital of Siam (Thailand) in the 17th century and up until its destruction by the Burmese in 1767. See also the separate entry for *Sião* and the image on p. 132.

BIBLIOGRAPHY

MANUSCRIPTS AND CHARTS

Amsterdam, Universiteitsbibliotheek van Amsterdam (Bibliotheek Universiteit van Amsterdam), O.K. 112, Hand-coloured printed map of the world by Pieter Plancius, 1592.

———, O.K. 130, Printed map of Sumatra, the Malay Peninsula, Borneo and Java by Cornelis Claesz, 1598.

———, O.K. 157, Printed map of Asia by Jocodus Hondius, 1615.

———, OTM Pfl. K. 26, Dutch pamphlet titled *Corte ende sekere beschrijvinghe* (Short and Accurate Description) published in 1604.

Brussels, Bibliothèque Royale, Ms. 39015A, Erédia, Manoel Godinho de, *Declaraçam de Malaca*, c.1613.

Leiden, Universiteitsbibliotheek Leiden, Icones 66, Portrait of the Dutch humanist Hugo Grotius, c. 1613.

Lisbon, Arquivo Nacional da Torre do Tombo (ANTT), *Aduertensia de Jaques do Couto ao Conde* ("Advice by Jacques de Coutre to the Count [of Linhares]"), unpublished manuscript (29 December 1628), Miscelâneas Manuscritas do Convento da Graça, Tomo VI–F, Cx. 3, fol. 52 verso–6 verso.

———, Collecção de São Vicente (CSV), Livro 19 (5 December 1623), fol. 171.

———, CSV, Livro 19 (25 January 1624), fol. 320–6.

———, CSV, Livro 19 (March 1624), fol. 253.

———, CSV, Livro 19 (12 March 1625), fol. 307.

———, Desembargo do Paço, Repartição da Justiça e Despacho da Mesa, Livro 14 (29 June 1632) fol. 202.

———, Documentos Remetidos da Índia (DRI), Livro 4 (8 February 1611), fol. 98.

———, DRI, Livro 6 (28 March 1613), fol. 153.

———, DRI, Livro 12 (9 February 1620), fol. 506.

———, DRI, Livro 19 (January 1624), fol. 18.

———, DRI, Livro 19 (January 1624), fol. 63 recto–verso.

———, DRI, Livro 19 (3 February 1624), fol. 173.
———, DRI, Livro 20 (19 February 1624), fol. 313.
———, DRI, Livro 21 (13 February 1625), fol. 163.
———, DRI, Livro 21 (21 February 1625), fol. 70 recto–verso.
———, DRI, Livro 22 (18 February 1625), fol. 49.
———, Inquisição de Lisboa, Processo 4941 (1 December 1610), fol. 101 verso–3.
Lisbon, Biblioteca Nacional de Portugal (BNP), Collecção Pombalina, no. 647, fol. 210–9.
London, British Library, Add. 15737 fol. 10, anonymous English map of the Old Strait.
———, Egerton, Ms. 1646, fol. 239.
Madrid, Biblioteca Nacional de España (BNE), Ms. 2780, *Vida de Jaques de Coutre.*
Munich, Bayerische Staatsbibliothek (BSB), Cod. Icon. 162, João Albarnaz I, *Plantas das Cidades, e Fortalezas da Conquista de Índia Oriental*, c.1648.
Simancas, Archivo General, Sec. Provinciales—XIII—Cód. 1498—Registro de despachos e cartas régias para a Índia no ano de 1608 (5 February 1602), fol. 13 verso, registry of grants conceded or refused, 5 February 1608.
The Hague, Nationaal Archief van Nederland (NAN), Collectie 102, Baron H. van Zuylen van Nyevelt, suppl. 2, no. 13 (2.21.179.01 no. 13), *Boeck Tracterende vande Wreede, Verradische ende Hostile proceduren der Portugesen In Oost-Indien.*
———, 4VELH.619, Vingboons Atlas.
———, VELH 156.I–II, Gerrit de Haan, *Lichtende Zeefakkel of de geheele Oost-Indische Water-Wereldt*, 1760–1.
Washington, D.C, Library of Congress, Map of the East Indies by Abraham Ortelius, c.1570.

BOOKS

Documentação Ultramarina Portuguesa, 2 vols. (Lisbon: Centro de Estudos Históricos Ultramarinos, 1960–02).
Nationaal Biographisch Woordenboek van België, 15 vols. (Brussels: Paleis der Academiën, 1964–96), vol. VI.
VOC Glossarium. Verklaringen van Termen, verzamelt uit de Rijksgeschiedkundige Publicatiën die betrekking hebben op de Verenigde Oost-Indische Compagnie (The Hague: Instituut voor Nederlandse Geschiedenis, 2000).
Allen, P.C., *Philip III and the Pax Hispanicam, 1598–1621. The Failure of Grand Strategy* (New Haven, Conn.: Yale University Press, 2000).

Alves, Jorge M. dos Santos, and Pierre-Yves Manguin, *O Roteiro das Cousas do Achem de D. João Ribeiro Gaio: Um olhar português sobre o norte de Samatra em finais do século XVI* (Lisbon: Comissão Nacional para as Comemorações dos Descobrimentos Portugueses, 1997).

Andaya, L., *The Kingdom of Johor 1641–1728: Economic and Political Developments* (Kuala Lumpur: Oxford University Press, 1975).

Baker, C., Dhiravat na Pombejra, A. van der Kraan and D.K. Wyatt, *Van Vliet's Siam* (Chiang Mai: Silkworm Books, 2005).

Barros, João de, and Diogo do Couto, *Da Ásia. Dos feitos que os Portuguezes fizeram no conquista, e descubrimento das terras e mares do Oriente*, 24 vols. (Lisbon: Na Regia Officina Typographia, 1777–78).

Birch, Walter de Gray, ed. and tr., *Commentaries of the Great Afonso Dalboquerque, Second Viceroy of India*, 4 vols. (London: Hakluyt Society, 1880).

Blair, E.H., and J.A. Robertson, ed., *The Philippine Islands, 1493–1898*, 55 vols. (Cleveland: A. H. Clark Co., 1903–09).

Bocarro, A., *Década XIII da História da Índia*, ed. Rodrigo José de Lima Felner, 2 vols. (Lisbon: Typographia da Academia Real das Sciencias, 1876).

Booy, A. de, ed., *De derde reis van de V.O.C. naar Oost-Indië onder het beleid van Admiraal Paulus van Caerden, uitgezeild in 1606*, 2 vols. (The Hague: Martinus Nijhoff, 1970).

Borschberg, P., *The Singapore and Melaka Straits: Violence, Security and Diplomacy in the 17th Century* (Singapore and Leiden: NUS Press and KITLV Press, 2010).

———, *Hugo Grotius, the Portuguese and Free Trade in the East Indies* (Singapore and Leiden: NUS Press and KITLV Press, 2011).

Borschberg, P., ed., *Journals, Memorials and Letters of Cornelis Matelieff de Jonge: Security, Diplomacy and Commerce in 16th- and 17th-century Southeast Asia* (Singapore: NUS Press, forthcoming).

Boxer, C.R., *Fidalgos in the Far East, 1550–1770: Fact and Fancy in the History of Macao* (The Hague: Martinus Nijhoff, 1948).

———, *The Portuguese Seaborne Empire, 1415–1825*, reprint (London: Hutchinson & Co., 1977).

———, *Opera Minora*, ed. Diogo Ramada Curto, 3 vols. (Lisbon: Fundação Oriente, 2002).

Boyajian, J.C., *Portuguese Trade in Asia under the Habsburgs, 1580–1640* (Baltimore and London: Johns Hopkins University Press, 1993).

Bracht, J. van, ed., *Verzameling van Pas-Kaarten, Dienende tot de Vaart naar Oost- en Westindien; Meest alle uitvoerig met de Pen getekent: benevens eenige Afbeelingen van voorname Eylanden, Steden en Sterktens, zo wel in de Spaansche, Engelsche als Nederlands Indien Gelegen: Alle zeer net naar 't Leven met Waterververn Geschildert. In order geschikt naar't Alphabeth*, facsimile edition of the Vingboons Atlas (Amsterdam: Fibula-Van Dieshoeck, 1981).

Brown, D.E., J.E. Edwards and R.P. Moore, *The Penis Inserts of Southeast Asia: A Bibliography, Overview and Comparative Perspective* (Santa Barbara: Department of Anthropology, University of California Santa Barbara, 1988).

Bruijn, J.R., Femme S. Gaastra and Ivo Schöffer, *Dutch-Asiatic Shipping in the 17th and 18th Centuries*, 3 vols. (The Hague: Martinus Nijhoff, 1979–87).

Bry, T. de, *Icones seu Gennuinae et Expressae Delineationes Omnium Memorabilium*, (Frankfurt am Main: 1607).

———, *Neundter Theil der Orientalischen Indien* (Frankfurt am Main: unknown publisher, 1612).

Burkhill, I.H., *A Dictionary of the Economic Products of the Malay Peninsula,* 2 vols. (Kuala Lumpur: Governments of Malaysia and Singapore, Ministry of Agriculture and Cooperatives, 1966).

Commelin, I., *Begin ende Voortgang Vande Vereenigde Neerlandsche Geoctroyeerde Oost-Indische Compagnie*, facsimile of the edition printed by Johannes Janssonius in 1646 in 4 vols. (Amsterdam: Facsimile Uitgaven Nederland, 1969).

Coolhaas, W.Ph., ed., *Generale Missiven van Gouverneurs-Generaal en Raden aan Heren XVII der Verenigde Oost-Indische Compagnie,* part I, 1610–38 (The Hague: Martinus Nijhoff, 1960).

———, ed., *Generale Missiven van Gouverneurs-Generaal en Raden aan Heren XVII der Verenigde Oostindische Compagnie,* part II, 1639–55 (The Hague: Martinus Nijhoff, 1964).

Corrêa (also Correia), G., *Lendas da Índia*, ed. R.J. de Lima Felner, 7 vols. (Lisbon: Na Typographia da Academia Real das Sciencias, 1858–66).

Coutre, J. de, *Aziatische Omzwervingen. Het levensverhaal van Jaques de Coutre, een Brugs diamantenhandelaar, 1591–1626*, ed. and tr. J. Verbeckmoes and E. Stols (Berchem: EPO, 1988).

———, *Como Remediar o Estado da Índia? Being the Appendices of the Vida de Jaques de Coutre (Madrid: Biblioteca Nacional, Ms. 2780)*, ed. Benjamin N. Teensma (Leiden: Centre for the History of European Expansion, 1989).

———, *Andanzas asiáticas*, ed. E. Stols, B. Teensma and J. Verbeckmoes (Madrid: História 16, 1991).

Cruysse, D. van der, *Louis XIV et le Siam* (Paris: Fayard, 1991).

———, *Siam and the West, 1500–1700*, tr. Michael Smithies (Seattle: University of Washington Press, 2002).

Cummins, J.S., ed., *The Travels and Controversies of Fray Domingo de Navarrete, 1618–86*, 2 vols. (London and Cambridge: Hakluyt Society and Cambridge University Press, 1960–62).

Dalgado, S.R., *Glossário Luso-Asiático*, 2 vols. (Coimbra: Imprensa da Unviersidade, 1919–21).

Dam, P. van, *Beschryvinge van de Oostindische Compagnie*, ed. F.W. Stapel, 8. vols. (The Hague: Martinus Nijhoff, 1931–43).

Dames, M.L., *The Book of Duarte Barbosa. An Account of the Countries Bordering the Indian Ocean and their Inhabitants, Written by Duarte Barbosa and Completed about the Year 1518 A.D.*, 2 vols. Facsimile edition printed by the Hakluyt Society, London, in 1918 (Nendeln: Kraus Reprints, 1967).

Danvers, F.C., *The Portuguese in India: being a history of the rise and decline of their Eastern empire*, 2 vols. (London: Frank Cass & Co., 1966).

Doursther, H., *Dictionnaire universel des poids et mesures anciens et modernes, contenant des tables des monnaies de tous les pays* (Amsterdam: Meridian Publishing Co., 1965).

Dunlop, H., ed., *Bronnen tot de Geschiedenis der Oostindische Compagnie in Perzië, eerste deel, 1611–1638* (The Hague: Martinus Nijhoff, 1930).

Erédia, M. Godinho de, *Malaca L'Inde Méridionale et le Cathay: Manuscrit original autographe de Godinho de Erédia appartenant à la Bibliothèque Royale de Bruxelles*, tr. M. Léon Janssen (Bruxelles: Librairie Européenne C. Muquardt, 1882).

———, *Suma de Árvores e Plantas da Índia Intra Ganges*, ed. J.G. Everaert, J.E. Mendes Ferrão and M. Cândida Liberato (Lisbon: Commissão Nacional para as Comemorações dos Descobrimentos Portugueses, 2001).

Farrington, A., and Dhiravat na Pombejra, ed., *The English Factory in Siam, 1612–1685*, 2 vols. (London: The British Library, 2007).

Fell, R.T., *Early Maps of Southeast Asia*, 2nd ed. (Singapore: Oxford University Press, 1991).

Flückiger, F.A., and D. Hanbury, *Pharmacographia: A History of the Principal Drugs of Vegetable Origin Met With in Great Britain and British India* (London: Macmillan and Co., 1874).

Foreest, H.A. van, and A. de Booy, ed., *De Vierde Schipvaart der Nederlanders naar Oost-Indië onder Jacob Wilkens en Jacob van Neck (1599–1604)*, 2 vols. (The Hague: Martinus Nijhoff, 1980–81).

Foster, W., ed., *Early Travels in India, 1583–1619* (London: Humphrey Milford and Oxford University Press, 1921).

———, ed., *The Voyage of Thomas Best to the East Indies 1612–1614* (London: Hakluyt Society, 1934).

Gaastra, F.S., *De Geschiedenis van de VOC*, 4th ed. (Zutphen: Walburg Pers, 2002).

———, *The Dutch East India Company: expansion and decline* (Zutphen, Walburg Pers, 2003).

Galvão (Galvano), A., *The Discoveries of the World from their First Original until the Year of Our Lord 1555*, tr. R. Hakluyt and ed. Adm. Bethume (London: Hakluyt Society, 1862).

———, *Tratado dos Descobrimentos* (Porto: Livraria Civilização Editoria, 1944).

Garnier, D., *Ayutthaya: Venice of the East* (Bangkok: River Books, 2004).

Grotius, H., *De Jure Praedae Commentarius: Commentary on the Law of Prize and Booty. A Translation of the Original Manuscript of 1604*, tr. G.L. Williams and W.H. Zeydel (Oxford: Clarendon Press, 1950).

———, *De Jure Praedae Commentarius: Commentary on the Law of Prize and Booty*, ed. M.J. van Ittersum (Indianapolis: Liberty Fund, 2006).

Guedes, M.A. Marques, *Interferência e integração dos Portugueses na Birmânia, ca. 1580–1630* (Lisbon: Fundação Oriente, 1994).

Guerreiro, F., *Relação anual das coisas que fizeram os Padres da Companhia de Jesus nas Suas Missões ... nos anos de 1600 a 1609*, 3 vols. (Coimbra: Imprensa da Universidade, 1930–42).

Guy, J., *Woven Cargoes: Indian Textiles in the East* (London: Thames and Hudson, 1988).

Haak, S.P., and A.J. Veenendaal, ed., *Johan van Oldenbarnevelt. Bescheiden betreffende zijn staatkundig beleid en zijn familie*, 3 vols. (The Hague: Martinus Nijhoff, 1934–67).

Hariharan, S., *Cotton Textiles and Corporate Buyers in Cottonopolis: A Study of Purchases and Prices in Gujarat, 1600–1800* (New Delhi: Manak Publications, 2002).

Hattendorf, J.B., *Encyclopaedia of Maritime History*, vol. 4 (Oxford and New York: Oxford University Press, 2007).

Hildebrandt, R., *Die Georg Fuggerischen Erben* (Berlin: Duncker & Humblot, 1966).

Hutchinson, E.W., ed. and tr., *1688. Revolution in Siam, The Memoir of Father de Bèze, S.J.*, 3rd impression (Bangkok: White Lotus Press, 2002).

Irwin, J.I., and P.R. Schwartz, *Studies in Indo-European Textile History* (Ahmedabad: Calico Museum of Textile, 1966).

Israel, J.I., *The Dutch Republic and the Hispanic World, 1606–1661* (Oxford: Clarendon Press, 1982).

———, *Dutch Primacy in World Trade, 1585–1740* (Oxford: Clarendon Press, 1989).

———, *Empires and Entrepots: The Dutch, the Spanish Monarchy and the Jews* (London: Hambledon Press, 1990).

Ittersum, M.J. van, *Profit and Principle: Hugo Grotius, Natural Rights Theories and the Rise of Dutch Power in the East Indies, 1595–1615* (Leiden: E.J. Brill, 2006).

Jonge, J.K.J. de, *Opkomst van het Nederlandsch gezag in Oost-Indië: Verzameling van onuitgegeven stukken uit het oud-coloniaal archief*, eerste reeks, 16 vols. (The Hague: Martinus Nijhoff, 1862–1925).

Kalus, M., *Pfeffer—Kupfer—Nachrichten. Kaufmannsnetzwerke und Handelsstrukturen im europäisch-asiatischen Handel am Ende des 16. Jahrhunderts*, Dissertation zur Erlangung des akademischen Grades doctor rerum politicarum (Jena: Wissenschaftliche Fakultät, Friedrich-Schiller-Universität, 2009).

Kaufmann, T. DaCosta and M. North, ed., *Artistic and Cultural Exchanges between Europe and Asia, 1400–1900: Rethinking Markets, Workshops and Collections* (Aldershot: Ashgate, 2010).

Kellenbenz, H., *Unternehmerkräfte im Hamburger Portugal- und Spanienhandel, 1590–1625* (Hamburg: Verlag der Hamburgischen Bücherei, 1954).

Keulen, J., and G. van, *De Nieuwe Groote Ligtende Zee-Fakkel*. Facsimile of the edition printed in Amsterdam 1716–53, 3 vols. (New York and Amsterdam: Da Capo Press and Theatrum Orbis Terrarum, 1970).

Kruijtzer, G, *Xenophobia in Seventeenth-Century India* (Leiden: Leiden University Press, 2009).

Lach, D., *Asia in the Making of Europe*, vol. I (Chicago and London: University of Chicago Press, 1965).

Lagoa, Visconde de, *Glossário Toponímico da Antiga Historiografia Portuguesa Ultramarina*, 4 vols. (Lisbon: Junta de Investigações Coloniais, 1950–04).

Leitão, H., and J.V. Lopes, *Dicionário da Linguagem de Marinha Antigua e Actual*, 2nd edn. (Lisbon: Centro de Estudos Históricos Ultramarinos da Junta de Investigações Científicas do Ultramar, 1974).

Linschoten, J.H. van, *Itinerario, Voyage, ofte Schipvaert van Jan Huygen van Linschoten naer Oost ofte Portugaels Indien, 1579–1592*, ed. H. Kern, 5 vols. (The Hague: Martinus Nijhoff, 1910–39).

———, *Itinerario. Voyage ofte Schipvaert van Jan Huygen van Linschoten naer Oost ofte Portugaels Indien, 1579–1592*, and *Reys-geschrift vande navigatiën der Portugaloysers in Orienten*, ed. H. Kern and J.C.M. Warnsinck, 2nd edn. (The Hague: Martinus Nijhoff, 1939).

Lombard, D., *Le Sultanat d'Atjéh au temps d'Iskandar Muda 1607–1636* (Paris: École français d'Extrême-Orient, 1967).

Loureiro, R.M., *Nas Partes da China: Colectânea de Estudos Dispersos* (Lisbon: Centro Científico e Cultural de Macau, 2009).

Ma, Huan, *Ying-Yai Sheng-Lan. The Overall Survey of the Ocean's Shores, 1433*, tr. and ed. J.V.G. Mills (Cambridge: Cambridge University Press, 1970).

MacLeod, N., *De Oost-Indische Compagnie als Zeemogendheid in Azië*, 2 vols. (Rijswijk: Blankwaardt & Schoonhoven, 1927).

Malekandathil, P., *The Germans, the Portuguese and India* (Münster: LIT Verlag, 1999).

———, *Maritime India: Trade, Religion and Polity in the Indian Ocean* (New Delhi: Primus Books, 2010).

Manguin, P.-Y., *Les Portugais sur les côtes du Viêt-Nam et du Campa: Étude sur les routes maritimes et les relations commerciales, d'après les sources portugaises (XVIème, XVIIème, XVIIIème siècles)* (Paris: École française d'Extrême-Orient, 1972).

Markham, C.R. ed., *The Voyages of Sir James Lancaster, Knight, to the East Indies with Abstracts of Journals of Voyages to the East Indies, during the Seventeenth Century, Preserved in the East India Office, and the Voyage of Captain John Knight (1600) to Seek the North-West Passage* (London: Hakluyt Society, 1877).

Mathew, K.S., *Indo-Portuguese Trade and the Fuggers of Germany: Sixteenth Century* (New Delhi: Manohar Publishers, 1997).

Meilink-Roelofsz, M.A.P., *Asian Trade and European Influence in the Indonesian Archipelago between 1500 and about 1630* (The Hague: Martinus Nijhoff, 1962).

Meteren, E. van, *Commentariën ofte Memoriën van den Nederlantsen Staet, Handel, Oorloghen ende Gheschiedenissen van onsen tyden, etc.*, 2 vols. (Gedruckt op Schotlant buyten Danswijck by Hermes van Loven, no date [c. 1646]).

———, *Historien der Nederlanden, en haar naburen oorlogen tot het jaar 1612: met heerelijker konterfeijtsels dan ooyt voor dezen verciert en verbetert* (Amsterdam: Jan Jacobsz Schipper, 1652).

Meuwese, M., *Brothers in Arms, Partners in Trade: Dutch-Indigenous Alliances in the Atlantic World, 1595–1674* (Leiden: E.J. Brill, 2012).

Milner, A., *The Malays* (Oxford: Wiley-Blackwell, 2008).

Moreland, W.H., ed., *Relations of Golconda in the Early Seventeenth Century* (London: Hakluyt Society, 1931).

———, ed., *Peter Floris, His Voyage to the East Indies in the "Globe" 1611–1615* (London: Hakluyt Society, 1934).

Morga, A. de, *The Philippine Islands, Moluccas, Siam, Cambodia, Japan and China at the Close of the Sixteenth Century*, ed. L.V. de Torres and H.E.J. Stanley (London: Hakluyt Society, 1868).

———, *Sucesos de las Islas Filipinas*, tr. and ed. J.S. Cummins (Cambridge: Cambridge University Press for the Hakluyt Society, 1971).

Münster, S., *Cosmographia Oder Beschreibung der gantzen Welt etc.*, facsimile reproduction of the Basel edition of 1628 (Lindau: Antiqua Verlag, 1978).

Naber, S.P. l'Honoré, *Reisebeschreibungen von Deutschen Beamten und Kriegsleuten im Dienst der Niederländisch West- und Ost-Indischen Kompanien, 1602–1797*, 13 vols. (The Hague: Martinus Nijhoff, 1930–33).

Nadkarni, K.M., *Indian Materia Medica, with Ayurveredic, Unani-Tibbi, Siddha, Allopathic, Homeopathic, Naturopathic and Home Remedies, Appendices and Indexes*, 2 vols. (Bombay and Panvel: Popular Book Depot and Dhootapapeshwar Prakashan, 1954).

Newitt, M., ed., *The First Portuguese Colonial Empire* (Exeter: Department of History and Archaeology, University of Exeter, 1986).

Opstall, M.E. van, ed., *De reis van de vloot van Pieter Willemszoon Verhoeff naar Azië, 1607–1612*, 2 vols. (The Hague: Martinus Nijhoff, 1972).

Parmentier, J., K. Davids and J. Everaert, *Peper Plancius en Porselein: De reis van het schip "Swarte Leeuw" naar Atjeh en Bantam, 1601–1603* (Zutphen: Walburg Pers, 2003).

Pato, Raymundo A. de Bulhão, and A. da Silva Rego, ed., *Documentos Remettidos da Índia ou Livros das Monções*, 10 vols. (Lisbon: Typographia da Academia Real das Sciencias and Imprensa Nacional—Casa de Moeda, 1880–1982).

Paulus, J., ed., *Encyclopaedie van Nederlandsch-Indië*, 2nd edn., 8 vols. (The Hague and Leiden: Martinus Nijhoff and E.J. Brill, 1917–39).

Pinto, P.J. de Sousa, *Portugueses e Malaios: Malaca e os Sultanatos de Johor e Achém, 1575–1619* (Lisbon: Sociedade Histórica da Independência de Portugal, 1997).

———, *The Portuguese and the Straits of Melaka, 1575–1619. Power, Trade and Diplomacy* (Singapore: NUS Press, 2012).

Pires, T., *The Suma Oriental of Tome Pires: An Account of the East from the Red Sea to Japan. Written in Malacca and India in 1512–1515*, ed. A. Cortesão, 2 vols. (London: Hakluyt Society, 1944).

Roques, G., *La manière de négocier aux Indies, 1676–1691. La compagnie des Indies de l'art du commerce*, ed. and tr. V. Bérinstain (Paris: École française d'Extrême-Orient—Maisonneuve & Larose, 1996).

Roux, P. le, B. Sellato and J. Ivanoff, ed., *Poids e mesures en Asie du Sud-Est—Weights and Measures in Southeast Asia*, 2 vols. (Paris: École française d'Extrême-Orient and Institut de Recherche sur le Sud-Est Asiatique, 2004–08).

Ruangsilp, B., *Dutch East India Company Merchants at the Court of Ayutthaya: Dutch Perceptions of the Thai Kingdom c. 1604–1765* (Leiden: Brill, 2007).

Saldanha, A. Vasconcelos de, *Iustum Imperium, dos tratados como fundamento do império dos portugueses no Oriente: estudo de história do direito internacional e do direito português* (Lisbon: Fundação Oriente, 1997).

Santos, J. dos, *Etiópia Oriental e Vária História de cousas Notáveis do Oriente*, ed. M. Lobato and Maria do Carmo Guerreiro Vieira (Lisbon: Comissão Nacional para as Comemorações dos Descobrimentos Portugueses, 1999).

Silveira, F.R., *Reformação da Milícia do Governo do Estado da Índia Oriental*, ed. Benjamin N. Teensma (Lisbon: Fundação Oriente, 1996).

Sinclair, W.F., and D. Ferguson, ed. and tr., *The Travels of Pedro Teixeira with His "Kings of Harmuz" and Extracts from His "Kings of Persia"* (London: Hakluyt Society, 1902).

Smithies, Michael, ed. and tr., *Impressions of Old Siam* (Kuala Lumpur and New York: Oxford University Press, 1995).

Sopher, D.E., *The Sea Nomads, a Study Based on Literature of the Maritime Boat People of Southeast Asia*, Memoirs of the National Museum, No. 5 (Singapore: The National Museum, 1965).

Staring, W.C.H., *De Binnen- en Buitenlandsche Maten, Gewichten en Munten van Vroeger en Tegenwoordig* (Arnmem: Gyspers & Van Loon, 1980).

Steensgaard, N., *The Asian Trade Revolution of the Seventeenth Century: The East India Companies and the Decline of the Caravan Trade* (Chicago and London: University of Chicago Press, 1974).

Stols, E., *De Spaanse Brabanders of de Handelsbetrekkingen der Zuidelijke Nederlanden met de Iberische Wereld, 1598–1648. Tekst en Bijlagen* (Brussels: Paleis der Academiën, 1971).

Sunait Chutintaranond, and C. Baker, ed., *Recalling Local Pasts: Autonomous History in Southeast Asia* (Chiang Mai: Silkworm Books, 2002).

Teensma, Benjamin N., *De politieke en economische ideeën van de Bruggeling: Jacques de Coutre (1575–1640), alsmede enige tekstkritiek* (Leiden, 1994).

Teeuw, A., and D.K. Wyatt, ed., *Hikayat Patani. The Story of Patani*, 2 vols. (The Hague: Martinus Nijhoff, 1970).

Teixeira, P., *Relaciones ... d'el origen descendencia y succesión de los Reyes de Persia, y de Harmuz* (Amberes: En casa de Hieronymo Verdussen, 1610).

Terpstra, H., *De Opkomst der Westerkwartieren van de Oost-Indische Compagnie (Suratte, Arabië, Perzië)* (Den Haag: Martinus Nijhoff, 1918).

———, *De factorij der Oostindische Compagnie te Patani*, Verhandelingen van het Koninklijk Instituut voor de Taal-, Land- en Volkenkunde van Nederlandsch-Indië, I (The Hague: Martinus Nijhoff, 1938).

Terwiel, B., ed. and tr., *A Traveler in Siam in the Year 1655: Extracts from the Journal of Gijsbert Heeck* (Chiang Mai: Silkworm Books, 2008).

Tiele, P.A., and J.E. Heeres, ed., *Bouwstoffen voor de Geschiedenis der Nederlanders in den Maleischen Archipel*, 3 vols. (The Hague: Martinus Nijhoff, 1886–95).

Unger, W.S., ed., *De Oudste Reizen van de Zeeuwen naar Oost-Indië, 1598–1604* (The Hague: Martinus Nijhoff, 1948).

Veen, E. van, *Decay or Defeat: An Inquiry into the Portuguese Decline in Asia, 1580–1645* (Leiden: Research School of Asian, African and Amerindian Studies, 2000).

Veen, E. van, and L. Blussé, ed., *Rivalry and Conflict: European Traders and Asian Trading Networks in the 16th and 17th Centuries* (Leiden: CNWS, 2005).

Wade, G., ed., *Southeast Asia-China Interactions: Reprint of articles from the Journal of the Malaysian Branch, Royal Asiatic Society* (Kuala Lumpur: MBRAS, 2007).

Wheatley, P., *The Golden Khersonese: Studies in the Historical Geography of the Malay Peninsula before A.D. 1500* (Kuala Lumpur: University of Malaya Press, 1961).

Winius, G., *Studies in Portuguese Asia, 1495–1689* (Aldershot: Variorum, 2001).

Wolters, O.W., *Early Indonesian Commerce: A Study of the Origins of Srivijaya* (Ithaca: Cornell University Press, 1967).

Yule, H., and A.C. Burnell, *Hobson-Jobson: A Glossary of Colloquial Anglo-Indian Words and Phrases*, reprint (Sittingbourne: Linguasia, 1994).

Zorn, W., ed., *Lebensbilder aus dem Bayerischen Schwaben* (Max Hueber Verlag, 1966).

ARTICLES AND CHAPTERS

Apius, M., "Incidente em Macau, 1601" ed. and tr. A. Pos, *Revista de Cultura* 12 (2004): 61–7.

Barendse, R., "Sources on Pre-1800 Asian History in Portugal and Spain", *Itinerario* 19 (1995): 144–60.

Barnes, W.D., "Singapore Old Straits and New Harbour", *Journal of the Straits Branch of the Royal Asiatic Society* 60 (1911): 24–34.

Bassett, D.K., "Changes in the Pattern of Malay Politics, 1629–1655", *Journal of Southeast Asian History* 10, 3 (1969): 429–52.

Blussé, L., "Brief Encounter at Macao", *Modern Asian Studies* 22, 3 (1988): 647–64.

Borschberg, P., "The Seizure of the *Sta. Catarina* Revisited: The Portuguese Empire in Asia, VOC Politics and the Origins of the Dutch-Johor Alliance (c.1602–1616)", *JSEAS* 33, 1 (2002): 31–62.

———, "A Portuguese-Dutch Naval Battle in the Johor River Delta", *Zeitschrift der Deutschen Morgenländischen Gesellschaft* 153, 1 (2003): 157–75.

———, "O comércio europeu de almíscar com a Ásia no inicio da edad moderna—The European Musk Trade with Asia in the Early Modern Period" (bilingual feature article, Portuguese-English), *Revista Oriente* 5 (2003): 90–9.

———,"Der Asiatische Ambra-Handel während der frühen Neuzeit" in *Mirabilia Asiatica II. Produtos raros no comércio marítimo*, ed. J.M. dos Santos Alves, C. Guillot and R. Ptak (Wiesbaden and Lisbon: Harrassowitz-Fundação Oriente, 2004), pp. 167–201.

———, "Luso-Johor-Dutch Relations in the Straits of Malacca and Singapore", *Itinerario* 28, 2 (2004): 15–33.

———, "O comércio de âmbar asiático no início da época moderna (séculos XV–XVIII)—The Asiatic Ambergris Trade in the Early Modern Period (15th to 18th Century)" (bilingual article, Portuguese-English), *Revista Oriente* 8 (2004): 3–25.

———, "The Seizure of the *Santa Catarina* off Singapore", *Revista de Cultura*, International Edition 11 (2004): 11–25.

———,"The Euro-Asian Trade and Medicinal Usage of Radix Chinae", in *European Travellers and the Asian Natural World*, part 1, ed. R.M. Loureiro, *Revista de Cultura*, International Edition 20 (2006): 102–15.

———, "The Trade, Forgery and Medicinal Use of Porcupine Bezoars in the Early Modern Period (c.1500–1750)" (bilingual article, Portuguese-English), *Revista Oriente* 14 (2006): 60–78.

———, "Jacques de Coutre as a Source for the Early 17th Century History of Singapore, the Johor River, and the Straits", *JMBRAS* 81, 2 (2008): 71–97.

———, "The Johor-VOC Alliance and the Twelve Years Truce", Institute for International Law and Justice (IILJ) Working Paper 8 (2009): 1–64.

———, "Ethnicity, Language and Culture in Melaka during the Transition from Portuguese to Dutch Rule", *JMBRAS* 83, 2 (2010): 93–117.

Boxer, C.R., "Uma raridade bibliográfica sobre Fernão Cron", *Boletim Internacional de Bibliografia Luso-Brasileira* 12, 3 (1971): 323–64.

Briggs, L.P., "Spanish Intervention in Cambodia, 1593–1603", *T'Oung Pao*, second series 39, 1/3 (1950): 132–60.

Coolhaas, W.Ph., "Een bron van het historische gedeelte van Hugo de Groots De Jure Praedae", *BMH* 79 (1965): 415–537.

Cummins, J.S., "Antonio de Morga and his *Sucesos de Las Islas Filipinas*", *JSEAH* 10, 3 (1969): 564–5.

Diguet, M.L., "Histoire de la cochenille au Mexique", *Journal de la Société des Américanistes* 6 (1909): 75–99.

Duyvendak, J.J.L.,"The First Siamese Embassy to Holland", *T'Oung Pao* 32 (1936): 285–92.

Frederiks, J.G., "Cornelis Cornelisz Matelieff de Jonge en zijn geslagt", *Rotterdamsche Historiebladen*, ed. J.H. Scheffer and Fr. D.O. Obreen, 3 afd., 1, 1 (1871): 204–357.

Gibson-Hill, C.-A., "Singapore: Note on the History of the Old Straits, 1580–1850", *JMBRAS* 27, 1 (1954): 165–214.

———, "Johore Lama and Other Ancient Sites on the Johore River", *JMBRAS* 28, 2 (1955): 126–99.

———, "Singapore Old Strait and New Harbour, 1300–1870", *Memoirs of the Raffles Museum*, no. 3 (Singapore: Government Printing Office, 1956): 11–115.

Halikowski-Smith, S., "Globalisation before Globalisation: the case of the Portuguese world empire, 1415–1808", *World and Global History: Research and Teaching*, ed. S. Jalagin, S. Tavera and A. Dilley (Pisa: Edizioni Plus—Pisa University Press, 2011), pp. 25–46.

Heeres, J.E., ed., "Corpus Diplomaticum Neërlando-Indicum. Verzameling van politieke contracten en verdere verdragen door de Nederlanders in het Oosten gesloten, van privilegiebrieven, aan hen verleend, enz.", eerste deel (1596–1650), *BKI* 57 (1907): 1–586.

Hervey, D.F.A., "François Valentyn's Account of Malacca", *JSBRAS* 16, 1 (1885): 289–301.

Irwin, J., "Indian Textile Trade in the Seventeenth Century, I. Western India", *Journal of Indian Textile History* 1 (1955): 5–33.

———, "Indian Textile Trade in the Seventeenth Century, II. Coromandel Coast", *Journal of Indian Textile History* 2 (1956): 24–42.

———, "Indian Textile Trade in the Seventeenth Century, III. Bengal", *Journal of Indian Textile History* 3 (1957): 59–74.

Ittersum, M.J. van, "Hugo Grotius in Context: Van Heemskerck's Capture of the *Santa Catarina* and Its Justification in *De Jure Praedae* (1604–1606)", *AJSS* 31, 3 (2003): 511–48.

Kalus, M., "Tracing Business Patterns in Sixteenth Century European-Asian Trade. New Methods Using Semantic Networking Models", XIV International Economic History Congress, 21–25 August, 2006. (Accessed 12 May 2012 at www.helsinki.fi/iehc2006/papers1/kalus.pdf)

Kellenbenz, H., "Autour de 1600: Le commerce du poivre des Fugger et le marché international du poivre", *Annales, Histoire, Sciences Sociales* 11, 1 (1956): 1–28.

———, "Cron, Ferdinand, 1559–1637", in J. Serrão, *Dicionário de história de Portugal*, I (Lisbon: Iniciativas Editoriais, 1963), pp. 752–3.

———, "Ferdinand Cron, 1559–1637" in *Lebensbilder aus dem Bayerischen Schwaben*, ed. W. Zorn, 9 (Munich: Max Hueber Verlag, 1966), pp. 194–210.

———, "Ferdinand Cron" in *Lebensbilder aus dem Bayerischen Schwaben*, ed. W. Zorn, 3, 9 (Munich: Max Hueber Verlag, 1974), pp. 95–6.

———, "German Trade Relations with the Indian Ocean from the End of the Eighteenth Century to 1870", *JSEAS* 13, 1 (1982): 133–52.

———, "From Melchior Manlich to Ferdinand Cron. German Levantine and Oriental Trade Relations (Second Half of 16th and Beginning of 17th Century), *Journal of European Economic History* 19, 3 (1990): 611–22.

Koninckx, C., "Review of Eddy Stols and Johan Verbeckmoes. Aziatische omzwervingen. Het leven van Jacques de Coutre, een Brugs diamanthandelaar 1591–1627", *Revue Belge de philologie et d'histoire* 70, 4 (1992): 1052–3.

Leupe, P.G., "The Siege and Capture of Malacca from the Portuguese in 1640–1641. Extracts from the Archives of the Dutch East India Company", tr. M. Hacobian, *JMBRAS* 14, 1 (1936): 1–178.

Linehan, W., "History of Pahang", *JMBRAS* 14, 2 (1936): 1–256.

Loureiro, R.M., "European Encounters and Clashes in the South China Sea", II, *Revista de Cultura*, International Edition 12 (2004): 1–154.

Mills, J.V., "Report on the Golden Chersonese", *JMBRAS* 8, 1 (1930): 228–55.

Milner, A., E.E. McKinnon and Tengku Luckman Sinar, "Aru and Kota Cina", *Indonesia* 26 (1978): 1–42.

Muijzenberg, O. van den, "Philippine-Dutch Social Relations, 1600–1800", *BKI* 157, 3 (2001): 471–509.

Pelliot, P., "Les Relations du Siam et de la Hollande en 1608", *T'Oung Pao* 32 (1936): 223–9.

Pinto, P.J. de Sousa, "Captains, Sultans and liaisons dangereuses: Melaka and Johor in the Late Sixteenth Century" in *Iberians in the Singapore-Melaka Area and Adjacent Regions, 16th to 18th Century*, ed. P. Borschberg (Wiesbaden and Lisbon, Harrassowitz—Fundação Oriente, 2004), pp. 131–46.

Rouffaer, G.P., "Was Malaka Emporium vóór 1400 A.D. genaamd Malajoer? En waar lag Woerawari, Ma-Hasin, Langka, Batoesawar?", *BKI* 77 (1921): 1–174 and 359–604.

Rubiés, J.P. "The Spanish Contribution to Ethnology of Asia in the Sixteenth and Seventeenth Centuries", *Asian Travel in the Renaissance*, ed. Daniel Carey (Malden and Oxford: Blackwell Publishing, 2004), p. 121.

Sinclair, W.F. and D. Ferguson, ed., *The Travels of Pedro Teixeira with this "Kings of Harmuz" and Extracts from his "Kings of Persia"* (Nendeln: Kraus Reprint, 1967).

Souza, T.R. de, "Embassies and Surrogates: Case Study of a Malacca Embassy to Siam in 1595", Fifth International Seminar on Indo-Portuguese History, Cochin I, *Indica* 26, 1/2 (1989): 39–55.

Subrahmanyam, S., "An Augsburger in Ásia Portuguesa: Further Light on the Commercial World of Ferdinand Cron, 1587–1624", *Emporia, Commodities and Entrepreneurs in Asian Maritime Trade, 1400–1750*, ed. Roderich Ptak and Dietmar Rothermund (Stuttgart: Franz Steiner Verlag, 1991), pp. 401–25.

———, "Manila, Melaka, Mylapore …: A Dominican Voyage through the Indies, ca. 1600", *Archipel* 57 (1999): 223–42.

———, "Holding the World in Balance: The Connected Histories of the Iberian Overseas Empires, 1500–1640", *The American Historical Review* 112, 5 (2007): 1359–85.

Swart, F., "Lambert Biesman (1573–1601) of the Company of Trader Adventurers, the Dutch Route to the East Indies, and Olivier van Noort's Circumnavigation of the Globe", *Journal of the Hakluyt Society* (2007): 1–21.

Teensma, B.N., "Literaire, filologische en moralistische bespielingen over de Siamese penisbel", *BKI* 147, 1 (1991): 128–39.

———,"Nederlandofobia en Goa a Principios del Siglo XVII", *Contactos entre los Países Bajos y el Mundo Ibérico*, ed. J. Lechner, III (Amsterdam: Editions Rodopi, 1992), pp. 125–32.

Tiele, P.A., "De Europeërs in den Maleischen Archipel", *BKI* part VI, 30 (1882): 141–242.

———, "Documenten voor de Geschiedenis der Nederlanders in het Oosten", *BMH* 6 (1883): 228–42.

———, "De Europeërs in den Maleischen Archipel", *BKI* part VII, 32 (1884): 49–118.

Tun, Aung Chain, "Pegu in Politics and Trade, Ninth to Seventeenth Centuries", S. Chutintaranond and C. Baker, ed., *Recalling Local Pasts: Autonomous History in Southeast Asia* (Chiang Mai: Silkworm Books, 2002), pp. 25–52.

Villiers, J., "*Review of Jacques de Coutre, Como Remediar o Estado da Índia*?, ed. Benjamin N. Teensma, Leiden: Center for the History of European Expansion, 1989", *JSEAS* 21, 2 (1990): 454–5.

Winius, G.D., "The Life of Jaques de Couttre: a Prime Source Emerges from the Shades", *Itinerario* 9 (1985): 137–44.

———, "Review of Miroslav Krása, Joseph Polišenský, and Peter Rakoš, 'European Expansion 1494–1519. The Voyages of Discovery in the Bratislava Manuscript Lyc. 515/18 (Codex Bratislavensis), Prague: Charles University, 1986", *The Hispanic American Historical Review* 68, 4 (1988): 821.

———, and C.C. Chorba, "Literary Invasions in *La vida de Jaques de Coutre*: do they prejudice its value as an historical source?", *A Carreira da Índia e as Rotas dos Estreitos. Actas do VIII Seminário Internacional de História Indo-Portuguesa,* ed. A.T. de Matos and L.F.R. Thomaz (Angra do Heroísmo: Barbosa & Javier, 1998), pp. 709–19.

Wolters, W.G., "Heavy and light money in the Netherlands Indies and the Dutch Republic: dilemmas of monetary management with unit of account systems", *Financial History Review* 15, 1 (2008): 37–53.

INDEX